Ritual and the Poetics of Closure in Flavian Literature

Trends in Classics –
Supplementary Volumes

Edited by
Franco Montanari and Antonios Rengakos

Associate Editors
Stavros Frangoulidis · Fausto Montana · Lara Pagani
Serena Perrone · Evina Sistakou · Christos Tsagalis

Scientific Committee
Alberto Bernabé · Margarethe Billerbeck
Claude Calame · Kathleen Coleman · Jonas Grethlein
Philip R. Hardie · Stephen J. Harrison · Stephen Hinds
Richard Hunter · Giuseppe Mastromarco
Gregory Nagy · Theodore D. Papanghelis
Giusto Picone · Alessandro Schiesaro
Tim Whitmarsh · Bernhard Zimmermann

Volume 147

Ritual and the Poetics of Closure in Flavian Literature

Edited by
Angeliki-Nektaria Roumpou

DE GRUYTER

ISBN 978-3-11-221405-3
e-ISBN (PDF) 978-3-11-077048-3
e-ISBN (EPUB) 978-3-11-077056-8
ISSN 1868-4785

Library of Congress Control Number: 2023939400

Bibliographic information published by the Deutsche Nationalbibliothek
The Deutsche Nationalbibliothek lists this publication in the Deutsche Nationalbibliografie;
detailed bibliographic data are available on the Internet at http://dnb.dnb.de.

© 2025 Walter de Gruyter GmbH, Berlin/Boston
This volume is text- and page-identical with the hardback published in 2023.
Editorial Office: Alessia Ferreccio and Katerina
Zianna Logo: Christopher Schneider, Laufen
Printing and binding: CPI books GmbH, Leck

www.degruyter.com

Acknowledgements

This collection of essays arises from a post-doctoral research project on "Religion and the Poetics of Closure in Flavian Epic Poetry", funded by the Swiss Government and held at the University of Geneva, Switzerland. Most of the papers were first presented at an online conference entitled "The Poetics of Release and Binding: Resolution and Constraint as Modes of Closure in Flavian Literature", which took place on the four Wednesdays in June 2021. Apart from the papers presented at the conference, a few more researchers in the area of Flavian literature have also contributed to the current volume and, in doing so, enhanced our perception of this particular subject. First, I would like to thank the Département des Sciences de l'Antiquité at the University of Geneva for its overall support and help in organising the online conference. I am particularly indebted to my project supervisor, Prof. Damien P. Nelis, for his constant support and encouragement throughout my post-doctoral studies at the University of Geneva, and for his immediate enthusiasm in putting together that online conference. I would also like to thank a number of people who provided me with their help and advice on specific matters regarding this volume: Antony Augoustakis, Darcy Krasne, Joy Littlewood, Spyridon Tzounakas, Sophia Papaioannou, Helen Lovatt, Margot Neger, Theodoros Antoniadis, Melissande Tomcik, Melanie Fitton-Hayward.

Warm thanks are also due to the Fondation Hardt in Geneva and to its generous and kind staff, in particular Gary Vachicouras and Sabrina Ciardo, for providing me with access to its specialised library during the tough years of the pandemic. Finally, my warmest thanks goes to all those who participated in the online conference as well as the contributors to this volume; it was a pleasure and honour for me to collaborate with such a kind and talented group of scholars. Last but not least, I am grateful to the Swiss Government for generous sponsorship, with which I was able to complete my post-doctoral studies and to work undisturbed on this specific project.

Contents

Acknowledgements —— V

Angeliki-Nektaria Roumpou
Introduction: Ritual and the Poetics of Closure in Flavian Literature —— 1

Jörg Rüpke
Ritual Closure and Transcendence: Mobilising Ritual Theory for Flavian Epic —— 13

Margot Neger
Religious and Social Rituals as Motifs of Closure in Martial's *Epigrams* —— 27

Alison Keith
Closural Poetics in Martial, *Epigrams* 10 —— 43

Laila Dell'Anno
Ritual and the Impossibility of Song in Statius' *Siluae* 5 —— 59

Sophia Papaioannou
Sacrifice, Death, and Closure in Valerius' *Argonautica* Book 1 —— 79

Clayton Schroer
Mansuri Compos Decoris? Scipio's *Reditus* and Exile in *Punica* 17 —— 95

Theodoros Antoniadis
Silius Italicus' False Rituals, Politics and Poetics: Mock Funerals and Triumphs as Closural Markers in the *Punica* —— 111

Helen Lovatt
Burning up, Melting down, Collapsing in: Fire Imagery, Narrative Articulation, Funerals, and the Incestuous Poetics of Statius' *Thebaid* —— 135

Michael Knierim
Narrative and Psychological Closure through Ritual at Cyzicus and Circe's Island —— 161

Marco Fucecchi
Compage soluta: Collapsing Universe and the Boundaries of Epic Poetry (Lucan, Silius, Statius and Claudian's *De raptu*) —— 181

Damien P. Nelis
Epilogue —— 201

List of Contributors —— 207
Bibliography —— 209
Thematic Index —— 233
Index of Sources —— 241

Angeliki-Nektaria Roumpou
Introduction: Ritual and the Poetics of Closure in Flavian Literature

The present volume offers two major claims about how Flavian literature relates to ritual and closure. It explores the role and significance of ancient religious practices, such as burial, funeral rites, prophecies, triumphal procession, purification etc., both in closing sections of literary texts (epigram, epic and occasional poetry) as well as in the overall closure of the text itself. It focuses on the problematic nature of Flavian literary endings by exploring ritual as a way to reflect on closure, and seeks to expand the scope of the scholarly discussion on the poetics of closure by providing new insights into the representation of ritual in the literature of the Flavian era.

The study of the closural section of classical texts in recent literary criticism has raised a discussion regarding the finality and the sense of an ending, readerly satisfaction and dissatisfaction, the coherence of narrative structures, and the sense of incompleteness arising from a lost ending or a deliberate tendency of some authors to leave matters as open-ended as possible.[1] One means of closure is achieved through the representation of a ritual ceremony: burials, lament, sacrifice or purification often work as closural acts. The performance of rituals at the end of the narrative, concluding books or episodes, offers resolution to problematic situations by providing a fitting solution to restore order that has been disrupted, and thus giving a sense of readerly satisfaction and completeness. For example, the religious act of oath-swearing is the prerequisite for the establishment of justice and order in human affairs:[2] oath-swearing practices can lead to the formation of treaties and alliances between peoples (see *Il.* 2.337–341) or can establish rules of war (see *Il.* 3.103–107); death practices, such as burials, provide closure and restoration, as for example, the burial rites of Hector which conclude the *Iliad* (24.785–804), and offer both restoration to the hero's soul and a sense of satisfaction to the reader's mind. However, rituals in narrative endings can be perverted and thwart closure, as in the end of

---
1 For the relevant bibliography, see below.
2 See Sommerstein/Torrance 2014, 18–19. The oath (ὅρκος, which, according to Eustathius, ad B 339; *Etym. Magn.*, cognates with ἕρκος, meaning 'fence', 'enclosure') had a binding function that connected peoples with each other, or people with the gods; in Latin, for the fulfilment of a vow the phrase used is *uotum soluit*, which illustrates the loosening of the bond between the human and the divine; see Meyer 1983, 64–66; also Neger's analysis in this volume, page 41.

the *Aeneid*, where a series of perverted rituals defy the restoration of the disrupted narrative order. For example, in the final lines of the *Aeneid*, when Aeneas is ready to kill Turnus, his use of the word *immolat* ('he sacrifices') at 12.949 (*Pallas te hoc uulnere, Pallas / immolat et poenam scelerato ex sanguine sumit*, 'Pallas it is, Pallas, who sacrifices you with this stroke, and exacts retribution from your guilty blood') impels us to read Turnus as a sacrificial victim. Therefore, the readerly expectations for ritual restoration at the end of the Virgilian epic are defied and formal closure is subsequently undermined.[3] The use of the word *immolat* impels us to read the end of the epic in sacrificial terms, which in turn opens up questions about whether sacrifice as ritual makes the ending 'complete' or at least 'unproblematic'.

On epic poetry specifically, the study of the relationship between ending and ritual has revealed that the epics, no matter how 'closed' they are, seem to lend themselves to continuation.[4] The incompleteness of epic has encouraged the production of continuations, observed as early as the cyclical epics of Archaic Greece and Homer's *Iliad*; the *Odyssey* and the *Aeneid* continue the *Iliad*, Silius' *Punica* continues the *Aeneid*, and so forth.[5] One such example is the ending of the *Iliad*: although the poem ends with a ritual and a funeral, its closure is not the end of the war. Indeed, a textual discrepancy relating to the last word of the *Iliad* creates a link to the cyclic poem that follows, the *Aithiopis* of Arctinus.[6] Hence, the *Iliad* does offer a degree of closure as a standalone epic but also becomes a link to further action within the epic cycle.[7] Similarly, Ennius' *Annales* has shown that closure was not (straightforwardly or lastingly) achieved in book 15 with the ritual of the triumphal procession for Fuluius Nobilior, since

---

3 Panoussi 2009, 75. As Panoussi has shown, in the *Aeneid* ritual is often perverted and fails to achieve restoration, which thus forces the reader to confront the problems inherent in Augustus' socio-political order that the poem seeks to assert.
4 See Simms 2018 who explores the ways that heroic epic narratives have been continued in the Greco-Roman and western classical traditions through prequels, sequels and retellings. See also Roberts 1997, for story aftermaths and endings beyond endings.
5 See Simms 2018, 1. For the *Punica* as a continuation of the *Aeneid*, see Bernstein 2018a.
6 The *Iliad* ends with Ὣς οἵ γ' ἀμφίεπον τάφον Ἕκτορος ἱπποδάμοιο ('Thus they busied themselves with the burial of Hector, tamer of horses.'). However, in some copies, in the last line of the poem there was an alternative ending Ὣς οἵ γ' ἀμφίεπον τάφον Ἕκτορος· ἦλθε δ' Ἀμαζών ('Thus they busied themselves with the burial of Hector; and the Amazon came.') which provided a transition to the *Aithiopis*, the next poem in the epic cycle, and moves on from the funeral of Hector to the new topic. For analysis, see West 2011, 428–430; 2013, 137–138.
7 For the discussion on the *Iliad*'s and the *Odyssey*'s continuations, see Hardie 1997, 139.

there is a new beginning with three additional books to create, eventually, an 18-book epic.[8]

Ritual perversion, defiance of closure and narrative open-endedness seem to be common characteristics in imperial literature. Rituals at the end of the texts or as concluding markers offer a rather complicated sense of ending; they can bring but mostly they hinder closure by alluding to new beginnings, reflecting the cyclical nature of war and the socio-political disruption caused at the post-civil war Empire. The collection of papers in this volume focuses on this problematic correlation between ending and ritual in Flavian literature and investigates its socio-political dimensions. Closure in the extant imperial literary tradition defies stereotyping, with several epics and literary collections being unfinished or incomplete: the fact that Lucan's *Pharsalia*, which was very influential on Flavian epic, avoids any kind of resolution reflects its epic subject of civil war without end.[9] Statius' *Achilleid* and Valerius' *Argonautica* end abruptly, whereas Silius Italicus' *Punica* and Statius' *Thebaid*, although complete, raise further questions at their conclusions instead of giving a sense of finality.[10] In Flavian literary culture, this problematic closure and sense of open-endedness is commented on in diverse ways by authors of the same period who respond to their current political situation by creating dynamic relationships with their texts as well as continuations.

In Flavian literature, ritual, sacrifice, death and burial are privileged as the macabre and grotesque take over the narrative,[11] but they do not seem to offer a proper and satisfactory resolution. For example, at the end of the *Thebaid*, the reader is unsure whether the burial of the Argive soldiers provides satisfactory closure to an epic which thematises fratricide and the Theban extinction.[12] This is somehow associated with the new regime and the new sociopolitical context, where religion is under crisis. In literature this crisis is reflected in the representation of the divine, especially after Lucan's epic: the end of *libertas* and the beginning of the empire bring the negation of divine providence and the eventual removal of the divine machinery in epic.[13] The gods in Lucan are unconcerned by human events (7.454–455 *mortalia nulli / sunt curata deo*, 'mortal

---

8 See Skutsch 1985, 563–565; Hardie 1997, 140–141.
9 Masters 1992, 259.
10 The *Thebaid* is the only extant epic of the Flavian period for which we can be reasonably sure that it was published at Rome in its final form under the supervision of the poet himself, and indeed Statius boasts of the care he took over the *Thebaid*; see Heslin 2009, 64.
11 Augoustakis et al. 2019, 483.
12 For analysis of this episode, see Augoustakis et al. 2019, 518–519.
13 Feeney 2007, 135; also Augoustakis et al. 2019, 483.

affairs are of no concern to any god') and the Romans have substituted them with the deified Caesars, a total disruption of order, according to Lucan. In Flavian literature, in Statius' *Thebaid*, Jupiter as guarantor of a providential plan is absent and replaced instead by Theseus, who offers the final resolution in the epic. Therefore, a human model of kingship as represented by Theseus proves superior to the divine model offered by the poem.[14] At the end of the *Thebaid*, as in the *Siluae*, Statius inverts the power relations between Jupiter and his earthly representative, the emperor. Moreover, the failed prayers in the *Thebaid* reveal a crisis between the human and the divine worlds,[15] and expose disruption in the social order.[16] In the *Achilleid*, ritual causes generic instability, as, for example, in the ritual activities of women — Bacchic rites, choral dancing, and collective worship of Pallas — whose exceptional power and agency poses a real threat to the full articulation of (the epic's) masculinity.[17] As Fucecchi observes in this volume, this construction of a new human authority as well as of a more 'human' power that can resist the forces of chaos reveals the inability of the Olympian gods in the Flavian literary world.[18]

The contributions in this volume treat the subject of closure in different ways: ritual could be a perfect kind of ending but it hardly ever seems to be; funeral rites in particular are firmly closural, but only in part, as they can be denied, perverted or mocked in different ways. In Flavian literature this is even more apparent because of the socio-political background under which these texts were produced. As stated above, after Lucan's distance from matters of religion and ritual in the *Pharsalia*,[19] there was a general ritual crisis and thus rituals are even more exposed to risk. Some examples of the findings of this volume include: that in Martial's epigrams, religion, where it appears, is often connected with the Imperial cult, especially Domitian's depiction as a deity, and that typically Martial's approach is more playful than serious;[20] that in Valerius' *Argonautica* there is a lack of catharsis at the end of book 1, as the incomplete

---

14 See Bessone 2013, 159; also Feeney 2007, 135.
15 For ritual as a communicative system between the human and the divine, see Rüpke 2001, 13–30 as well as his paper in this volume.
16 Hubert 2013. Significant research has been done on the representation of religion in Flavian epic, such as the role of the gods by Feeney 1991, Criado 2000, or the role of sacrifice by Hardie 1993.
17 Panoussi 2013, 337. The same generic instability is caused at the end of the *Thebaid* with the ritual lament by the women; see Voigt 2016.
18 See Fucecchi's paper, page 200.
19 Augoustakis et al. 2019, 483.
20 See Neger's analysis in this volume.

sacrifice and the multiple ritual perversions (the employment of witchcraft; suicide) anticipate and prohibit, yet eventually replace, perverted (human) sacrifice;[21] in Silius' *Punica*, Scipio's triumph at the end of the epic, although it provides a sense of closure, finally speaks of a *reditus*, implying a possible return and a new beginning;[22] or that burial scenes, where used as concluding markers, are often mocked and therefore distorted in order to create a "false" end.[23]

Ancient religious practices in the closing sections of Flavian texts help us create connections between endings and (new) beginnings, order and disorder, binding and loosening, structure and dissolution, all of which reflect the structure of the Empire in Flavian Rome: "The endless new beginnings of imperial literature are also the endless new beginnings of the Roman Empire, the hopeful yet hopeless attempt to ground both closure and continuity in politics".[24] As Fowler explains, the Flavian epic is characterised by its expansive, digressive nature: "they go on a bit but they refuse to get down to it".[25] The current volume shows that this Flavian tendency to *mora*,[26] the refusal to move towards the end, is related to the cyclic nature of civil war and the endless disasters in post-civil war times: in order to create meaningful political change, it is necessary to radically erase existing structures. The contributions in this volume show that endings and rituals apply to all generic contexts, from epic to occasional poetry, and to different textual spaces, at the end of a literary work or at the closing section of a literary text alluding to an open-ended story. Although a great deal of theory on poetic closure and on the relationship between religion and political power has already been done,[27] the current collection of papers focuses on the study of the poetics of closure through different religious practices in Flavian literature. It thus introduces a new interdisciplinary approach to a wide

---

21 See Papaioannou in this volume and also Papaioannou 2021, 70.
22 See Schroer in this volume.
23 See Antoniadis in this volume.
24 Fowler 1997, 8 on Hardie's book *The Epic Successors of Virgil*. See also Fucecchi in this volume.
25 Fowler 1997, 16.
26 Fowler 1997, 16.
27 See for example Kermode 1966, Herrnstein Smith 1968, Grewing/Acosta-Hughes/Kirichenko 2013. Individual research has been done first on the examination of the closure of the epics of the 1st c. CE with the most significant being Braund 1996, Dietrich 1999, Hardie 1997 and West 2007. Don Fowler opened the complicated discussion of endings in ancient texts, set the foundations for the study of closure, and discussed internal divisions that complicate further the sense of an ending; see Fowler 1989 and 1997. Augoustakis 2013 offers discussions on the Flavians' perception of cults, rituals, religious activities and the role of the seer-poet.

range of ancient texts and authors, which are important but not well-trodden in scholarship on Latin literature, and which are still in need of further research.[28]

Ultimately, the main goal of this volume is primarily to offer new perspectives on the relationship between literary closure and ritual, destruction, renewal and continuation in the Roman Empire, by bringing together both established and young researchers in the field of the Flavian literature. Overall, the studies in this book offer a new tool for studying literary endings through ritual, which will promote our understanding of Flavian culture and politics as well as creating a new perception of the use of religion and ritual in Flavian literature: instead of giving a sense of closure, this volume argues that ritual is a medium which increases complexity, exposes ritual actors and projects a generic riskiness of ritual actors also onto the epic actors who are acting in a ritual scene. Therefore, ritual provokes more questions than answers; it does not create resolution or closure, but rather a structural and cultural disruption in a correspondingly socially and politically disrupted post-civil war world.[29]

This volume explores ritual and closure in all genres developed in the Flavian era: epic, epigram and occasional poetry. As the table of contents show, the lion's share of the discussions involved herein concern epic poetry. For this reason, I decided to situate the papers that deal with non-epic poetry — Martial and Statius' *Siluae* — after the introduction, and then devote the rest of the volume to the epic genre particularly. The contributors explore key aspects of the essential interconnections between literature, religious studies and psychology as well as anthropology.

The volume opens with an introductory paper by Jörg Rüpke, who focuses on theoretical approaches and definitions of ritual, and examines how ritual is used in structuring literary compositions. Rüpke reviews insights from ritual studies and ritual theory; he interprets ritual as a highly dynamic way of constructing relationships between people, time, space, and a transcendence created by such an action. He focuses on the temporality of ritual and on the third-person phenomenon produced by the transcendence of given social constellation through ritual communication. As an historian of religion, Rüpke presents a reflection on what ritual actually is, and offers a concept of ritual that is useful as a tool for literary analysis. In order to illustrate his theory, Rüpke applies his approach to passages with complex treatments of rituals (death, burial and mourning) at the beginnings and endings of books of Statius' *Thebaid*. Rituals,

---

[28] See Nelis' paper about ideas for further research.
[29] Lovatt in this volume, for example, analyses how in Statius' *Thebaid* fire imagery in rituals causes catastrophic destruction and inner collapse.

he claims, are seen as sites of creativity and conflict rather than unanimously accepted social devices of affirming pre-conceived social and cosmic order.

The rest of the contributions explore examples of ritual at closing parts of Flavian texts and discuss how ritual opens up further questions instead of giving a sense of finality. After Rüpke's theoretical approach of ritual, the first literary genre treated is epigram; this particular genre is closely connected with the performance of rituals with its original function as inscription, or when it accompanies objects in rites such as dedications or funeral ceremonies. Ritual is the poetic matter of the *Siluae*, which records an accumulation of various rites of passage. The contributions of Margot Neger and Alison Keith focus on epigram and the one by Laila Dell'Anno deals with the *Siluae*.

In her paper Margot Neger explores several of Martial's books of epigram that begin and end with images of various rituals (such as the rituals of banqueting and gift-exchange during the Saturnalia at 14.223; 4.88; 5.84 and of commemorating the deceased at 1.114 and 116), both religious and social. She shows that Martial uses social and religious rituals as images conveying "a sense of an ending" to his books but, in many cases, religious practices such as oath making (at 8.81 and 12.90) are depicted in satirical contexts, and the characters who perform these rituals are ridiculed and mocked. On the other side, in epigrams regarding Martial's patrons and friends, rituals are often presented with a more serious tone.

Alison Keith explores the connections between religion, ritual, and literary closure in Martial's tenth book of epigrams. In Martial's final epigrams, ritual practices are associated with the poet's career end; they engage a series of social and religious rituals that propose the end of the poet's sojourn in Rome. More specifically, epigram 10.92 exhibits several closural features (a change in life; the poem's philosophical/ Epicurean frame, a gaze both retrospective and prospective; a dedication and the successful performance of religious ritual involving both sacrifice and prayer), and dovetails neatly with the closing programme of Martial's revised tenth book, anticipating the poet's departure from Italy and retirement to Spain. Therefore, according to Keith, 10.92 is part of the book's movement toward the end of Martial's revised tenth collection of epigrams and also as part of the poet's movement toward the close of his Italian career.

Keith's discussion on the interconnection between ritual and poetic production and the association of book closure with the end of Martial's poetic career leads us to the next contribution by Laila Dell'Anno, who focuses on Statius' *Siluae*. Dell'Anno first considers the editorial authenticity of book 5 of the *Siluae*, which has been disputed for decades, and then draws parallels between this particular book and Ovid's poetry of exile relating to their closural dynamics.

She discusses the tension between ritual and poetry by comparing Ovid's alleged loss of Latin and poetic aphasia caused by the absence of Rome in his exilic poetry, with Statius' impossibility to continue his poetry due to his grief of a *puer*'s death, which leads him to end his *Siluae*. At 5.5, the final poem of the *Siluae*, the collection, and with it Statius' poetic activity, comes to an abrupt end. As Statius progressively retreats from producing poetry, there is also a gradual disappearance of ritual description in the text, as there is no mention of any ritual for the boy's passing at 5.5. Hence, Dell'Anno argues that book 5 enacts a correspondingly gradual withdrawal from writing the *Siluae*, that is, from writing ritual. Through reference to the funerary rites at the end of the *Thebaid*, the ritual act of mourning itself in *Siluae* 5.5 comes to function as a closural device, since it is linked to the impossibility of narration. However, despite ritual's character as a closural device, ritual thus leads the author in a failure of poetic creation and continuation.

The rest of the papers focus specifically on the epic genre, i.e. Statius' *Thebaid*, Valerius Flaccus' *Argonautica* and Silius Italicus' *Punica*. There are some references to the *Achilleid*, the very incomplete Flavian epic, and Claudian's *De raptu*. The first three papers deal with rituals that can have an ambiguous or incomplete feeling of closure which thus creates a sense of open-endedness. First, Sophia Papaioannou focuses on Valerius' unfinished *Argonautica* and discusses the prominence of ritual as a traditional sign of epic closure. Papaioannou shows a connection between the unfinished final section of the *Argonautica* in book 8 and the meticulously crafted closure of the first book of the epic; book 1 shares certain important formal and thematic correspondences with book 8, the final book of the epic, which generates a 'ring composition' effect for the poem overall. She explores the politics of closure in Valerius by focusing on the final episode of the first book of the *Argonautica*, the murder of Aeson and Alcimede by Pelias, an episode that builds on the opposition between chaos and order, which dramatises a fraternal conflict, and develops around an impressive ritual (a necromancy) and a climax of sacrilege. She argues that the Aeson and Alcimede episode has been a Valerian addition to the Argonautic legend, is a self-standing narrative, and although it little influences the development of the story, it features the main closural themes expected at the end of a traditional heroic epic: ritual, death, emotional intensity, and open-endedness. According to Papaioannou, this premature ending provides a sense of resolution with an underlying political message ever present in the imperial era — the many faces of internecine conflict — and the proper closure that is missing from the Latin *Argonautica*.

In Flavian epic the common imagery related to funeral rites and triumphs is often reversed or perverted in a way that undermines their obvious function as public spectacle and artistic representation. This is particularly evident in the closing scenes of several books of Silius Italicus' *Punica*, where different aspects of ritual are often collated to create a sense of an ending that is ambiguous and incomplete. Such poetics of closure fuse resolution and constraint so as to undercut the establishment of order supposedly achieved by ritual performances and religious practices on an individual and public level. First, Clayton Schroer explores Silius Italicus' *Punica*, a finished epic but with many smaller narratives remaining open, thus raising further questions about its closedness. Schroer demonstrates how Silius uses the ritual of the *reditus* — the ritual celebration of a victorious general coming back to Rome — as a closural strategy to make a distinction between the exiles of Scipio and Hannibal, with Scipio's triumphal "return" proleptically remedying his future exile: Hannibal's intended (but failed) *reditus* corresponds to the connotations of exile that Scipio's triumph creates at the *Punica*'s conclusion. Schroer argues that in the *Punica*'s denouement Silius does not completely dismiss Scipio's future removal from Rome, thereby hinting in this one ritual to both the closure and continuation of his narrative, causing open-endedness.

The next chapter explores the (anti-) closural function of 'false rituals' in Silius Italicus' *Punica*. Theodoros Antoniadis demonstrates that the religious element is often used by Silius to create an ambiguous and unsettling closure to several episodes of the epic with symbolic import. Antoniadis focuses on the problematic rituals in books 2, 5 and 17. First, the mass suicide of the Saguntines and the subsequent pollution implicated in book 2 increase readerly dissatisfaction and an atmosphere of chaos and disorder as a result of human decadence. In book 5 Flaminius is denied the customary funeral rites while the only tomb he is granted is made up of the cadavers of Roman soldiers. Finally, Hannibal's disappearance from Scipio's triumphal parade at the end of book 17 creates a sense of emptiness, which thus transforms the ritual celebration into a mock funeral. According to Antoniadis, these 'false rituals' as public spectacles embodied in an epic can be further construed as equivocal responses to the extreme theatricalisation of religious ceremonies under Nero. Therefore, when funerals and triumphs take place in Silius' epic, this is only to confirm that in the Flavian culture ritual had been gradually transformed from a religious ceremony into ritual discourse.

The next chapter by Helen Lovatt builds on existing work on funerals, lament, and closure in the *Thebaid* to reveal how fire imagery contributes to the complexity of the poem's narrative articulation, ritual scenes and their relationships to the Theban poetics of incest and politics of resistance. Lovatt shows that the *Thebaid* is structured not just by a series of deaths but also by a series of problematic, refused, incomplete or unsatisfying funerals. She explores the relationship between fire, ritual and narrative articulation in Statius' *Thebaid* to argue that funeral ritual, and other rituals associated with fire do not provide secure transition in spatial, temporal, spiritual or narrative terms in the epic, but that the accumulation of failed rituals creates rather a collapse inwards of the epic's structure itself. She finally shows that in the middle of the epic, Statius creates an imagery of both opening and closing, so that every part of the poem can be read as simultaneously beginning, middle and end. This destabilisation of ritual practice, and the blurring of narrative divisions and thematic ideas, fundamentally setting epic teleology on fire, suggests, according to Lovatt, a dark political vision in the Flavian era.

The final two chapters discuss the metaphors of release — opening — dissolution and binding — closure — reconstruction in the epic genre, allowing further discussion of political restoration in Imperial times. First, Michael Knierim examines ritual and closure in Valerius' *Argonautica*, through the lens of modern literature on trauma and moral injury. Knierim applies the moral injury theory to Valerius' Cyzicus episode, where Jason and the Argonauts are paralysed by guilt and grief after unintentionally killing their hosts in a night-battle until Mopsus acts like a forgiving authority figure of moral injury and heals the group with a communal ritual. Even the funeral ritual, helpful though it might be, fails to produce psychological or literary closure as the Argonauts still remain emotionally paralysed. The quest and the poem itself cannot proceed until a further ritual is performed by a legitimate moral authority figure whose explanatory conversation helps Jason and whose ritual reinforces the unity of the Argonauts, helping them to lay aside their memories and finally close off the Cyzicus episode. Knierim considers Medea, first Valerius' more hopeful version, then Apollonius' Circe episode which isolates Medea rather than reintegrating her. According to Knierim, both purification rituals mark an end: the one in Valerius brings a healing closure to the Argonauts' feelings of guilt and grief from the moral injury of the slaying of their hosts; the Circe episode in Apollonius marks the end of Medea's relationship with her family, her people and her language as well as the intensification of her suffering from moral injury. Valerius Flaccus in particular points a positive way forward embodying many of the principles of current moral injury research with effective community action, whereas Apollonius shows us the effects of its absence. Finally, Knierim argues that Valerius' positive way leads to a refreshing feeling of release for the

Argonauts and the reader as well as some hope for restoration for a Flavian world full of the wounds of civil war.

In the final chapter of the volume Marco Fucecchi analyses the phrase *compage soluta* which illustrates the loosening of the very structure of the cosmos as often occurs in texts dealing with civil war, such as Lucan's *De bello ciuili*, Statius' *Thebaid*, Silius' *Punica* and Claudian's *De raptu Proserpinae*. Fucecchi creates a dialectical tension between images of release — opening — dissolution, on the one hand, and binding — closure — (re)construction on the other, situating the phrase within a Stoic conceptual frame and asserting its influence throughout the epic tradition. He starts by analysing Lucan's use of *compage soluta* at 1.72, he then explores the storm of the Amyclas episode at book 5 which he considers an instance of the cosmic collapse where the heaven's framework was shaken (*soluta compage*) announced by the poem's first simile, while at the same time, it also reenacts — and even overturns — other 'chaotic' epic openings, such as *Aeneid* 1. Fucecchi demonstrates that images of cosmic dissolution characterise crucial points — mostly openings and closures — of Latin war epic since the 1st c. CE. Historical characters (such as Caesar, Hannibal) or the gods of the underworld, like the Furies and Hades also seem undaunted by cosmic dissolution, and display the ambition to take control over the entire universe. The gods are proved unable to tame the forces of chaos, and the gods' ultimate target (starting with Flavian epic, at least) is the construction of a new (human) authority as well as of a more 'human' power (mirrored in epic characters like Statius' Theseus or Silius' Scipio) that can actually resist the forces of chaos. And this is what, according to Fucecchi, will ensure the renewal and perpetuation of the Empire.

The volume's denouement comes with a contribution by Damien Nelis, who provides an overview of the beginning of the study of closure, and stresses the importance of defining the term 'ritual' before any scrutiny of the subject of closure in the Flavian texts. He finally writes down his thoughts on how the subject of Ritual and Closure can be expanded and developed in different genres and periods.

While the contributions in the volume provide a meticulous study of specific episodes of ritual and closure in Flavian literature, the subject can be studied further in other episodes of Flavian literature. I believe that the volume has at least shed some light in the investigation of such a complicated subject and I aspire the volume to advance the current scholarship on Flavian literature and culture.

Jörg Rüpke
Ritual Closure and Transcendence: Mobilising Ritual Theory for Flavian Epic

Abstract: Closure of epic books is related to the conventions and necessities of recitation as much as to the articulation of narrative progress and structure. Starting from the occasional but significant presence of descriptions of, or references to, rituals at the end of epic books, this paper uses insights from ritual studies and ritual theory to identify testable hypotheses for this pattern. Focussing on ritualisation rather than on the repetition of scripted rituals, the creative use of ritual as a strategy and a tool to solve problems of loss, threats or insecurity by establishing new relationships, new social and material constellations, will be foregrounded. Special emphasis will be given to the temporality of ritual and to the so-called 'third-person phenomenon' produced by the transcendence of given social constellations through ritual communication. Such insights, it will be argued, help to better understand Statius' positioning and his short or deliberately complex treatments of rituals at the ends and beginnings of books of his *Thebaid*. Rituals, the chapter claims, are seen by Statius as sites of creativity and conflicts rather than unanimously accepted social devices of affirming pre-conceived social and cosmic order.

1 Endless Rituals

Closure of epic books is related to the conventions and necessities of recitation as much as to the articulation of narrative progress and structure. Research following the landmark study of Roberts/Dunn/Fowler,[1] and furthered in this volume has analysed the careful mediation of continuity and interruption in ongoing narrative and the struggle of Latin epic poets of finding their solution

---

I am grateful for the invitation by Angeliki-Nektaria Roumpou to bring together research on rituals and epic closure and her many interventions and clarifying additions to my text. The theoretical approach taken here reflects research supported by the German Science Foundation (DFG) in the framework of the International Research Training School "Resonant socioreligious practices in ancient and modern societies" at the Universities of Erfurt and Graz (GRK 2283).

1 Roberts/Dunn/Fowler 1997, especially Fowler's introduction.

in their attempts to position themselves in texts which were regarded as tainted by problems of ending. Such problems included the possibility of loss of text in textual transmission and illegitimate additions as in the case of Homer. Epic narrative of recent and contemporary history was ended and continued afterwards by the same author several times, as Ennius' *Annales* illustrate. Or epic authors might opt for deliberately open endings as is illustrated by Virgil's *Aeneid* and Ovid's *Metamorphoses*, perhaps also by Lucan.[2] It is, however, not the *very* end of epic oeuvres that offers my point of departure here. That the epic form has a recurring pattern of beginnings and endings whenever the length of a "book", that is scroll, is transcended means that the challenges associated with epic closure are repeatedly met, and it is these interim endings on which this article focuses. Many ancient epics – in contrast to *epyllia* – were not consumed in the convenient hard-or paperback forms of today but rather in piecemeal fashion. To roll your scroll and return it to the shelf or to have endured an hour of recitation might well have been the typical point of "calling it a day" and postponing continuation of reading or listening to subsequent days – some professionals including the prolific Flavian, but not epic, Pliny the Elder excepted, who famously enjoyed nightly reading – *lucubrationes* (*HN* 19.173). Dawn and dusk, daylight and night are probably the most frequent marker of the epic book structure,[3] and this holds true also for Flavian epics.

This chapter starts by observing the occasional but significant description of, or references to, rituals at the end of epic books. Subsequently, I aim to review insights from ritual studies and ritual theory to identify testable hypotheses for this pattern. Special emphasis will be given to the temporality of ritual and to the third-person phenomenon produced by the transcendence of given social constellation through ritual communication.

Yet as this volume attests, rituals, too, are frequently in prominent positions of epic books. In Statius' *Thebaid*,[4] an epic that I will later use as a reference point, nearly all books conclude on a ritual, preparation of a ritual, or a religious communication – I will identify these terms shortly.[5] Books 6 and 7 show *omina* or *prodigia* in these positions, book 8 an epiphany of Athena. Although the ending of book 10 might not be as clear-cut, I interpret the duel of Capaneus

---

[2] See in particular Hardie 1997.
[3] Thus Rüpke 2012, 238; see also Sacerdoti 2019.
[4] See in general the still useful analyses of Kytzler 1955; Cancik 1965; Juhnke 1972; Ahl 1986; Henderson 1993; for rituals in Statius, see Leibinger 2000; Augoustakis 2013.
[5] For Statian endings, Schetter 1960, 64–71; Braund 1996; for *Thebaid* book 1, see Newlands 2009a.

and Jupiter (10.883–939, the scene starts at 837), as a silent but quite intensive form of human – divine interaction.⁶ The obvious exception is book 11 – the penultimate book directly leading into the epic finals of book 12. While ritual or its equivalent, according to my definition, often acts as a structural marker to the endings of books, it features much more rarely in their beginnings. Rather than marking new beginnings, the books' openings instead indicate attempts to interlace books with preceding ones: the extensive funeral festivities for the divinised infant Opheltes in book 6 (1–248), the epiphanies of book 7 (1–226) and the Plutonian rituals and dialogues of book 8 (1–126) after the engulfment of Amphiaraus, as well as the negation of ritual of the beginning of book 9 (1–31), reacting to the sacrilege of Tydeus' act of cannibalism at the end of book 8 (760–767). Their dominance in the middle, the "Durstsrecke", of the long epic might show the poet's keen awareness for the reading or listening experience of his audience; the intensification of attention by narrating rituals would then be used for quicker reconnection to the already complex narrative, which had been interrupted by the mechanical (and probably also temporal) interruption of the ending of scrolls.

Recent literary criticism as displayed in this volume has dealt intensively with such phenomena and more expert scholars will continue to do so. What I am able to offer, as an historian of religion, is a reflection on what ritual actually is. More precisely, I will offer a concept of ritual that might be useful as a *tool* for literary analysis. In the following lines, I will develop this concept,⁷ and at the very end I will return to my reference point, the *Thebaid*, and offer some literary hypotheses to stimulate further investigation.

2 Ritual

Religious action establishes a relationship between human actors and addressees, such as ancestors, spirits, divinities or non-transparent objects that are attributed agency in the given situation, beyond the usual context of social interaction. Such a move on the part of the instigators might be culturally well established and plausibilised by objects, place and time, but might also be a daring move against the expectation of the bystanders. Such addressees receive their special or "divine" status – and this by no means necessarily includes

---

6 Cf. Dominik 2012; Chaudhuri 2014; Pontiggia 2018.
7 That section is based on translated passages from Rüpke 2021.

their personalisation[8] — precisely through the special actions of those who want to address them and introduce them as such special participants in the situation, i.e. through "ritualisation". From the perspective of the actors, successful ritual action depends on a temporal and spatial framing that qualifies communication directed at transcendent actors and makes it successful in attracting their reactions. This is part of "ritualisation". Times, but above all spaces created by social action and material objects seem to have been very important in this respect. Such objects, times, and spaces may have already been charged by earlier religious acts in processes which I call "sacralisation". Conversely, it is such spaces, times and material or immaterial representations of addressees — sanctuaries, holidays, altars or images — that invite ritualised action and influence the choice not only between strategies, but indeed the choice to employ a religious strategy at all.

It is in such religious practices that relationships between the self and the world are experienced, practised and institutionalised. The "world" addressed is not just a political community and its deities, but includes the self, the social, things (objects) and transcendence. Establishing a relationship to this world relies on initiative and creativity in the use of ritual as a strategy and a tool to solve problems of loss, threats or insecurity by establishing new relationships. It is from this that many social and material constellations and traditions emerge rather than being based on preceding institutionalisations and standardisations. In such a view of ritual, its initiators and their social and institutional positions and their interests are of importance, indeed analysing rituals might also reveal the actors' aims. The analysis of ritual communication needs to inquire into the investments made by the originators into such a strategy or tool in the form of media created or employed. These serve to ensure the primary communicative success by attracting attention to woo the divine counterparts. Thus, they serve to control a relationship to a section of the world that is hardly open to direct observation, to establish a reputation as a pious person or radical. In this way, religious rituals gain a materiality that determines the later historical traditions as well as the contemporary perception of religion for participants and observers alike. It is precisely here that resonance theory, as I have recently suggested on the basis of the work of my colleague Hartmut Rosa, becomes

---

8 Such personalisation or even anthropomorphisation is a consequence rather than a prerequisite of religious communication attributing agency on the model of human agency; aniconic objects or abstract ideas of transcendental order can also be addressed thus stressing the specialness by their divergence of human models without any reduction in agency.

helpful as an analytical concept.⁹ Resonance theory is a type of relational sociology, which looks into the mutual constitution of subjects and objects (or other subjects) in their many relationships. Built on the assumption that humans need relationships of a particular, namely resonant quality (instead of mute or repulsive relationships), resonance theory postulates conditions for resonance to occur: attribution of agency and being attributed agency, self-empowerment and self-effacing, listening and being heard, including and touching the other, but also being addressed and touched by social and material others. Finally trusting in the reaction of the addressed and controlling their reaction, producing and experiencing transformation are important. In difference to ritual theory, resonance theory however does not regard resonance as a tool that can be easily produced and applied but as a specific and intensive outcome of an encounter that cannot be forced to happen (*unverfügbar*).

In the expansion of the sociality to include the material, the more recent scholarship focuses on things that are not regarded just as "objects" and on the effect of their materiality on, and entanglement with, human actors.¹⁰ In his more recent work, Bruno Latour has characterised religion in particular as a cultural practice, a mode of existence, shaped by such materiality and its impact.¹¹ For the study of rituals, this opens up a perspective that no longer has to see the material in ritual, from tools to communication media (i.e. gifts), to the material and architectural environment, only from a semiotic perspective.¹² Thus, their function and functionalisation as carriers of memory, as triggers of experience, as well as their structuring effect on ritual movements and temporal divisions, their affordance, move into the foreground.¹³

The material dimension is closely intertwined with the spatial. In ritual action, space is differentiated, is sacralised temporarily or permanently to varying degrees. Such space is productive, creating meanings, relationships and religious roles.¹⁴ Cultural geographic concepts of space, as developed by Benno Werlen or Jacques Lévy, suggest space functions as an instrument of closure of ritual action or simply as a necessary and stabilising component of ritual

---

9 Rüpke 2021 with reference to Rosa 2019.
10 Appadurai 1986; Gosden/Marshall 1999; Hodder 2012; for religion, e.g. Chidester 2018; Promey 2014; Weinrich 2020.
11 Rosa 2016b, 556–559; 2016a; Latour 2011.
12 This approach still dominates in religious archaeology, see for example Insoll 2001; 2004; 2009; 2011, cf. by contrast Raja/Rüpke 2015b. For the use of media in successful religious communication, see Rüpke 2018, 64–65.
13 Raja/Rüpke 2015a; 2015c; Rieger 2016; 2018; 2020.
14 See Tweed 2011.

action.¹⁵ It is not Cartesian space, a geographical point where rituals take place, but rather an environment considered relevant and effective through the networking and processing of an assemblage of things and people. Conversely, it creates for the actors a relevant environment from the perspective of other, overlapping structures: the ritual in the temple interior space is not only an act of communication intended as a temple ritual by its initiators, but also part of the sacralised atmosphere of those who act or experience in the temple forecourt. A temple would not be a "house of God", but only a "house", and a religious action only an action, if it did not ascribe agency to addressees in that situation and thus significantly influence the non-Cartesian layout of the space of action. A primarily horizontal definition of space is problematised when there is an emphasis on the vertical or a gesture of pointing or invoking addressees far beyond the metrics of the accessible or visible. The spatial arrangement of material things, which can be plainly viewed or experienced by all participants, can serve to store knowledge as well as a trigger of memories and experiences, evoking emotions or even just memories of emotions: euphoria as well as dejection.

Let me clarify a further point. Religious action can be understood as a form of communication with specific actors (sometimes objects), often conceived as gods or deities, ancestors or demons. Actual religious communication is not only characterised by a verbal inclusion of the "special" actors defined above.¹⁶ Through the performance of such communicative acts and their particular contents, these special actors are granted a power of action, an agency, that is not plainly plausible beyond doubt for the other social actors involved.¹⁷ Since this interaction is based on assumptions open to criticism from points of view like etiquette, economic judgement, priority of written law or political decisions rather than religious claims about divine will, many decisions during this process can elicit criticism from observers clinging to the divergent norms just listed, either at the time of address or after it: the decision to use religious communication at all in a *particular situation,* to use *this kind* of religious communication or to address *this particular addressee.* Every act of religious communication is therefore a risky form of communication, even if religious communication as such

---

15 See for example Lévy/Lussault 2013; Suarsana/Werlen/Meusburger 2017; Werlen 2008; 2021 (each without reference to religion).
16 The concept of the special is introduced in Taves 2009.
17 One example is offered by Antoniadis in this volume: the Carthaginian Hannibal at *Punica* 10 is the only one that offers burial to Roman Paulus, hence he is described as *unus sat decoris laudator* (568–569), i.e. the absolute religious actor who therefore outshines his opponents in terms of religious communication and effect.

is considered acceptable in the respective historical context, i.e. if actors and audiences do not question the existence of effective ancestors or deities *per se*.

The risk factor just mentioned is a consequence of the social embedding of religious communication. Communication with or about such divine actors is a standard part of human action, it creates or alters social relations and changes power relations across the complex web of instigators, participants, mere observers and those who are distant yet understand what they are witnessing. In the eyes of such spectators or observers, it is the specific addressees who provide their human worshippers with agency and opportunities to act. Obviously, the attribution of superior power now also to human actors in certain material, spatial, temporal and social constellations can challenge or even overcome the constraints of everyday life: health, (re)production capacities, spatial or social constraints and hierarchies. Such constellations and the experience provided by them, that is, a satisfying or encouraging experience of the malleability of some segments of the world is sought after in rituals. Such rituals include the fundamentally uncontrollable practices denounced by contemporaries as magic, but they also include initiation ceremonies or opportunities to monopolise priestly roles or to monopolise religious knowledge. Both extremes, the concealed practice as well as the ostentatious, pragmatically function through the collaboration of human counterparts who criticise such action precisely because they fear its efficacy. At the same time, ritual actors are sensitive to criticism, creative alternatives or non-compliance of further human participants. In the face of such risks, which can affect even a high-ranking actor, a ruler for instance, religious action requires safeguarding through further techniques.

Religious action must also be strengthened for another reason. If religious communication occurs between mortal and divine actors, I have so far emphasised the risks that come from the human side. But as much as human actors remain outside of all-encompassing social control, even in small and so-called traditional societies, the not tangible actors are not entirely transparent figures. The very communication that brings the divine actors into real situations for the mortal here and now must construct the deities as independent from the human participants.

This is where the concept of ritualisation comes into play and, I suggest, only as a shorthand term, the concept of ritual. In order to become recognisable and effective, communication with special actors must be different from everyday communication (on which it is modelled). How can the pragmatic efficiency of this communication, which is notoriously difficult to evaluate, as well as its plausibility, to which the other participants in active and passive forms must agree, be ensured? For those who initiate the communication as well as for the other participants including those playing a passive bystander role beyond language and gestures, material things are also used intensively, objects that function as a communication medium. The act of communication and the variety of media involved thus promote the existence of the otherwise invisible addressees.[18]

The media intensity of religious communication is by no means the least important reason for its presence, indeed overrepresentation, in the material tradition. I propose to understand sacralisation as actions and processes that incorporate elements of the situation — objects, space, time — into the ritual act and thereby ascribe special meaning to them. Sacrality is thus something that can be given different degrees of intensity. Such processes have a temporal dimension. Sacralised objects (and places or times constituted as sacral, which are marked with these objects) thus create the conditions to control the interpretive processes associated with communicative action and to control the risks presented: the sacralised space provides knowledge and sedimented emotions that form part of memory and stimulates their use, memory or reproduction.[19] The reuse of objects or places or the inclusion of new objects in the process of framing can strengthen and intensify the religious character of an event. Sacralisation is a matter of quantity and scale.[20]

The position of ritual actors can be enhanced through the use of previously sacralised objects or through their positioning in previously sacralised spaces, that is, the deliberate layering and linking of ritually constructed spaces.[21] Praying in a temple, sacrificing on a holiday, preaching in a priest's robe — all can serve to enhance religious authority as long as the actor's position of power allows him or her to use these means.[22] And it is precisely such repetition or

---

[18] See Rüpke 2007.
[19] On the 'places of memory' in Judeo-Christian rituals, Kranemann 2017; on the secondary memory of places of memory, Leonhard 2005; on the turn to the ritual place itself exemplarily, see Triplett 2010. On negative and erased memories, see Östenberg 2019; on the concept in general, see Nora/Ageron in recourse to Halbwachs 1925.
[20] Thus, concepts such as "sacred topography" or "sacred landscape" (for example Cancik 1985; Ando 2001; Caseau 1999; Ceccarelli 2008; Hahn/Gotter 2008; MacCormack 1990; Steinsapir 2005) must also be discussed in terms of the degree of sacralisation — as well as visibility, legibility and intentionality.
[21] For example, after his victories at the Greek festivals, Nero arrived in Rome at 67 CE riding the same triumphal chariot that Augustus had used to celebrate his military victories, with a mocking effect though.
[22] For a detailed discussion, see Patzelt 2018 (on praying) or Rüpke 2013 and Rüpke 2018 (for sanctuaries). For the notion of religious authority, see Blidstein 2018; Bowden 2013; Cheong/Huang/Poon 2011; Gordon 2013; Kolb 1994; Strathern 2019.

consolidation, often combined with the reminder of the explicit purpose of such constructions of space, time and body, that turns these entities into (in these cases, intensely) sacralised spaces, times, things. This is a process of negotiation and appropriation, a process in which the body is the most important connecting link.[23]

We must keep in mind that religious action itself is a strategic decision of the actors; of course, such a "strategy" can also be habitualised or even consciously institutionalised and therefore seem almost without alternative in a particular given situation. In such a constructivist perspective, the religious actors assert (to very different degrees) the effectiveness of communication while at the same time postulating (again to very different degrees) the agency and the self-will of the addressees and thus the risk level, the likelihood of success and failure, of their own actions. Specific things can be done to increase the likelihood of success, for example heightening the ritualisation of the action. Words and colours that bring good luck, pleasant scents and food, locked rooms and bids of silence are supposed to ensure success, which is continuously checked by means of divination procedures, the enquiry of the god's will in the intestines, light effects and so on. In this way, the self-efficacy of the actors is to be strengthened and affirmed in a situation characterised by a high degree of constitutive unavailability, the impossibility of achieving goals in a way that can be planned.

The question of the relationship between the self and world of the ritual actor intensifies the attention to the subjectification that takes place in the ritual. For this, I refer to research that has examined the self-referential and emotional quality of rituals,[24] but also work that considers rituals as tools of religious reflection rather than faith, and not as mere expressions of belief or social order.[25] The degree of plausibility of the "special" agents to which actor quality or "agency" is attributed opens up a broad field of ritual analysis, despite the seemingly narrow starting point from a substantialist definition of "religion", that is a single definition, that refers to "special" or "divine" actors. Such religious action can certainly be analysed as communication employing a massive amount of media. The relational analysis proposed here goes however beyond

---

[23] Werlen 2017, 41 with reference to Schütz 1981.
[24] For Mediterranean religions, see Barchiesi/Rüpke/Stephens 2004; Rüpke 2005; Stavrianopoulou 2006; Borgeaud 2009; Rüpke/Scheid 2010; Favro/Johanson 2010; Georgoudi/Koch/Schmidt 2012; Brandt/Iddeng 2012; Raja/Rüpke 2015b; for precedence for Greek rituals see Chaniotis 2009; 2011; 2013a; 2013b.
[25] For example, see Insoll 2004; 2009; 2011; Scheid 2005a; 2005b.

such instrumental function of the material components. It also inquires into the form and qualities of the relationships between objects, addressers and addressees and the actor quality of all in jointly spanned space and time redeems the breadth of the relational programmatic. The self-referentiality of religious ritual is the only way to achieve a categorical other at all. But beyond this other, relations are thus created with a changing world, relations that are not only directed towards the world but also listen to it and are modified by it, not in lofty reflection but quite pragmatically. How far a concise concept of resonance can be used for such investigations will have to be examined.

3 Doing ritual and writing ritual

My extensive development of a theory of ritual was intended to invite consideration of ritual as a highly dynamic way of constructing relationships between people, times, spaces, and a transcendence created (even if not *de nouo*) by such action. The dynamic and risky character is reflected in, and helps us to understand, several features of the *Thebaid*'s rituals.

– They are not just natural occurrences, but might be highly contested. Burial for instance, is demanded or negated; Tydeus, close to his heroisation at the end of book 8, is denied burial at the beginning of book 9 due to his indulging in cannibalism (gnawing on Melanippus' brains; 8.760). Minerva begs Jupiter to grant Tydeus immortality (8.715). Upon her return to the battlefield with a positive response from her father (8.759 *miser decus immortale ferebat*), she sees Tydeus' act of cannibalism. Due to this act of sacrilege, her promise is annuled (8.762–767/end of book). At the beginning of book 9, the Thebans try to take over Tydeus' body to avenge Melanippus and prevent his burial by the Argives (9.1–31). The Thebans' intentions are made clear through the simile likening them to vultures attracted by rotting bodies (9.27–31 esp. 29 *sine funere mortes*). Therefore, in this case funerary rituals for Tydeus are denied.
– The elaborate funeral of Opheltes[26] at the beginning of book 6 needs a process of decision to be materialised at the end of book 5. The case is complex again. In the case of Opheltes, immediately after the child's accidental death, his immortality had been acknowledged by the seer Amphiaraus at the end of book 5 (5.750–752) and he had called for a proper funeral and the

---

[26] For the literary precedences, see Vessey 1973, 138–143.

instauration of an actual cult to the divinised baby (5.741–743 *mansuris donandus honoribus infans / et meruit; det pulchra suis libamina uirtus / manibus*). The funeral rites then take place at the beginning of book 6 (24–250) and a festival, the Nemean games, is inaugurated in his honour. Therefore, the ritual of burial is not doubted; the point instead resides in the instauration of lasting rituals which has been demanded by Amphiaraus.

– Rituals are themselves frames of highly dynamic communication and interaction. Even if prayer might be taken as a basic form, typically rituals are not monologues indexed by a positive assent or silence at the end. For example, at the end of book 3, Argia's prayer-like addressing of her father Adrastus to help Polynices regain his throne by waging war on Thebes (*da bella, pater* at 696) is followed by Adrastus' answer that he agrees to support Polynices (3.712–720).[27] Evidently, the interaction between human daughter and father is modelled on religious rituals and religious semantics.

– While references to seemingly standardised rituals do exist, for example the animal sacrifice by a priest very early in book 4 (4.13–15) or the conclusion of a treaty very late in book 12, these are mentioned in passing rather than conveying structural force. In book 12, the treaty is only summarily referred to, but it quickly develops into a brief and hasty but vivid description of widespread mourning and multiple rituals.[28] The fleeting reference to the standard form of treaty between the Thebans and the Athenians after the death of Creon (12.782–785) is followed by a description of the mourning Argive women who burst onto the battlefield in search of their husbands (12.789–796). The mention of both forms of rituals (the Thebans' peace treaty and the Argives' funeral) are likened to Bacchic rituals through similes (12.787–789; 791–793). Therefore, excessive rituals supersede the 'standard' ones.

– In the more developed examples, the degree of ritualisation is quite diverse. The prayer to the river Nemea, voiced by an (deliberately) unknown speaker (4.824 *aliquis regum*), which concludes book 4 (825–843), is hardly ritualised — as the only mention of a religious action is the intention of celebrating the river at feasts (4.839–841 *festasque super celebrare mensas*) — it is instead embedded into the pragmatic act of fighting thirst, that is, drinking water. Therefore, priority is given to pragmatic matters rather than dwelling

---

27 See Pepe/Moretti 2015 on funerary rhetorics.
28 See Sterbenc Erker 2009 for the role of women shedding tears. On funerary rites in general, Hope 2009; Hope/Huskinson 2011.

- on ritualisation. The focus is here on the even more intensive relationship to water stimulated by thirst than typical ritual practices.
- Similar is the complex epiphany of divinities and the preceding exchange between the gods at the beginning of book 7 (1–226). Among themselves, gods do not need ritualisation. The same holds true to a lesser degree in the netherworld at the beginning of the subsequent book (8.1–126).
- Rituals bring together many and, at times, very different people. Here, elaborate ritualisation creates a bubble in space and time very different from the spatio-temporality around it — referred to occasionally by a "meanwhile". These people form a temporary community — to come together later again or to dissipate forever.
- In a text so interested in materiality and above all the corporeal, it is warfare, wounding, killing and dying that are primary means to explore the body. Rituals accrue, however. These include the dedication of arms to a tree (*exuuias* 726 f.) at the end of book 2, where Tydeus erects a trophy to Minerva to thank her for his victory over the soldiers sent by Eteocles to ambush him (2.704–742), thus presenting the mere shell of a warrior's body. To this the many funerary rites have to be added, including the imagination of splitting and dissipating one's own body in a ritual manner given to Parthenopaeus at the end of book 9 (885–907).[29] As he is dying, Parthenopaeus cuts a lock of his hair and sends it to his mother as a replacement of him after his death (9.901 *hunc toto pro corpore crinem*; 903 *huic dabis exequias*).

No doubt, Statius has his protagonists doing rituals for good reasons and various effects. Let me gloss over the structural issues that are focused on in this volume and I will certainly reach some clearer observations. Instead, I would like to end on a hypothesis that might shed some light on the relations established between Statius and his readers by the poet's written[30] rituals. One of the most frequently invoked (even if hardly very well understood)[31] effects of communication via mass and social media is the so-called "third-person effect". Let me quote from the founding father of the notion, W. Davison:

> people will tend to overestimate the influence that mass communications have on the attitudes and behaviour of others. More specifically, individuals who are members of an audience that is exposed to a persuasive communication (whether or not this communication is intended to be persuasive) will expect the communication to have a greater effect

---

29 See Borg 2014 on the contemporary dramatisation of death on sarcophagi.
30 See Nasse 2012 on that perspective.
31 See Tsfati 2011.

on others than on themselves. And whether or not these individuals are among the ostensible audience for the message, the impact that they expect this communication to have on others may lead them to take some action. Any effect that the communication achieves may thus be due not to the reaction of the ostensible audience but rather to the behaviour of those who anticipate, or think they perceive, some reaction on the part of others.[32]

All observations discussed and explained through this concept relate to the modern world. Let me postulate validity for antiquity, too. According to my model of ritual as religious communication, rituals are intended and perceived as "persuasive communication". In the face of much explicit critique of and debate about particular rituals as well as formalised ritual and sacrifice in general, such a third-person effect might explain the high degree of conformity reflected by the overall success and long survival of many rituals and ancient ritual systems. This, however, is not at issue here. If Statius' listeners and readers themselves were subject to the third-person effect, they would have imagined rituals not from the point of view of people, for whom such practices were customary and unquestionable, but as contended and only precariously successful courses of action. Thus, rituals do not operate as a calming reduction of complexity but rather bring about a narrative increase of discrepant layers of positions, intentions, and actions, of relationships of very different qualities and hence an increase in reflection and tension. Rituals would make a causal narrative,[33] typically moving into nightly torpor, more complex. They provide a question mark rather than a full-stop.

---

32 Davison 1983, 3.
33 Cf. Narlikar 2020.

Margot Neger
Religious and Social Rituals as Motifs of Closure in Martial's *Epigrams*

Abstract: Several of Martial's epigram books begin and end with images of various rituals, both religious and social. The epigrammatic genre itself is closely connected with the performance of rituals: in their original function as inscriptions, epigrams accompanied objects with important roles in rituals such as dedications or funeral ceremonies. As the paper argues, images of rituals are exploited by Martial in many ways: already the preface to Book 1 suggests that reading the epigrams corresponds to participating in the cheerful festival for the Roman goddess Flora. The same book ends with a different atmosphere when two epigrams (1.114 and 116) present a father performing the funeral rites for his deceased daughter. Moreover, the Saturnalia are another prominent festival which marks both the beginning and closure of several books, especially Books 2, 4, 5, 7 and 11, or is even the subject of two entire volumes (13 and 14, the *Xenia* and *Apophoreta*). The act of swearing an oath is another closural motif which appears at the end of Books 8 and 12 where characters making vows are ridiculed in satirical epigrams.

Modern scholarship has long recognised that Martial's epigram books are not a randomly produced collection of individual poems, but artfully composed textual units.[1] In this context, Martial's techniques of book closure have also been studied in several contributions.[2] Besides the question of book composition, the depiction of Roman society and social practices in Martial's epigrams is another topic to which a fair amount of scholarship has been dedicated.[3] The role of religion in Martial's poems, on the other hand, has not yet been systematically studied.[4] Whereas social rituals, especially those connected with the patron-client-relationship (such as the *salutatio* early in the morning, the exchange of gifts, the dedication of poetry to a patron or the invitation to the *cena* in the

---

[1] See Merli 1993; Fowler 1995; Merli 1998; Scherf 2001; Holzberg 2004/05; Lorenz 2004; Höschele 2010, 38–68; Lorenz 2019.
[2] See Fowler 1989; Canobbio 2007; Höschele 2013; cf. Gunderson 2021, who studies the political valence of Martial's closural practices. See also Keith in this volume.
[3] See White 1972; 1975; Nauta 2002; Spisak 2007; Flores Militello 2019; see also the relevant bibliography in Lorenz 2003 and 2006.
[4] First attempts were made by Kaliwoda 1998.

https://doi.org/10.1515/9783110770483-003

evening) are omnipresent in the collection, religion and religious rituals are a topic which one encounters less frequently in the epigrams. When religion appears, it is often connected with the Imperial cult, especially Domitian's depiction as a deity.[5] Moreover, in those epigrams where Martial deals with religious matters, his approach is often more playful than serious. Take, for example, epigram 3.24, where Martial describes a sacrifice for Bacchus which did not go as planned due to a misunderstanding.[6] The Tuscan priest's assistant, a simple peasant, by mistake cut off the testicles of the priest instead of the actual victim, a he-goat which was supposed to be sacrificed to the god. Thus, the *Tuscus aruspex* was transformed in a *Gallus aruspex* (13–14 *sic, modo qui Tuscus fueras, nunc Gallus aruspex, / dum iugulas hircum, factus es ipse caper*, "So, soothsayer, recently Tuscan but now Gaul, in slaughtering a goat you yourself became a gelding"),[7] not an actual priest from Gaul, but one of Cybele's priests (γάλλοι) who used to castrate themselves.[8] In Martial's world, the combination of religious topics with coarse jokes on body parts does not seem to be problematic, as one can also see in epigram 12.77 about a prayer to Jupiter in the Capitolium:[9] while Aethon was praying to the god, he had to fart due to his strenuous posture during the prayer (3 *Aethon in Capitolio pepedit*). The offended deity punished Aethon for this sacrilege with three nights of *domicenium*, i.e. dinner at home instead as a guest at a patron's banquet (6 *adfecit domicenio clientem*).[10] Thus, the embarrassing disturbance of the religious ritual was punished by the deity with Aethon's exclusion from a social ritual.[11] From this day on, Aethon always went to the latrines before visiting the Capitolium and farted ten to twenty times, but still he continued praying to Jupiter *compressis natibus* ("with clenched buttocks").

The present chapter investigates to what extent rituals – social and especially religious ones – are used as closural markers in Martial's epigram books. From all the rituals mentioned in the collection, the festival of the Saturnalia has probably received most attention by scholars.[12] Several of the epigram books

---

5 For Martial's epigrams on Domitian, see Lorenz 2002; Leberl 2004; Gunderson 2021, 29–188.
6 See Kaliwoda 1998, 205–206; Fusi 2006, 235–243.
7 The text of Martial follows Lindsay 1929, the translations Shackleton Bailey 1993 with slight adaptions.
8 For the wordplay with *Gallus*, see Fusi 2006, 242–243.
9 For this poem see Rodríguez-Almeida 1989, 249–254; Patzelt 2018, 230–231.
10 For the fear of Roman clients of having to eat at home cf. Mart. 2.14; 5.78.
11 On the risky nature of the ritual communication due to disturbances or mistakes, see Rüpke in this volume; for the ritual communication in general, see Rüpke 2016, 124–128; 2018, 15–21.
12 See Citroni 1989; 1992; Döpp 1993; Lejavitzer 2001; Grewing 2020.

are characterised as Saturnalian products and contain poems where the time of the festival is presented as the ideal occasion for reading the epigrams — particularly Books 4, 5, and 7 as well as Books 13 and 14 (the *Xenia* and *Apophoreta*), the latter two even entirely dedicated to the Saturnalia.[13] In the *Xenia* and *Apophoreta* the reader is cast into the role of a guest at a dinner party (14.1.5–6 *diuitis alternas et pauperis accipe sortes: / praemia conuiuae det sua quisque suo*, "accept these lots, alternately for the rich man and the poor man; let each one give his guest the appropriate prize"),[14] a banquet which continues until the early morning and ends at first cockcrow, as the last poem of Book 14 suggests (223):

> *Adipata*
> *Surgite: iam uendit pueris ientacula pistor*
> *cristataeque sonant undique lucis aues.*

> Children's Dainties
> Rise. Already the baker is selling boys their breakfast,
> and the crested birds of daybreak sound from every side.

The Saturnalia are over, as the boys at the break of dawn are on their way back to school, stopping at the bakery to buy their breakfast, the *adipata*. This pastry with high fat content[15] as a final image of Book 14 implies that the *libellus* has also become fat enough and it is time to stop now.[16] Scholars have already observed that in this epigram Martial also evokes several other literary closures, among them Virgil's tenth *Eclogue* (75 *surgamus*), Horace's first satire (119 *cedat uti conuiua satur*) and Plato's Symposium (223 C πρὸς ἡμέραν ἤδη ἀλεκτρυόνων ᾀδόντων).[17] The epigrams of Books 13 and 14 are imagined as labels for gifts which the *conuiuae* exchange during the festival and thus become part of a social ritual themselves. As is well known, the epigrammatic genre itself from its origins onwards is closely connected with the performance of rituals: in their original function as inscriptions, epigrams accompanied objects playing

---

13 For the Saturnalia, see 2.85; 4.14; 4.19.3; 4.46; 4.88; 5.18; 5.19.11–14; 5.30; 5.49.8–10; 5.84; 6.24; 7.28.7–8; 7.36; 7.53; 7.72; 7.91; 10.18; 10.29; 10.87.6–7; 11.2; 11.15; 12.62.11–16; 12.81; for the *Xenia* and *Apophoreta*, see Leary 1996 and 2001.
14 Cf. Leary 1996, *ad loc.*
15 See Leary 1996, 292.
16 For the Callimachean antithesis of fat (παχύς) and slim (λεπταλέος), as expressed in the prologue to the *Aetia*, (*Aet.* Fr. 1.23–24 Pf.) see Asper 1997, 156–189. On Martial's play with — and against — Callimachus' poetic ideas, see Neger 2012, 77–87.
17 See Citroni 1989, 210–211; Fowler 1995, 55–56; Leary 1996, *ad loc.*; Roman 2001, 132–133; Barchiesi 2005, 328–329; Neger 2012, 29–30.

important roles in rites such as dedications or funeral ceremonies.[18] The tradition of the dedicatory epigram is varied in Martial's collection where not only the gods, but also various members of Flavian society are the recipients of objects with accompanying poems.[19]

Both the *Xenia* and *Apophoreta* start with references to the clothing which is appropriate or inappropriate for the festival. The incipit of Book 13 is *ne toga* (13.1.1) and the *Apophoreta* begin with *synthesibus* (14.1.1). Instead of the *toga*, the Romans used to wear lighter apparel, the *synthesis*.[20] In 13.1.1, the *toga* is used metaphorically for the papyrus which might end up as paper used for wrapping food such as tuna and olives, as Martial jestingly expects that his *libellus* will disappoint the readers.[21] In this light, one might also read the *synthesis* at the beginning of Book 14 as a metapoetic symbol, referring not only to the garment of Roman knights and senators (14.1.1 *eques dominusque senator*), but also to Book 14 as a literary composition (σύνθεσις).[22] In contrast to the idea of putting together a text stands the title of the collection, *Apophoreta*, which implies splitting and dissolving.[23]

A Saturnalian atmosphere is also created in other books. In 4.14, for instance, Martial tries to convince the epic poet Silius Italicus to read the epigrams during the festivities in December (7–8 *dum blanda uagus alea December / incertis sonat hinc et hinc fritillis*, "while December goes hither and thither with his seductive hazard and on all hands the doubtful dice boxes clatter").[24] The festival is imagined as being over at the end of Book 4 where the idea is expressed that both poet and readers now have to return to business as usual, i.e. serious matters of Roman everyday life. Martial complains that his friends have failed to send him gifts during the festival. In 4.88.1–4 he writes to an anonymous addressee:

> *nulla remisisti paruo pro munere dona*
>   *et iam Saturni quinque fuere dies.*
> *ergo nec argenti sex scripula Septiciani*
>   *missa nec a querulo mappa cliente fuit.*

---

18 On the origins of epigram, see Day 2019.
19 For gift-giving in Martial, see Spisak 1998.
20 Cf. Leary 1996, 51.
21 For the motif of the papyrus ending up as wrapping paper cf. Catull. 95.8; Hor. *Epist.* 1.20.12; 2.1.269–270; Ov. *Pont.* 1.1.72; Mart. 6.61.7; 14.37; Stat. *Silu.* 4.9.10 ff.
22 See Barchiesi 2005, 327; *LSJ* 1716 s.v.
23 See Roman 2001, 135–136; Höschele 2010, 62; Neger 2012, 23–25.
24 On this poem, see Moreno Soldevila 2006, 177–186; Neger 2012, 301–304; Mindt 2013, 146–148 and 204–206; Neger 2019, 93–97.

> You have sent me no gifts in return for my little present, and already Saturn's five days are past and gone. So didn't you have six scruples of Septician silver or a napkin sent you by a grumbling client...?

Martial first complains about not having received any presents in return from his addressee and then continues the poem with a catalogue of gifts which his anonymous friend or patron could have sent if he wanted. It is tempting to assume that Martial's *paruum munus* (1) is the collection of *Epigrams* 4,[25] and that the numbers mentioned in the penultimate poem of the book not only refer to the days of the festival[26] and number or character of gifts (2–3 *quinque … sex … Septiciani*), but also indirectly announce the continuation of the epigrammatic collection with the publication of Books 5, 6 and 7. Moreover, the name of the god Saturnus and the formulation *iam Saturni* (2) recall the genre of satire and the Horatian *iam satis est* at the end of the first *sermo* (120), a passage to which Martial also alludes in the final poem 4.89 (1; 9 *Ohe, iam satis est, ohe, libelle*).[27]

Martial's frequent references to the Saturnalia also imply the idea of binding and loosening as the cult statue of Saturnus used to be tied with woolen bonds which were loosened only during the time of the god's festival.[28] The end of the Saturnalia and the return to normal life is also the topic of the final poem of Book 5 (84):[29]

> *Iam tristis nucibus puer relictis*
> *clamoso reuocatur a magistro,*
> *et blando male proditus fritillo,*
> *arcana modo raptus e popina,*
> *aedilem rogat udus aleator.*   5

---

25 Moreno Soldevila 2006, 537 instead thinks of the garment (*endromis*) which Martial mentions in 4.19 (3–4 *sordida...dona*) as a present for an anonymous friend.
26 Under Domitian, the Saturnalia lasted five days, sometimes also seven days are mentioned; see Moreno Soldevila 2006, 537–538.
27 Moreno Soldevila 2006, 541.
28 Stat. *Silu.* 1.6.4 *Saturnus … compede exsoluta* ("Saturn with his bonds released"); Macrob. 1.8.5 *Cur autem Saturnus ipse in compedibus uisatur … Saturnum Apollodorus alligari ait per annum laneo uinculo et solui ad diem sibi festum id est mense hoc Decembri* ("As for why Saturn himself is seen to be in bondage: … Apollodorus says that Saturn is bound throughout the year with a woolen bond and is released on the day of his festival, that is, in this month of December"; transl. by Kaster [2011]); see Nilsson 1921, 203; Martial's poem 3.29 where a certain Zoilus dedicates his shackles to the god Saturnus suggests that slaves might have dedicated their chains to the god on the occasion of the festival during which they enjoyed more freedom than usually; see Fusi 2006, 258–263.
29 For this poem, see Canobbio 2011, 589–593.

> *Saturnalia transiere tota,*
> *nec munuscula parua nec minora*
> *misisti mihi, Galla, quam solebas.*
> *Sane sic abeat meus December:*
> *scis certe, puto, uestra iam venire*   10
> *Saturnalia, Martias Kalendas;*
> *tunc reddam tibi, Galla, quod dedisti.*

Now the schoolboy sadly leaves his nuts, recalled by the clamorous master, and the boozy gambler, betrayed by an all too alluring dice box and just hauled out of a secret tavern, is pleading with the aedile. The Saturnalia are over and done with, and you sent me no small presents, Galla, not even smaller ones than you used to send. Very good, so pass away my December. Methinks you surely know that *your* Saturnalia are coming soon, the Kalends of March. Then I shall return to you, Galla, what you gave.

The last poem of Book 5 envisions a boy sadly returning to school and a drunken gambler being forced by the aedile to leave the tavern as the Saturnalia, together with the permission of enjoying light entertainment, are over now. In the following lines, Martial complains to a certain Galla[30] that she had forgotten to send him a present and announces that he will pay her back at the beginning of March, the date of the festival of the Matronalia, by not sending to her any presents either. Martial explicitly draws a parallel between the end of the book and the end of December (9 *sic abeat meus December*), a literary strategy which, together with other factors, has led scholars to the assumption that Book 5 was published during the Saturnalia 89 AD.[31] Martial on the one hand nostalgically looks back to the merry time of Saturnalian lightness and on the other hand looks forward to the beginning of March where Roman women used to celebrate the Matronalia in honour of Juno Lucina.[32] Coleman reads this as a hint that Book 6 might have been published during the Matronalia of the year 91 AD instead of summer/autumn 90 AD, arguing that "the Matronalia of AD 91 would provide a convenient mid-point between the publication of Book 5 in December 89 and Book 7 in December 92."[33] Scholars usually follow Friedländer's chronology of Martial's XII *Epigrammaton libri* according to which the poet published

---

[30] Most probably a fictitious character who appears in several other epigrams with sex and money as subject matters, sometimes characterised as a prostitute or *uetula*; cf. 2.25; 2.34; 3.51; 3.54; 3.90; 4.38; 4.58; 7.18; 7.58; 9.4; 9.37; 9.78; 10.75; 10.95; 11.19; Canobbio 2011, 591–592; Moreno Soldevila et al. 2019, 248–250.

[31] Citroni 1989; 1992; Coleman 2005; Canobbio 2011, 32–40.

[32] Martial mentions this festival, which coincided with his birthday, also in 9.90.15 and 10.24.1–3; cf. Coleman 2005, 27.

[33] Coleman 2005, 27.

roughly one book per year between 85 and 102 AD,[34] and further attempts were made to narrow down the publication dates to certain seasons or occasions.[35] Independent from these efforts to date the publication of single books, one can say with more certainty that Martial tries to create the impression of temporal progression on an intradiegetic level.[36] Therefore, if we follow the logic of epigram 5.84 with its topic of (failed) gift-exchange, it would be more reasonable to assume that Martial refers to the Matronalia which are immediately following the Saturnalia of poem 5.84 and where he wants to return Galla's "favour" by sending her nothing. Book 6 itself does not contain any hints to the Matronalia, but still there might be a link between the *Martias Kalendas* of 5.84.11 and the beginning of Book 6. Instead of the first of March, we encounter in poem 6.1 another Martialis who is first, this time Iulius Martialis, a friend to whom the epigrammatist dedicates Book 6 (2 <u>in primis</u> mihi care <u>Martialis</u>, "Martialis, dear to me above all men").[37]

Martial repeatedly links the production and reception of his epigrams to social and religious rituals which are characterised by lightness and merriment. Apart from the carnivalesque festival of the Saturnalia, Martial also draws a parallel between his poetry and mime performances[38] as well as the festival of the goddess Flora, the *ludi Florales*, which were celebrated at the end of April and beginning of May.[39] In the preface to Book 1, Martial announces that "epigrams are written for those who are accustomed to watch Flora's games" (1 *praef.* 14–15 *epigrammata illis scribuntur qui solent spectare Florales*). Martial concludes the first preface with an epigram which alludes to an *exemplum* by Valerius Maximus, according to which the Younger Cato left the theatre during the mime performances of the Floralia because the crowd was ashamed to demand the traditional striptease of the actresses in his presence and Cato did not want to disturb the custom of the show (Val. Max. 2.10.8 *populus ut mimae nudarentur postulare erubuit ... discessit e theatro, ne praesentia sua spectaculi consuetudinem impediret*, "the people blushed to ask that the actresses be stripped naked ... he left the

---

[34] Friedländer 1886, 50–67.
[35] See the discussion in Coleman 2005, 23–26.
[36] Martial himself numbers his books; cf. 2.93.1 (*liber iste secundus*); 5.2.5–6 (*lasciuos lege quattuor libellos / quintus cum domino liber iocatur*); 6.1.1 (*sextus...libellus*); 8 *praef.* (*hic tamen, qui operis nostri octauus inscribitur*); 8.3.1–2 (*quinque satis fuerant. nam sex septemue libelli / est nimium*); 10.2.1 (*decimi ... libelli*); 12.4(5).1 (*undecimi ... decimique libelli*); see Lorenz 2019.
[37] Cf. Grewing 1997, *ad loc.*
[38] See Gaffney 1976; Neger 2012, 223–235.
[39] From April 28th to May 3rd; cf. Citroni 1975, 11; Howell 1980, 100–101; cf. Ov. *Fast.* 5.183–378; Bömer 1957/58, 304–313; Brookes 1992, 109–179.

theatre, not wishing that his presence should interfere with the custom of the show").⁴⁰ Whereas Cato is praised as an *exemplum maiestatis* by Valerius Maximus, Martial mocks him as the embodiment of the stern reader and calls on him either not to come to the theatre at all or, once he has entered, to stay and watch the show (1 *praef.* 15–16 *non intret Cato theatrum meum, aut si intrauerit, spectet*).

In contrast to the wantonness and merriment associated with Flora's festival and the mime at the beginning of Book 1, the end of the same book leads us to death and rituals connected with mourning for the deceased. Before Martial concludes the book with two metapoetic poems (1.117–118), we encounter a couplet of epigrams about a father who had to bury his prematurely deceased daughter (1.114 and 116).

> *Hos tibi uicinos, Faustine, Telesphorus hortos*
> *Faenius et breue rus udaque prata tenet.*
> *condidit hic natae cineres nomenque sacrauit*
> *quod legis Antullae, dignior ipse legi.*
> *ad Stygias aequum fuerat pater isset ut umbras:*
> *quod quia non licuit, uiuat, ut ossa colat.*

This place near town, Faustinus, neighbour to yours, with its parcel of land and water-meadows, belongs to Faenius Telesphorus. Here he buried his daughter's ashes and consecrated the name you read, Antulla's; it were more fitting that his own be read. In justice the father should have gone to the Stygian shades. Since that was not to be, may he live to cherish her bones.

> *Hoc nemus aeterno cinerum sacrauit honori*
> *Faenius et culti iugera pulchra soli.*
> *hoc tegitur cito rapta suis Antulla sepulchro,*
> *hoc erit Antullae mixtus uterque parens.*
> *si cupit hunc aliquis, moneo, ne speret agellum:*
> *perpetuo dominis seruiet iste suis.*

This wood and beautiful acres of cultivated soil Faenius consecrated to the eternal honour of his dead. By this tomb is covered Antulla, snatched from her family too soon, and in this will be mingled both Antulla's parents. If any man desire this plot of land, I warn him not to hope; it will serve its lords in perpetuity.

Both poems are of equal length, each one consisting of three elegiac distichs. Whereas the first of the two epigrams is addressed to Martial's friend Faustinus and informs him about Faenius Telesphorus, the owner of a property with a

---

40 Translation by Shackleton Bailey 2000; cf. Ov. *Fast.* 5.349: *turba quidem cur hos celebret meretricia ludos*; Themann-Steinke 2008, 559–564.

kepotaphium adjacent to Faustinus' estate, the second poem is imagined as the actual verse epitaph inscribed on Antulla's tombstone.⁴¹ As Larash has demonstrated, the two poems are artfully woven into the closing sequence of Book 1, a section comprising epigrams 1.112–118 and arranged symmetrically around poem 1.115. Moreover, the two funeral poems pick up the first poem of Book 1, where "Martial uses epitaphic conventions to cast the book as a monument to his own *fama* during his lifetime".⁴² Instead of the whole world which knows Martial's name (1.1.2 *toto notus in orbe Martialis*), the setting is now a private grave-garden outside the metropolis where Antulla's name has been immortalised by her father (1.114.3 *nomenque sacrauit*). By closing his book with the image of a funeral monument, Martial varies the *monumentum* topos famously established by Horace in *Carm*. 3.30. This literary appropriation of Antulla's tomb — which might really have existed⁴³ — is not surprising in light of the metaliterary poems surrounding the two epigrams.⁴⁴ Moreover, Faustinus, the addressee of 1.114, has been introduced to the reader as a poet himself in 1.25 where Martial summons him to finally publish his *libelli* and not wait for posthumous fame.⁴⁵ The motifs of death and posthumous renown (1.25.8 *cineri gloria sera uenit*, "glory comes late to the grave") connect this poem with both epigram 1.1 (5–6 *decus ... rari post cineres habent poetae*) and the poems on Antulla (1.114.3 *natae cineres*; 1.116.1 *aeterno cinerum sacrauit honori*).

The Greek name of the girl's father, Telesphorus, with its meaning of "bringing fulfilment", fits well at the end of the first book.⁴⁶ Regardless of his possible historicity, as an epigrammatic character performing funeral rites Telesphorus serves as an agent who brings the first book to its closure. In the first of the two epigrams on Antulla, Martial creates the impression that he and Faustinus are visiting Telesphorus' garden adjacent to Faustinus' own *uilla suburbana* (1.114.1 *hos tibi uicinos ... hortos*) which was located at Tibur, as other epigrams reveal.⁴⁷

---

41 For funerary poems in Martial, see Manzo 1995; Henriksén 2006; Lorenz 2009; for epitaphs on children, cf. Mart. 1.88; 6.28–29; 7.96; 9.86; Galán Vioque 2002, 505.
42 Larash 2010, 43; for epigram 1.1 and the tradition of the epitaph, see Citroni 1975, 14–15.
43 A Faenius Telesphorus is also known from an inscription found near Tibur and dating from the first century AD (*CIL* XIV.3762 = *Inscr. Ital.* I.321); see Howell 1980, 342–343; Moreno Soldevila et al. 2019, 49 and 230.
44 In 1.113 Martial reflects on his juvenilia, in 1.117 he gives instructions where to buy a copy of his book and 1.118 deals with the length of the book.
45 See Citroni 1975, *ad loc.*; Howell 1980, *ad loc.*; on Faustinus in Martial's epigrams, see Moreno Soldevila et al. 2019, 231–232.
46 Cf. *LSJ*, 1771, s.v. τελεσφόρος; Larash 2010, 50.
47 For Faustinus' villa at Tibur, cf. 4.57; 5.71; 7.80.12; Howell 1980, 342–343.

Telesphorus' *breue rus* (2) fits the epigrammatic ideal of *breuitas*. After the first distich has outlined the spatial setting, the second one implies that Martial and Faustinus have encountered Antulla's tomb during a walk and are reading her name on the tombstone (3–4 *nomenque ... quod legis*), with Martial serving as a kind of "travel guide" who informs his companion about the history of this monument. The poem concludes with Martial's comment that it would have been more just if the father had died before his daughter and with the wish that, now Antulla is dead, Telesphorus may continue to live in order to take care of her commemoration (6 *uiuat, ut ossa colat*).

It might not surprise us that in a poem addressed to another poet Martial alludes to various literary models. The wording of 1.114.3, *condidit hic natae cineres nomenque sacrauit*, is reminiscent of Virg. *Aen.* 5.46–48 on the first anniversary of Anchises' death:[48]

annuus exactis completur mensibus orbis
ex quo reliquias diuinique ossa parentis
condidimus *terra maestasque* **sacrauimus** *aras.*

With the passing of the months the circling year draws to an end since we laid in earth the dust, all that was left, of my divine father, and hallowed the altars of grief.[49]

Whereas in the *Aeneid* it is the son who buries the father and takes care of his commemoration, in Martial's epigrams the situation is reversed. Virgil's reference to the completion of one year (5.46 *annuus ... completur ... orbis*) resembles the Homeric phrase εἰς ἐνιαυτόν (*Il.* 19.32; *Od.* 4.86), a model which Martial's epigram evokes with the name Telesphorus.[50] After recalling *Aeneid* 5 in the third line of epigram 1.114, line 5 imagines Telesphorus' own *katabasis* (5 *ad Stygias ... pater isset ut umbras*), thus reminding us of *Aeneid* 6. In addition to Virgil, Ovid might also be hidden in this epigram: Martial's wish that Telesphorus may live (6 *uiuat*), together with the future tense *uiues* in the following epigram (1.115.7), can be read as a variation of the famous closure of Ovid's *Metamorphoses* (15.879 *uiuam*).[51] In an epigram on the praxis of commemorating the dead, Martial also activates the literary memory of his readership.

---

48 Citroni 1975, *ad loc.*
49 Translation of Virgil by Fairclough 1916; cf. Fratantuono/Smith 2015, 153–156.
50 For Martial's play with Homeric phrases cf. 1.45 (τὸν δ' ἀπαμειβόμενος) and 1.50 (μίστυλλόν τ'ἄρα τἆλλα); Neger 2012, 277–279.
51 Cf. Stat. *Theb.* 12.816: *uiue, precor*; Bömer 1986, 490–491.

Whereas poem 1.114 outlines the topography of Antulla's tomb, epigram 1.116 is to be imagined as the actual epitaph, a text which forms an important part of the ritual of commemorating the deceased. The first distich draws attention to Faenius' property (1–2 *hoc nemus .... iugera*), whereas the second one, continuing the *hoc*-anaphora, focuses on the family's tomb. The girl's name, which Faustinus is reading in the previous epigram (1.114.3–4 *nomenque ... quod legis Antullae*), is mentioned twice in the central distich of poem 1.116 (3–4). Martial stylistically underlines the image of Antulla being covered by the tomb through the hyperbaton *hoc ... sepulchro* which frames Antulla's name in line 3. Antulla's ashes one day will be mixed with the remains of her parents (4 *mixtus uterque parens*). In the final distich, which advises individuals interested in the property to give up their hopes, Martial varies the common epigraphic formula *hoc monumentum heredem non sequitur* ("this monument does not pass to the heir", abbreviated with H.M.H.N.S.) by pointing out that the *agellus* will always remain the property of Faenius Telesphorus and his family.[52]

At the end of Martial's book, death is juxtaposed with eternity (1.116.6 *perpetuo*) and closure with a new beginning. Whereas the first Antulla-epigram contained reminiscences of Virgil's *Aeneid* and the end of Ovid's *Metamorphoses*, the second poem evokes the beginning of Tibullus' elegies: Faenius' *culti iugera pulchra soli* remind us of the *culti iugera multa soli* of Tibullus 1.1.2.[53] Moreover, the following epigram 1.117 entertains the idea of reading the book from the start again, when Martial meets a certain Lupercus who would like to borrow the volume (3 *epigrammaton libellum*) and return it immediately after reading (4 *lectum quem tibi protinus remittam*). From a *kepotaphium* outside the city Martial leads us back to the urban centre in 1.117 when he explains to Lupercus the way through Rome to the bookstore where one can purchase a copy of the epigrams.[54] Also here visitors can read inscriptions: instead of epitaphs, the doorposts are inscribed with the names of the poets whose works are sold inside the store (10–12 *taberna / scriptis postibus hinc et inde totis / omnis ut cito perlegas poetas*, "a shop with its doorposts completely covered by advertisements, so that you can read the entire list of poets at a glance").

In addition to the rituals of banqueting and gift-exchange during the Saturnalia (cf. 14.223; 4.88; 5.84) and of commemorating the deceased (1.114 and 116), Martial also uses the motif of the oath as a signal of closure. Book 8 which is dedicated to the emperor Domitian (8 *praef.*) begins with the image of *religiosa*

---

52 Howell 1980, 348.
53 Cf. 1.85.2; Howell 1980, 347.
54 Cf. Larash 2010, 47–48; Neger 2012, 16–17.

purificatio (8 *praef.* 16, "religious lustration"),⁵⁵ a necessary ritual before entering a temple — in this case, the epigram book has been cleaned of its otherwise characteristic licentiousness in order to be able to approach the house of the *dominus et deus* (cf. 8.1). At the end of the book, Martial again addresses Domitian in two epigrams (8.80 and 8.82) which are separated by a satirical poem on a certain Gellia⁵⁶ who is so fond of her pearls that she used to invoke them instead of the gods when swearing an oath (8.81.1–7):

> *Non per mystica sacra Dindymenes*
> *nec per Niliacae bouem iuuencae,*
> *nullos denique per deos deasque*
> *iurat Gellia, sed per uniones.*
> *hos amplectitur, hos perosculatur,*
> *hos fratres uocat, hos uocat sorores,*
> *hos natis amat acrius duobus.*

> Gellia does not swear by the mystic rites of Dindymene, nor by the bull of Nile's heifer, nor in fine by any gods or goddesses, but by her pearls. These she embraces, these she covers with kisses, these she calls her brothers, these she calls her sisters, these she loves more passionately than her two children.

Gellia worships her pearls (*uniones*) more than any gods. The priamel in lines 1–4 (*non ... nec ... nullos ... sed*) moves from Cybele (1 *Dindymene*) via Isis and Apis/Osiris (2 *Niliacae bouem iuuencae*) to gods and goddesses in general (3 *per deos deasque*) before it ends at the core subject of the poem, Gellia's pearls (4 *per uniones*). The anaphora of *hos* (5–7) might be read as an imitation of the repetitive style of prayers and hymns, reminiscent of the hymnic *Du-Stil* and *Er-Stil*.⁵⁷ Martial's catalogue of deities, as it seems, is inspired by Ovid's second *Epistula Heroidum* where Phyllis writes to Demophoon and complains about the false oath which he had sworn to her (35–45):⁵⁸

> *per mare, quod totum uentis agitatur et undis,*
>   *per quod nempe ieras, per quod iturus eras,*
> *perque tuum mihi iurasti—nisi fictus et ille est—*
>   *concita qui uentis aequora mulcet, auum,*
> *per Venerem nimiumque mihi facientia tela*

---

55 For the religious language dominating the preface to Book 8, see Johannsen 2006, 87–97, esp. 90 with no. 85.
56 On this character, see Moreno Soldevila et al. 2019, 257.
57 These terms characterising religious language were tagged by Norden 1956, 143–176.
58 Schöffel 2002, 678.

> —altera tela arcus, altera tela faces—
> Iunonemque, toris quae praesidet alma maritis,
>   et per taediferae mystica sacra deae.
> si de tot laesis sua numina quisque deorum
>   uindicet, in poenas non satis unus eris.

> By the sea, all tossed by wind and wave, over which you had indeed sailed, and were to sail once more; and by your grandsire — unless he, too, is but a fiction — by your grandsire, who calms the windwrought wave, you swore to me yes, and by Venus and the weapons that wound me all too much — one weapon the bow, the other the torch; and by Juno, the kindly ward of the bridal bed; and by the mystical rites of the goddess who bears the torch. Should all the many gods you have wronged take vengeance for the outrage to their sacred names, your single life would not suffice.[59]

Phyllis' list of witnesses by whom Demophoon swore his oath is more extensive than Martial's, containing the sea (35–36), grandfather Neptune (37–38), Venus and Amor (39–40), Juno (41) and a *taedifera dea* not mentioned by name (42). Ovid's verse epistle is the only other Latin text which contains the phrase *mystica sacra* (42); it is usually believed to refer to Ceres who searched for her daughter, Proserpina, with a torch (*taedifera*).[60] However, torches also played an important role in the iconography of Cybele,[61] and therefore it might not be surprising that Martial replaces (or interprets) Ovid's *taedifera dea* with Dindymene when referring to the secret rites of the goddess. Whereas Phyllis confronts Demophoon with all the gods whose names he invoked when swearing to return back to her, the intertextual humour of the epigram is based on Martial's emphasis that Gellia does *not* need to invoke so many deities (cf. Ov. *Her.* 2.44 *tot ... numina*), but that her pearls replace them when she has to swear an oath.

Making a vow is a motif which also appears near the end of Book 12, again in a satirical context. In 12.90, Martial mocks a legacy hunter as follows:

> Pro sene, sed clare, uotum Maro fecit amico,
>   cui grauis et feruens hemitritaeos erat,
> si Stygias aeger non esset missus ad umbras,
>   ut caderet magno uictima grata Ioui.
> coeperunt certam medici spondere salutem.
> ne uotum soluat nunc Maro uota facit.

---

59 Translation of Ovid by Showerman 1914.
60 Cf. Ov. *Fast.* 3.786; Bömer 1957/58, 197–198; Knox 1995, 121–122.
61 For example, in Greek dedicatory reliefs for Kybele from the 4th century BC, Antikensammlung Berlin, Sk 691 and 692; see Kunze 1992; Ovid's *taedifer* is a translation of the Greek δαιδοφόρος which is attested as an epithet of Hecate and the Furies rather than Demeter; Knox 1995, 122.

> Maro made a vow, made it loud and clear, for an aged friend suffering from a severe, burning semitertian, that, if the sick man was not sent to the shades of Styx, a welcome victim would fall to great Jupiter. The doctors have begun to guarantee a certain recovery. Maro now makes vows against having to pay his vow.

A legacy hunter named Maro[62] is pretending to wish for an old man's recovery from a heavy fever[63] by ostentatiously (1 *clare*) making a vow,[64] and promising a sacrifice to Jupiter.[65] What he does not expect at this point is that the *senex* could recover from his disease; when the doctors pronounce that the old man will survive instead of being sent to the Styx, Maro regrets his first vow and now makes another one where he tries to avoid the promised sacrifice (which would have cost him some money). The epigram can be divided into three distichs, each one forming a narrative entity: Exposition of the situation (1–2), Maro's vow in indirect speech (3–4), the doctors' prognosis and Maro's reaction (5–6). The last words of the epigram (6 *Maro uota facit*) pick up the beginning (1 *uotum Maro fecit*), thus creating a cyclic structure which, together with the *polyptoton* (*uotum…uotum…uota*), might imitate the repetitive style of a prayer.[66]

Martial's epigram on a character named Maro who ostentatiously makes a vow in order to appear as a righteous individual could be read as a variation of a passage in Horace's letter 1.16 where a similar problem is discussed (57–62):[67]

> *uir bonus, omne forum quem spectat et omne tribunal,*
> *quandocumque deos uel porco uel boue placat,*
> *"Iane pater!" clare, clare cum dixit, "Apollo!"*
> *labra mouet metuens audiri: "pulchra Lauerna,*
> *da mihi fallere, da iusto sanctoque uideri,*
> *noctem peccatis et fraudibus obice nubem."*

---

62 A fictional character who also appears in 4.80; 9.33; 11.34; 11.67; Virgil is also frequently called Maro in Martial's poems; see Moreno Soldevila et al. 2019, 372–373.
63 For the *hemitritaeos* as a fever recurring on the third day see Bowie 1988, 385; cf. Mart. 2.40; 4.80 (where Maro himself is suffering from this disease).
64 However, a true friend should not make a vow secretly, as Martial points out in 1.39.5–6 *si quis erit recti custos, mirator honesti, / et nihil arcano qui roget ore deos* ("if one there be that guards the right, admires virtue, and asks nothing from the gods with secret lips"); Citroni 1975, *ad loc.*; Bowie 1988, 383.
65 The phrase *uictima grata* is Ovidian, cf. *Fast.* 1.440; Martial also uses it in epigram 3.24.2 discussed above.
66 One could compare the prayer to Mars transmitted in Cato's *De Agricultura* 141 *Mars pater, te precor quaesoque … uti tu morbos uisos inuisosque … prohibessis defendas auerruncesque … Mars pater*; see Petersmann 1973.
67 Cf. Bowie 1988, 384.

This "good man," for forum and tribunal the cynosure of every eye, whenever with swine or ox he makes atonement to the gods, cries with loud voice "Father Janus," with loud voice "Apollo," then moves his lips, fearing to be heard: "Fair Laverna, grant me to escape detection; grant me to pass as just and upright, shroud my sins in night, my lies in clouds!"

Similar to Martial's Maro, Horace's *uir bonus* (an ironic designation) invokes Ianus and Apollo in public with a loud voice (59 *clare, clare*), but secretly prays to Laverna, the Etruscan goddess of the thieves, to help him conceal his sins and lies.[68] The general criticism of *peccata* and *fraudes* in Horace's epistle is transformed into a satiric epigram on a legacy hunter in Martial's collection. Both texts are linked through the motif of ostentatious prayers in public versus vows made secretly. Additional humour is generated by the fact that an epistle written by Horatius Flaccus serves as the intertext for Martial's epigram on a character named Maro.[69]

The fulfilment of a vow, for example by dedicating a votive offering to a deity, is usually expressed in Latin with the formula *uotum soluit*, in inscriptions usually abbreviated as *V.S.L.M.* (*uotum soluit libens merito*).[70] Fulfilling a vow by delivering a promise in form of a sacrifice, dedication or other, implies the idea of loosening a bond which has been created between the human being and the deity through the act of *uotum facere*. Martial's Maro made a vow (1 *uotum fecit*), but he had no intention to fulfil it (6 *ne uotum soluat*). Martial's epigram 12.90 thus wittily reverses the customary language of votive inscriptions.

The image of loosening is also used by Martial in another context at the end of his books: in 9.102, the penultimate poem of Book 9, Martial uses the verb *soluere* with the meaning "to pay". At the end of Book 11, Martial addresses a reader who asks for more epigrams but does not want to pay for them (11.108.4): *lector, solue. taces dissimulasque? uale* ("Pay up, reader. You say nothing and pretend not to hear? Goodbye").[71] In this poem, the material aspects of literary exchange are foregrounded, presenting the relationship between poet and reader and the consumption of the epigrams as a form of trade.[72]

This short survey of selected passages should have demonstrated how Martial, besides other closural motifs, also uses social and religious rituals as images

---

68 See Mayer 1994, 227–228.
69 For Martial's play with Virgil's cognomen Maro, see Holzberg 2011; Heil 2013.
70 See Meyer 1983, 64–66.
71 See Kay 1985, *ad loc.*; as Höschele 2010, 53–54 argues, the reader wants to avoid payment by delaying the completion of the book.
72 See Roman 2001, 126–129.

conveying "a sense of an ending" to his books. In many cases, religious practices are depicted in satirical contexts, the characters who perform these rituals being ridiculed and mocked. On the other hand, in the context of epigrams concerning Martial's patrons and friends, rituals are often presented with a more serious tone, as in the case of the epitaphs on Antulla. Modern scholars will probably be more careful with trying to deduce the religious attitude of the historical Martial from the content of the epigrams.[73] But a more comprehensive and systematic study on Martial's literary approach on religious matters is necessary and would be most welcome.

---

[73] See Kaliwoda 1998 on "die persönliche Religiosität Martials".

Alison Keith
Closural Poetics in Martial, *Epigrams* 10

Abstract: This paper explores Martial's closural poetics in *Epigrams* 10 in relation to religious ceremonies, elite social conventions, and ritual practices. The collection announces Martial's physical removal from Rome and retirement to Spain, as the final epigrams engage in a series of social and religious rituals marking 'the end' of Martial's Roman sojourn: expression of desire to resign the rituals of a client (10.74, 96); a propempticon to Macer on his assumption of the governorship of Dalmatia (10.78); the end of Laurus' passion for playing ball; the assignment of the Nomentan farm and its cultic rites to his friend Marrius (10.92); the anticipation of a return to Bilbilis and the religious rituals familiar from his youth (10.103); and the dedication of his finished book to Spanish friends (10.104). This study proposes that Martial buttresses his closural strategies in *Epigrams* 10 by evoking ancient religious practices (such as sacrifices and oaths), but that his archive of ritual imagery supports an 'open' closure that allows for his resumption of epigram composition, whether on his arrival in Spain or upon a return to Rome.

Martial prefaces his tenth book of *Epigrams* with a poem explaining the collection as a second edition, containing a few previously published epigrams newly 'polished with a recent file' (10.2.3 *nota leges quaedam sed lima rasa recenti*), but a greater number still of entirely fresh poems (10.2.4 *pars noua maior erit*).[1] In his description of the original collection as 'too hurried earlier', the epigrammatist implicitly justifies the reissued volume as a work of greater literary care (10.2.1–2) *Festinata prius, decimi mihi cura libelli / elapsum manibus nunc reuocauit opus* ('Too hurried earlier, the care of my tenth little book has now recalled a work

---

I am grateful to Angeliki-Nektaria Roumpou for the invitation to participate in the original conference on "The Poetics of Release and Binding: Resolution and Constraint as Modes of Closure in Flavian Literature", and her assured editorial guidance; and to Margot Neger and Jovan Cvjetičanin for their helpful feedback on an earlier draft of this chapter: all have saved me from numerous errors. Thanks also to my fellow conference participants for their discussion of the oral version of this paper, especially Damien Nelis and Jörg Rüpke.

1 I cite Martial's *Epigrams* from the Loeb edition of Shackleton Bailey 1993; translations follow or adapt Shackleton Bailey 1993.

https://doi.org/10.1515/9783110770483-004

that slipped from my hands').² Yet a political motive for the reissue in 98, under Trajan, of a collection originally put into circulation in 95, under Domitian, is not far to seek. Martial hints at the recent regime change at the end of the second epigram, where a personified Rome reflects on the immortality of her poet's epigrams, by contrast with the mortality of statesmen's monuments (10.2.9–12) *'marmora Messallae findit caprificus et audax / dimidios Crispi mulio ridet equos: / at chartis nec furta nocent et saecula prosunt, / solaque non norunt haec monumenta mori'* ('The fig tree splits Messalla's marble tombstone and the bold muleteer laughs at Crispus' halved horses: but thefts don't harm your pages and the centuries do them good. These are the only memorials that cannot die'). Scholars have therefore connected Martial's reflection on the destruction of partisan memorials over the passage of time not only to the important literary model of Horace's famous *envoi* to his three-book collection of *Odes* (3.30), but also to the contemporary political erasure of Domitian's name from his monuments as a result of the senatorial vote of *damnatio memoriae*.³

Complementing the literary and political motivations for the reissue of a revised tenth collection is the important autobiographical motivation implicit in the announcement of the poet's physical removal from Rome and retirement to Spain, a theme which comes increasingly to dominate the book.⁴ The first intimation of Martial's departure comes in 10.13, an epigram which adumbrates a disjunction between city and countryside that is all too easily mapped onto a contrast between the imperial metropolis and any provincial hinterland. But the poet's impending departure from Rome to Spain is also implicit in the epigrams praising the Italian villa retreats of Martial's friends Domitius (10.12), Apollinaris (10.30), and Maternus (10.37), whose withdrawal to his country villa Martial explicitly sets in counterpoint to the motif of his own impending retirement to Spain (10.37.3–4):⁵ *municipi, Materne, tuo ueterique sodali / Callaicum mandas si quid ad Oceanum* ('if you entrust anything to your fellow townsman and old companion for the Galician ocean').

---

2 Holzberg 2002, 140–148 has expressed doubt about the second edition of Book 10; see also Lorenz 2002, 219–231. I thank Margot Neger for the references.
3 Fearnley 2003; Rimell 2008, 66.
4 On Martial's retirement to Spain, see Howell 1998; Citroni 2002; Keith 2021.
5 Cf. 10.37.19–20, where line 20 repeats line 4: *omnis ab urbano uenit ad mare cena macello. / Callaïcum mandas si quid ad Oceanum.* ([In Italy,] 'every dinner comes to the sea from the urban market. If you entrust anything for the Galician ocean'.) On 10.37, see Kolosova 2000; Scherf *apud* Damschen and Heil 2004, 152–155; Buongiovanni 2012, 183–233. On the identification of Maternus, see Buongiovanni 2012, 199–202, *contra* Kolosova 2000.

In the closing movement of the book, moreover, Martial repeatedly returns to the disparities between imperial capital and provincial hinterland, between his busy life of *clientela* at Rome and his prospective retirement to Epicurean *otium* in Spain,[6] and he articulates the contrasts in both literary and ritual frameworks. The final epigrams engage a series of social and religious rituals that often implicitly, but occasionally explicitly, propose 'the end' of the poet's sojourn in Rome. Thus, Martial renews his expressions of desire to resign the rituals of a client (10.74, 96); offers a propempticon to Macer on his assumption of the governorship of Dalmatia (10.78); records the end of Laurus' passion for playing ball (10.86); assigns his farm property near Nomentum, along with its cultic rites, to his friend Marrius (10.92); anticipates his return to Bilbilis and the religious rituals familiar from his youth (10.103); and commends his finished book to Spanish friends when he sends it off on the journey to Spain (10.104). This study explores Martial's closural poetics in relation to ritual practices and religious emblems in his most tightly scripted collection of epigrams. In this way, I hope to illuminate the connections between religion, ritual, and literary closure in Martial's tenth book of epigrams.[7]

We may begin by considering epigram 10.74, in which Martial expresses his frustration with the Roman social ritual of the client's morning call on his patron (10.74.1–6):[8]

Iam parce lasso, Roma, gratulatori,
lasso clienti. quam diu salutator
anteambulones et togatulos inter
centum merebor plumbeos die toto,
cum Scorpus una quindecim graues hora
feruentis auri uictor auferat saccos?

Spare at length the weary congratulator, Rome, the weary client. How long shall I be a morning-caller, earning a hundred coppers in a whole day, among escorts and petty clients, when Scorpus in a single hour carries off as victor in the arena fifteen heavy bags of gold hot from the mint?

The epigrammatist contrasts the poor return on his services as a morning caller (*gratulator*, 1; *salutator*, 2), indistinguishable amongst others' clients who likewise wear the toga while clearing the path of a great man (*anteambulones et*

---

[6] See Keith 2021.
[7] On closure in Martial's epigram books, see Canobbio 2007, with only brief discussion of *Epigrams* 10 however.
[8] On Mart. 10.74, see Schramm *apud* Damschen and Heil 2004, 268–270.

togatulos inter, 3),⁹ with the riches secured by the star charioteer Scorpus in a single race.¹⁰ Success in the arena makes a mockery of the established social rituals of Roman *clientela*, which offer such a low return on the client's investment of time. But Martial also develops a secondary contrast between wealth in coin, such as accrues to Scorpus for his performances in the arena, and wealth from landholdings in Apulia, Hybla, Egypt, and Setia (10.74.7–12):

> *non ego meorum praemium libellorum*
> *— quid enim merentur? — Apulos uelim campos;*
> *non Hybla, non me spicifer capit Nilus,*
> *nec quae paludes delicata Pomptinas*
> *ex arce cliui spectat uua Setini.*
> *quid concupiscam quaeris ergo? dormire.*

> I would not want the plains of Apulia as a reward for my little books — what do they deserve, after all? Hybla does not attract me, nor corn-bearing Nile, nor the dainty grape that surveys the Pomptine marshes from the top of Setia's slope. Do you ask what I crave then? Sleep.

With characteristic irony,¹¹ Martial concludes that his verses do not deserve remuneration in land, such as the Sabine farm for which Horace thanks his patron Maecenas. Yet the geographical panorama of Rome's territorial holdings — southern Italy (Apulia and Campania), Attica, Egypt — notably omits Spain, the site of Martial's planned retirement, which receives so much favourable attention elsewhere in the revised tenth book. This omission is particularly striking for re-readers of the collection, with their knowledge of the epigrammatist's paean to life in retirement in 12.18, where Martial boasts of enjoying 'an enormous, indecent amount of sleep, often unbroken till past the third hour, and pay[ing] himself back in full for his vigils of thirty years' (12.18.13–16 *ingenti fruor improboque somno / quem nec tertia saepe rumpit hora, / et totum mihi nunc repono quiquid / ter denos uigilaueram per annos*).¹² Since 'the *salutatio* took place in the first and second hours, often forcing the client to leave home before dawn',¹³ the retired poet's claim to enjoy sleeping in until 'the third hour'

---

9 On Martial's distaste for the *toga*, cf. 10.47.5, and see further George 2008.
10 On the historical charioteer Flavius Scorpus (*PIR* 2 F359; *RE* 3.1.a, 609–611; *CIL* 6.10048, 10052, 9729), see Vallat 2008, 91, 115, 352; Fusi 2011; Tafaro 2016; Moreno Soldevila et al. 2019, 542–543.
11 On Martial's playful literary humility, ironising Callimachean poetics, see Rimell 2008, Index s.v. 'Callimachean aesthetics'.
12 On epigram 12.18, see Bowie 1988, 101–113.
13 Bowie 1988, 106 *ad* 13 ff., *tertia hora*.

(*tertia hora*, 8 or 9 am) underlines his release from the duties of a client in Rome. Martial's humourous insistence on the sleep he enjoys in Bilbilis in 12.18 functions as an intratextual cross-reference to 10.74,[14] and confirms the implicitly closural function of 10.74 in the revised tenth collection.

The epigrammatist openly broaches the theme of retirement from *clientela* in epigram 10.96, addressed to an Avitus of Spanish origin like himself.[15] The opening couplets contrast city life in Latium (i.e., Rome) with provincial life in Spain (10.96.1–6):

> *Saepe loquar nimium gentes quod, Auite, remotas*
> *   miraris, Latia factus in urbe senex,*
> *auriferumque Tagum sitiam patriumque Salonem*
> *   et repetam saturae sordida rura casae.*
> *illa placet tellus in qua res parua beatum*
> *   me facit et tenues luxuriantur opes:*

Does it surprise you, Avitus, that I, who have grown old in Latium's city, often speak of very far-off peoples, that I thirst for gold-bearing Tagus and my native Salo, that I am going back to the rough fields of a well-stocked cottage? Give me a land where a small competence makes me wealthy and narrow means are a luxury.

The client's hustle, Martial complains, barely supports him in a costly city and he contrasts urban poverty in Rome with an idealising image of the provender his resources could supply in Spain (10.96.7–12):

> *pascitur hic, ibi pascit ager; tepet igne maligno*
> *   hic focus, ingenti lumine lucet ibi;*
> *hic pretiosa fames conturbatorque macellus,*
> *   mensa ibi diuitiis ruris operta sui;*   10
> *quattuor hic aestate togae pluresue teruntur,*
> *   autumnis ibi me quattuor una tegit.*

Here the soil is supported, there it supports. Here the hearth warms with a grudging fire, there it is bright with a huge blaze. Here hunger is costly, and the market makes men bankrupt, there the board is spread with the riches of its own countryside. Here four or more gowns wear out in a summer, there one covers me through four autumns.

---

14 As implied by Bowie (1988, 106 *ad loc.*) in his use of the commentator's 'genially open' reference, 'cf. 10.74'.
15 Hernández González 2008, 38; Balland 2010, 234 n. 33. See also Moreno Soldevila et al. 2019, 72–73.

The juxtaposition of the client's need for several *togae*, just to get through one summer of social calls in Rome, with the single toga that lasts four years in Spain (11–12) sums up the appeal of provincial living for the jaded epigrammatist, and resumes the thematic through-line of disengagement from the imperial metropolis (including the requisite round of social rituals of *clientelae*) that unifies the revised collection. The final couplet makes the point explicitly (13–14) *i, cole nunc reges, quidquid non praestat amicus / cum praestare tibi possit, Auite, locus* ('Go now, pay court to royal patrons, Avitus, when a place can provide you with all that a friend does not'). In a powerful denunciation of the toils of *clientela* in imperial Rome, Martial sarcastically enjoins his readership to cultivate kings (10.96.13 *cole nunc reges*), echoing Catullus' disavowal of his noble friends out of disillusionment with Roman politics (28.13 *pete nobiles amicos*).[16] The epigram builds on Catullus' model, and Martial's own intratextual record of disdain for the required social calls symbolised in the wearing of the toga,[17] to articulate the epigrammatist's closural programme of retirement from Rome.

By contrast with the social rituals from which Martial would resign in 10.74 and 10.96, religious emblems and ritual practices are the focus of the poet's articulation of his closural poetics in epigram 10.92.[18] In the poem Martial entrusts his beloved Nomentan farm, the gift of a wealthy patron, to his dear friend Marrius of Atina, characterised as an Epicurean fellow-traveller in the opening line of the epigram at 10.92.1: *Marri, quietae cultor et comes uitae* ('Marrius, cultivator and companion of the quiet life').[19] For his friend's benefit,

---

16 Bianconi 2005 has shown that words like *rex* and *dominus* are used for patrons in a derogatory sense. I am grateful to Jovan Cvjetičanin for his suggestion that the verb *colere* here (10.96.13) problematises patron-client relationships still further, in part through its religious valence since Martial elsewhere expresses distaste for clients who treat their patrons as gods.
17 Cf. 10.73, where Martial records the gift of a toga and lauds the donor, even if he 'cannot love the gift' (10.73.7 *possem nisi munus amare*); on the theme, see George 2008. I thank Jovan Cvjetičanin for reminding me that in the preceding couplet, Martial directly compares gift-giving to sacrifice (10.73.5–6): *uilior haec nobis alio mittente fuisset;/ non quacumque manu uictima caesa litat* ('I should have valued it less if another had sent it. Not slaughtered by every hand does the sacrifice find acceptance'). He notes that in this couplet 'the client is the one who is like a god and is given the agency to accept or reject a patron's gift, whereas the opposite might be expected'.
18 On 10.92, see Albrech *apud* Damschen and Heil 2004, 328–330; Fantham 2009, 158–159.
19 On the interlinked themes of retirement and Epicurean withdrawal in Martial's tenth book, see Keith 2021.

Martial lists his Nomentan estate's cult-statues and tutelary divinities, whom he reveres in sacrificial rituals (10.92.3–12):[20]

has tibi gemellas barbari decus luci
commendo pinus ilicesque Faunorum
et semidocta uilici manu structas   5
Tonantis aras horridique Siluani,
quas pinxit agni saepe sanguis aut haedi,
dominamque sancti uirginem deam templi,
et quem sororis hospitem uides castae
Martem, mearum principem Kalendarum,   10
et delicatae laureum nemus Florae,
in quod Priapo persequente confugit.

To you I commend these twin pines, ornament of a rough copse, and the holm oaks of the Fauns, and the altars of Jupiter and bristly Silvanus, constructed by my bailiff's half-skilled hand, which the blood of a lamb or kid has often bedewed, and the virgin goddess, mistress of her holy shrine, and he, whom you see, his chaste sister's guest, the god Mars, ruler of my Kalends, and the laurel grove of dainty Flora, into which she fled from Priapus' pursuit.

From the outset, Martial signals the religious valence of the epigram, with a succession of trees and sacred groves: twin pines, ornament of a sacred grove (3–4); the sacrosanct holm-oaks of the Fauni (4); the wood-god Silvanus' altars (6); and a laurel grove consecrated to Flora (11). The words *lucus* (3) and *nemus* (11) both come into Latin with the sense of 'sacred grove', or 'sanctuary'. Servius explains the former as 'a throng of trees with a sense of the presence of supernatural power' (Serv. *ad Aen.* 1.310 *lucus est arborum multitudo cum religione*),[21] while Isidore glosses the latter as 'named for divinity (*numen*),

---

20 On 'sacralisation', see Rüpke in this volume.
21 Ernout/Meillet 1994 [1959], 368 s.v., records its specialisation in religious language, in the sense of '*bois sacré*', 'sacred grove', citing Servius' etymology *ad Aen.* 1.310. Given the cultic context, Martial may gesture specifically to the religious etymology of *lucus* from *luceo*, 'light by ritual torches', preserved by Isidore (*Etym.* 14.8.30): *potest et a conlucendo crebris luminibus dici, quae ibi propter religionem ... fiebant*. ('It is also possible that the word is derived from the lighting of many lights, which were kindled there because of pagan beliefs and rituals'. Cf. Isid. *Etym.* 17.6.7 *siue a luce, quod in eo lucebant funalia uel cerei propter nemorum tenebras* ('or *lucus*, 'sacred grove', is named from *lux*, 'light', because in it torches or candles used to give off light against the darkness of the grove', tr. Barney et al. 2006). Servius rejects this etymology in his acceptance of the now better-known antiphrastic etymology of the noun, *lucus a non lucendo* (*ad Aen.* 1.441): *lucus ... dicitur quod non luceat, non quod sint ibi lumina causa religionis, ut quidam uolunt* ('a grove is so called because there is no light, not because there are lights there because of religion, as some want it to be understood'). On this famous etymology

because pagans set up their idols there' (*Etym.* 17.6.6 *nemus a numinibus nuncupatum, quia pagani ibi idola constituebant*).²² Martial underlines the religious valence of both terms by juxtaposing them with his farm's resident deities in this passage.

The specific trees that Martial identifies on the property also enter the epigram freighted with religious significance. Stefanie Albrecht notes the rich traditions of classical myth that cluster about the pine (10.92.4).²³ Thus, Dionysus' thyrsus is topped with a pine cone, while the tree also played an important role in the cults of Attis and Cybele. Catullus evokes the goddess' association with forest shade in his reference to her sacred 'places crowned with woods' at the outset of *Carm.* 63 (3 *opaca siluis redimita loca deae*), and it is reported that her worshippers carried pine tree branches in their rites. In Roman ritual, the cults of Attis and Cybele were combined in the attachment by the Magna Mater's *dendrophoroi* of an 'effigy of Attis to this tree in their procession up the Palatine Hill in Rome'.²⁴ The tree was also of paramount importance in the iconography of Silvanus,²⁵ invoked two lines later (10.92.6).

Although the same level of religious and mythological symbolism does not inhere in holm-oaks (10.92.4), they bring with them the literary symbolism of Virgil's Epicurean pastoral (*Ecl.* 6.54, 7.1) and, according to Albrecht, 'they compete with the cypress as a symbol of imperishability, [being] holy to the Erinyes and stand[ing] under the protection of Jupiter',²⁶ as Servius attests (*Aen.* 5.129 *frondente ex ilice*) *haec enim arbor in tutela Iouis est*.²⁷ Martial, however, here links the tree with the Fauni, rustic divinities of the wild Italian countryside associated from ancient times with 'flocks and forests'.²⁸ Faunus himself, moreover, along with his father Picus, is reported to have frequented a

---

κατ' ἀντίφρασιν, see O'Hara 1996, 43, with n. 244, and 66. On etymologising in Martial, see Grewing 1998.

22 Translation from Barney et al. 2006. *OLD* s.v. notes that *nemus* is cognate not only with ancient Greek νέμος, but also with Old Irish *nemed*, 'holy place', 'sanctuary'; cf. Ernout/Meillet 1994 [1959], 437 s.v.
23 Albrecht *apud* Damschen and Heil 2004, 328.
24 Dorcey 1992, 17 n. 16.
25 Dorcey 1992, 17–19.
26 Albrecht *apud* Damschen and Heil 2004, 328.
27 In the *Aeneid* passage, Aeneas uses a leafy branch of holm-oak as the turning post of the chariot race, on the model of Hom. *Il.* 23.327–328, where Nestor characterises the turning point in the chariot race 'as a dry stump six feet high of oak or pine' (Williams 1960, 72 at *Aen.* 5.129 *metam*). Martial seems to take up the Homeric alternates of oak and pine in his collocation *pinus ilicesque* (10.92.4).
28 Horsfall 2000, 78 at *Aen.* 7.47.

holy spring in a sacred *ilex*-grove at the foot of the Aventine in Rome (Ov. *Fast.* 3.295–299):[29]

> *lucus Auentino suberat niger ilicis umbra,*
>   *quo posses uiso dicere 'numen inest'.*
> *in medio gramen, muscoque adoperta uirenti*
>   *manabat saxo uena perennis aquae:*
> *inde fere soli Faunus Picusque bibebant.*

> Under the Aventine there lay a grove black with the shade of a holm-oaks; at sight of it you could say, 'There is a divine spirit here'. There was a grassy knoll in the midst, and, veiled by green moss there trickled from a rock a rill of never-failing water. At it Faunus and Picus were wont to drink alone.

The rustic conjunction of holm-oak grove and pastoral divinities in the heart of urban Rome, the characteristic setting of Martial's epigrams, has even led to the suggestion that the Roman site furnished the source of Martial's image.[30] Whether or not the historical grove on the Aventine inspired Martial's imagery in this epigram, it is notable that the Augustan poet insists on the religious significance of the Aventine holm-oak grove in his playful etymologising collocation *lucus ... ilicis* (*Fast.* 3.295) and interpretive etymological gloss at the end of the next line, *numen inest* (*Fast.* 3.296).[31] We may therefore be confident that the classical literary tradition of etymological wordplay informs Martial's depiction of the farm's sacred groves, and underlines the sanctity of his cult observances there.

Given the numinous import of the Italian woods, home to so many rustic divinities, it is not surprising to find on Martial's farm property altars to both Jupiter Tonans and Silvanus (10.92.6), as also the ritual practice of blood sacrifice associated with their use (10.92.7). Jupiter, the sky god, was the supreme deity of the Roman world, honoured under the cult title 'Tonans' with a temple on the Capitol in Rome at which, as here, sheep were sacrificed (Ov. *Fast.* 2.69–70) *ad penetrale Numae Capitolinumque Tonantem / inque Iouis summa caeditur arce bidens* ('at Numa's sanctary, at the Thunderer's shrine on the Capitol, and on the summit of Jove's citadel a sheep is slain'). More at home

---

[29] I cite Ovid's *Fasti* from the Loeb edition of Frazer 1976; translations follow or adapt Frazer 1976.
[30] Albrecht *apud* Damschen and Heil 2004, 328.
[31] On typical features of Virgilian etymological wordplay, applicable to Martial by extension, see O'Hara 1996, 57–102; for the collocation *lucus ... umbra* in Virgilian as a reference to the etymology κατ' ἀντίφρασιν, *lucus a non lucendo*, see O'Hara 1996, 125 and 167.

in the countryside is the rustic divinity Silvanus, who took his name from the woods, *silua*, and was associated 'with forest and uncultivated land'.[32] He was worshipped as the protector of the woods, especially of the plantation, the field and farm, but also (like Faunus) of the flocks.[33] The adjective *horridus* indicates his rustic appearance, bristling with beard and long hair, and his standard iconography shows him wearing a garland of pine on his head, carrying a pine branch in his left and often sporting a pine cone on his cloak, symbolising reproduction.[34]

In addition to the altars of Jupiter Tonans and Silvanus, Martial locates on the farm a precinct sacred to Diana (8), goddess of the hunt and of fertility for both human women and wild nature.[35] In war, she was invoked for protection against the dangers of battle and in this context she was linked with the war gods Victoria, Fortuna, and Mars himself.[36] Albrecht accordingly proposes that this association accounts for the appearance of the war god here (10.92.9–10).[37] Yet Mars' presence on the farm and in the poem may have had less to do with his martial character than with his early Italian origin as a god of agriculture and animal husbandry and with the poet's own self-fashioning in his epigrams.[38] We may note Martial's emphasis on his own special relationship to Mars through his birth on the Kalends of March (10.92.10), the god's day (Ov. *Fast*. 3.1–2), from which the poet M. Valerius Martialis, derived his cognomen.[39] Especially suggestive, however, in the context of Martial's country estate, are the god's associations with both herds and crops. Already in the mid-republican period, the elder Cato reports that sacrifice was offered to Mars for the health of

---

[32] In general, on the cult of Silvanus, see Dorcey 1992. He follows Meid 1957 in viewing the god's name Silvanus as an emphatic form of the noun *silua*, rather than as an adjective derived from the noun. Dorcey 1992, 83 notes Silvanus' frequent appearance on reliefs and inscriptions in the company of Jupiter Optimus Maximus.

[33] Albrecht *apud* Damschen and Heil 2004, 328.

[34] Albrecht *apud* Damschen and Heil 2004, 329. Dorcey 1992, 16–24 discusses the evidence for the iconography of the god.

[35] Albrecht *apud* Damschen and Heil 2004, 329. Dorcey 1992, 83 observes that 'Diana is [Silvanus'] most common female companion' in extant inscriptions and reliefs.

[36] Albrecht *apud* Damschen and Heil 2004, 329.

[37] Albrecht *apud* Damschen and Heil 2004, 329.

[38] Albrecht *apud* Damschen and Heil 2004, 329.

[39] Albrecht *apud* Damschen and Heil 2004, 329. Margot Neger reminds me that the evocation of this date links the closural section of Book 10 with the closure of Book 5, where the Kalends of March are also mentioned (5.84).

the herd and the growth of the crop.⁴⁰ Moreover, he apparently conflates Mars with Silvanus in his instruction to farmers to 'perform the vow for the health of the cattle' by making 'an offering to Mars Silvanus in the forest' (Cato *Agr.* 83) *Votum pro bubus, uti ualeant, sic facito. Marti Siluano in silua interdius in capita singula boum uotum facito... Hoc uotum in annos singulos, si uoles, licebit uouere* ('perform the vow for the health of the cattle as follows: Make an offering to Mars Silvanus in the forest during the daytime for each head of cattle... You may vow the vow every year if you wish').⁴¹ This ancient association of Mars with Silvanus is implicit in Martial's juxtaposition of Jupiter with Silvanus and Diana with Mars in the epigrammatist's roster of the Nomentum farm's tutelary divinities. In this connection, it is striking that Cato repeatedly petitions 'father Mars' in his recitation of the prayer that accompanied the farm's annual purification ceremony, the *lustratio*, which was prefaced by the invocation of Janus and Jupiter (Cato *Agr.* 141):

> ... *Ianum Iouemque uino praefamino, sic dicito:*
> **'Mars pater te precor quaesoque**
> *uti sies uolens propitius*
> *mihi domo familiaeque nostrae;*
> ...
> **Mars pater,**
> *eiusdem rei ergo*
> *macte hisce suouitaurilibus*
> *lactentibus immolandis esto.'*
> ...
> *Nominare uetat* **Martem** *neque agnum uitulumque. Si minus in omnis litabit, sic uerba concipito:*
> **'Mars pater**, *quod tibi illoc porco neque satisfactum est, te hoc porco piaculo'.*

Make a prayer with wine to Janus and Jupiter, and say: "Father Mars, I pray and beseech thee that thou be gracious and merciful to me, my house, and my household... Father Mars, to the same intent deign to accept the offering of these suckling offering." ... If favourable omens are not obtained in response to all, speak thus: "Father Mars, if aught hath not pleased thee in the offering of those sucklings, I make atonement with these victims." If there is doubt about one or two, use these words: "Father Mars, inasmuch as thou wast not pleased by the offering of that pig, I make atonement with this pig".'

---

40 Albrecht *apud* Damschen and Heil 2004, 329. Dorcey 1992, 8–10 discusses the passage in connection with other evidence for the ritual sphere of the god Silvanus.
41 The Latin text and English translation are from Hooper rev. Ash 1934.

Martial's epigram offers evidence for the durability of Mars' operations in the agricultural sphere, in conjunction with so many other deities of the Roman rustic pantheon.

The roster of the Nomentan farm's divinities concludes with the mention of a laurel grove on the property sacred to the goddess Flora (10.92.11), an Italian divinity of plants, especially grain crops.[42] Although the laurel tree was sacred to Apollo and also a secondary attribute of Dionysus,[43] Martial's laurel sanctuary belongs to Flora not only as the site of her refuge from Priapus' assault but also in her capacity as a goddess of vegetation and produce. The goddess had long had her own priest (*flamen Floralis*) at Rome and had received annual games at a festival in her honour (*Floralia*), at least from the mid-republic. In Martial's day, however, she was associated above all with prostitutes, who claimed the Floralia as their own, reportedly dancing naked in the games' spectacular conclusion, to riotous approval from the crowd.[44] In the prose epistle that heads his first collection of epigrams, moreover, Martial introduces her as the inspiration for his sexually licentious genre (*Praef.* 12–21):[45]

> si quis tamen tam ambitiose tristis est apud illum in nulla pagina latine loqui fas sit, potest epistula uel potius titulo contentus esse. Epigrammata illis scribuntur qui solent spectare Florales. non intret Cato theatrum meum, aut si intrauerit, spectet. uideor mihi meo iure facturus si epistulam uersibus clusero:
> > Nosses iocosae dulce cum sacrum Florae
> > festosque lusus et licentiam uulgi,
> > cur in theatrum, Cato seuere, uenisti?
> > an ideo tantum ueneras, ut exires?

However, should any man so flaunt his prudery that Latin cannot be spoken on any page in his presence, he can make do with my letter, or better, my title. Epigrams are written for those who are accustomed to watch Flora's games. Let Cato keep out of my theatre; or if he comes in, let him watch. I think I shall be within my rights if I conclude my letter in verse:
> You knew of sprightly Flora's ritual fun,
> the festal jests and licence of the rout.
> Then why, stern Cato, come to watch? Have done.
> Or did you come in simply to walk out?

---

42 Albrecht *apud* Damschen and Heil 2004, 328. Dorcey 1992, 83 notes that the god Silvanus is never paired with Flora, which is the case here too, of course; but it is instructive to see both gods' inclusion in Martial's rustic pantheon.
43 Albrecht *apud* Damschen and Heil 2004, 328.
44 Keith 2018, 84, citing Scullard 1981, 110–111; Richlin 1992a, 6–10; Edwards 1993, 119–121; cf. also Edwards 1994, with further bibliography.
45 On the passage, see Citroni 1975, 11–12; Howell 1980, 100–101.

Flora's numinous presence on Martial's Nomentan farm should thus also be connected with her role as (one of) the tutelary god(s) of his epigrams, which she oversees almost from the very outset of his collections. Indeed, an early epigram in the first book highlights her thematic importance to Martial's verse by reference to Priapus as well (1.35):

> *Versus scribere me parum seueros*
> *nec quos praelegat in schola magister,*
> *Corneli quereris: sed hi libelli,*
> *tamquam coniugibus suis mariti,*
> *non possunt sine mentula placere.*
> *quid si me iubeas thalassionem*
> *uerbis dicere non thalassionis?*
> *quis Floralia uestit et stolatum*
> *permittit meretricibus pudorem?*
> *lex haec carminibus data est iocosis,*
> *ne possint, nisi prurient, iuuare.*
> *quare deposita seueritate*
> *parcas lusibus et iocis rogamus,*
> *nec castrare uelis meos libellos.*
> *gallo turpius est nihil Priapo.*

Cornelius, you grumble that I write risqué verses, not the sort a school master would dictate in class. But these little books are like husbands with their wives — they can't please without a cock. You might as well tell me to sing a wedding song without using wedding song words. Does anybody put clothes on Flora's festival or allow whores the modesty of the matron's robe? There's a law laid down for merry verses: they can't be good for anything unless they itch. So please put prudery aside and spare my jests and jollities; and don't try to emasculate my little books. There's nothing uglier than a neutered Priapus.

Flora's laurel sanctuary on his Nomentum estate perfectly instantiates the goddess' pride of place both in Martial's literary corpus and on his country estate.

The story of Priapus' intended rape of the goddess Flora (10.92.12) is not elsewhere preserved and has been supposed to be either a local tradition or an invention of Martial himself.[46] In its lineaments, however, it is reminiscent of myths related by Ovid in the *Fasti* concerning Priapus' lustful approaches to the nymph Lotis (*Fast.* 1.391–440) and the goddess Vesta (*Fast.* 6.319–348). On both occasions, the Lampsacene god is thwarted in his intentions by the braying of Silenus' ass, which alerts the sleeping goddesses (*Fast.* 1.391, 433–444; 6.339–344); and it seems that on a third occasion too, Priapus' sexual aggression is

---

46 Albrecht *apud* Damschen and Heil 2004, 329. On Priapus in Latin poetry, see Fantham 2009, 133–159.

foiled, this time when Martial's tutelary goddess takes refuge in the laurel grove on his farm.[47] Albrecht notes that the poet's inclusion of Priapus concludes the roster of deities of agricultural fertility in the poem, as his image frequently stood in gardens and vineyards, which were entrusted to his protection.[48] As the agricultural instantation of raw physical desire, he is also completely at home in the epigrammatist's literary garden.[49]

Martial characterises the cohort of divinities on his little farm (*agelli paruuli*) as constituting a 'gentle godhead' (*mite numen* 13), and as nature gods on his rural estate they offer him the peace and relaxation he seeks from the hustle and bustle of city-life, which he now intends to leave behind on his retirement to Spain. On his country property he has conducted the religious rites owed to the gods of nature and agriculture, and in preparation for his departure from Italy he entrusts the continuing care of his farm and its tutelary divinities to his dear friend Marrius (10.92.13–19):

> *hoc omne agelli mite paruuli numen*
> *seu tu cruore siue ture placabis;*
> *'ubicumque uester Martialis est,' dices,*   15
> *'hac ecce mecum dextera litat uobis*
> *absens sacerdos; uos putate praesentem*
> *et date duobus quidquid alter optabit.'*

All this gentle godhead of my little plot you will propitiate with blood or with incense, and say: 'Wherever your Martial is now, see, by my hand he along with me makes you acceptable offering, an absent priest. Think of him as present, and give to both whatever either shall pray for'.

The estate owner's formal role as priest in the performance of his ritual obligations to the rural gods continues even during his absence (17), in Marrius' commitment to cultivating both Martial's farm and its tutelary divinities. Indeed, Marrius' provision of an acceptable offering to the gods (16) is predicated on Martial's own recommendation of an appropriate guardian for his country estate (4).[50]

---

[47] I thank Margot Neger for noting that the connection between a mythological story of a rural god chasing a goddess/nymph and the estate of a Roman contemporary also appears in Stat. *Silu.* 2.3 on the *arbor Atedi Melioris*. There it is Pan who chases the nymph Pholoe, and the story is the aition for a strangely shaped tree next to the pond on the estate of Statius' friend.
[48] Albrecht *apud* Damschen and Heil 2004, 329. On Priapus, see esp. Richlin 1992b.
[49] In addition to his appearance in 1.35, where we have already met him, Priapus appears in epigrams 3.58.47, 6.72–73, 8.40, 11.18.22, 11.72, 14.70; cf. 6.16, 6.49, 7.91.4, 11.51.2.
[50] See Rüpke in this volume.

Albrecht views Marrius' pious observance of the country gods' rites, whether in an offering of blood sacrifice or of incense (14), as testimony to the friends' shared love of an Epicurean ideal of the peaceful life.[51] Certainly, Marrius' epithets *quietae cultor* and *comes uitae* (1) are drawn from the Latin lexicon of Hellenistic Greek philosophy and are particularly suggestive of Epicureanism in their idealisation of *quies* (= ἀταραξία),[52] country living on a small property (cf. *agelli paruuli*, 13),[53] and friendship (*comes*)[54] in the enjoyment of the good life (*uita* = βίος). If Marrius were of an Epicurean temperament, as I have argued was the case for Martial,[55] the concord of their prayers, which the closing lines of the epigram rehearse (15–18), is easily understood.[56] Whether or not we are inclined to see an Epicurean valence in the poem's celebration of a peaceful life in the countryside, however, the poem's philosophical frame sounds another closural note, inasmuch as Roman writers often propose to move on to philosophical study as the appropriate end to a literary career.[57]

Epigram 10.92 thus exhibits many of the closural features which literary critics have catalogued in poetry: a change in life; a gaze both retrospective and prospective; a dedication (or commendation); and the successful performance of religious ritual involving both sacrifice and prayer.[58] In the commendation of his farm to Marrius, Martial ritually binds his friend to the Nomentan property and simultaneously releases himself from it.[59] In this respect, the epigram dovetails neatly with the closing programme of Martial's revised tenth book, anticipating the poet's departure from Italy and retirement to Spain. As Don Fowler has observed, in the case of literary closure operating beyond the level of the individual poem or collection, 'supertextual closure is often marked by a parallelism

---

51 Albrecht *apud* Damschen and Heil 2004, 328 and 330.
52 On Epicurean ἀταραξία, see O'Keefe 2010, 111–116.
53 Diogenes Laertius records Epicurus' saying that the wise man 'will love the countryside' (Diog. Laert. 10.120a).
54 *KD* 27–28; *VS* 23, 39, 52, 66, 78. Diogenes Laertius (10.120b) discusses how Epicurus reconciled the pleasures of friendship with his utilitarian views. On Epicurean friendship, see Rist 1980; O'Keefe 2010, 147–154.
55 Keith 2018 [2019] and 2021.
56 Diogenes Laertius records Epicurus' exemplary 'piety toward the gods' (Diog. Laert. 10.10) and quotes him as saying that the wise man 'will enjoy himself more than others at state festivals' (Diog. Laert. 10.120a) and 'will set up statues (Diog. Laert. 10.12ab). On the gods in Epicurean philosophy, see O'Keefe 2010, 155–162.
57 Cf., e.g., Prop. 3.5.25–46, 21.25–26; VSD 35.
58 Smith 1968; Roberts/Dunn/Fowler 1997; Kermode 2000 [1966]; Fowler 2000a [1989] and 2000b.
59 See Rüpke in this volume.

between the progress of a writer's life and of his poetry'.[60] Here we can see 10.92 as part of the book's movement toward the end of Martial's revised tenth collection of epigrams and also as part of the poet's movement toward the close of his Italian career.

In the book's penultimate epigram (10.103), Martial recalls the end of his cult observance in Spain on his departure for Italy and holds out the possibility of his resumption of ritual participation in his natal community on his proposed return to Bilbilis. Addressing his fellow townsmen (10.103.1–2), the poet dates his departure for the imperial capitol by reference to the goddess Ceres' annual rites (103.7–8): *quattuor accessit tricesima messibus aestas / ut sine me Cereri rustica liba datis* ('a thirtieth summer has joined four harvests since you first gave Ceres your rustic cakes without me'). In keeping with the closural placement of the epigram, second from the end of the book, Martial marks his departure from Bilbilis, thirty-four years previously, according to the agricultural ritual calendar, in the annual dedication of sacred cakes to the goddess of the harvest. Within the tenth book, the poet's reference to the conclusion of his ritual observance of Ceres' cult at Bilbilis briefly recalls his elaborate invocation of the gods of his Nomentan farm in 10.92 and the transferal of their rites to the care of his friend Marrius. In this way, Martial amplifies the ritual resonances of the book's closural programme, even as he simultaneously proposes the renewal of his participation in Ceres' rites upon his return to Spain. The generic openness and fluidity of epigram allows Martial to draw on religious emblems and cultic rites in the articulation of both closure and renewal in the poetic design of his revised collection.

---

60 Fowler 2000a, 247 [= 1989, 83–84].

Laila Dell'Anno
Ritual and the Impossibility of Song in Statius' *Siluae* 5

Abstract: The first part of the paper shows that all the silvan occasions, as varied as they may be, describe at their core what modern anthropology calls a rite of passage. In this context, this paper proposes a fundamental reappreciation of Book 5 of Statius' occasional poems, exploring how the involvement of the poet's persona in the ritual activity and its change in the final book brings about the closure of the *Siluae* and perhaps the Statian oeuvre altogether. For the literary self-fashioning spanning over the entire collection, and especially the closing volume, Ovid will prove a decisive model and underline the final book's claim to authenticity: just like Ovid's exilic poetry, *Siluae* 5 expresses a deep personal and poetic crisis.

It may surprise some to find a text on Statius' *Siluae* in a volume on closure, given that they neither have a narrative — in a stricter sense — that could come to a close, nor a (textually) certain end. With the present article, I will aim to counteract precisely this preconception, by following ritual as an overarching narrative framework for the *Siluae*-collection and ultimately showing how its evolution over the course of the five books acts as an instrument in bringing about closure. For this, the two elements in question, ritual and closure, will need to be considered separately. The latter will require a reappraisal of the fifth and final book by identifying it as a complete and authentic, rather than a posthumous and fragmentary edition.[1]

1 Ritual in the *Siluae* — the *Siluae* as rituals

As the title suggests, the *Siluae* are characterised by their varied and heterogeneous nature,[2] and are as such hardly feasible as a unity. A common feature to

---
[1] For my reading of the *Siluae*, the context of book-publication is fundamental: I would contend that we can only speak about closure because of the arrangement of Statius' occasional poems as *Siluae* in a series of volumes. The importance of the prefaces and the book-context will be discussed at length in my PhD thesis.
[2] For possible implications of the title *Siluae*, see Malaspina 2006; 2013; Wray 2007; Lévy 2013.

https://doi.org/10.1515/9783110770483-005

all of the thirty two compositions, however, is their occupation with ritual: whether public rites like games and Saturnalia festivities, or private ones like birthday celebrations or funerary rites, each of the poems describes what in today's terminology would be called a rite of passage,[3] a particular moment or event in the lifespan of an individual that, for its structural importance in their life, is celebrated in an often socially and religiously institutionalised manner. The *Siluae* function as poetic records of these rites. Scanning the mere titles of the individual pieces, such a claim is immediately feasible for the *epithalamium* (*Silu.* 1.2), the birthday poems (e.g. *Silu.* 2.3 and 2.7) or the *epicedia* (e.g. *Silu.* 2.1; 2.6; 3.3; 5.3; 5.5). At other times, the ritual occasion is more difficult to individuate, as when, for instance, the construction of a new temple to Hercules becomes the deity's re-birth in *Silu.* 3.1,[4] or when in *Silu.* 4.6 the acquisition of a statuette by Novius Vindex is fashioned into the aggregation of a new *amicus* into his circle.[5]

As a particularly speaking example, *Silu.* 4.2 illustrates this dynamic: in the framework of the *eucharisitikon* to Domitian for an invitation to the palace, the poet describes the sight of the emperor during the dinner as a quasi-religious experience (4.2.10–16):

> *mediis uideor discumbere in astris*   10
> *cum Ioue et Iliaca porrectum sumere dextra*
> *immortale merum. steriles transmisimus annos;*
> *haec aeui mihi prima dies, hic limina uitae.*
> *tene ego, regnator terrarum orbisque subacti*
> *magne parens, te, spes hominum, te, cura deorum,*   15
> *cerno iacens?*

---

[3] On rites of passage, see van Gennep's 1909.
[4] For the fact that the foundation days of temples were considered their birthdays, see Hardie 1983, 128; Rüpke 2004, 32; Feeney 2007, 148.
[5] There is no room for a detailed discussion of how the *Siluae* reproduce the fundamental structure of the rite of passage. Suffice to say at this stage that the temporal dichotomy at the basis of each rite of passage, i.e., the emphasis on one single moment in time that will have an impact on the *longue durée* (e.g. the wedding-day engenders a long-lasting change), is reproduced in virtually every poem of the *Siluae*. This aspect also constitutes one of the major differences of Statius' occasional poetry from Horace's, who, unlike his successor, stays focussed on the *hic et nunc* while the *Siluae* consciously look beyond the moment. I analyse this temporal structure in detail in my PhD thesis. Since a detailed overview of every poem and its corresponding rite of passage would exceed the scope of this article, I hope that the reader will content themselves with these few examples and follow my argumentation from here onwards. One noticeable exception to the correspondence of the individual poems to rites of passage is *Silu.* 5.4 on *Somnus*, to which I have not been able to attribute a rite.

I seem to be reclining with Jupiter among the stars and taking immortal liquor proffered by Ilian hand. Barren are the years behind me, this is the first day of my span, here is the threshold of my life. Do I behold you as I lay here, sovereign of the lands, great parent of a world subdued, you, hope of mankind, you, care of gods?[6]

The poem here uses an encomiastic strategy well established in the Statian *oeuvre*, namely equating the emperor, duly addressed in the *Du-Stil* characteristic of prayer, to the *optimus maximus*,[7] thus enhancing the overall religious atmosphere of the moment: such is the ritual impact of Jupiter–Domitian's presence that the poet emerges from the scene reborn. Identifying the moment of the imperial banquet as *limina uitae* ('threshold of my life'), the author renders it a *locus* of ritual passage. This instance is paradigmatic for Statius' treatment of events: where *a priori* no ritual or religious framework is given, the structural importance of the moment, its long-lasting impact on the individual's life, is highlighted so as to reproduce the dynamics of the rite of passage. In the case of *Silu.* 4.2, participation in an imperial banquet becomes a sort of initiation rite for the author. In this sense, the *Siluae* collectively can be read as a series of rites, many of which are to be celebrated in their annual recurrence, an aspect that is not only enhanced by the preservation of the rites in the books, but also by the pieces' vaguely calendrical order in each volume.[8] But as heterogeneous and as variegated as the *Siluae* might be — indeed just as varied as the year itself — there is a red thread running through the collection: the poet.

As the one constant presence in all the pieces, the author-persona 'Statius' is an especially revealing figure with regard to the larger structure or, if you will, narrative frame, of the collection, over the course of which he takes on various roles.[9] Whereas the *eucharistikon* describes a rite of passage for the poet himself, over the first four books he mostly appears as either participant in a rite or as external observer and commentator. A telling example in this regard is *Silu.* 2.1, an *epicedion* for Melior's boy Glaucias. Melior, as addressee of no less than three poems, and the entirety of Book 2, stands out as one of Statius' most

---

6 The Latin text and all translations with slight alterations are from Shackleton Bailey 2015.
7 On Domitian as *Iupiter terrestris* ('earthly Jupiter') in *Silu.* 4.1, see Hulls 2010, 97.
8 Book 4 especially adheres to this order, opening with a composition presented in January and closing with a Saturnalia poem gifted in December. On this, see Parker 2014, 118; Newlands 2009b; 2010, 165. Book 1 equally closes with December, Book 2 with November. In my thesis I discuss the influence of the calendar and Ovid's calendar poem in detail.
9 When, in the subsequent pages, I will speak of 'the author' or 'Statius', I am not referring to the real-world author Publius Papinius Statius but rather to the persona of the poet as he appears in the framework of his texts.

important *amici*.¹⁰ It is hardly surprising, then, that the author takes an active part in a rite that marks such a pivotal moment in the friend's life without, however, being himself its main actor (*Silu*. 2.1.1–35):

> *Quod tibi praerepti, Melior, solamen alumni*
> *improbus ante rogos et adhuc uiuente fauilla*
> *ordiar?* [...]
> *cum iam egomet cantus et uerba medentia saeuus*   5
> *confero, tu planctus lamentaque fortia mauis*
> *odistique chelyn surdaque auerteris aure.*
> [...]
> *lacrimis en et mea carmine in ipso*   17
> *ora natant tristesque cadunt in uerba liturae.*
> *ipse etenim tecum nigrae sollemnia pompae*
> *spectatumque Urbi (scelus heu!) puerile feretrum*   20
> *produxi.*
> [...]
>   *nec te lugere seuerus*   34
> *arceo, sed confer gemitus pariterque fleamus.*

> How shall I begin, Melior, to console you for the foster child that Fate has snatched away from you as I stand before the pyre and the embers still glow [...] While I cruelly weave song and words of healing, you prefer beating your breast and loud lament, hating the lyre and turning deaf ears away. [...] See, my face too swims with tears even as my song proceeds and sad blots fall on the page. For I myself led forth the black-garbed funeral procession by your side, the childish bier (alas the crime!) watched by all Rome. [...] I do not tell you sternly not to mourn; but mingle your groans and let us weep together.¹¹

The author has a double role: as a friend, he grieves with Melior (17–21; 34–35); as a poet, he composes a consolation (1–7). Here, mourning and making poetry go hand in hand, as this *Silua*, the poetic record of both actions, testifies. By virtue of the close bond with the bereaved, the author is able to recount this rite from a privileged vantage point. As an *epicedion*, the poem remembers the dead and consoles the survivor; it is as such testimony of and instrument for this particular passage in Melior's life. At the same time, the poem self-consciously reflects on its aptitude for this context: while Statius appears in the scene in his capacity as poet — as indicated by his *insignia*, lyre and fillets — this is not what the friend is looking for. Therefore, he is compelled temporarily to abandon these poetic attributes (26–28) *et nunc heu uittis et frontis honore soluto* /

---

10 Stat. *Silu*. 2 *praef*. 1–4.
11 For 2.1.20 I follow the emendation proposed by Ker and adopted by Shackleton Bailey 2015 and Newlands 2011.

infaustus uates uersa mea pectora tecum / plango lyra, "and now alas! a poet of ill omen, I cast off the fillets that dignify my brow, I turn my lyre over and with it beat my breast along with you". He thus makes way for amicable compassion instead of professional vocation. In this instance, Melior's grief only for a short while hinders the author's poetic activity and soon enough, as the very existence of the poem indicates, it is taken up again. Although in the front row, the poet is not himself implicated in this particular rite of passage, which therefore only indirectly affects him.

It can be gleaned that, in turn, the degree of the author's personal involvement in a rite has direct consequences on the poem produced from a passage in *Silu.* 1.6. Having dedicated nearly a hundred lines to the festivities for the Saturnalia, the overabundance of food and wine enjoyed during the festival starts to have effects on the poet as he is describing it (1.6.93–97):

> *Quis spectacula, quis iocos licentes,*
> *quis conuiuia, quis dapes inemptas*
> *largi flumina quis canat Lyaei?*   95
> *iamiam deficio tuoque Baccho*
> *in serum trahor ebrius soporem.*

> Who should sing the shows, the unbridled jests, the banquets, the viands unbought, the rivers of lavish Lyaeus? Now, now my strength fails, and your Bacchus draws me tipsy into tardy slumber.[12]

During the process of composition, the author has evidently taken part in the ritual festivities he is recounting, with a detrimental effect on his composition which breaks off before the rite comes to an end. It is already becoming apparent that, although I have characterised the *Siluae* as textualised rites of passage, rite and poetry are not always in harmony. In fact, the poet must carefully calibrate the degree of participation in ritual activity in order to pursue his primary poetic vocation. While the mourning with Melior, like the Saturnalian wine-frenzy, only lasts a short while and is overcome in the following piece, a more radical picture emerges in the last volume of the collection. However, before I will turn to the nexus I am ultimately interested in, the intersection of ritual and closure, I shall leave the subject of the *Siluae* as rites of passage, and consider the editorial authenticity of the last book, which has been disputed for decades.

---

[12] I accept the emendation of *tuaque* at 96 to *tuoque.*

2 Reappraising *Siluae* 5

That the fifth and final book of the *Siluae* was not edited by Statius himself but put together and published after the author's death is the common scholarly opinion up to this day.[13] This claim can be traced back almost three centuries to Jeremiah Markland's commentary on the *Siluae* collection.[14] Over the years, Markland's hypothesis has enjoyed great popularity in subsequent scholarship,[15] up to the most recent publications in the field, which tend to treat *Siluae* 5 as unauthentic, sometimes even excluding it from critical discussion altogether.[16] While the main arguments in favour of a posthumous edition, the missing preface, the heterogeneous nature of *Silu.* 5.3–5, and the fragmentary status of the last poem, are indeed valid points to raise,[17] not enough effort has been dedicated to find alternative explanations for these questions, a fact that, especially given the troubled textual transmission of the *Siluae*, is more than problematic.[18] In the following I will therefore address these concerns showing that the design, if not the publication itself, of the fifth book could well be authentically Statian.

In contrast to the four prefatory letters to Books 1–4, the epistle to Abascantus, placed at the corresponding position in the fifth book, cannot make a claim at the same scope, for neither does the author mention a *quintus liber* or indeed the *Siluae* at all, nor is there any direct reference to the other poems contained in the volume, let alone a request for publication of them. While the absence of a proper preface is reason enough for many to suspect that *Siluae* 5 was not published by Statius, who had adhered to this particular mode of publication

---

[13] As upheld prominently by Gibson in his 2006 commentary on the very book. Cédric Scheidegger Laemmle has proposed a reading of the poems of Book 5 as part of Statius' literary politics; see Scheidegger Laemmle (forthcoming).
[14] Markland 1827 [1728], 342.
[15] E.g. in the monumental commentary by Vollmer 1898; Newmyer's 1979 volume on the design of the collection, or in the commentaries by Laguna Mariscal 1992; Liberman 2010; and Newlands 2011.
[16] Thus Johannsen 2006, 300; Bitto 2020; 2018, 289–290: "Ich möchte jedoch nicht den Buchkontext als sinntragendes Moment aktivieren, da mir eine postume Edition allein schon aufgrund der fehlenden *Praefatio* als zwingende Annahme erscheint." — 'I will not use the context of the book's publication as a meaningful element [of my argument], since a posthumous edition appears to be urgently implied by the mere absence of the preface.' (Transl. LDA).
[17] On these arguments, see Markland 1827, 342; Vollmer 1898, 4 n. 7; Laguna Mariscal 1992, 11–12; Gibson 2006, xxviii–xxiv; Liberman 2010, 158.
[18] For the manuscript tradition of the *Siluae*, see Reeve 1977.

for the first four parts, there are some observations to be made about the letter to Domitian's *ab epistulis* that may give way to reconsidering its status and scope in the collection.

First of all, the question of textual transmission cannot be disregarded: given that the *Siluae* have come down to us through one manuscript alone,[19] their textual integrity is more than dubious. Of the four prefaces, two very probably are fragmentary to a certain extent: while the second preface is only missing a closing formula, the first one breaks off in mid-sentence. To assume a similar destiny for the collection's last epistle — which, incidentally, is significantly shorter than the others and does not feature a final salutation — does not seem unreasonable. Furthermore, even the complete absence of an introductory epistle does not exclude the possibility of a publication during the author's lifetime, which is demonstrated by the fact that the prefatory letter to the *Thebaid* — attested by Statius himself (4 *praef*. 16–19) — has not been transmitted.

Moving on from the letter-preface to the design of the book itself, there is nothing that would suggest anything out of the ordinary with respect to the extant volumes. On the contrary, the neat rhythm of the *epicedia* is coherent with the design of Book 1, where personal poems occur in alternation with descriptive texts.[20] Likewise, the triad of compositions focusing on the lyric 'I' at the close of the volume mirror the two groups of poems in *Siluae* 2 and 4.[21] That such an arrangement could have been realised by a posthumous editor is of course possible, but there is another structural link between the pieces that makes an intended authorial design of the volume more probable: a verbal echo of and thematic reference to *Siluae* 5.1 in the subsequent piece.

In the closing section of *Siluae* 5.2, the poet beholds — in a mimetic stance — the arrival of a messenger appointing Crispinus to the office of military tribune (*Silu*. 5.2.168–174):

*Sed quis ab **excelsis** Troianae collibus Albae,*
unde suae iuxta prospectat moenia Romae
*proximus ille deus, **fama uelocior** intrat*   170
***nuntius** atque tuos implet, Crispine, penates?*
*dicebam certe 'uatum non inrita **currunt***
auguria.' en ingens reserat tibi limen honorum
Caesar et Ausonii committit munia ferri.

---

[19] See Reeve 1977, 202.
[20] See Newmyer 1979, 124; Newlands 2009b, 238.
[21] The poet points out these triads at 2 *praef*. 15–18 for *Silu*. 2.3–5 and 4 *praef*. 1–4 for *Silu*. 4.1–3.

But who is the messenger from Trojan Alba's lofty hills, where close at hand our god here present looks out upon the walls of his Rome? Swifter than Fama he enters and fills your home, Crispinus. Did I not say so? Not idle run poet's auguries. Behold! Mighty Caesar unbars for you the doorway to office and entrusts you with the duties of Ausonia's sword.

Compare the hyperbolic finale to the description of Abascantus' tasks as *ab epistulis* (*Silu.* 5.1.101–107):

> *cunctaque si numerem, non plura interprete uirga*
> **nuntiat ex celsis** *ales Tegeaticus astris*
> *quaeque cadit liquidas Iunonia uirgo per auras*
> *et picturato pluuium ligat aera gyro*
> *quaeque tuas laurus uolucri, Germanice,* **cursu**   105
> *fama uehit praegressa diem tardumque sub astris*
> *Arcada et in medio linquit Thaumantida caelo.*

> If I were to enumerate all, not more messages does the winged Tegean announce from the high stars with his go-between wand, nor Juno's maiden as she falls through the liquid air and binds the rainy atmosphere with her coloured arc, nor Fama that bears your laurels, Germanicus, outstripping the sun in her rapid flight, leaving the slow Arcadian beneath the stars and Thaumas' daughter in mid sky.

The comparison with *Fama* along with a number of verbal parallels link the passages on a micro-textual level and draw the readers' attention to the fact that the *nuntius* (5.2.171) probably delivers the epistle written by Abascantus, whose task as *ab epistulis* it is, *inter alia*, to announce the appointment of tribunes (5.1.94–97) *fidos dominus si diuidat enses, / pandere [...] quem deceat clari praestantior ordo tribuni [...]*, "Furthermore, if our lord should be distributing his faithful swords, to announce [...] who is right for the higher rank of a Tribune [...]". Significantly, the metonymy of the sword for military posts activated in this passage also returns at 5.2.177 *[...] cuique sacer primum tradit Germanicus ensem*, thus further reinforcing the reference to the preceding piece.[22]

This connection between the only two addressees in Book 5 is hardly coincidental. Rather, with the first pair of poems, Statius proposes an encomium of the imperial state apparatus, where pious officials elect worthy men for office. By adding a second encomiastic poem after the extensive first one, the author makes good on the promise he made in the — prefatory — letter, namely to "oblige any appendage of the Divine House."[23] A closer look at the structure of *Siluae* 5 reveals its thorough design, down to the micro-level of verbal echoes

---

22 Gibson 2006 *ad loc.*
23 5 *praef.* 8–9.

between compositions. Paradoxically however, it is not the unity, but the heterogeneous nature of the last three *Siluae*, at which scholars have long taken offence,[24] that points to a volume consciously composed for closure, and to which I will now turn.

3 Closing a collection (Statius and Ovid)

Last books often undergo particular scrutiny when it comes to the question of publication. The unfinished Book 10 of Lucan's *Bellum ciuile*, for instance, has been suspected of posthumous publication, as has Valerius Flaccus' *Argonautica*.[25] Ovid's final collection of letters *ex Ponto* likewise cannot claim the same certain status of a polished and published book as its three forerunners. Significantly, *ex Ponto* 4 raises, in terms of publication, much the same questions as *Siluae* 5:[26] next to the volumes' excessive length, the fact that the last book includes poems from a larger timespan than the previous[27] suggests that it might be an amalgamation of compositions left unpublished after the author's death. In a recent article, Franklinos has argued that *Pont.* 4 was, if not published, then still designed by Ovid himself.[28] Structure and coherence between the single poems, Franklinos' main focus in his analysis of Ovid, is an important aspect in Book 5 of the *Siluae* too, as illustrated above, yet it has not been accepted as evidence for a design by its author. Instead, the coherence and thorough design is attributed to an anonymous editor.[29] So why are scholarly debates so intent on exposing a work as *imperfectum*? Why are last books under such critical pressure if they do not follow their predecessors in every single detail? If Ovid's fourth Book *ex Ponto* produces a change of paradigm of some sort, closing

---

24 See Liberman 2010, 158.
25 See Zissos 2019, 534.
26 For Statius, see Liberman 2010, 33; for Ovid, see Holzberg 1997, 197–200; Wulfram 2008, 259–278; Franklinos 2018, 289.
27 In the case of *Pont.* 4 poems written between AD 13 and 16, *Siluae* 5 between the composition of *Silu.* 5.3 somewhere between 79 and 90 and 95 for the other poems.
28 See Franklinos 2018.
29 See Gibson 2006, xxx. This rather far-fetched hypothesis warrants the use of Wulfram's criticism regarding the publication of *Pont.* 4 (2008, 277): "Die Einführung einer solchen zusätzlichen [Editor-] Instanz erweist sich [...] meiner Ansicht nach als gänzlich überflüssig, ja als methodologisch bedenklich." – "Introducing such an additional [editor] authority proves itself, in my opinion, wholly superfluous, and indeed, methodologically questionable" (Transl. LDA).

off a multi-book collection published in several instalments, why cannot the same be true for Statius' *Siluae* 5? Might it not be worth considering that stepping back from established patterns could be part of the larger poetic strategy? Could *Siluae* 5 not be the poet's farewell to, and subsequent recusal of, poetry?

A double parallel can be drawn between Ovid's and Statius' last books, because not only is a rehabilitation of this work by critical research similar to Franklinos' undertaking, but the two final books are also very similar in terms of content and structure. Given the palpable influence of Ovid over the entire *Siluae* collection,[30] it will be useful to point out some overlaps between the two 'late works' in order to illustrate the closural dynamics more clearly. For *Siluae* 5, Ovidian exile-poetry functions as a double reference: on the one hand, the publication and uncertain status of the last book *ex Ponto* show significant parallels with the volume in question; on the other hand, it is *in toto* a model for Statius' last book insofar as it presents a more self-conscious, introspective kind of poetry that deals with crisis and suffering experienced by the author-persona.

Ovid is a recurring presence throughout the *Siluae*, and in his last book Statius glances, with its opening *me miserum!* at *Silu.* 5.5.1 towards the elegiac *persona* of the *Amores*.[31] But looking back on his oeuvre from a moment of personal and poetic crisis, he recalls first and foremost Ovid's exilic poetry. That such a reflection happens at a crucial moment, namely at the end of a five-book collection, makes sense against the background of Ovid's works but also in terms of *Werkpolitik* more generally:[32] it is at the end of the *Georgics* that Virgil looks back to the *Eclogues*; it is in *Carm.* 3.30 that Horace reflects on his future fame,[33] and, likewise, the *Thebaid* is closed off by a metapoetic epilogue. In short, a review of an oeuvre and the weighing of one's poetic glory does not happen at random, but the shift of focus away from the main poetic subject towards a meta-discourse on his poetic glory is a clear marker that Statius is about to close at least this particular poetic chapter of his life.[34]

As an *epicedion*, *Silu.* 5.3 fits, at first glance, seamlessly into the collection, not least because in a much earlier poem, Statius had already alluded to this composition.[35] But besides the *laudatio* of the deceased, the poem has yet another

---

[30] On Ovidian intertexts in Statius, see Lühr 1880, 48–55.
[31] On *me miserum* as an intertext, see Hinds 1998, 29–34.
[32] On *Werkpolitik* in Ovid and other classical authors, see Scheidegger Laemmle 2016.
[33] Lovatt 2007, 154 remarks the echo of *Carm.* 3.30 in *Silu.* 5.1.12 and 15.
[34] Perhaps one could even conceive of *Silu.* 5.3–5 as an extended *sphragis*, a metapoetic coda or an annexe to the other poems.
[35] *Silu.* 2.1.33–34. Incidentally, this earlier reference to the *epicedion in patrem* is an argument in favour of a Statian publication, following Heslin's claim (2009, 58–59) that a mention of the

rhetorical purpose. In terms of dating, it is the most complex poem not only in Book 5 but in the entire collection. Gibson's meticulous analysis of chronological indicators reveals that this piece was very probably composed in multiple phases.[36] It is also the only one in this book to have been written – or at least drafted – much earlier than *Silu.* 5.1. Thus, under the premise that Statius himself chose to publish *Silu.* 5.3 as part of his last book of extempore poems, it must have been particularly important to him. This is corroborated by the fact that the piece is the main source of biographical information about Statius (and his father), and as such de facto constitutes the poet's autobiographical legacy. In this respect it is particularly akin to *Trist.* 4.10, Ovid's most extensively autographic piece.[37] Just as this poem is a condensation of the collection's general atmosphere of retrospection and introspection, Statius' review of his life and career reflected through his father[38] is indicative of the tenor of the last three pieces. The marked opening of *Trist.* 4.10, *ille ego qui*, is thus echoed not only at *Silu.* 5.3.10 (*ille ego magnanimum qui facta attollere regum / ibam altum spirans Martemque aequare canendo*)[39] but also at 5.5.38 and 40,[40] which testifies to the poet's ongoing occupation with, and reflection on, his present situation and the consequences for this poetry. This Statian autography also holds the only direct mention of the poet's *Nachruhm* in the framework of the *Siluae*: whereas earlier in the collection, the lyric 'I' repeatedly claimed the longevity of his small pieces,[41] and along with it implicitly his own fame, here he specifically looks towards the *fama* as a poet many years after his death (5.3.213–214). Although evoked in a *Silua*, this much more ample kind of renown is not strictly tied to Statius' occasional production but to the sum of his poetic achievements, especially the

---

Achilleid in the *Siluae* only made sense because parts of it were already published. The same must be true for this piece.

36 Gibson 2006, *ad loc.*

37 Gibson 2006, xxxviii; Rosati 2013, 83. On Ovid's *Tr.* 4.10 and Statius' *Siluae* see also Klodt 2005. The term "autography" is used in Barchiesi/Hardie 2010 and elaborated in Barchiesi 2020a, 137: "[...] the idea of 'autography', a construction where poetry is the self-conscious expression of an interaction between poetics and biography."

38 Who Rosati 2013, 83 fittingly calls Statius' "avatar". This is also indicative of what Barchiesi explains in reference to autography (2020a, 144): "[...] if you want to represent yourself in public you need a model, and this model will always be someone else: my life needs to be someone else's life first."

39 Gibson 2006 follows Markland's suggestion to read *ille* instead of M's *certe*. Courtney 1990 prefers *certe*. Even if one reads *certe*, the phrasing and look back to the golden years of a poetic career clearly show the affinity.

40 Johannsen 2006, 333.

41 See *Silu.* 1.1.91–94; 3.3.37–39; 5.1.10–15.

Thebaid and the victories in the Neapolitan and Alban games. The *epicedion* for the father thus becomes a space for Statius to reflect on his life and poetic career as well as on his future posthumous fame.

This movement towards introspection in itself may not constitute a strong link with Ovid's exile poetry, but the fact that self-reflection occurs in a context of grief is decidedly Ovidian: at a moment of crisis, the poet is unable to live up to his former productions and looks back on his oeuvre perhaps in an attempt at self-consolation. Central in this context is the motive of unlearning of the poetic composition, present both in Ovid and Statius: compare *Silu.* 5.3.5–7 *Corycia quicquid modo Phoebus in umbra, / quicquid ab Ismariis monstrarat collibus Euhan, / dedidici*, "Whatever Phoebus had lately shown me in Corycian shade, whatever Euhan from Ismarian hills, I have unlearned", and *Tr.* 3.14.45–46 *dicere saepe aliquid conanti — turpe fateri — / uerba mihi desunt dedidicique loqui*, "Often when I try to say something — it is shameful to admit — words fail me, and I have unlearned to speak." This echo of Ovid who, exiled from Rome, has unlearned the Latin language, is a sign that Statius' occasional poetry is drawing to a close, especially since the idea expressed in this passage resurfaces again in the last poem at *Silu.* 5.5.49–52 *absumptae uires et copia fandi / [...] inferior uox omnis et omnia sordent / uerba*, "My strength is exhausted, I have no store of speech, my mind finds nothing worthy of such a thunderbolt." The loss of the mother tongue in the *Tristia* is an expression of the progressive recusal of poetry, and the same is true for the poet, who enacts his own gradual retreat from (this kind of) poetry. While in Ovid's exile poetry the absence of Rome causes his loss of Latin and poetic aphasia, in the *Siluae* it is the confrontation of the poet with his own grief.

4 Ritual and song — or silence?

In the first part of this article, I have argued that the *Siluae* are poetic expressions of various rites of passage, or more boldly put, that ritual is the poetic matter of the *Siluae*. This is no different in the fifth book, as the accumulation of *epicedia* clearly displays. And although the chapter has also noted that too much overlapping of ritual and poetry can counteract Statius' poetic endeavour, in the first four books this only leads to temporary interferences. With the last book however, this aspect changes, and the tension between poetry and ritual, built up from the beginning of the collection, collides with the closural introspection of Ovidian coinage.

While in the first four volumes, as has been shown, the poet takes a marginal, if not external place with regard to the rites he is singing, *Silu.* 5.3 brings about a change of paradigm, given that, with the death of his own father, the poet now finds himself at the very centre of the rite, as becomes apparent in the following passage from the *epicedion in patrem suum* (5.3.47–63):

atque utinam fortuna mihi dare manibus aras,
par templis opus, aeriamque educere molem
Cyclopum scopulos ultra atque audacia saxa
Pyramidum, et magno tumulum praetexere luco.   50
illic et Siculi superassem dona sepulchri
et Nemees lucum et Pelopis sollemnia trunci.
[...]
sed Phoebi simplex chorus en frondentia uatum   56
praemia laudato, genitor, tibi rite ligarent!
ipse madens oculis, araeque animaeque sacerdos
praecinerem gemitum, cui te nec Cerberus omni
ore nec Orpheae quirent auertere leges.   60
atque ibi me moresque tuos et facta canentem
fors et magniloque non posthabuisset Homero,
tenderet aeterno <et> Pietas aequare Maroni.

And would it were my fortune to build an altar to your spirit, a work to match temples, and raise high an airy mass, outdoing the Cyclopean cliffs and the bold stones of the Pyramids, and screen your tomb with a great grove! There would I have surpassed the gifts bestowed on the Sicilian sepulchre, and Nemea's forest, and the rituals of maimed Pelops. [...] only Phoebus' choir (behold!) would duly bind the leafy prize of poets on your lauded brow, my father. I myself moist-eyed would lead the dirge, priest of the altar and of your soul. Not Cerberus with all his mouths nor laws of Orpheus could turn you away from it. And as I there sang your ways and deeds, Piety mayhap would have accounted me not inferior to mighty-mouthed Homer and striven to match me with immortal Maro.[42]

In the image of thoroughly poetic funerary rites, poetry and ritual merge into one, with the figure of Statius-*sacerdos* as its embodiment at the centre. Indeed, each ritual element is given an extra poetic spin, from the altar that, as an *aeria moles*, not only echoes the collection's opening poem,[43] but also gestures towards the metapoetic proem of *Georgics* 3 as well as Horace's *Carm.* 3.30, to the strictly poetic funerary *ludi*, as such outdoing the games of *Aeneid* 5 and the

---

[42] For this textually uncertain passage I follow Shackleton Bailey 2015. On the difficulties in the various lines, see Gibson 2006 *ad loc.*
[43] *Silu.* 1.1.1–3 *Quae superimposito moles geminata colosso / stat Latium complexa forum? caelone peractum / fluxit opus?*

Nemean games of Statius' own *Thebaid*.⁴⁴ And while Statius' imaginary poetic *agon* surpasses all the previous ones, it is his father, in whose honour the games are held, who carries off the victory (l. 57 *praemia laudato, genitor, tibi rite ligarent*). As a priest in a position *supra partes,* Statius himself, just like his father, stands out as the best of poets. And while the poetic *agon* as part of the funerary rites remains reverie, the poet's role as *sacerdos* extends beyond this particular scene, insofar as this very composition is the funerary offering he is giving to the deceased (*Silu.* 5.3.41–45): *hic ego te* [...] / *inferiis cum laude datis heu carmine plango / Pierio,* 'Here do I alas! lament you in Pierian song, making offering and praise'. While the *hic* in line 41 can be read as referring to the location of the father's grave (36–40), it also designates, and I would argue most relevantly so, the ritual space of the present poem.

The double mandate Statius' *sacerdos* takes on in this composition, of poet and mourner, is similar to the one encountered in *Silu.* 2.1 earlier in the chapter. Inherent in this twofold role is a paradoxical tension created by two opposite movements: one towards poetry, which takes the form of the ritual offering, the other one away from it, for the father's death "takes away song" (l. 18 *carmine sublato*) and clouds the poet's mind (l. 14). How can Statius be presenting a text, in spite of having initially declared that he was not able to produce poetry? The answer may lie in the fact that the object of grief is, in the form of his father, poetry itself. On a par with Orpheus, best of all poets, and source and reason for Statius' poetic career, the father is the embodiment of poetry. Therefore, since the centre of his mourning is song, its ritual configuration can only manifest itself in such a form. Just as when Melior can think only of the lost boy, Statius' mind is entirely focused on the lost poetry (*carmine sublato*).

But the escalating crisis of poetry must not be disregarded, despite the overly long poem 5.3, for only two poems further on, the *Siluae* come to an abrupt end, and with them Statius' poetic activity. Already the first lines of *Silu.* 5.5 mark the poem as the collection's last one:

*Me miserum! neque enim uerbis sollemnibus ultra*⁴⁵
incipiam nunc Castaliae uocalibus undis
inuisus Phoeboque grauis.

---

44 Perhaps the mention of the Olympian games also serves as a reference to Pindar, who is an important model for the *Siluae*.
45 For *M*'s *ulla* Gibson 2006 reads *ultro*. I would follow Barth and read *ultra*. This would be consistent with the author's use of the same word e.g. at *Silu.* 1.2.114. For an intransitive use of *incipere* cf. *Silu.* 3.1.114 and 4.3.120.

Wretched me! For I will not begin anything with solemn words beyond this, now that I am hated by the sounding waves of Castalia and a burden to Phoebus.

While the situation and the tone of the piece are similar to the previous *epicedion*, this time the impact of loss cannot be compensated and the reason is clearly stated: because it is the poet himself who is experiencing it, and thus remains speechless, as emphasised by the following passage (5.5.46–52):

> *nimirum cum uestra modis ego funera maestis*
> *******
> *increpitans: "qui damna doles aliena, repone,*
> *infelix, lacrimas et tristia carmina serua."*
> *uerum erat. absumptae uires et copia fandi*
> *nulla mihi dignumque nihil mens fulmine tanto*   50
> *repperit. inferior uox omnis et omnia sordent*
> *uerba.* [...]

Certainly, when your funerals in sad tones I [...] reproaching me: 'You who grieve for the losses of others, keep back your tears, unlucky one, and conserve your grim songs.' It was true: my strength is exhausted, and I have no store of speech, my mind finds nothing worthy of such a thunderbolt. All utterance falls short all words are mean.

At this moment of personal loss, the poet must concede that, while bewailing the suffering of others (l.47 *aliena damna*) might have come easily — and indeed the reminiscence of his friends' defensive stance recalls Melior's reluctance to listen to the consoling poet in the first *epicedion* 2.1.15–18 — this ease of composition so characteristic of the *Siluae* has now vanished entirely: not a trace of the programmatic *uoluptas festinandi* or *audacia stili* advertised in the first and third prefaces survives.[46]

Comparing this poem with 5.3 and asking why the death of the boy, rather than the loss of the father, signifies the end of the *Siluae*, two hypotheses can be advanced: first, that, as I have argued above, the impact of this rite of passage for Statius is so strong and engaging that there is no room for poetry. Secondly, and I shall come back to this in the last part of my chapter, that the boy, like the poet to his father, represents an *alter ego* of Statius and with his death the poet too, and his *Siluae*, perish. In contrast to the previous *epicedion*, the subject matter of the poem does not act as a motor for poetry, but leaves the poet completely empty, so that, in a one-off movement he has no choice but to look to the *amici*, the *Siluae*'s primary audience, for help (5.5.43–45):

---

[46] 1 *praef.* 3; 3 *praef.* 4. The author mentions the speediness of his composition for Glaucias in 2 *praef.* 7–9.

> *nunc tempus, amici*
> *quorum ego manantes oculos et saucia tersi*
> *pectora. reddite opem, saeuas exsoluite grates.* 45

> Now is the time, friends, whose streaming eyes I have dried and wounded breasts I have healed. Return the help, pay back the cruel gratitude.

In the framework of this last composition, the roles have been reversed: after having celebrated and mourned the happy and unhappy events in the lives of his circle of friends over 31 pieces, the poet now finds himself at their place, in need of *their* help.

By reaching out to an extratextual authority, the author sends a clear sign that his poetry has come to an end. Again, it is important to underline how ritual and singing, or rather the impossibility of song, are interconnected, for, by moving himself into the passive position at the centre of the rite of passage — ritual mourning in this instance — he must forfeit his former active role of commentator or, in *Silu.* 5.3, as priest. Whether the death of the *puer* did in fact chronologically coincide with the end of Statius' poetic activity, whether this boy in truth existed or not, or whether all of this is a poetic *mise en scène* to bring about closure, cannot be known for certain. That Statius' minor poetry breaks down with and after this composition, however, is a certainty, and can be gleaned not only from its abrupt end, but also from the fact that, although clearly still in a religious framework, there is no description of it whatsoever. Parallel to the intensifying poetic crisis, ritual gradually disappears from the texts: while the *epicedion* for Priscilla dedicates a lengthy passage to the funeral procession and her tomb (208–246), the rites for the father, as argued above, merely take place in the poet's imagination, and finally there is no mention of any ritual for the boy's passing. Book 5 thus enacts a gradual withdrawal from writing *Siluae*, that is, from writing ritual.

Perched between the *epicedia* is a short hymn to the god of Sleep which in its intertextual complexity cannot be discussed in full in the present framework.[47] The conspicuous absence of an external occasion is down to the fact that the piece *in toto* is a "metapoetical reflection on Statius' literary production",[48] its occasion being the poetic crises thematised in the circumferent compositions. As a motive, sleeplessness occurs throughout the collection in connection

---

[47] For literature on *Silu.* 5.4, see Pomeroy 1986; Laguna 1990; Gibson 1996; Augoustakis 2008; Ambühl 2010; Bitto 2018.
48 Bitto 2018, 285.

with various occasions and is thus closely linked to Statius' poetic activity.[49] In *Silu.* 5.4, however, the poet laments his incessant insomnia, imploring the god Somnus to grant him some relief. The thematic nexus of sleep, poetry, and death opened in this piece strongly gestures towards closure.[50] At the same time, its hymnic mode appears almost paradoxical in the context of religious crisis: I would argue that Statius fashions his metapoetic lullaby, as it were, as a hymn, in order to demonstrate the vainness of addressing the gods. Indeed, the reference to Ovid's Argus episode, in which Hermes' song, rather than Somnus, overcomes the giant,[51] suggests that Statius is trying to sing himself to sleep. Thus, the adapted *recusatio* of lines 11–13 exemplifies the poet's convoluted situation: his personal grief leaves him sleepless, yet he does not have the poetic strength — nor will — to continue his silvan lament. The hymn to Somnus is thus a densely metapoetic interlude between the two pieces which openly display the closure of silvan poetry. With the futility of its poetic elaborateness and against the background of the author's personal crisis, the piece gestures again towards the implosion of poetry which has lost all its strength: *omnia sordent uerba.*

While the retreat from poetry, as I have tried to show over the course of this chapter, is a gradual process, it is nevertheless undeniable that the fifth poem, and with it the last book and the entire collection, finds an abrupt end. Whether this is due to the textual tradition or, as I would argue, to the stylistic device of *aposiopesis* remains open. The appropriateness of the last sentence, however, as the last utterance in a closural composition should be underlined, since with it, Statius takes up a long-established closural motif, namely the terminal *sphragis.*[52]

Going once more back to Ovid, Franklinos discusses the importance of the name in his last book *Ex Ponto*:[53] naming or not naming someone is decisive for the survival of that person's memory. This is of course true beyond Ovid, beyond poetry even, and throughout the *Siluae* Statius makes sure to recall the names of the deceased, who will live on by virtue of his poetic sepulchres. With one marked exception: nowhere is there any mention of the name of his slave boy, the one he allegedly cherished beyond all others. This is remarkable in two regards: first of all, even if the child did not have a name apt for poetry, he

---

49 Cf. for example Sacerdoti 2014, 26–29 who illustrates that sleepless nights are a recurring motive in the *Siluae*.
50 Pace Augoustakis 2008, 342 who reads this piece as a request for inspiration for the subsequent poem.
51 Augoustakis 2008, 345.
52 Zissos 2019, 555–556.
53 Franklinos 2018, 290.

might have chosen to call him a pet name, like Ursus' slave "Philetus" in *Silu.* 2.6, but he does not.⁵⁴ Secondly, the poet does seem actively to draw attention to this *lacuna*, recalling at the very end of the poem that the boy's first word was his (i.e., Statius') name: (*Silu.* 5.5.86) *nomen uox prima meum*, replacing thus the memory of the deceased's name with his own.⁵⁵ The *Siluae* leave the reader with the mental image of the Papinian *nomen*, not only in the words of the nameless child but in the remembrance of his father who carries the same name. With this ingenious indirect *sphragis* at the end of his collection, Statius follows the tradition instituted by Virgil, Horace and Ovid, and even outwits them: when Ovid writes at the end of his epic *nomenque erit indelebile nostrum* (*Met.* 15.876), Statius goes one step further by taking away all of the name's materiality and with it any possibility of erasing it. At the same time, the *uox prima* enclosed in the verse structure by his name also refers the reader to the first word of the *Siluae* they encounter: the author's name on the cover, thus closing the collection with a *sphragis* referring back to its very beginning.⁵⁶

5 Afterthought: another uncertain end

We do not really know anything about the end of Statius' life; it is usually associated with Domitian's death in AD 96, given several poems dating to the year 95 act as *terminus post quem*.⁵⁷ The composition of the last poem, considered unfinished at the poet's death,⁵⁸ is thus dated to the year 96. But the *Siluae* are of course not the only work Statius labours over in the last years of his life, left behind at least seemingly unfinished. As was the case for the *Thebaid*, the composition of the small poems between the years 94 and 95/96 ran parallel to a major epic project. But, although we know as little about the progress of composition of the *Achilleid* as we do about the last of the *Siluae*, the extant part of the epic has in recent years received a lot of positive attention: its status of 'fragment' has been rightfully revoked, and its literary quality and complexity have

---

54 On the problem of versifying names cf. Ov. *Pont.* 4.12, 4.14 and Mart. 4.31. Perhaps there is an echo in *Silu.* 5.5.72 *inserui uitae* from Mart. 4.31.4 *inseruisse chartis*. Statius uses *inserere* twice in the prefaces (2 *praef.* 21; 4 *praef.* 24). Gibson 2006, *ad loc.* remarks the unusualness of the construction.
55 On the (missing) family links in *Silu.* 5, see Henderson 2007.
56 On the signification of the *sphragis* at the margin of a text, see Peirano 2012.
57 *Silu.* 4.3; 4.4; perhaps 5.1.
58 Heslin 2009, 58; 62.

been underlined. Heslin proposes to conceive of the known parts of the *Achilleid*, i.e., those that exist, as a "prospectus for patrons".[59] He contrasts this second epic, which he sees closing at a logical point, with *Silu.* 5.5 to which he ascribes an abrupt, that is, not intended, end. Most recently, Barchiesi has commented on the almost paradoxical status of the *Achilleid*, which is an unfinished work ("poema incompiuto") but at the same time is perfectly polished and much more 'finished' than, for instance, Virgil's *Aeneid*. Another argument in favour of considering the *Achilleid* an *opus(culum)* rather than a fragment is the fact that there are no indices whatsoever that anything might have been lost in transmission.[60] Indeed, already in *Silu.* 4.7 (i.e., in 94 CE) the reader is informed that "Achilles is stuck at the first turning point" (4.7.23–24 *primis meus ecce metis / haeret Achilles*). Perhaps this was as far as he would get.[61] So while the *Achilleid* has been rehabilitated, why is the same not true for the *Siluae*? When Heslin writes about the *Achilleid* and the *Fasti* that "both texts have suffered from the presumption that they only exist as the result of an accident beyond their author's control", he forgets that the *Siluae* are still suffering that fate.[62] All of the above arguments could just as well be applied to Book 5: if Statius has worked on the epic up to his death and still managed to close it off harmoniously (maybe he saw what was coming), could this not be the case for the *Siluae* as well? Yes, there are a number of *lacunae* and uncertainties in the last book, but this can easily be ascribed to the textual transmission.[63] There are, however, no half-lines, or alternative versions of any of the poems. As to the 'abrupt' end of *Silu.* 5.5,[64] this might very well have been, as I have argued, an aesthetic choice.[65] In the volume *Classical Closure*, Hardie argues in relation to the end of the *Thebaid* that the abrupt passage to the closing topos of the ship in the harbour (12.809) in conjunction with the hundred tongues topos (808) leaves the

---

[59] Heslin 2009, 61.
[60] Barchiesi 2020b, 287; 2021, 59.
[61] In *Silu.* 4.4, which was supposedly composed after 4.7, the poet certainly does not seem to be working on the epic with a lot of drive (4.4.94–96 *Troia quidem magnusque mihi temptatur Achilles / sed uocat arcitenens alio pater armaque monstrat / Ausonii maiora ducis.*). The *Achilleid* is again mentioned in *Silu.* 5.2 but Statius does not comment on the progress of composition. Perhaps he was just reciting parts of the first book.
[62] Heslin 2009, 66. Rather paradoxically, Heslin 2009, 62 himself mentions the possibility of an echo from *Silu.* 5.5 in Mart. 9.48, which was published before Statius' death.
[63] See at *Silu.* 5.5.24–27 where the manuscript has a large *lacuna*.
[64] Which Heslin 2009, 58 calls a "fragment".
[65] Also suggested by Henderson 2007, 245–246.

poem open-ended.⁶⁶ What Statius interrupts is, in Hardie's words, "nothing less than a whole epic of mourning."⁶⁷ Is this not exactly what the poet is doing in *Silu.* 5.5? After having found pleasure in his own grief (5.5.33–34 *iuuat, heu iuuat, illaudabile carmen / fundere et incompte miserum laxare dolorem* — "I am fain, fain alas, to pour out song that none can praise and ease the cruel pain in clumsy sort."), as the Theban women did at *Theb.* 12.793–794,⁶⁸ the author sets a limit to his lament, his poem, and perhaps his poetic activity altogether.⁶⁹

---

66 Lovatt 1999, 146 reads the final book of the *Thebaid* as rendered "endless [...] through excess".
67 Hardie 1997, 154–155.
68 On this passage, see also Hardie 1997, 154.
69 Similarly, Barchiesi 1997, 200 asks: "Are we so sure that the *Fasti* is just an interrupted utterance and that the interruption cannot be a communicative 'gesture'? The personal situation of the author invests the damaged year with at least a potential metaphorical meaning: the time of Ovid's life is severed like the structure of the poem." On the poet's lament at the end of the collection see Lovatt 2007, 160. Incidentally, the scholarly conception of *Siluae* 5 as posthumous edition speaks for the persuasiveness of the Statian narrative of overpowering grief.

Sophia Papaioannou
Sacrifice, Death, and Closure in Valerius' *Argonautica* Book 1

Abstract: The *Argonautica* is a celebrated case of an open-ended text: book eight breaks midway, at a point where intertextuality (the script of the abandoned heroine by her lover and beneficiary, which Medea and Jason engage in) seems to anticipate a breach with tradition. Precisely because of its very incompleteness, Valerius' epic creates a diverse interpretative potential in the whole work. In the present chapter I argue that part of this interpretative potential may rest with the dialogue between the closure of the entire *Argonautica* and the closure of the first book of the epic. I identify in the closing section of *Argonautica* 1 themes and motifs that feature also in the closing episode of the epic, and I stress the prominence of ritual in the articulation of these themes. The closing episode of *Argonautica* 1 further exhibits indisputable motifs of closure, namely, death and a katabasis, both of which are entwined with ritual: sacrifice, magic, and a necromancy. All these motifs appear again in the portrayal of Medea in Book 8.

Epic closure in the surviving imperial epic tradition is the exception rather than the norm: influenced by the dissatisfying and in several respects open conclusion of the *Aeneid*, first-century CE Latin epics, with the exception of Statius' *Thebaid*, tend to eschew definite closure.[1] As such, the question of epic endings is an irresistible one for critics of Latin epic, especially when the ending clearly does not exist, as is the case of Valerius' *Argonautica*, a tantalisingly open-ended text: book eight breaks midway, at a point where intertextuality (the script of the abandoned heroine by her lover and beneficiary, which Medea and Jason engage in) seems to anticipate a breach with tradition. Precisely because of its incompleteness, Valerius' epic creates a richly diverse interpretative potential for the whole work,[2] which may be imprinted in the dialogue between the

---

[1] On open-endedness in imperial Latin epic, see Hardie 1997, expanding on Hardie 1993, chapter 1. On imperial Greek epic, especially Quintus, see Greensmith 2020, 280–344.
[2] According to Hershkowitz 1998, 34, the very incompleteness of the Roman *Argonautica* (vis-à-vis the already known closure of the Argonautic legend and of the Greek literary model of Apollonius) provides for a work that is ever receptive to new interpretations. Buckley 2018a discusses the various attempts of the Renaissance scholars to compose the closural section of

unfinished final section of the *Argonautica* and the meticulously crafted closure of the first book of the epic. The last part of book 1 features a section that embraces themes and motifs markedly closural, which, further, recur in the fragmented closure to the entire epic, but also interact with specific passages of Valerius' intertexts, most notably the *Aeneid*, which operate similarly as epilogic units.³ In addition, it stresses the prominence of ritual, a traditional sign of epic closure.

Book 1 is remarkably favoured by critics: the only book of a Flavian epic that has received no less than four commentaries within less than 10 years (Spaltenstein 2002 in French, Kleywegt 2005 and Zissos 2008 in English, and Galli 2007 in Italian) — a predilection on the part of the scholarly community that bespeaks the significance of the opening book for the understanding of the epic overall. For the purposes of the present study, it is important to acknowledge that book 1 shares certain important formal and thematic correspondences with book 8,⁴ which generate a 'ring composition' effect for the poem overall.⁵ In the words of Andrew Zissos, "each book [1 and 8] features Jason abducting — I would say, seducing — a royal child (Acastus, Medea) and

---

Valerius' epic, focusing more specifically on Giovan Battista Pio's furtherance of the Roman *Argonautica*.

3 The closural character of the murder of Aeson has been noted already in light of its correspondence to the murder of Turnus at the end of the *Aeneid*. For McGuire (1990, 29) the description of Aeson's death at 1.825–826 (*horruit Aeson / excedens memoremque tulit sub nubibus umbram*, "Aeson shuddered, passing away, and bore his mindful share beneath the clouds") recalls that of Turnus at *Aen.* 12.951–952 (*ast illi soluuntur frigore membra / uitaque cum gemitu fugit indignata sub umbras*, "but his limbs are loosened by coldness, and with a groan his life fled, indignant, beneath the shadows"). Then Hershkowitz (1998, 12 n. 41) notes that when Pelias decides to kill Aeson, he is described as *furiis iraque minaci / terribilis* ("terrible with madness and threatening anger", 1.722–723), and recalls the description of Aeneas before he kills Turnus as *furiis accensus et ira / terribilis* ("inflamed by madness and terrible in his anger", *Aen.* 12.946–947). For Hershkowitz, these verbal overlaps are deliberate as to "set up the end of *Argonautica* 1 as a would-be end of the *Aeneid*, foiled by Aeson's suicide"; and "could anticipate the end of the epic, when the episode is enacted successfully with the role reversal of Pelias from Aeneas-figure and with the heroic Jason now as Aeneas".

4 On Valerius' *Argonautica* 8 no fewer than three commentaries appeared recently in a little over a decade: C. Lazzarini and T. Pellucchi both published commentaries (in Italian) in 2012 (Lazzarini covers only part of the book, lines 1–287); Castelletti 2022 constitutes the first commentary in English.

5 Repeatedly pointed out in Zissos 2008, xxxi; and in his *Commentary* on 34–36, 61–63, 272–273, 723–724; also Barich 1982, 104–107. Zissos 2008, 380–381, illustrates the ring composition structure that determines the organisation of the Aeson and Alcimede episode in the context of *Arg.* 1.

narrowly escaping by sea, with the local tyrant rushing troops to the shore in a vain attempt to forestall departure, followed by a parental lament over the abducted child (1.700–721, 8.134–174). Likewise, both books contain accounts of a storm at sea, incited by a hostile divinity in order to thwart a specific nautical expedition (1.574–658, 8.318–384). Finally, [and] each [book] features a divinatory scene in which Mopsus foresees the tragic aftermath of the voyage, including Medea's infanticide (1.211–226, 8.247–251)".[6] In addition to the above important parallels with book 8, the concluding episode of book 1 develops around a set of themes that signify closure: death, including suicide and the murder of innocent victims, and interaction with the world of the dead are observed in markedly closural sections across the epic tradition, and are revisited in the portrayal of Medea. Their closural function is underlined through ritual: sacrifice and magic.[7] The prominence of ritual at the end of a unit enhances its tragic character: ritual in general is expected to feature at the end of tragedies (it is either celebrated, established, or just described). The two sections are bound together and aligned with epic literature of the imperial era by the distinct presence of allusions to civil war, seen in terms of a fraternal conflict.

Prior to examining the emphatic articulation of closural motifs in the ring composition structure of the *Argonautica*, it is useful to focus on the astounding death of Aeson and Alcimede, and underscore the significance of this episode for the comprehensive appreciation of the epic overall, which is stressed, oddly, by means of its parenthetical character next to its closural placement. Valerius' account of the death of Jason's parents, which draws on an obscure version reported, according to Diodorus Siculus (4.50) and Apollodorus (1.9.27), in the lost historiographical text of Dionysios Scytobrachion, and features in the epic tradition for the first time in the Roman *Argonautica*,[8] emphasises further the function of the entire episode as a coda to book 1, a loose addition with practically no association to the progression of the narrative: Jason never finds out about their death in the course of the epic. This information is produced at the opening five lines of book 2 (V. Fl 2.1–5):[9]

Interea scelerum luctusque ignarus Iason
alta secat. Neque enim patrios cognoscere casus

---

[6] Zissos 2008, xxxi–ii.
[7] The most detailed treatment of the entire episode is Zissos 2008, 397–420; complete list of earlier important studies is recorded in Zissos 2008, 379.
[8] On the suicide of Jason's parents in a ritual context, see Bernstein 2013, 236–237.
[9] All translations of Valerius' *Argonautica* are from Mozley 1934, with adaptations when necessary; the Latin quotations from the *Argonautica* are from Ehlers' 1980 Teubner text.

> *Iuno sinit, mediis ardens ne flectat ab undis*
> *ac temere in Pelian et adhuc obstantia regis*
> *fata ruat placitosque deis ne deserat actus.*

> Meanwhile Jason cuts through the deep, knowing nothing of the crime and of the sorrow. For Juno does not allow him to know about his parents' deaths, for fear he should turn back, in rage, midway, and hurl himself blindly against Pelias and his royal destiny that still opposed, for fear too that he should abandon the task decreed by heaven.

This brief section is crafted to serve dual narrative: first, it wraps up the Aeson and Alcimede coda and, at the same time, underscores its parenthetical function. The wrap-up is stated by means of ring composition. The narrator carefully notes that the news about the death of Aeson and Alcimede never reached Jason; should it did so, Jason would no doubt cancel his expedition – the Argonautic journey, and Valerius' own epic, in other words, would never have happened. The last mention of Jason in book 1, at *Arg.* 1.693–699, pictures Jason in fearful preoccupation about his parents; having manipulated Pelias' young son Acastus into joining the Argonautic expedition, Jason fears that Pelias would take his anger and pain out on Jason's family, as if anticipating the murder of Jason's family about to follow. Second, by means of the use of '*interea*' in the same way it features in the *Aeneid* at the opening of a book to denote, "first and foremost, continuation of an action continuing for some time loosely coextensive with a number of events to mark out an interval",[10] it signals the end to the Aeson and Alcimede digression and a return to the *Argonautica* narrative proper as reported in the leading model of Apollonius.[11]

Closing book 1 with a para-narrative goes against the Latin epic tradition – in earlier epics, including most prominently the *Aeneid* and the *Metamorphoses*, but also Lucan's *Bellum Ciuile*, the end of book 1 emphatically reaches forward to book 2 by means of a narrative bridge. Valerius ingeniously transforms this mechanism of smooth transition into an emphatic statement of closure, by stressing the impending death of Pelias upon the return of Jason – something that is not going to happen in the course of the *Argonautica* – by double reference, the first three lines prior to the end of book 1 (1.847) and the other four lines into book 2 (2.4).

---

10 Reinmuth 1933, 325; for Reinmuth this is the most frequent of the six overall uses of '*interea*' in Virgil's poetry.
11 Krasne 2018a, 239: "Book 2's immediate return to the Argonautic voyage and to the moment of [the] earlier departure from the Argonautic narrative… thus marks an end to this extended digression, and it simultaneously concludes a major divagation from Apollonius Rhodius' version…".

This unsuitably positioned episode features extraordinary events that underscore its outstanding character: the gruesome death of Jason's parents preceded by a necromancy.[12] As the enraged and deeply wounded Pelias is preparing to murder Aeson and extract revenge for the secret departure of Acastus to join Jason and the Argonauts, Alcimede initiates the performance of a sacrificial rite in order to raise Aeson's father, Cretheus, from the dead and consult him about the future (1.730–740). The ghost of Cretheus has good news about Jason (he will conclude successfully his expedition) but informs Alcimede that she and Aeson will soon die (1.741–748). Not soon afterwards, Aeson and Alcimede do resolve to die, and upon hearing that Pelias and his army are on their way to their residence, commit suicide by drinking bull's blood (1.749–817). Pelias and his army break in Aeson's residence, find the elderly couple dead or almost dead and murder additionally their younger son, Promachus (1.818–826). The closing scene of the unit (and book 1) is set in the Underworld following the souls of the dead entering the domain of death through the gate reserved for great heroes, where they are received by Cretheus; simultaneously it is foretold that Pelias will die and enter the world of the dead through the "left-hand gate", to eternal torment (1.827–850).[13]

This necromancy stands out in the tradition of the literary topos. Topographically speaking, it lacks the dreary, fear-inducing elements distinguishing the setting that typically hosts the ritual: necromancies were performed near the tomb of the deceased to be invoked, or in special oracles established for the very practice in locations near caves and certain rivers that were believed to lead to the Underworld.[14] Further, it inverts the epic *katabasis* motif at the same time it inverts the necromancy ritual (the ghost of the dead ancestor here crosses onto the world of the living). In Latin epic, the most celebrated necromantic ritual features in Lucan and builds around Erichtho (Luc. 1.730–751), Valerius' primary model. Not least, the particular ritual replaces the funeral of Jason's family: the ritual of burial is the type of closural ritual par excellence. The *Iliad* is the classic example. The funeral that ought to follow affirms closure, through mourning which at once transcribes and confines inside socially constructed

---

12 On the necromancy and *katabasis* episode in Valerius, see Zissos 2008, 379–382.
13 On the episode in general, see Vessey 1973, 245–248; Adamietz 1976, 26–29; Perutelli 1982; Franchet d'Espèrey 1988, 193–197; Hershkowitz 1998, 128–136; Ripoll 1998a, 204–205, 376–382, 393–394; Manuwald 2000; Spaltenstein 2002, 274–305; Kleywegt 2005, 425–492; Zissos 2008, 379–420.
14 Details in Ogden 2019.

limits the survivors' grief.¹⁵ In the *Aeneid*, the closest model for the episode at hand, Aeneas' *katabasis*, closes with a ritual funeral (of his nurse, Caieta), which is set prominently at the opening of the second half of the epic, as at once a closural and an opening marker. The absence of Jason and the fratricidal nature of the death of Aeson's family cancels the funeral lament ritual. The proper reception of the souls of the murdered family to the Underworld, however, has been anticipated by the (ritually problematic) necromancy,¹⁶ which has assigned to the ghost of Cretheus the part of the principal ritual actor.¹⁷

By the end of the episode, Alcimede, the ritual performer, and her family are dead and descending to the world of the dead, taking a place among the souls of the blessed, thus realising the epic *katabasis* themselves. The brevity of the descending route corresponds to the closure of *Aeneid* 6, which records the exact opposite journey, Aeneas' return to the world of the living. The important details shared by the two journeys seem to substantiate the dialogue between the Valerian and the Virgilian passages. The detailed description of the topography of the Underworld at 832–845 draws upon three passages from *Aen.* 6.893–897 (~ V. Fl. 1.832–839; twin gates of sleep), 660–665 (~ V. Fl. 1.835–842; the souls of the blessed), 637–644 (~ V. Fl. 1.842–845; the Elysium).¹⁸ The above intertextual associations ascertain that the closural character of the final episode of *Argonautica* 1 is emphasised through the evocation of pivotal imagery from the particularly powerful closural section at the end of the first half of the *Aeneid*, and, as it will be presently shown, from reaching forward to the closing section of the *Argonautica*, as well.

The end of the *Argonautica* is conspicuously missing — the epic breaks off with Medea's Dido-like appeal to Jason lest he considers abandoning her, while her marriage ceremony toys at once with Dido's perverse *coniugium* and the semiotics of a Roman wedding,¹⁹ her portrayal as a Roman matron evoking the spousal devotion of Alcimede, who, according to Hershkowitz befits that of a Roman matron.²⁰ Alcimede's leading role and the vocabulary applied to her in

---

15 See Roberts 1993 on death and ritual as markers of closure or transition in (Greek) epic and tragedy.
16 See Roberts 1993, 586 on the problematic ritual as typical in Greek tragedy.
17 On the idea of religious actor, see Rüpke in this volume.
18 The clear presence of the Virgilian model has been noted already in Summers 1894, 30, and more recently in Barich 1982, 143–144, though Valerius has improved on the *Aeneid* text (see Feeney 1991, 336–337, on notable differences).
19 Buckley 2016.
20 Hershkowitz 1998, 134–135, who further specifies that Alcimede calls to mind Virgil's Creusa.

the necromancy episode exhibits motifs that are observed in subsequent episodes in the characterisation and act of Medea. Twice Jason's mother is referred to as "Thessalian", at 1.736–737 (*grandaeua... Thessalis*) and a little later at 1.780. The emphasis on Alcimede's Thessalian origin is interconnected with allusions to magic qualities: Thessaly was traditionally a land of witches in antiquity. Alcimede's ties to sorcery is corroborated by her appellation at 1.755 f. as *sacerdos*, a term typically describing witches and sorcerers.[21] In particular in Roman poetry, Thessalian witches are notorious for their power over the netherworld, including their skill in raising the ghosts of the deceased, a detail noted at V. Fl. 6.446–448, when Valerius turns his focus on Medea's magic powers. Lucan's Erichtho, obviously is intentionally evoked— a witch who also is from Thessaly, performs a necromantic ritual, and is repeatedly called *Thessalis* (e.g. 6.605, 762) and *Thessala uates* (6.628, 651).[22]

V. Fl. 6.446–448 comprises the closing lines to a section that features in detail the qualities putting together Medea's sorceress profile from the perspective of Juno (V. Fl. 6.439–448):

> *sola animo Medea subit, mens omnis in una*
> *uirgine, nocturnis qua nulla potentior aris.*   440
> *illius ad fretus sparsosque per auia sucos*
> *sidera fixa pauent et aui stupet orbita Solis.*
> *mutat agros fluuiumque uias, †suust† alligat ignis*
> *†cuncta sopor†, recolit fessos aetate parentes*
> *datque alias sine lege colus. hanc maxima Circe*   445
> *terrificis mirata modis, hanc aduena Phrixus*
> *quamuis Atracio lunam spumare ueneno*
> *sciret et Haemoniis agitari cantibus umbras.*

Medea alone comes to her mind, all her thoughts are centered on the maiden only, than whom is none more potent at the nightly altars; for responsive to her cry and to the juices she scatters in desolate places the stars are halted trembling and the Sun, her grandsire, is aghast as he runs his course; she changes the aspect of the fields and the tracks of the rivers, all things are bound fast by flames in their own deep slumber, old folk she seethes again

---

21 Paule 2014. On the association of Alcimede and Medea on the basis of their common practice of witchcraft, see also Scott 2012, 112–122. Hershkowitz 1998, 132 believes that the necromancy in *Argonautica* 1 is performed by an anonymous professional witch, not Alcimede herself.

22 The association of the two witches is convincingly established in Finkmann 2019, 767–769. The presence of a third witch is implied in imperial epic, also in the context of a necromancy: in Statius, *Theb.* 2.19–22, as the ghost of Laius is escorted out of the underworld by Mercury, he is seen by another ghost who presumes that a necromancy is performed by some Thessalian witch (2.21–22 *sacerdos / Thessalis*); see Finkmann 2019, 770 n. 95.

to youth and lawlessly assigns them yet more spindles; at her did Circe, mightiest in the ways of terror, at her did the stranger Phrixus marvel, though he knew that Atracian poisons made the moon to foam and that spells of Haemonia were rousing up the ghosts.

According to Juno, Medea's magic powers affect the course of celestial bodies and can turn back rivers to their source. A niece of Circe, the archetypal epic sorceress and first necromancer of classical literature, Medea has surpassed her aunt in the art of witchcraft: Valerius' Circe looks at her niece's power in wonder (*mirata*, 446). The ritual peculiarities that distinguish Alcimede's necromantic performance similarly underlines her exceptional status. Jason's mother is nowhere beyond this closural section reported to have expertise in sorcery. Even though necromancies in ancient epic are typical, the performer in charge always is a professional *uates* (Circe in Homer; Tiresias in Statius' *Thebaid*, where he is assisted by his daughter, Manto, also a sorceress; Erichtho in Lucan, indubitably the strongest intertextual influence behind the portrayal of both Alcimede and Medea in Valerius;[23] the Sibyl in both Virgil and Silius Italicus, though in the former she bears the name Deiphobe, while in the latter she is called Autonoe), Valerius' Alcimede is an exception: but as a native Thessalian woman she is familiar with the art of sorcery.[24] This association of sorcery and Thessalian origin in book 1, recurs in Medea's own words: the latter, in a time of hardship, feels insecure about the effectiveness of her magic, and wishes for expert assistance from no other than Jason's mother or wife: '*si tibi Thessalicis, nunc si tua forte uenenis / mater et heu siqua est posset succurrere coniunx!*' ("if only your mother, or perhaps your wife (if — alas! — you have one) were now able to help with Thessalian poisons", 7.198–199). This statement is doubly ironic: Medea unknowingly, on the one hand, connects Jason's mother,[25] whom she has never referred to earlier in the poem, to sorcery, and, on the other, envisions for him a wife, who likewise would be a sorceress herself! To the suspecting reader, the ties between Medea and Alcimede may be observed even in details seemingly minor. Valerius follows Apollonius 1.46–47 in identifying Jason's mother by a

---

[23] Finkmann 2019, 767: Alcimede is "an intertextual allusion to Lucan's Thessalian witch Erichtho".
[24] Because of the violation of the necromancer pattern, critics have suggested the possibility that Valerius' necromancy also is being performed by some anonymous professional *sacerdos*. Finkmann 2019, 750 n. 10.
[25] Castelletti 2022, 130–131, 133 notes the similarities between Alcimede and Medea's mother in the latter's *suasoria* at 8.144–170.

name signifying "strong thought" (ἀλκή + μήδομαι),[26] and thus sharing the same etymology with the name of Medea (the thoughtful, brainy one, from μήδομαι).

A few additional elements that point to the end of the *Argonautica* may be identified in the Aeson and Alcimede episode. The appearance of the ghost of Cretheus foremost foretells the successful outcome and triumphant return of Jason (741–746): thus, the readers are reassured, along with Jason's parents, that the Argonautic expedition will have a fitting closure with success and a homecoming. This piece of information seems to anticipate the fragmented end to Valerius' epic and hastens to furnish the desired cathartic ending to the story that is missing from the narrative as recorded.

An intriguing correspondence to Medea of book 8 seems to justify the rather awkward lion simile employed at V. Fl. 1.757–761:

> quam multa leo cunctatur in arta
> mole uirum rictuque genas et lumina pressit,
> sic curae subiere ducem, ferrumne capessat
> imbelle atque aeui senior gestamina primi   760
> an patres regnique acuat mutabile uulgus.

Even as a lion hemmed round by a thick mass of men will hesitate a long while, and with huge gaping jaws wrinkles up cheeks and yes, so do doubts crowd upon the prince — is he to seize a feeble sword? shall he in his old age wield the weapons of early youth? shall he stir up the elders and the fickle folk of the kingdom?

In the simile Aeson is likened to the trapped lion, as he weights his chances to confront dynamically Pelias' impending murderous attack. This is the first of a total of seven lion similes in the *Argonautica*, the last of which is set at 8.455–457, just ten lines prior to the abrupt ending of the epic. In this final lion simile, the lament of Medea is compared to the growling sound of a hungry lion (V. Fl. 8.453–457):[27]

> tunc tota querellis
> egeritur questuque dies eademque sub astris
> sola mouet, maestis ueluti nox illa sonaret   455
> plena lupis quaterentque truces ieiuna leones
> ora uel orbatae traherent suspiria uaccae.

---

26 Zissos 2008, 222 ad 296–298.
27 On the simile, see Castelletti 2022, 248–250.

Then all day is spent in weeping and complaint, and alone beneath the stars she makes the same lament, as though that night were full of the dismal howling of wolves, and savage lions were hungrily roaring, or cows lowed sadly for their lost ones.

Both similes are ill-suited to the circumstances they presumably underline. In Aeson's case the encircled lion simile aims at valorising Aeson's suicide performance — in traditional epic, the lion simile distinguishes the epic hero preparing a vigorous response to pressing physical danger, and goes as far back as Homer.[28] Aeson's lack of options, however, his infirmity due to age and his proximity to the altar evokes the tragic death of Priam at the altar by Neoptolemus in *Aeneid* 2 — a death that is an extreme expression of ritual since the old king takes the place of the sacrificial victim upon the altar.[29] Eventually, Aeson will abstain from following either epic model, but will take his own life instead by drinking bull's blood.[30] Still, unlike the pathetic death of the Virgilian Priam, his suicide is heroic in an appropriately Roman way, because it harmonises with the premises that dictate and justify the Stoic suicide. The Stoic character of Aeson's suicide has been discussed by Andrew Zissos, for whom Aeson is the ideal Stoic wise man who serenely takes his own life and views death as liberating for the soul when living has become too painful.[31] The Stoic subtext of the episode is enhanced by the portrayal of Pelias as the quintessential Stoic villain, the tyrant who can never find peace, rules with terror, and in turn is ruled by anxiety.[32] Be as they may, Aeson's expectations are overturned: his suicide which he staged to serve as a memorable act of bravery for his younger son, eventually takes place after the latter's tragic death before Aeson's eyes. In Buckley's words, "it is the horrified spirit-Aeson who is left to bear away the

---

[28] Zissos 2008, 392 listing several comparable epic paradigms from the Greek tradition. The inappropriate employment of the lion simile for the feeble and ambushed Aeson is noted in Perutelli 1982, 116–127; Zissos, however, *o.p.*, notes that the lion simile is an effective way to "achieve a convergence of heroic modes, to valorise Aeson's suicide, its essential passivity notwithstanding, through intertextual association with the great martial heroes of earlier epic".
[29] Zissos 2008, 392 ad 759–761; Ripoll 1998a, 379.
[30] For the tragic character of the episode, see Ripoll 2008.
[31] Zissos 2014, 274–277 offers an excellent discussion on the transformation of Aeson in Valerius Flaccus from a feeble old man to a Stoic wise man, focusing foremost on his suicide. Zissos (2008, 393, with references) also argues that Alcimede's decision to follow her husband's paradigm calls to mind comparable double suicides of spouses during the early Empire.
[32] Zissos 2008, 95 citing the discussion in Scaffai 1986, 234–235 on Pelias as the Stoic tyrant. See also Fucecchi in this volume for Lucan's Caesar and Silius' Hannibal who embody paradoxical versions of the Stoic *sapiens* when they show indifference towards death.

memory of Promachus' death (*Arg.* 1.823–826)",[33] yet this overturn is what ultimately brings Aeson and the Virgilian Priam next to each other for having witnessed the deaths of their sons shortly before their own.

Similarly complex in meaning and experimenting with canonical epic is the application of the lion simile in book 8 to describe the reaction of the scorned Medea. The angry lion is just one of the wild animals to which Medea is compared, a pattern of similes that echoes the description of her furious tragic counterpart in Seneca's *Medea* 800 ff., and 862 ff.[34] In the simile the cries of three different animals in distress are employed to express the complexity of Medea's emotional distress upon realising that Jason is about to leave her behind. Since Homer, the employment of similes, especially animal similes, became a means of exhibiting artistry and originality, and by the time of imperial epic, rhetorical mastery. The animals identified in Valerius' final simile, the wolves, the lions, and the cattle, each in a different emotional state, which elicits its own epic intertext, never before in the epic tradition appear together to reflect, even offer a synesthetic expression to the emotional state of a single individual in a particular situation. Medea is at once angry, desperate, confused, unable to react, helpless and lonely, and this complex emotional confusion, effected through an unprecedented confluence of epic intertextuality, vocalises her cognitive impasse (she does not know how to plan her next move). Her anxiety reminds of Pelias' own in book 1, but unlike the king of Iolkos, Medea's reaction successfully cancels the Argonauts' plan to depart and leave her behind.

Medea in book 8 is too infirm to influence the situation and, by extension, fashion the next episode of the epic. Death officiates closure for Aeson, and abrupt fragmentation of textual continuity causes Medea to stall. Even though the heroine does not cross to the netherworld, the cave at Peuce where she stays and prepares to consummate her marriage to Jason is qualified similarly to a location of death: the adjective *infausto* has firm associations to the Underworld (*OLD* s.v. *infaustus* 2). Also, the island of Peuce is significantly described as triangular by Apollonius (4.310), and as such calls to mind Sicily, the more famous triangular mythological island and location of the rape of Proserpina. It is worth noting that already at V. Fl. 5.341–349, just prior to her first encounter with Jason, Medea and her handmaids were compared to Proserpina. Even though expectations of literary intertextuality dictate some depiction of the goddess in the company of her friends picking flowers, Valerius' Proserpina is

---

33 Buckley 2018b, 96.
34 The proximity of the two heroines in their state of frenziness is noted in Corrigan 2013, 255. Cf. also Grewe 1998, 173–190 and Castelletti 2022, 250.

unquestionably the queen of the underworld, depicted on her way to her annual visit from her royal residence onto the world of the living:

> *his turbata minis fluuios ripamque petebat*
> *Phasidis aequali Scythidum comitante caterua.*
> *florea per uerni qualis iuga duxit Hymetti*
> *aut Sicula sub rupe choros hinc gressibus haerens*
> *Pallados, hinc carae Proserpina iuncta Dianae,*   345
> *altior ac nulla comitum certante, priusquam*
> *palluit et uiso pulsus decor omnis Auerno;*
> *talis et in uittis geminae cum lumine taedae*
> *Colchis erat nondum miseros exosa parentes.*

> Distracted by these threatening signs she sought the banks of Phasis' stream amid a band of Scythian maids, her peers in age. As Proserpina in spring-time led the dance over Hymettus' flowery ridges or beneath the cliffs of Sicily, on this side stepping close by Pallas, on that side hand in hand with her beloved Diana, taller than they and surpassing all her fellows, before she grew pale at the sight of Avernus and all her beauty fled: so fair also was the Colchian in her sacred fillets by the twin torches' light, while she had not hated her hapless parents yet.

The particular simile and the pairing of Proserpina to Diana draws into the structuring of Medea's character several famous intertexts in addition,[35] and most notably Virgil's Dido, primarily in the setting of her first appearance in the *Aeneid*, at 1.496–506, but also in the scene of the thunderstorm in *Aeneid* 4.160 ff., which led to the queen's infamous "wedding" (*Aen.* 4.172 *coniugium uocat*)[36] to Aeneas in a cave[37] and under circumstances no less ominous since it inaugurated a chain of events that would end in death (*Aen.* 4.169–170 *ille dies primus leti primusque malorum / causa fuit*, "that day was the first of her death, the first of her misfortunes"). The associations to death are corroborated by the formulation of the sound and visual effects that herald the outbreak of the storm, which recalls the description of the cave of the winds in *Aen.* 1.55, another Underworld landscape,[38] as they are about to be set loose by Aeolus.

---

[35] On Medea's intertextual character see Hinds 1993, 46.
[36] The parallelism between the union of Jason and Medea at Peuce (8.243–260) and Roman wedding rituals has been noted in Williams 1958; and Hersch 2010, 20, 120, 186.
[37] For caves as traditional entrance to the underworld, see Nelis 2001, 244.
[38] Adler 2003, 166; Jenkyns 2013, 279. The adjective *ater*, "black", the colour of the Underworld par excellence is the first colour adjective recorded in the *Aeneid* and significantly describes the dark caves that keep imprisoned Aeolus' winds (*Aen.* 1.60); on *ater* see Edgeworth 1992, 74–82.

The presence of Virgil's Dido in Valerius' subtext does not limit itself to the intertextual nexus behind Medea.[39] It contributes even more visibly to the characterisation of the maddened Pelias in book 1. Pelias' reaction at V. Fl. 1.700–703 to the departure of Acastus presupposes knowledge of the helpless Ariadne of Catullus 64 watching Theseus' ship moving out of her sight (Catull. 64.53–55) and, more importantly for the present argument, the furious Dido[40] sensing that Aeneas stealthily prepares to sail away. The relevant texts from Valerius and Virgil are listed below (V. Fl. 1.700–703; *Aen.* 4.300–303):

Saeuit atrox Pelias inimicaque uertice ab alto
uela uidet nec qua se ardens effundere possit.
nil animi, nil regna iuuant; fremit obice ponti
clausa cohors telisque salum facibusque coruscat.

Savage Pelias rages as from a high peak he beholds the sails of his enemy, and knows not how his anger can find vent. Nor courage, nor the kingdom offer any help; hemmed in by the barrier of the sea his army chafe, and the brine sparkles with their weapons and torches.

[Dido] saeuit inops animi totamque incensa per urbem
bacchatur, qualis commotis excita sacris
Thyias, ubi audito stimulant trieterica Baccho
orgia nocturnusque uocat clamore Cithaeron.

Her mind weakened, she [Dido] raves, and, on fire, runs wild through the city: like a Maenad, thrilled by the shaken emblems of the god, when the biennial festival rouses her, and, hearing the Bacchic cry, Mount Cithaeron summons her by night with its noise.[41]

Pelias' rage soon will lead him to crime, but in the particular moment and under the influence of the double intertext he triggers compassion: the aching and deserted father briefly replaces the cruel and deceitful king. And his decision to murder Aeson and Alcimede is described as motivated by irrational, bacchic-like fury for revenge, which brings the king next to the Carthaginian Dido. Medea's maenadic frenzy, with which the Latin *Argonautica* break off, similarly reaches back to Dido, and temptingly is paired to Pelias' own, in tragic anticipation of

---

39 On Dido in Valerius Flaccus and in the final book in particular in relation to Medea, see Heerink 2020; and Castelletti 2022, *passim*.
40 On the broad similarities of the curse of Valerius' Pelias to Dido's curse at *Aen.* 4.590–627, see Eigler 1988, *ad loc.* 27–28. Kleywegt 2005, 408; Adamietz 1976, 28 n. 65, observe structural resemblances between the Aeson episode and the end of *Aeneid* 4 ("place of departure, last scene of the book, curses, suicide"); see also Spaltenstein 2002, 273–274.
41 The translations of the *Aeneid* passages follow Kline 2002.

the heroine's assuming in turn the part of Pelias and murdering her family to extract revenge for what she considered to have been Jason's betrayal (V. Fl. 8.444–449):[42]

> sic fata parantem
> redde<re> dicta uirum furiata mente refugit
> uociferans. qualem Ogygias cum tollit in arces
> Bacchus et Aoniis inlidit Thyiada truncis,
> talis erat talemque iugis se uirgo ferebat
> cuncta pauens;

So spoke she, and while the hero strove to answer she fled away in a mad fury, crying aloud upon him. Like a Thyiad when Bacchic frenzy dries her to the Ogygian hills and dashes her against Aonian trees, so was she then, so madly raged the maiden upon the thwarts, in fear of all that might befall.

I have left for last the interaction of both closural passages with the theme of civil war. The murder of Aeson by Pelias at the end of book 1 comes at the end of a series of cases of internal conflict: the dispute between Aeson and Pelias at 1.21–37 is the catalyst that brings about the Argonautic expedition;[43] the golden fleece itself, the target of this mission, was taken to Colchis in the aftermath of the bitter strife between Ino and her stepchildren (1.277–282; also 2.585–612); while the deadly fraternal encounter between Pelias and Aeson is preceded by the discord between Jupiter and Sol (1.498–567),[44] which further similarly features a belligerent vs. peaceful brother dichotomy: Sol objects to Argo's voyage (his speech at 1.503–527), arguing that his son Aeetes, like Sol himself, has embraced peace (520); Sol's plans however clash against Jupiter's own desire to cause a war that would eventually translate the *socer — gener* conflict into grand-scale warfare among the nations of East vs. West (Jupiter's speech at 1.536–556).[45] Fraternal conflict frames Jason's arrival at Colchis, for it coincides with the war between Aeetes and his brother Perses, which spreads over the most part of book 6 and offers Jason the opportunity to ingratiate himself with Aeetes and gain access to his court and the golden fleece. The last episode in this chain of fraternal feuds that maintain the dominance of the civil war theme

---

42 On Dido's many echoes in V. Fl. 8.444–449, see Castelletti 2022, 244–245.
43 Zissos 2008, 123–124, 392–393. Zissos pointedly notes that Jason decides to undertake the expedition precisely because of his aversion to insurrection and civil war.
44 For civil war as fraternal conflict and vice versa, see Fantham 2010; also Armitage 2017, 88–89.
45 See Stover 2012, 90 n. 32.

throughout the Latin *Argonautica* is the clash between the Argonauts and the pursuing Colchians on the Peuce island in book 8 (8.217–467). The Peuce episode, in addition to the war between Aeetes and the Argonauts, comprises the wedding of Jason and Medea and the altercation between Jason and Medea, with which the *Argonautica* breaks off, and has already been examined in relation to its closural function.[46] Sanderson has recently shown that every unit in this episode is studded with vocabulary and phraseology that portrays the various conflicts as conflicts among kin of various types (fraternal, familial, and marital, and by extension socio-political).[47] The most explicit interfamilial fight and the one closest to the feud between Aeson and Pelias is, of course, the fight between Medea and her brother, Absyrtus, who, in Valerius' version, is the leader of the Colchian fleet pursuing her (V. Fl. 8.312–314), while their sibling status is mentioned repeatedly (8.263, 277, 312–317). As a result of Medea's marriage to Jason, further, the Minyans and the Colchians have become kindred people, hence the war about to break out is projected to be a civil one.[48]

To conclude, Valerius Flaccus' *Argonautica* conspicuously lacks a closure, provoking different readings and even encouraging the composition of literary supplements in later centuries. The presence of ritual, specifically a marriage celebration, undermines the abandonment script which Medea and Jason seem to engage in. In the present chapter I argued that it is possible to study the politics of closure in Valerius Flaccus by focusing on the final episode of the first book of the *Argonautica*, the murder of Aeson and Alcimede by Pelias, an episode that builds on the opposition between chaos and order, dramatises a fraternal conflict, and develops around an impressive ritual (a necromancy) and a climax of sacrilege. In addition, the concluding episode of book 1 and the end of book 8 share common themes, including civil war, fratricide, and allusions to death. The Aeson and Alcimede episode has been a Valerian addition to the Argonautic legend, is a self-standing narrative and influences little the development of the story, but features the main closural themes expected to appear at the end of a traditional heroic epic: ritual, death, emotional intensity, and open-endedness. This premature ending provides a sense of resolution with an underlying political message ever present in the imperial era, i.e., the many faces of internecine conflict, and the proper closure that is missing from the Latin *Argonautica*.

---

46 Hershkowitz 1998, 1–34; Pellucci 2012, v, xii–xxi.
47 Sanderson 2022.
48 Sanderson 2022.

Clayton Schroer
Mansuri Compos Decoris? Scipio's *Reditus* and Exile in *Punica* 17

Abstract: Silius Italicus ends his *Punica* by describing Scipio Africanus' triumphal *reditus* to Rome, with the hero defined by feats that make him incomparably superior to other Roman saviours like Camillus. Scholars have noted that the closural force of the poem is hereby frustrated, since heroes like Camillus (and Scipio himself) are also exiled by the state they once saved. Such readings, however, fail to observe the ways in which the ritual "return" (*reditus*), i.e. the notional remedy of the state of exile, that we find in Scipio's triumph effects the poem's closure, and in a way that proves particularly Flavian in its imagery and symbolism. At the same time, Silius leaves room for us to doubt the efficacy of such a closural strategy; although the narrator promises that Scipio knows the *decus* he provides his patria will "remain for all time" (17.625), we have already been told that it is precisely this same *decus* that will depart Rome when the hero is exiled (13.515).

Many parts of the final book of Silius Italicus' epic seem to come rather abruptly: we will think of the transition between lines 17.289 and 17.292,[1] when the narrative suddenly turns from Hannibal's storm-blown return to Africa to the battle at Zama. Or we will think of the immediate shift from Hannibal's retreat from the battlefield to Carthage's surrender and Scipio's return to Rome with the words at 17.618–619. These lines also constitute a sudden and unexpected shift in the narrative, despite their Virgilian pedigree (618 *hic finis bello*, cf. *Aen.* 1.223 *et iam finis erat*)[2] and ring structure hearkening back to the epic's opening lines (618 *reserantur protinus arces*, cf. 1.14: *reserauit...arces*).[3] In spite of such narrative urgency, the epic's denouement nonetheless accomplishes a notable sense of resolution, and its closural strategies have therefore drawn much comment. As Philip Hardie says in a seminal study of the epic's conclusion, the *Punica*

---

[1] Perhaps because of a *lacuna* in the text, either after 290 (Drakenborch and Summers) or 292 (Barth and Heinsius), although Delz sees no *lacuna* in the text. See further Roumpou 2018, 13; Spaltenstein 1990, 464.
[2] Cf. also Sil. 10.208 *hic tibi finis erat* with Roumpou 2018, *ad loc.*
[3] Cf. Roumpou 2018, *ad loc.* As Hardie 1997, 158 aptly notes, we have in these lines "a close immediately followed by...[an] opening."

"plays with the possibilities of reopening stories that seem to have reached a conclusion" by making "the final victory of Scipio Africanus...a decisive ending of a war, but...only a stage in the much larger history of Rome".[4] As we see throughout the present collections of essays, Silius' *Punica* is hardly alone in combining a successful sense of closure with the notion that the narrative could also be continued.

This chapter focuses on the closural elements at the conclusion of the *Punica* based on a ritual that bridges "the final victory of Scipio Africanus" and the other "stage[s] in the much larger history of Rome." Bridging these two narrative possibilities is no mean feat, for Scipio's immediate and more remote futures at the epic's conclusion differ dramatically from one another. Scipio will be remembered as one of the greatest generals of Republican Rome's history, the first to take a *cognomen* memorialising his military accomplishments (17.626). In the concluding lines of the poem, Silius commemorates Scipio's ascendant position in the political and military spheres of early 2nd century BCE Rome as he celebrates a triumphal procession (17.651–654):

> *salue, inuicte parens, non concessure Quirino*
> *laudibus ac meritis non concessure Camillo:*
> *nec uero, cum te memorat de stirpe deorum,*
> *prolem Tarpei mentitur Roma Tonantis.*

> Hail, unconquered father, destined never to yield to Quirinus in praiseworthy deeds, nor ever to yield to Camillus in worthy ones. And indeed, when she commemorates you descended from the lineage of the gods, Rome does not lie that you are the progeny of the Tarpeian Thunderer.[5]

For all of this praise, we are tempted to forget that the future these lines herald for Scipio is not at all as bright as they suggest. As this volume's editor, Angeliki Roumpou, has keenly observed, in Scipio's triumph "the final model to which he is compared, Camillus, is the only one that will be exiled — exactly as Scipio will be in the future. But whereas Camillus will be recalled to Rome, Scipio will not".[6] The topic of Scipio's exile,[7] and the way that Silius navigates it in the closure of his epic, demands further investigation.

---

4 Hardie 1997, 158.
5 Translations throughout are my own unless otherwise noted.
6 Roumpou 2018, 405
7 Scipio escaped prosecution most likely in 184/3 BCE by going into self-imposed exile at his estate in Liternum where he died shortly later in the very same year that Hannibal also died in exile; see: Scullard 1973, 290–303 (cf. MRR 1.378) and Briscoe 2008, 176, 395.

In this chapter, then, we must address two related interpretive cruxes that present themselves in accounting for the impact of Scipio's exile on the conclusion of the poem. On the one hand, there remains no consensus on how we are to understand Silius' allusion to Scipio's displacement. Marks has argued that Silius makes a kind of *apologia* out of the allusion, claiming that the "comparison between Scipio and Camillus in 17.652 is not on their shared experience of exile, but on…their shared devotion in spite of their exiles";[8] McGuire, however, argues that the point of this line is precisely to draw attention to "Scipio's growing personal power and its impending consequences."[9] On the other hand, we must also account for the fact that Hannibal and Scipio both die in exile — indeed, even in the same year. In that way, the conclusion of the narrative, which leans so heavily on a strong distinction between victor and defeated, threatens to collapse.[10] In this chapter, I argue that Silius uses the ritual of the *reditus* — the celebration of a victorious general coming back to Rome — as a closural strategy to make a distinction between the exiles of Scipio and Hannibal, with the Roman general's triumphal "return" proleptically remedying his future displacement. As I demonstrate, a Flavian audience would have been particularly attuned to noticing the importance and nuances of the *reditus*. In this way, the epic attains a sense of closure by maintaining a distinction between the winner and the loser of the narrative. All the same, I also show that Silius does not completely dismiss Scipio's future removal from Rome, thereby hinting in this one ritual to both the closure and continuation of his narrative.

1 Cultural Contexts: The reditus in Domitianic Rome and literary expectations

The milieu in which Silius composed his *Punica* points to the cultural relevance of our reading. The poem's contemporary audience would have been well-attuned to noticing elements of the *reditus*, as the ceremony played an important role in Domitian's military triumphs and propaganda. While the *reditus* was not technically a part of the triumphal rites, even before the high imperial period the two rituals were linked in theory, if not in practice. For example, *Aen.*

---

8 Marks 2005, 203.
9 McGuire 1997, 101–102. For more on this issue, see: Ahl/Davis/Pomeroy 1986, 2555; Laudizi 1989, 139; Tipping 2010, 162, 187; Roumpou 2018, *ad loc.*; Schroer 2020, 156–170.
10 Also noted by Roumpou 2018, 405.

11.54 (*hi nostri reditus exspectatique triumphi?*) reveals the notional proximity of return and military victory: in this and other passages from the Latin textual tradition, the *reditus* and the *triumphus* form a kind of hendiadys in the Roman imagination.[11] This trend continues in the Domitianic period, when the *reditus* became an important visual and literary element of imperial propaganda. For instance, we have two Domitianic friezes that display *reditus*-processionals, one of them Relief B of the Cancelleria Reliefs and the other a relief now housed at Michigan's Kelsey Museum.[12] We also see the importance of the triumphal *reditus* in Domitian's dedication of a temple to Fortuna Redux (recalling a similar Augustan altar to the same goddess),[13] which Martial (viz. *Ep.* 8.65) associates with the *Porta Triumphalis* and Domitian's all-but triumphal return after the Second Pannonian War in 93.[14] This goddess, it is worth noting, also features prominently in the coinage of the Flavian emperors.[15]

The temple of Fortuna Redux and Flavian imagery attached to her, moreover, alerts us to the polyvalence of returns; after all, as an abstraction or a goddess, (*F/f*)*ortuna* oversaw the destiny and return not just of victorious generals, but also of exiled persons. Indeed, the goddess' function as patroness of the displaced can be observed within Flavian literature, for instance in the poet Statius' *epicedion* for the father of his patron Claudius Etruscus in *Silu.* 3.3. In that poem, Statius praises the younger Etruscus for his work in successfully securing his father's return from exile in Campania,[16] but laments the fact that

---

11 The link between the two can be traced as far back as Ennius' *Annales* (viz. with Skutsch 1985, 477, *Ann.* 9.299: *Liuius inde* **redit** *magno mactatus* **triumpho**). In Livy, Silius would not have failed to notice the regularity of the phrase *triumphans redit* (Liv. 1.38.4; 4.10.7; 5.49.7; 41.28.9; 44.22.17; 45.39.11; cf. 9.5.9).

12 For the debate on what the Cancelleria Reliefs depict, see Darwall-Smith 1996, 172–174 with bibliography and the interpretation of Augoustakis 2010, 242–246; for the other relief, see Koeppel 1969, 138–140 and 1980, 18.

13 On the temple (whose placement and context are heavily debated), see most recently Goldman-Petri 2021, 46–50 with further bibliography.

14 Domitian celebrated between 2 and 4 triumphs; see Griffin 2000, 63 and the relevant testimonia cited by Hulls 2011, 173 n. 21.

15 For Vespasian, see RIC2.1 573 p. 101; for Titus, RIC2.1 421 p. 87; cf. Carradice/Buttrey 2007, 20–22 with items 11 and 33 for early examples and pp. 59, 61, 63, 65, 71, 75, 78–79, 84, 87, 101 with nn. 108, 103, 122, 124, 131, 142, 144, 146, 148 all only on Vespasianic coinage to my knowledge. We do not seem to have any coins minted by Domitian with the epithet *Redux*. He instead seems to have preferred other epithets such as *Publica* and *Augusti*; see, e.g. Carradice/Buttrey 2007, 302 with n. 55.

16 *Fortuna* also oversees the plight of the elder Etruscus in an earlier poem when Statius obliquely alludes to displacement of his patron's father (*Silu.* 1.5.64–65: *tecum ista senescant, / et tua iam melius discat* **fortuna** *renasci!*).

the elder Etruscus died shortly after *Fortuna* secured his return to the city Rome (*Silu.* 3.3.182–183 *cur nos, fidissime, linquis / **Fortuna redeunte**, pater?*).[17] What's more, Silius reveals his awareness of this irony in the way he describes the tragic return of Satricus (Sil. 9.66–177). Satricus, a prisoner of war from the First Punic War, escapes his captors and, having armed himself unwittingly in the armour of one of his slain sons, is killed by his other son, named Solymus, who mistakes his father for the enemy who killed his brother. Silius makes it clear in various ways that we are to think of Satricus as an exile, such as by likening him to the exiled poet Ovid.[18] Just as importantly, Solymus' words to his dying father reveal that the goddess Fortuna oversaw Satricus' unhappy return (Sil. 9.157–158): *sicine te nobis, genitor, **Fortuna reducit** / in patriam*? The wordplay patent in the collocation of *Fortuna reducit* would have been all the more obvious to a generation of readers familiar with Domitian's cultivation of the goddess *Fortuna Redux*: Satricus' return from exile is anything but triumphant.

The Satricus episode therefore parodies the associations ancient audiences might have drawn between the exilic *reditus* and the military triumph, and yet such a parody suggests that the connection between the two was one Silius' contemporaries could notice. Compare, for instance, how Silius himself observes that the hero Camillus earned a triumphal *reditus* precisely because he came back from exile to dislodge the Gauls from their siege (Sil. 1.625–626 *Gallisque ex arce fugatis / arma **reuertentis pompa** gestata Camilli*). Our poet's language in these lines is telling: we know from Cicero that *uertere* is one of the key legal words denoting the state of exile (e.g. Cic. *Quinct.* 60 *qui exilii causa solum uerterit*), thus leaving *reuertere* to denote return from displacement; moreover, that verb's collocation with the word *pompa*, denoting the triumphal "procession,"[19] recalls the language of Silius' model Livy at 5.49.7 (*triumphans redit*). Indeed, Silius further develops this association between Camillus' return from exile and triumph over the Gauls in an extended simile in book 7 (Sil. 7.557–563).[20]

Westall has argued that Roman audiences were attuned in their readings of history and literature to regard triumphs as moments of closure; what's more, he briefly points to the concluding scene of the *Punica* as evidence of this

---

17 For *Fortuna*'s oversight of exile elsewhere in Flavian literature, cf., e.g., Mart. 2.24.1–4 and (also of Claudius Etruscus) 6.83.1–2.
18 See Marks 2020, 91–93 and *passim*.
19 See Feeney 1982, *ad Pun.* 1.626 and TLL 10.1.2595.
20 See further Schroer 2021, 203–206.

trend.[21] Silius' audience, therefore, was culturally attuned to noting imagery associated with the triumphal *reditus* as an element of literary closure, while also remaining keenly aware that returns (overseen by the goddess Fortuna) occurred in many different contexts beyond the martial, such as in the *reditus* from exile. These cultural contexts allow us to unlock further meanings in characters like Satricus and Camillus; particularly for the latter, we will notice that the two times our poet mentions him before the *Punica*'s conclusion, Camillus' triumphal and exilic returns are associated with one another. In sum, returns from exile and successful military campaigns, in both Flavian culture and the *Punica* more specifically, were recognisably linked *topoi*.

2 Camillus, Scipio, and the exilic *reditus*

Given this literary and cultural nexus, we bring our attention back to the return described in the final lines of the poem. We will notice, however, that at no point does Silius explicitly call Scipio's celebration a *reditus*; it is only described as a *triumphus* at 17.628. Nonetheless, the language of the surrounding lines suggests that the usual hendiadys of "return" and "triumph" remains operative in this scene (Sil. 17.625–628):

> *mansuri compos decoris per saecula rector*
> *deuictae referens primus cognomina terrae*
> *securus sceptri repetit per caerula* Romam
> *et patria* **inuehitur sublimi** *tecta* **triumpho**.

> Assured of a glory that would remain throughout the ages, the commander — the first to come back having the cognomen of a conquered land — returns over the ocean to Rome assured of his reign and **rides** into the walls of his fatherland **in lofty triumph**.

True to form, our poet's words display a clear Livian pedigree (Liv. 30.45.1 Romam *peruenit* **triumpho**que *omnium* **clarissimo** *urbem est* **inuectus**).[22] As often, however, the differences between the two are more telling than the similarities. Silius, for instance, departs from his model by emphasising that Scipio's

---

21 Westall 2014, *passim* and especially p. 37.
22 Spaltenstein 1990, 484; Spaltenstein and Roumpou 2018, *ad Pun.* 17.626 also note the correspondence between 30.45.7 (**primus** *certe hic imperator* **nomine uictae** *ab se gentis est nobilitatus*) with Silius' 17.626 (*deuictae referens* **primus** *cognomina terrae*). Hardie 1997, 159 compares *Aen.* 8.714–715 (*at Caesar triplici inuectus Romana triumpho / moenia*)

triumph is also a *reditus*. The repetition of the prefix *re-* and simply the denotations of *referens* (*OLD* s.v. 1c) and *repetit* (*OLD* s.v. 1) advertise that Scipio is "returning" to Rome.[23] We will find no parallel for this language in the Livian source. Moreover, Silius is curiously insistent on the geography of Scipio's return: Scipio comes back both "to Rome" (*Romam*) and to "the walls of his fatherland" (*patria tecta*). On the one hand, this repetition does recall Livy's *Romam* and the parallel repetition in *urbem*; however, the phrase *patria tecta* is arresting for how uncommon it is, and especially in comparison to *tecta patriae*. In either case, we will observe in the Latin literary tradition that one far more commonly leaves the walls of one's father(land) (e.g. V. Fl. 7.163 *patriis... euadere tectis*; 7.440 *patriis...excedere tectis*), often in exile (e.g. Ov. *Met*. 13.421 *patriae fumantia tecta relinquunt*; *Pont*. 1.2.48 *aspicio patriae tecta relicta meae*) than one enters them. Put more simply, one cannot mention Scipio entering his *patria tecta* without reminding us that Scipio will be exiled from these same walls.

Rare though it is to mention someone entering their *patria tecta*, Silius does have his eye on one of his most important poetic models: his epic forebear Lucan. The Neronian poet's narrator laments, in the third book of his poem, the way in which Caesar "entered the walls of his fatherland" (Luc. 3.73 *tecta petit patriae*; cf. Sil. 17.627–628 *repetit.../ patria...tecta*).[24] We can be all but certain that Silius had his eye on this passage, as in it Lucan's narrator recounts how much better it would have been if Caesar had "returned" (*remeasset*) with a conquered people like the Gauls in tow (Luc. 3.73–74), a likely allusion to the Camillus-myth and rhetorical connections made between Caesar and the Gauls.[25] In that way, Lucan's passage anticipates Silius' own allusion to Camillus in the triumph of Scipio. Furthermore, Lucan's passage also deals with (the denial of a) triumph, since Caesar could have earned such a great triumphal procession (Luc. 3.75 *pompa*, 3.79 *triumphum*) by fighting Rome's enemies instead of her own citizens. Silius will have been attracted to this passage not only for the language of return and use of the Camillus-myth, but also the way that he can have Scipio's triumph proleptically correct the sin of future civil discord by representing violence properly directed against foreign enemies instead of

---

[23] Noted also by Hardie 1997, 158.
[24] To my knowledge, these words occur in such close proximity to one another only once elsewhere beyond Lucan and Silius (cf. Sen. *Phoen*. 322–324). For more on Silius' engagement with Lucan in the poem's final lines, see especially Hardie 1997, 159–160.
[25] See Gaertner 2008, esp. 49–51, on Lucan's use of a motif likely stretching back to Livy and Pompeian rhetoric.

the Roman state. On one level, then, this passage fits into a pattern of antiphrastic Lucanian allusions that according to Marco Fucecchi demonstrate how Rome has "the necessary 'antibodies'...to face the difficult trials of the future" related to civil war.[26]

Silius' word choice and allusive programme in the *Punica*'s denouement make it clear that he is interested in connecting Scipio's triumph to the *reditus* (both military and exilic) of his heroic antecedent, Camillus. Our poet accomplishes this by adapting his Livian source and supplementing it with the language of return. Such imagery suggests a proleptic connection with, even a correction of Scipio's future disgrace in exile. Readers might also sense in Silius' allusion to Lucan's anti-triumph that Scipio's triumph is meant to serve as a remedy for the mistakes of the future, be those mistakes his own resulting in his exile or Julius Caesar's resulting in civil discord. In this way, Silius' use of the ritual of *reditus* provides a sense of closure, alleviating the concerns that readers might have over what a continuation of the epic's historical narrative might bring with it.

3 *Syncresis* and exile?

In the lines we have just examined, there remains one further strategy that Silius employs to emphasise the way that Scipio's triumph is a closural *reditus*. The noun *reditus* occurs only once in *Punica* 17, at a point when Hannibal is contemplating a return to Italy just after he has departed. Our poet is at pains to link these two scenes intratextually; observe how Hannibal's state of mind looks forward to Scipio's serene awareness of his coming glory (Sil. 17.625), *mansuri compos decoris* (Sil. 17.220–223):

> *nullaque iam Hesperia et nusquam iam Daunia tellus,*
> *hic secum infrendens: 'Mentisne ego* compos *et hoc nunc*
> **indignus reditu,** *qui memet finibus umquam*
> *amorim Ausoniae?*

---

26 Fucecchi 2018, 32; cf. also Marks 2018 and 2010, esp. 151 ("Unlike Lucan, who offers few positive models of heroism, Silius offers many."). I say "seemingly" because, like myself, many scholars remain unconvinced that Silius expresses such optimism unambiguously and without qualification; see, e.g., the discussion of the phrase *securus sceptri* (Sil. 17.627) at Roumpou 2018, *ad loc.* with bibliography (adding now Dominik 2018, 289), although cf. the optimistic reading of Marks 2005, 114 and 201–206.

> Hannibal kept grinding his teeth in rage, since there was no more of Italy or Daunus' land to see. He said: "<u>Am I in my right mind</u>? And am I now **unworthy of this return**, I who never removed myself from Italy?"[27]

The intratextual repetition of *compos* linking these two scenes alerts us to still deeper connections between the two scenes. We will notice that the two passages share the language of return, and we will further observe that in both passages there are both exilic and martial/ritual connotations. Here, Hannibal announces his intention to return to the land of Italy, which he has just left. Crucially, Silius follows his model Livy in likening that departure to one of exile. Just before these lines, a departing Hannibal looks back on Italy "as if he were expelled, leaving his fatherland and dear home, and as if he were an exile being dragged to sad shores" (Sil. 17.216–217 *haud secus ac patriam pulsus dulcesque penates / linqueret et tristes exul traheretur in oras.*). Much has been written about these and the surrounding lines, how they liken Hannibal and his conflicted sense of identity to a Roman and to Aeneas.[28] But for our purposes, it is enough to note that Hannibal fails at securing a kind of exilic *reditus* (*indignus reditu*) to Rome in a way that contrasts with Scipio's return in the poem's conclusion.

Throughout the remainder of the epic's closing scene, we see allusions in the language of Hannibal's intended return that make us think of Scipio. For example, we will note Hannibal's aims to come back to Italy, *remeabo Anienis ad undas* (Sil. 17.233), and to force Scipio to be recalled to a fortified Rome, *uallata reuocetur Scipio Roma* (Sil. 17.235); ironically, *reuocetur* is part of the legal lexicon of exile, denoting one's formal "recall" to Rome (*OLD* s.v. 3b).[29] Hannibal, to put this more simply, is wishing for the very thing, a pseudo-exilic return to Rome, that Scipio gets at the end of the poem. We get further proof of this contrast in the language Jupiter uses to deny Hannibal his *reditus*, using the very same verb of return used later in book 17 to describe Scipio's at poem's end (Sil. 17.381–382 **repetat** *neue amplius umquam / Ausoniam*; cf. 17.627 **repetit** *per caerula Romam*).

In this way, Hannibal's intended (but failed) *reditus* corresponds to the connotations of exile that Scipio's triumph creates at the *Punica*'s conclusion. We will also note that Hannibal's use of the word *reditus* above to describe his return to Italy summons to mind the word's martial-ritual associations. A Roman audience will not have failed to understand the phrase *indignus reditu* as

---

27 On the difficulty of the sense and syntax of 17.223–224, see Fucecchi 2020, 273 n. 30 with bibliography; I have adopted the translation of Augoustakis and Bernstein 2021 for these lines.
28 See most recently Schroer 2022 with further bibliography.
29 Cf. also Sil. 17.378 (*redeuntibus armis*).

an allusion to the ritual of the triumphal return to the city: "worthy triumphs" constitute a key formula in literary descriptions of the *triumphus*.³⁰ Particularly for a Flavian audience, these words may have carried a special relevance: nearly half of the references just cited in note 30 were composed during the Domitianic period. We may just be catching a hint of Domitian's presentation of his military successes in this language of the worthy, or indeed in this case unworthy, triumphs and the way that later detractors questioned those assertions. We might think of Pliny the Younger all but explicitly laying such an accusation at Domitian's feet in the *Panegyricus* (*Pan.* 16.3), looking to a time when the Capitol will welcome an "emperor returning with real glory" (*imperatorem ueram...gloriam reportantem*) rather than "mock chariots and images of empty victory" (*mimicos currus...falsae simulacra uictoriae*).³¹ Let me be clear that I am not implying that Silius is expressing sympathy with such rhetoric in relation to Domitian with the phrase *indignus reditu*; rather, I am arguing that the language of (un)worthy triumphs would have been a noticeable feature of the text to a contemporary audience versed in the politics of the final years of Domitian's reign.

Silius in this way appears to insist on the differences between Hannibal and Scipio in their returns. Hannibal, by this reading, seems to act almost as an exilic scapegoat, representing all the negative consequences of his and Scipio's shared futures in displacement. By contrasting Scipio with Hannibal, Silius can use the ritual of the *reditus* to correct for Scipio's future in exile: the starkly drawn line between victor and defeated reveals that it is Hannibal, and not Scipio, who is exiled from Italy and Rome, that it is him alone who cannot triumphally "return" to the city that expelled him. This ritual act therefore grants a sense of closure to the epic, acknowledging but also remedying the possibility of future complications for the hero of the narrative.

And yet, I know that some readers will protest that a reading like this posits the creation of a stark distinction between Scipio and Hannibal that amounts to poetic a fiction, something that is not true — I know this because I am one of those readers. Whatever distinctions between the two leaders that Silius creates, we cannot ignore the fact that their shared fate of exile ultimately erases the line

---

30 The phrase "worthy of a triumph" (albeit in Greek) is cited as if it were a common phrase at Suet. *Cal.* 47. See also: Cic. *Phil.* 13.9, *Att.* 6.3.3; Liv. 7.11.11, 31.20.3, 45.39.2; Ov. *Am.* 2.12.5; St. *Theb.* 12.579, *Silu.* 3.3.171; Mart. 5.19.3, 8.65.11.

31 On Pliny's words and their engagement with Domitianic propaganda, see Östenberg 2009, 29–30; Strunk 2017, 44–45 examines Tacitus' similarly biting criticism of Domitian's false triumph at *Ag.* 39.1 and compares it to Pliny's in the *Panegyricus*, also adding Dio's 67.7.4 accusation that the emperor purchased people to play the roles of captives in his German triumph.

between Scipio and Hannibal, between winner and loser; in fact, by a remarkable accident of history, both men would die in exile within a year of one another. Livy makes this point most famously in his own coda to the tale of the two antagonists (Liv. 38.50.7):

> *duas maximas orbis terrarum urbes ingratas uno prope tempore in principes inuentas, Romam ingratiorem, si quidem uicta Carthago uictum Hannibalem in exilium expulisset, Roma uictrix uictorem Africanum expellat.*

> The two greatest cities in the world were found at nearly the same time to have been ungrateful towards their leaders, but Rome all the more so seeing as Carthage in defeat had driven out the defeated Hannibal into exile, but Rome in victory would expel the victorious Africanus.

It is no novel claim to take a generally syncretic reading of Scipio and Hannibal, as Silius adopted this trend from his Livian model.[32] However, fewer have followed Livy in comparing the two generals in terms of their exile (even though Silius himself does this in *Punica* 13);[33] what is more, to my knowledge only Angeliki Roumpou has used Livy's comparison in a discussion of the closing lines of the *Punica*. In her words, the poem's final allusion to Camillus "works also as a reminder of Hannibal's and Scipio's interchangeability: surely it is not a coincidence that Scipio and Hannibal shared the same fate in exile."[34]

Surely not. But Roumpou's point requires further investigation. On the one hand, such a claim demands evidence: it is not immediately clear why an allusion to Camillus, on its own, should summon to mind an exilic comparison of Hannibal and Scipio, especially since Silius otherwise is at pains, as we have seen, to distinguish the two men. In other words, if we are meant to compare the two in this way, there should be some evidence that supports our doing so. And indeed, we will find that evidence if we examine Silius' last description in his epic — not of Scipio, but of Hannibal (17.643–644):

> *sed non ulla magis mentesque oculosque tenebat,*
> *quam uisa Hannibalis campis fugientis imago.*

---

32 On the syncresis of Scipio and Hannibal in the *Punica*, see especially Stocks 2014, 182–217 and Voisin 2016 with further bibliography; on the same in Livy, see most prominently Rossi 2004.
33 See von Albrecht 1964, 151, 209; Juhnke 1972, 292; Reitz 1982, 9–11, 46; Marks 2003; Jacobs 2009, 293–296; Van der Keur 2015, xi–xviii, 456 with n. 35; Augoustakis 2015b, 167; Schroer 2020, *passim*.
34 Roumpou 2018, 405.

> But no other image held the attention of those watching more than the one of Hannibal that seemed to be fleeing from the field.

This distich intratextually connects Hannibal's exile with Scipio's in two ways. On the one hand, these lines subtly hint that Hannibal's "flight," *fugientis*, from the field also alludes to his future in *fuga*, in exile. In this way, Silius continues his pattern of alluding to Hannibal's death in exile as a closural strategy at the end of his epic as well as at the end of books 2 (2.699–707) and 13 (13.874–893).[35] Furthermore, this image of being in flight, *imago fugientis*, in turn recalls the other *imago fugiens* of book 17, the phantom of Scipio summoned by Juno to lead Hannibal away from the battle at Zama (17.538 *dat terga et campo **fugiens** uolat ales **imago***). The martial *fuga* of both empty images therefore looks ahead to and links together the exilic *fuga* of Scipio and Hannibal.[36]

Secondly, we will note that Hannibal's captivating *imago* recalls another artistic representation of one led in chains and demanding the attention of all who look upon it (6.689–691):[37]

> *haec inter iuncto religatus in ordine Hamilcar,*
> *ductoris genitor, cunctarum ab imagine rerum*
> *totius in sese uulgi conuerterat ora.*

> Amidst these things Hamilcar, the general's father, bound in a linked row of prisoners, had drawn the eyes of the entire crowd to himself from the image of all the other things.

Of course, Hamilcar was never really led in defeat as a captive bound in chains, just as Hannibal never was.[38] Yet in these lines, with the general looking upon his father *religatus*, we also catch a hint of Hannibal's future after his own defeat, of Hannibal *relegatus*, i.e. of Hannibal in exile. And we certainly cannot forget that Hannibal looks upon these images at Liternum, the very place where Scipio would spend the end of his life in exile away from Rome.[39] An allusion to the scene at Liternum in the *Punica*'s final lines summons to mind the very exilic forces that Scipio's *reditus* mediates.

---

[35] I would like to thank Marco Fucecchi for pointing this out to me.
[36] As Roumpou 2018, 44–46 points out, Hannibal's *imago*, and by extension Scipio's, points not just to things that are, but also of things that are yet to come with respect to the epic's narrative time.
[37] The intratextual connection is also noted by Marks 2003, 133 and Stocks 2014, 221, who also notes that "the visit to Liternum recalls Scipio's future exile."
[38] Hamilcar in fact escaped, having watched over the battle from nearby Mt. Eryx.
[39] *Pace* Marks 2003 who argues that Silius does not use the scene at Liternum to hint at the place's negative connotations given Scipio's exile there.

4 Conclusion

These intratextual markers hint at forces operating contrary to the closural ones we examined above: here, Scipio's and Hannibal's exiles are linked to one another, and the boundary between winner and loser begins to fade away. The apologetic readings that find redemption for Scipio's exile in the figure of Camillus cannot account for these darker hues in the epic's closure. Reckoning with the *Punica*'s closural strategy of Scipio's exile and triumphal *reditus* requires readers to notice a certain degree of ambivalence. Our poet can insist that his poem accounts for and corrects Scipio's future in disgrace, but only for so long as the poem's version of history is told. Scipio's *reditus* is the final word in Silius' story, but not of Scipio's.

In conclusion, let us return to a line we have already examined above (17.625):

> *mansuri compos decoris per saecula rector*

> Assured of a glory that would remain throughout the ages, the commander...

In this line, Hardie observes that the phrase *mansurum decus* translates the Homeric ideal of κλέος ἄφθιτον to the glory of the Roman triumph.[40] Compelling as such a reading may be, *mansurum* carries meanings that ἄφθιτον cannot adequately convey; in the context of Scipio, in particular, the phrase *manere per saecula* raises some ambiguity, for it leads us to ask where, precisely, Scipio's *decus* is destined to remain. Can it really remain at Rome, since the hero dies in exile? That question is a meaningful one, for Silius only once refers to the exile of his hero, using language that looks ahead to the line we are investigating (13.514–515):

> *pudet urbis iniquae*
> *quod post haec decus hoc patriaque domoque carebit.*

> Shame on this unjust city! For after these events this man's glory will lack both his fatherland and his home.

Both passages tell us something about Scipio's place (figuratively and literally) in Roman history, *post haec* ≈ *per saecula*, but our poet tells a conflicting story of what that future-past has in store for the Roman hero and his people. On the

---

40 See Hardie 1997, 158 and Roumpou 2018, *ad loc.*

one hand, at the end of the poem it is clear that Scipio's glory, *decus*, has a "staying power," *manere*, among the Romans; stories like the *Punica* serve as a literary monument to the lasting nature of the lessons Scipio can impart to Rome.

And yet we know that Scipio's glory cannot remain at Rome into the future, at least not in any literal sense: our poet himself says that Scipio's exile by the unjust city Rome was also an exile of his *decus*. This earlier line, in other words, appears to directly conflict with the claim made at the end of poem. This ambiguity is a hallmark of the "staying power" of Scipio and the lessons his glory has to teach other Romans throughout the epic. When the young leader had been confronted after the battle at Cannae with the plot of Metellus to abandon Rome (10.415–448), or to go into exile as Silius puts it (10.420 *dux erat exilio... Metellus*), Scipio dissuades them by holding forth his own exemplary intent: he will never leave Rome "so long as some life <u>remains</u> in him" (10.438–439 *numquam Lauinia regna / linquam...dum uita <u>manebit</u>*).[41] There, as at poem's end, we are forced to confront the exemplarity of Scipio's actions and their "staying power" with the reality that he will not remain in Rome. We know, if Scipio does not, that he *will* leave Rome before his death, disgraced in exile.

Michael Putnam has called literary moments like these "dream[s] of a time to come," prophetic utterances that are too good to be true. These utterances express a praiseworthy hope for a future that a poet nonetheless knows cannot come to pass in any real sense.[42] Silius displays just this kind of thinking in his optimistic presentation of Scipio's future at the closure of the poem. Our poet can correct for the future exile of his hero, but only for so long as his narrative fiction lasts; in the *Punica*'s conclusion, this "dream of a time to come" sees a world in which Scipio comes back to Rome in the ritual of his triumphal *reditus*, his glory never to leave (17.625 *mansuri...per saecula*) and his status as returning

---

41 Silius has adopted the irony of Scipio's oath from his Livian source (Liv. 22.53.10–12), see further Schroer 2020, 66–79; cf. also Val. Max. 5.12.7, Front. *Strat.* 4.7.39, Dio 15.28–29. The geographic precision of *Lauinia regna* is, I suppose, open to interpretation; if the phrase expresses Rome's imperial sway on the Italian peninsula, then Camillus' exile to Ardea and Scipio's to Liternum do not, in a literal sense leave the sphere of the *Lauinia regna*. But looking back as this collocation does to Verg. *Aen.* 1.2–3 (*Italiam fato profugus Lauiniaque uenit / litora*), Silius' *Lauinia* almost certainly implies a greater degree of geographic specificity (the city of Rome or, more specifically and distinctly, Lavinium), just as Vergil's use of the word did; on the geographic specificity of Vergil's *Lauinia litora*, see Servius and Austin 1971 *ad* Verg. *Aen.* 1.2.
42 Putnam 2011, 14 uses this phrase to describe the famous prophecy (or better, *adynaton*) in book 1 of the *Aeneid* that under Augustus' reign, "Romulus will make laws together with his brother Remus" (*Aen.* 1.292–293).

victor contrasting him with the image of Hannibal in *fuga*. But Silius also hints in his intratextual nods that he knows his "dream of a time to come" is just that: a dream, a version of history contrary to what actually happened. Ritual, then, yields in the poem a sense of satisfactory closure, one that acknowledges but also attempts to rectify the problems that would be inherent in the continuation of the narrative. But even the master of this fiction himself knows — indeed, makes it explicitly known through his intratexts — that only his story, and not history, displays such tidy endings.

Theodoros Antoniadis
Silius Italicus' False Rituals, Politics and Poetics: Mock Funerals and Triumphs as Closural Markers in the *Punica*

Abstract: In ancient Roman culture and ritual, funeral processions and triumphs have been found to share many features as public ceremonies not just of purification, but also of demonstration both of individual glory and Rome's imperialist enterprise. Seneca captures the symbolic capital these complex social institutions may endorse as tropes of power and prestige by referring to Drusus' funeral as *funus simillimum triumpho* (*Marc.* 3.1). However, it is rather in the Flavian epics that the common imagery related to funeral rites and triumphs is often reversed or perverted in a way that undermines their obvious function as public spectacles and artistic representations. This is particularly evident in the closing scenes of several books of Silius Italicus' *Punica*, where different aspects of ritual are often associated to create a sense of an ending that is ambiguous and incomplete. Such poetics of closure fuse together resolution and constraint to undercut the establishment of order supposedly achieved by ritual performances and religious practices on individual and public level. From this point of view, Silius may reflect upon the extreme subjectification and ritualisation of public spectacles under Nero and Domitian, who indulged themselves in playing the role of religious actors during their rule.

1 Introduction

In one of the most debated scenes of the siege of Saguntum in *Punica* 2, Silius has Hercules, the acclaimed patron deity of the Spanish city, resort to the assistance of the personified Fides in a desperate attempt to save his beleaguered people from what is almost a foregone conclusion based on the epic's historical background: the destruction by Hannibal's forces of Rome's most reverent ally, which in the Roman tradition offered an exemplum of *fides* and *uirtus* for the steadfast loyalty of its inhabitants to the Italian capital. This moment in Silius' narrative is therefore very critical, since the Saguntines, having given up all hope of Roman aid (460), are starving to death, their bodies being deformed from plague and famine (465–474). For all its intertextual 'grotesqueness', Silius' description of their helpless state is very touching.[1] However, Fides' response to Hercules' supplication is rather not what most readers might have expected (Sil. 2.494–503):

> 'Cerno equidem nec pro nihilo est mihi **foedera rumpi,**
> statque dies ausis olim tam tristibus ultor.   495
> sed me **pollutas** properantem linquere **terras**
> sedibus his tectisque Iouis succedere adegit
> fecundum in fraudes hominum genus; **impia** liqui
> et, quantum terrent, tantum metuentia regna
> ac furias auri nec uilia praemia fraudum   500
> et super **haec ritu horrificos** ac more ferarum
> uiuentes rapto populos luxuque solutum
> omne decus multaque oppressum nocte pudorem.

> Indeed I see this. Not for nothing are *my treaties broken*, and the day that avenges such dire ambitions stands fixed long since. But the race of mankind, fertile in crime, led me to hurry away from the *polluted earth* and occupy this seat and Jupiter's dwelling. I left behind *wicked* kingdoms, as frightened as they are terrifying, and madness for gold and rewards not small for crime. On top of this, there were people with *horrifying customs*, living on plunder like beasts; all glory dissipated in self-indulgence and all sense of shame buried in deep darkness.[2]

While Fides obviously recognises the Carthaginian treachery (494 *foedera rumpi*) and points to the inevitable punishment awaiting traitors like Hannibal (495), the condemnatory tone of her speech and her overall rhetoric extend beyond the historical circumstances of the present episode. Once we focus on her exact wording, we see that religious terms and associations abound in her somewhat ritual denouncement of the polluted lands (496 *pollutas...terras*), of the impious kingdoms (498–499 *impia...regna*) and, above all, of the people who have compelled her to abandon the earth in haste (496) because of their horrific rites and bestial behaviour (501–502 *ritu horrificos ac more ferarum / uiuentis rapto populos*). In their recent translation of the *Punica*, Augoustakis and Bernstein render *ritu horrificos*, which matters most to us here, simply as "horrifying ways," removing from the phrase most of the religious undertones that Duff's choice of "customs" (for *ritu*) retains in the Loeb edition. However, Tacitus' strong

---

[1] See especially Ovid's description of the personified Fames at *Met.* 8.801–804 and Luc. 3.342–350, 4.253–336, 6.80–116 with Bernstein 2017, 210.
[2] For the Latin text, I have used Delz's edition (1987). With the exception of minor adaptations, all translations of the *Punica* are taken from Augoustakis/Bernstein 2021.

condemnation of the "polluted ceremonies" (*Hist.* 1.2 *pollutae caerimoniae*), especially at the end of Nero's reign and his notable anxiety concerning the events that followed suit after his fall, demands a closer look at Fides' tirade. Thus, while her pessimistic attitude may indeed draw upon the common Hesiodic motif of the human decline from the Golden to the Iron Age, and is further aligned with the Stoic view of an utterly corrupt world,[3] in what follows I shall argue that the religious element is often used by Silius to create a much ambiguous and unsettling closure to several episodes of his epic with symbolic import. Based on this premise, a final case will be made that these 'false rituals', aside from their obvious political function and exploitation as public spectacles embodied in an epic, can be further construed as equivocal responses to the extreme theatricalisation of religious ceremonies under Nero.

2 Pollution without purification in *Punica* 2

Thus far, Fides' ambiguous response to Hercules' plea and her even more ambivalent support of her devotees have triggered much discussion among scholars, most of whom have rather failed to observe that her *Weltanschauung* does not actually concern just the Carthaginian side, but most significantly extends to the Saguntine and, particularly, the Roman side as well.[4] Furthermore, in addition to the proverbial perfidy of the Carthaginians, and Hannibal's impiety in particular, which readers in the past were much preoccupied to expose,[5] the Saguntines' collective suicide has also raised some legitimate doubts concerning the perverse or even hollow display of their exemplary *fides* and *pietas*.[6] The surrounding debate gathers special interest when scholars engage in a political contextualisation based on Saguntum's conventional identification with Rome either as its distant counterpart or as its sacrificial stand-in.[7] Above all, what

---

[3] See Hes. *Op.* 109–201, Sen. *De ira* 3.26.4, *Ben.* 5.17.3 with Vessey 1974, 32.
[4] Note Fuccechi 2019 who explores how the traditional "polarisation" between the perfidious Carthage and the morally charged Rome as a symbolic embodiment of *fides* is undermined in the *Punica*. On *Fides* as an ambivalent ally and her equivocal stance, see Bernstein 2018b, 186–191. On her various representations in Flavian literature and culture, see Stocks 2019.
[5] See Sil. 1.8–11, 268, 296–302 and the most recent approach by Marks 2019, 171–176.
[6] On the interconnectedness of *fides* and *pietas* in the *Punica* and the programmatic force especially of their corresponding vices, *perfidia* and *impietas* at the outbreak of hostilities at Saguntum, note Marks 2019.
[7] Note especially Dominik 2003, 474–480; 2018, 273–280; Bernstein 2018b, 181.

Roman historiography is supposed to represent as an exemplary act, in Silius' account is 'contaminated' by a series of family crimes on the Saguntines' part as they become maddened and kill each other in order not to fall into Hannibal's hands.[8] In their perverted thinking after Tisiphone's manipulations (Sil. 2.526–542),[9] Rome's allies essentially chose death by suicide (i.e. civil war) over death by fighting and dying gloriously against the enemy (i.e. the "normal" way in war). This idea is reinforced by the poet's trenchant characterisations of their misdeeds as *nefas* (618), *laudanda monstra* (650) and *immania facta* (656), which point to a highly disputable martyrdom that will lead to an internecine carnage with no funeral rites for the dead.

Displaying her full awareness of the Saguntines' drama, Fides eventually commits herself to following the Saguntines' souls to the netherworld in a last-ditch attempt to bring a resolution to their sufferings and a greater sense of "release", a liberating closure, to the whole episode (Sil. 2.510–512):

> *quod **solum nunc fata sinunt** seriesque futuri,*
> *extendam **leti decus** atque in saecula mittam*
> *ipsaque laudatas ad manes **prosequar** umbras.*

> This is *the only thing that the Fates* and the order of future events now *permit*. So I shall extend their *deaths' glory* and pass it on to coming ages. I myself *shall follow* their praiseworthy souls down to the shadows.

As Bernstein duly observes, the religious connotations of *prosequar* allude to a funeral procession without the prospect of burial.[10] This notable absence of religious duties and obsequies to the deceased Saguntines is supplanted by a heart-rending scene where Rome's allies decide to erect a pyre in order to burn all their heirlooms (Sil. 2.599–608), an act which has been found to represent a "fake funeral" of their past.[11] For Augoustakis, in particular, the destruction of Saguntum's heritage and the loss of its historical identity in effect constitute a reversal not only of the city's foundation myth, but also of traditional funerary customs.[12] Silius' poignant remark on the aftermath of the massacre corroborates

---

8 See the excellent analysis by Bernstein 2018b.
9 At first glance Fury's intrusion recalls that of Virgil's Allecto who instigates war in the *Aeneid* (7.331–440); see Bernstein 2017, 148, 225–226.
10 See Bernstein 2017, 224. For the religious connotations of *prosequor*, see *OLD* (s.v. 2b); for *prosequor* as 'escorting' in funeral processions, see *OLD* (s.v. 1b).
11 Augoustakis 2017, 300.
12 Augoustakis 2010, 131: "this is a funeral pyre without subsequent burial, without hope for future rest of souls, ensured by the return of the dead to the mother-earth".

this approach further as Hannibal's army enters a ghost-town full of half-burned corpses that can hardly be distinguished from each other (Sil. 2.681–682):

semambusta *iacet nullo discrimine passim*
infelix obitus permixto funere turba

A crowd of *half-burned* cadavers, luckless in their death, lay everywhere with no distinction, corpses thrown together

The readerly dissatisfaction caused by the previous imagery of a pyre as a mass-grave of Saguntum's "Roman self" now culminates as the poet implements various intertexts to complement his poetics of the 'false ritual'.[13] Above all, through their perverse cremation, funeral and disposal, the dead Saguntines present a risk of ritual pollution in strictly Roman terms. Not only there will be no funerary rituals to separate them from the world of the living, and consign their spirits to the underworld, but it is Tisiphone who eventually leads a ceremony with them to the Underworld (Sil. 2.693–695):

tum demum ad manes perfecto munere Erinys
*Iunoni **laudata** redit magnamque **superba***
***exsultat** rapiens secum sub Tartara **turbam**.*

Then, her task at last complete, the Fury returned to the shades
with Juno's *praise. Exulting in pride*, she drove a huge *crowd*
along with her to Tartarus below.

Tisiphone earns Juno's praise not only for eliminating all the Saguntines, but also for foiling Fides' plan to accompany their souls to the Underworld. As a result, no funeral rites are conducted to grant Rome's allies an honourable transition from the upper to the lower world. Quite the opposite, their bodies are left half-consumed by fire and unburied. No heir is left to sprinkle their ashes with wine, gather them along with any traces of bone, place them in a cremation urn

---

13 As Augoustakis 2015a, 347–348 has shown, the entrance of the Carthaginian army into a city already dead resonates with the final scene of Valerius Flaccus' *Argonautica* Book 1 (818–826), where Jason's parents, Aeson and Alcimede, having performed the standard rites to consult the shade of Cretheus, resolve to end their lives before Aeetes' soldiers break into their home and slaughter them. However, in contrast to Valerius' comforting closure to *Arg.* 1, where the souls of Aeson and Alcimede are inducted into Elysium, after they have both met a decent death (V. Fl. 1.827–847), there will be no such soothing option for the Saguntines; on the ritual aspects of this episode in Valerius, see Papaioannou in this volume. Another source of inspiration for Silius is probably the Lemnian massacre at the end of *Argonautica* 2.

and inter them as would be the case with Roman dead.¹⁴ As for their sacrifice, though it supposedly denies Hannibal a triumphal entrance into a city of dead people, it perversely grants the Fury the chance of an iconoclastic triumph in the Underworld. It appears, therefore, as if a mock-ritual has taken the place of another one; a quasi-funeral procession is replaced by a quasi-triumphal one.¹⁵

All in all, even if Silius' farewell to the Saguntines' souls indeed succeeds in rehabilitating Rome's allies as a venerable *uulgus* deserving of a place among the innocent souls in Elysium (Sil. 2.696–707), the problematic rituals in which the Saguntines are implicated increase readerly dissatisfaction by evoking the *pollutas…terras* (2.496) and the atmosphere of chaos and disorder Fides had castigated in her speech as a result of human decadence.

3 Doomed rituals in *Punica* 5

The idea that religious practices utterly fail to secure a better prospect for the Romans and their allies in their war against Hannibal, despite his self-evident and much provocative impiety, continues to unsettle readers in Book 5. At its end, it is Silius' gruesome account of Flaminius' death at Trasimene that epitomises the general's earlier demonstrated irreverence toward rituals, providing another book closure in the *Punica* where the imagery of a false ritual is employed in order to 'seal' the Romans' complicated relationship with the divine. More specifically, on the eve of the battle at Trasimene, a series of prodigies and ill omens takes place in the Roman camp, generating a tension between the consul Flaminius and a certain Valerius Corvinus, whose figure is probably Silius' creation to further dramatise the historical controversy between the Roman officials as recorded by Livy and Polybius.¹⁶ In the *Punica* episode (5.24–129) the disagreement does not so much concern military and strategic issues, since Corvinus focuses his criticism on Flaminius' impiety and rashness in his

---

14 At the time Silius composed his epic, cremation was such a commonplace among the Romans that Tacitus in his *Annals* (16.6) referred to it as *Romanus mos*; see further Toynbee 1996, 40.
15 Fucecchi 2019, 193 observes another kind of perversion here inasmuch as Tisiphone signals "the final victory of the anti-*fides* (the perverted *fides* that comes from hell and is embodied on earth by Hannibal) over the real and 'positive' *fides*, represented by the Saguntines".
16 On Silius' use of his historical sources (especially Livy 22.3.4–14 and Polybius 3.80.3–82.8) in Flaminius' portrayal, see particularly Chaudhuri 2014, 214–218.

'fatal' defiance of the omens (5.77–91).[17] This assigns a particularly religious character to the *agon* between the two men over the validity of the omens, which indeed draws upon a long-standing epic *topos* from Homer's *Iliad* to Flavian epic.[18]

In his failure to respond comprehensively to the ominous warnings of the rituals and the divine manifestations, Flaminius is envisaged as an anti-*uates* who engages in a dialectic confrontation over religious practices with Corvinus. At the end of the day, Flaminius' precipitousness and his total disregard of the omens facilitates the plans of Juno, who is said to have chosen him to bring about this defeat to the Roman camp (Sil. 4.709–710). Thus, when the Carthaginian Ducarius rushes up to slaughter the consul in the final scene of the battle, Silius' narrative brings forth another false ritual in the sense of a mock sacrifice in which Hannibal's soldiers are invited to take part (Sil. 5.652–655):

> nec uos paeniteat, populares, fortibus umbris
> hoc **mactare** caput. nostros hic curribus egit
> insistens uictos alta ad Capitolia patres.
> ultrix hora uocat.   655

> Don't have any regrets, my countrymen, in *offering* this man's head to the souls of the brave dead. This is the man who led our defeated ancestors, driving them before his chariot, to the lofty Capitoline hill. The hour of revenge calls!

Ducarius' exhortation to his fellow combatants to offer Flaminius' head "to the souls of the brave" points with utmost irony to the potential abuse of his body. Yet, while *mactare* (653) is applied here in its common metaphorical sense to denote killing and slaughtering, it still retains its religious associations to mark Flaminius' imminent death as another perverse ritual.[19] Most notably, Ducarius invokes Flaminius' own triumphal celebration for his victory over the Boii (654)

---

17 Chaudhuri 2014, 214 notes that Silius appears to exaggerate the nature and the amount of the unsettling prodigies he recounts; see Sil. 5.66–69, 70–74 with Liv. 22.2.11–13 and Cic. *Div.* 1.77–78.

18 See the similar dispute between Hector and Polydamas in Homer's *Il.* (12.233–243) and that in Statius' *Theb.* (3.653–655) between Capaneus and Amphiaraus with Chaudhuri 2014, 220–221 who observes an underlying link between perverted rituals and civil war in the episodes of the Flavian epics.

19 Within the religious sphere, the verb denotes a sacrifice of a human or an animal in honour of the gods; see Lucr. 3.52–54: *et nigras mactant pecudes et manibus diuis / inferias mittunt multoque in rebus acerbis / acrius aduertunt animos ad religionem*, Ov. *Met.* 13.448 *placet Achilleos mactata Polyxena manes*.

as a ritual event that calls for revenge through a 'counter-ritual', that is, the general's mock burial, which takes place at Sil. 5.655–666:

> *pariter tunc undique fusis* 655
> *obruitur telis nimboque ruente per auras*
> *contectus nulli dextra iactare relinquit*
> *Flaminium cecidisse sua. nec pugna perempto*
> *ulterior ductore fuit. namque agmine denso*
> *primores iuuenum laeua ad discrimina Martis* 660
> *infensi superis dextrisque et cernere Poenum*
> *uictorem plus morte rati, super ocius omnes*
> *membra ducis stratosque artus certamine magno*
> *telaque corporaque et non fausto Marte cruentas*
> *iniecere manus.* **sic densi caedis aceruo** 665
> **ceu tumulo texere uirum.**

Then misSiles hurled simultaneously from all directions overwhelmed Flaminius. A cloud of arms rushing through the air struck him and left no man able to boast that Flaminius had fallen at his hand. There was no further fighting once the consul was killed. The first of the young men formed a close-packed line for battle's unlucky conflict. They were angry at the gods and their own fighting hands; they thought it worse than death to see the Carthaginians victorious. Swiftly they all rushed to hurl over the consul's corpse limbs prostrate from the huge combat and weapons and bodies and hands bloody from a battle that had gone against them. And so they packed in and covered the man in a heap of slaughter like a burial mound.

Flaminius' downfall brings Silius' narrative of the Roman disaster at Trasimene to a grotesque finale that encapsulates the undermining function of ritual imagery as an anti-closural marker. As the consul's body is virtually buried under a cloud of Carthaginian arms rushing through the air (655–656), the Romans are piling up all kinds of human limbs scattered in the battlefield on his corpse to erect a fake tomb (666 *ceu tumulo*). For McClellan "Flaminius is haunted by a ghost-army of the unburied Roman soldiers from Trebia (5.127–129), and is himself only granted a 'tomb' through the corpses of his own suicidal troops (5.658–666)".[20] Indeed, this is another iconic mass grave of mutilated bodies hardly discernible from each other (665 *densi caedis*) that digs into the distressing imagery of the Saguntines' abused bodies in *Punica* 2.[21] A particular appropriation of Theron's slaughter by Hannibal may also apply here; although Flaminius' death is not as humiliating as that of Hercules' priest, whose corpse is abused

---

20 McClellan 2019, 246.
21 See Sil. 2.681–682 quoted above and Sil. 2.686–688 *incubat* [sc. *leo*] *atris / semesae stragis cumulis aut murmure anhelo / infrendens laceros inter spatiatur aceruos.*

and left to become fodder for birds (Sil. 2.264–269), the consul is also denied the customary funeral rites while the only tomb he is granted is made up of the cadavers of Roman soldiers.[22] Moreover, in both episodes an inauspicious death (Theron's and Flaminius') instigates the destruction of the Saguntine/Roman army, thereby exposing the unresolved issue of the Romans' problematic relation to ritual and religion in the *Punica* that continues to intrigue readers as we move towards the major disaster at Cannae.[23]

4 From Cannae to Zama: Hannibal's funeral rites and Scipio's triumph

The rituals examined so far, mock, false, reversed or perverted, convey the impression that Silius is employing the religious element in order to set up a closure that is partially ambiguous and unsettling. Fabius' *aristeia* in Book 7 and the thanksgiving feast with which it culminates appear to constitute a notable exception to this rule. Nevertheless, the Cunctator's exemplary *fides* and *pietas* do not suffice to alter the 'anti-ritual' climate in the *Punica*.[24] In the next books Hannibal is still scoring some 'cheap religious points' through a series of self-fashioned rituals after his military triumph at Cannae and some of his late wins. More specifically, we see him offering obsequies for Paulus, Gracchus, and Marcellus in an attempt to show off his *humanitas* and his due respect to *Romanitas*.[25] Silius' various references to Hannibal's eulogies appear to expand especially on

---

22 On the intertextual and intratextual dynamics of Theron's death, see McClellan 2019, 100–106, 246.
23 John Jacobs reminded me here of the final scene of Sallust's monograph, where Catiline's half-dead body is said to have been found among the dispersed corpses of his Roman fellows and enemies, illustrating how Silius succeeds in sustaining a parallel link with civil war; see further Sall. *Cat.* 61 *Catilina uero longe a suis inter hostium cadauera repertus est paululum etiam spirans ferociamque animi, quam habuerat uiuus, in uoltu retinens.*
24 Commenting on Sil. 7.6–8 (*tot milia contra / Poenorum inuictum ducem, tot in agmina solus / ibat et in sese cuncta arma uirosque gerebat*), Littlewood 2011, 40 moves beyond the obvious metapoetic subtext of *arma uirosque* by reading Fabius' stance as "an inverted form of the sacrifice of *deuotio*". Note also her discussion (2011, 250) of the victory feast at Sil. 7.746–750 for which she finds no parallel as a closural theme in Roman epic.
25 On Paulus' burial, see Sil. 10.518–520 with Liv. 22.52.6. On Gracchus' funeral, see Sil. 12.473–474 with Liv. 25.17.4–7. On Marcellus' obsequies, see Sil. 15.385–387, 394–396 with Cic. *Sen.* 75; Liv. 27.28.1–2; App. *Hann.* 50; Plut. *Marc.* 30.1–2. See especially Augoustakis 2017, 305–315 and Pagán 2000; Stocks 2014, 29–31.

the *laudatio funebris* that Valerius Maximus reserves for these most prominent Roman generals.[26] Interestingly enough, though, it was Lucan who first envisaged the Carthaginian as a religious actor in the *Pharsalia* by comparing his homage to Paulus' dead body with Caesar's shocking decision to host a banquet amid the corpses of his fellow-citizens after Pharsalus.[27]

Silius' choice to invest further in the Lucanian intertext is particularly evident in his own elaborate account of Paulus' funeral after Cannae at Sil. 10.503–577, where Hannibal inspects a battlefield strewn with abused corpses (Sil. 10.449–453):

> atque ea dum Rutulis turbata mente geruntur,
> **lustrabat** campos et saeuae tristia dextrae   450
> facta recensebat pertractans uulnera uisu
> Hannibal et magna circumstipante caterua
> **dulcia** praebebat trucibus **spectacula** Poenis

> The Romans' minds were troubled as they did these things. Meanwhile, Hannibal *surveyed* the battlefield and reviewed his savage hand's grim deeds and ran over the combats in his mind's eye. He showed the fierce Carthaginians the *sweet spectacles* as a huge throng of men packed around him.

For Victoria Pagán both texts constitute a standard example of 'an aftermath narrative'.[28] According to her definition, this is the case when a battlefield full of decaying corpses, weapons and debris is inspected by the generals whose responsibility it is to collect and bury the corpses of high-ranking men as well as those of the ordinary soldiers. However, since "this inspection is an intermediate step between the destruction of war and the funeral rites", as Pagán argues, the application of *lustrare* by both poets outside its religious context to signify just the inspection of the battlefield comes in stark contrast to the pollution of the unburied corpses for which both Hannibal and Caesar are considered responsible. In other words, just as Caesar hosted a nefarious banquet amid dead

---

26 See Sil. 10.572–574, 15.383–387~Val. Max. 5.1. ext.6. with McClellan 2019, 243.
27 See Luc. 7.789–794 *cernit propulsa cruore / flumina et excelsos cumulis aequantia colles / corpora, sidentis in tabem spectat aceruos / et Magni numerat populos epulisque paratur / ille locus uoltus ex quo faciesque iacentum / agnoscat*. This obscene feast obviously constituted a grotesque inversion of the Roman custom of the family banquet that was held after the funeral near the ancestral tomb as a means of purification for the community. On the idea of religious actor, see Rüpke in this volume.
28 See also Pagán 2000, 430–439 who adduces several parallels from Roman historiographers (Sallust, Livy, Tacitus) before exploring the same motif in the narrative aftermath of Statius' *Theb.* 12 (also to be discussed here).

Roman soldiers, Hannibal now is provokingly offering the *dulcia...spectacula* (453) of Roman corpses to his soldiers.²⁹ From this point of view, the Cannae aftermath narrative suggests a light version of the ritual *nefas* committed either in Pharsalus or in Saguntum and Trasimene. When Hannibal in the most provocative and perverse way claims the right to conduct and sanction Paulus' burial rites, that must have been a tough read for a Roman (Sil. 10.518–523, 558–569):

'at, cui fortia et hoste
me digna haud paruo caluerunt corda uigore,
funere supremo et tumuli decoretur honore.   520
quantus, Paule, iaces! qui tot mihi milibus **unus**
maior laetitiae causa es. cum fata uocabunt,
tale precor nobis salua Carthagine letum.'

....

**hinc citus ad tumulum donataque funera Paulo
ibat** et hostilis leti iactabat honorem.
sublimem eduxere pyram mollesque uirenti   560
stramine composuere toros. superaddita dona,
funereum decus: expertis inuisus et ensis
et clipeus, terrorque modo atque insigne superbum,
tum laceri, fasces captaeque in Marte secures.
non coniunx natiue aderant, non iuncta propinquo   565
sanguine turba uirum, aut celsis de more feretris
praecedens prisca exsequias decorabat imago,
omnibus exuuiis nudo iamque Hannibal **unus**
sat decoris laudator erat.

[518] "But this man Paulus' heart was brave and worthy to face me as his enemy. It blazed with no little strength. Let him *be acclaimed with a final funeral ceremony and the honour of a tomb*. Paulus, how great you are as you lie in death! *As just one man*, you are a greater cause of happiness for me than so many thousands of dead. When my fate will call me, I pray for such a death for myself while Carthage stands safe." [...]

[558] From there, *he went swiftly to the tomb and the funeral offerings made to Paulus*. He boasted of the honour shown to his enemy in death. His men built the pyre high and made a soft bier from the green grass. In addition, they brought gifts as honour for the dead: a sword hated by those who had met it and a shield. These were once a terror and a proud symbol; now they were shattered. They also brought the fasces and the lictor's axes captured in war. Paulus' wife and children were not there, nor the crowd of relatives closely

---

29 Pagán 2000, 424. See Luc. 7.794–799 *iuuat Emathiam non cernere terram / et lustrare oculis campos sub clade latentes / Fortunam superosque suos in sanguine cernit./ Ac, ne laeta furens scelerum spectacula perdat, / inuidet igne rogi miseris, caeloque nocenti / ingerit Emathiam*. See Littlewood 2017, 200.

connected to him by blood. Nor did the ancestors' ancient wax masks go before his high bier, as was the custom, and give honour to his funeral procession. For Paulus, who had been stripped of all his gear, having Hannibal as his *sole* eulogist was glory enough now."

The erection of a tomb (520, 558) and a pyre (560), the offerings (561), the demised general's weapons brought as gifts (562–563), the fasces and the axes (564) framed by a touching *laudatio funebris* split into two sections (521–523, 572–575) constitute one of the most religious moments in the *Punica* as well as one of the fullest accounts of a funeral ceremony in Roman epic.[30] Even if self-aggrandisement and personal gain is Hannibal's "only real goal" behind these funerals, as most readers believe,[31] in my view there is sheer irony in the fact that the whole ritual is conducted not by a Roman but by Rome's absolute enemy and a conspicuous *contemptor deorum* whom we remember earlier in the epic denying funeral rites for his non-Roman opponents such as the Saguntine Theron.[32] This impression is sustained by Silius' extreme 'subjectification' of the ritual through the emphatic application of the synecdochic *unus* to indicate both Hannibal's and Paulus' 'singularity'/uniqueness in the ceremony. As *milibus unus* (521), Paulus is touchingly singled out not as a 'standard' synecdochic hero like Fabius in *Pun.* 7,[33] but as the synecdochic 'deceased' who receives the funeral rites on behalf of the many thousands of insignificant Roman warriors killed at Cannae. On the other hand, as *unus sat decoris laudator* (568–569), Hannibal does not simply fulfil the role of a kinsman of Paulus by being his sole eulogist but, in essence, is ironically envisaged as a religious actor *par excellence* who outshines or, more literally, outperforms his opponents in terms of religious communication and effect.[34] In *Pun.* 13, when Scipio informs the ghost of the slain Paulus in the Underworld that Hannibal sought to gain glory by erecting a tomb for his dead body, the general's emotional outburst indicates how

---

[30] See further Augoustakis 2017, 308–309.
[31] See Silius' sour comment on Hannibal's similar attempt to seize the praise for burying Gracchus at Sil. 12.478 *laudemque Libys rapiebat humandi* with McClellan 2019, 243, 247.
[32] See Sil. 2.264–269 and see the abuse of the corpse of the Spanish king Tagus by Hasdrubal at Sil. 1.152–154 with McClellan 2019, 245–246.
[33] On the singularity of Fabius (see *Pun.* 7.1, 6–7) but also of Marcellus (*Pun.* 14) and Scipio in *Pun.* 13, 15–17 see Littlewood 2017, 132 who notes in contrast the "catastrophic dualism" of the consuls at Trasimene (*Pun.* 5) and Cannae (*Pun.* 8–10). On Hannibal as a synecdochic hero, see Marks 2005, 79; Stocks 2014, 84.
[34] Augoustakis 2017, 308 notes that, according to Polybius (6.53.1–3), the *laudatio funebris* was usually performed by the son of the deceased or a close relative. On the formal strategies for the successful ritual communication, see Rüpke 2018, 15–21 as well as his paper in this volume.

bitter such an honour might have been for a Roman especially when bestowed by an enemy.³⁵

However, this is neither the only nor the main cause for the readers' dissatisfaction with the Cannae aftermath narrative. In a previous scene, we see Paulus' body recovered by Hannibal's troops amid heaps of abused corpses of other fallen warriors and their weapons (Sil. 10.504–506): *permixta ruina / inter et arma uirum et lacerata cadauera Pauli / eruerant corpus media de strage iacentum* ("amid the men's weapons and torn corpses all mixed together in a heap, they pulled Paulus' body from the middle of the pile of fallen soldiers").³⁶ This disparaging spectacle evokes Flaminius' mock-tomb as another gory compilation of "arms and men" at Sil. 5.658–666, while it substantiates the belief that the Romans and their allies still undergo false rituals. Silius' poignant reference to the absence of Paulus' wife, children and close relatives from his obsequies (10.565–566), and his despair at the fact that there was no funeral procession with wax masks of his ancestors in front (10.566–567) leaves no doubt that the whole ritual is flawed, if not essentially 'unRoman'. A comparison with Lucan's emotional account of Pompey's humble funeral is particularly applicable here. At Luc. 8.728–742 the lack of a funeral procession and the standard rites as well as the absence of his wife Cornelia are counterbalanced by the presence of Cordus, an otherwise unknown Roman soldier who laments at Pompey's grave and is struggling to create a genuine Roman atmosphere in the obsequies he offers in a foreign land in honour of Pompey.³⁷ This spirit is totally absent from Paulus' funeral, as Hannibal is striving to manipulate a Roman ritual both ideologically and politically by transforming it into a self-fashioned spectacle to serve his

---

35 See Sil. 13.714–716 "...*tum tibi defuncto tumulum Sidonius hostis / constituit laudemque tuo quaesiuit honore." / dumque audit lacrimans hostilia funera Paulus, / ante oculos iam Flaminius, iam Gracchus et aegro / absumptus Cannis stabat Seruilius ore*. Not accidentally at all, in the same scene the soul of Paulus is accompanied by the shades of Gracchus and Flaminius who, as already seen, also suffered from Hannibal's 'false rituals'. On these lines, see Augoustakis 2017, 310–315.

36 See McClellan 2019, 251–252.

37 See Mayer 1981, 171. Cf. Luc. 8.729–742 '*Non pretiosa petit cumulato ture sepulchra / Pompeius, Fortuna, tuus, non pinguis ad astra / ut ferat e membris Eoos fumus odores, / ut Romana suum gestent pia colla parentem, / praeferat ut ueteres feralis pompa triumphos, / ut resonent tristi cantu fora, totus ut ignes / proiectis maerens exercitus ambiat armis...Sit satis, o superi, quod non Cornelia fuso / crine iacet subicique facem conplexa maritum / imperat, extremo sed abest a munere busti / infelix coniunx nec adhuc a litore longe est.*' On the funeral rites in the case of a Roman general, see Alexiou 1974, 178–181.

own agenda.³⁸ Ironically enough, the more time the Carthaginian spends in Italy as the war progresses, the *more* Roman he essentially becomes as a religious actor to the constant dissatisfaction of Silius' readers. This sentiment is further substantiated by the funeral rites Hannibal will conduct later in the epic in honour of Gracchus and Marcellus that have been found to underscore not just his humanity but also his assimilation in the Roman culture and landscape after so many years of fighting in Italy.³⁹

To sum up before we move on, Hannibal's false rituals appear to serve much more than his mere self-aggrandisement as Rome's proverbial enemy. The casualties he has inflicted on the Romans and their allies so far in the epic have standardised death as part of his self-fashioned rituals in his obsession to conquer Italy both as a military and as a religious figure. Beyond the extreme subjectification and the high degree of self-referentiality of these rituals, a disconcerting sense of open-endedness is sustained through the relentless threat the Carthaginian poses to the Romans. In fact, with the exception of the Romans' 'ritualised celebrations' in honour of Fabius at the end of Book 7 discussed above, Hannibal's prevalence at least as a ritual 'performer' remains rather unchallenged, unless one gives special credit to Scipio's odd lecture on burial customs to Appius' ghost at Sil. 13.466–487.⁴⁰ Thus, in order to deconstruct the Carthaginian's military and religious predominance in the first half of the epic, the "Scipiad" of Books 13–17⁴¹ must finish with a ritual super-closure, where a Roman protagonist and a radically different type of ritual are featured as a response to Hannibal's hegemonic presence as religious actor so far in the epic.

Undoubtedly, Scipio's triumph furnishes the finest narration of Rome's most iconic, prestigious and self-referential war ritual. At the same time, it affords perhaps the most effective closure in Flavian epic together with a glimpse into a lost reality.⁴² Richard Westall has explicitly illustrated how this event, which normally marked the culmination of warfare, was perceived by the Romans

---

38 Cf. Luc. 4.503–504, where Volteius stages his imminent suicide as a *deuotio* expressing his grudge that his sacrifice will not take place in the presence of family members and relatives: *abscidit nostrae multum fors inuida laudi, / quod non cum senibus capti natisque tenemur*. On his perverse claim, see Hardie 1993, 54. On ritual perversion in Lucan's epic, see McClellan 2019, 115–169.
39 On Hannibal's "eagerness to seize the *laus humandi* with Gracchus' burial at Sil. 12.473–478 and with that of Marcellus at Sil. 15.381–396, see the discussion in Augoustakis 2017, 310–315 who supplies the relevant scholarship.
40 On this puzzling passage, see Augoustakis 2017, 303–304; Van der Keur 2015, 251–259.
41 See Hardie 1993, 97.
42 See Westall 2014, 34.

as a fundamental and enduring public event furnishing any sort of closure, religious, political or literary.[43] In the case of the *Punica*, the narration of a triumphal ritual may further symbolise the literary triumph of the largest of all Roman epics. This metapoetic touch becomes a pivotal one once we turn to the triumphal parade of Scipio at Sil. 17.625–654, which Westall rightly characterises as "the best-preserved example of historical epic that deploys triumph to effect closure".[44]

Silius' account begins with the display of Carthage's wealth, weaponry and elephants (17.618–624) and culminates with a raucous ceremony of prominent captives (Syphax and Hanno), subjugated peoples (the Moors, the Numidians, the Garamantes etc.) and the effigies of all the war's theatres (Carthage, Gades, Calpe, Baetis), mountains (Pyrene) and rivers (Ebro) (17.635–642). Above and beyond these effigies, however, it is the emblematic *imago* of his enemy at war and antagonist in the ritual act that seizes the spectator's attention by alluding to a pseudo-funeral (17.643–644):

> *sed non ulla magis mentesque oculosque tenebat,*
> *quam uisa Hannibalis campis* ***fugientis imago***
>
> But no other *image* attracted more people's minds and eyes than Hannibal's *as he left the field.*

Hannibal, the former religious actor, is now found in the place of a religious object, while his very effigy calls to mind those statuettes featuring in a Roman funeral procession.[45] For all its pejorative overtones and its symbolic import, his *imago* as a *fugiens* in essence denies Scipio the opportunity to outshine the Carthaginian as a ritual actor of triumph and – possibly – as a conductor of his own funeral. This is because, in military and political terms, the capture of the enemy leader was often regarded as the ultimate proof of the end of the war and the pacification of the enemy territory.[46] In the particular case of the Second

---

43 Note for instance the triumphs attributed to Cincinnatus (Liv. 3.26.29), C. Marius (Sall. *Iug.* 114) and Scipio Africanus the Younger (Liv. 30.45) which matters to us the most here. For the examination of triumph as the subject of closure in Graeco-Roman historiography, see Westall 2014.
44 Westall 2014, 36.
45 This idea is further corroborated by Silius' ending to his narrative of the clash at Zama some lines above (Sil. 17.618 *hic finis bello*) which resonates with his closure to Paulus' funeral (*Sil.* 10.305 *hic finis Paulo*).
46 Cf. Vell. Pat. 2.12.1 with Lange 2016a, 39. Quite the opposite, Dio (Zonar. 8.17) picks up the naval triumph of Lutatius Catulus in 241 BC after the Roman victory that marked the end of the

Punic War, the historical fact that Hannibal did survive after Zama was enough to provide Roman historiographers with some conflicting evidence regarding Scipio's very triumph in 206 BC.[47] Thus, whether the Senate had voted for Scipio's triumph or not, any literary representation of it was to a certain extent undermined by a sense of emptiness (inasmuch as you cannot have a 'superb triumph' when your most prominent enemy has escaped death), which in our case may even transform the ritual celebration into a mock funeral. Even more, as the *imago* of *Hannibal fugiens* seizes the spectator's minds and eyes (643 *sed non ulla magis mentesque oculosque tenebat*), Silius' readers are anxiously reminded of Jupiter's commitment to Venus (Sil. 3.572–573 *tenet longumque tenebit / Tarpeias arces sanguis tuus*) that Hannibal will continue to pose a threat to Rome for many years. Overall, if death suggests an indispensable element of the rituals in the *Punica* so far, Hannibal, dead or alive, constitutes the most conspicuous absence from Scipio's triumph.[48] Actually, at the end of the epic Hannibal and Scipio do not even face each other in single combat, as they presumably should have according to the rules of ancient war and especially ancient epic (see e.g. Achilles/Hector and Aeneas/Turnus). Instead, both can claim their own version of "victory" in the war. The whole issue is ultimately not at all irrelevant to Silius' ambiguity concerning Scipio's self-centred and much equivocal portrayal as *securus sceptri* (Sil. 17.627) that appears to undercut the liberating effect of his divinisation and the optimistic associations of his triumph.[49] As is often the case, the political and cultural context of a poet's era, to which we shall now turn, may provide some possible explanations considering what we have traced as mock or false rituals at the end of several books/episodes of warfare in the *Punica* and their unsettling associations.

Silius' emphasis on the permanence of Scipio's power (Sil. 17.625 *mansuri compos decoris*) remains largely undisputed in most scholarly discussions so far. There is good reason for this, as his account of the triumphal procession

---

First Punic War, as an example to emphasise the symbolic capital of triumph as a ritual to end wars. See Lange 2016b, 95.

47 Cf. Polyb. 11.33.7, App. *Hisp.* 38 with Liv. 28.38.4–5, Val. Max. 2.8.5, Dio frag. 57.56; see further Beard 2007, 78; Lange 2016a, 35.

48 This is the case, *mutatis mutandis*, with the final episode of Statius' *Thebaid*, which has been found in the core of some considerably challenging intertextual readings between the two epics. There the panegyrical character of Theseus' triumphal invasion of the city is undermined by the pessimistic overtones of endless mourning of the Theban women. See Pagán 2000, 446–448 and Hardie 1997, 156.

49 See McGuire 1997, 95–103 and, more recently, Dominik 2018, 290–291 whose argument for the unfavourable connotations of the phrase I share.

indeed suggests a clear allusion to Virgil's description of Augustus' triple triumph as the peak moment of Roman history in the ecphrasis of Aeneas' shield at *Aen.* 8.714–728.⁵⁰ The same goes for Scipio's comparison to the triumphant Bacchus and Hercules (Sil. 17.647–650), who are also said to have been rewarded with deification for their service to mankind in Anchises' panegyric of Augustus at *Aen.* 6.801–805.⁵¹ Ultimately, this closural celebration has been thought to nominate Scipio as a proto-princeps (or a proto-autocrat) within the model of gods and heroes, that is, a Republican precursor of an emperor, whether one identifies the latter with Augustus, Vespasian or Domitian.⁵²

Be that as it may, the on-going debate over whether Scipio's parade is packed with pro-Flavian clues or serves quite an anti-monarchical agenda seems rather misleading. After all, in the collective memory of Silius and his readers, triumph was a ritual exclusively limited and linked to the royal house and, as a result, any literary or mythological figure conducting a triumph would be unavoidably envisaged as an emperor and evoke memories of the Principate. More relevant, instead, is the question of what kind of memories these could be among those Romans who, as we shall see, had experienced a kind of 'ritual crisis' in the last years of Nero's reign, the year-long civil war that followed suit until the rise and fall of the Flavian dynasty and its last emperor Domitian.

5 False rituals in the age of Nero

Our study of Silius' various modes of ritual 'binding and release' appears to reflect the common premise that, in ancient Roman culture and ritual, funeral processions and triumphs shared many features as public ceremonies not just of purification, but also of demonstration both of individual and public glory. Recent scholarship has shed light on the monopolisation of the triumph as a medium of negotiating status and prestige within the highly competitive aristocratic

---

50 Cf. Sil. 17.627–628 *repetit per caerula Romam / et patria inuehitur sublimi tecta triumpho* ~ *Aen.* 8.714–715 at *Caesar triplici inuectus Romano triumpho / moenia* with Hardie 1997, 158–159; Westall 2014, 39–40.
51 The triumph of Bacchus serves as a closural motif also in Sil. 7.748–749 discussed above as well as Statius' *Theb.* 12.787–788. See further Hardie 1997, 153–159. On the instability of Bacchus and particularly Hercules as moral exemplars in the *Punica*, see Tipping 2010, 183–184; McGuire 1985, 152–159, 165–167; Roumpou 2019, 392–394.
52 See Fucecchi 1993; Ripoll 1998a, 351–355; Marks 2005, 230–235; Tipping 2010, 211–218; Dominik 2018, 292–293; see also Schroer in this volume.

society of the Republic and, of course, under the Principate.[53] Dio confirms that the transition from the Res Publica to the Empire was marked by major changes especially in the ritual of the triumph.[54] Indeed, Augustus' triple triumph in 29 BCE was a turning point in the history of this ritual as it transformed it into an exclusive prerogative of the court. As we have just seen, however, the literary reflections of this most prestigious of all Roman rituals are also very important, particularly when they incorporate the death element through its own concomitant ritual, the funeral, which was of special political significance to the Romans. In his *Consolatio ad Marciam*, Seneca had aptly captured the symbolic capital these complex social institutions endorsed and shared as tropes of power and prestige by referring to Drusus' funeral as *funus simillimum triumpho* (3.1). On the other hand, Silius' false/mock rituals seem to convey the distorting effect of the political exploitation of such rites, probably as a result of the poet's personal experience after his active involvement in politics. More generally, this was a period when people could hardly tell the difference between sacrilege and triumph, as Seneca again observes in a letter to Lucilius (*Ep.* 87.23–24):

> *nam **sacrilegia minuta puniuntur, magna in triumphis feruntur** [...] nam si, ut dicitis, ob hoc unum sacrilegium malum est, quia multum mali adfert, si remiseris illi supplicia, si **securitatem spoponderis**, ex toto bonum erit. atqui maximum scelerum supplicium in ipsis est.*

> For petty sacrilege is punished, but sacrilege on a grand scale is honoured by a triumphal procession [...] For if, as you object, sacrilege is an evil for the single reason that it brings on much evil, if you but absolve sacrilege of its punishment *and pledge it immunity*, sacrilege will be wholly good. And yet the worst punishment for crime lies in the crime itself.
> (transl. M. Gummere)

Seneca's sardonic perception of triumph as a provocative celebration of an enormous sacrilege was meant to provide the starting point for Mary Beard's now classic study on what she calls "the most lavish of all Roman rituals". For Beard, Seneca here does not merely question the morality of some of Rome's glorious victories against its enemies, but he castigates the extravagance of those lofty parades through the city that displayed "the fruits of sacrilege as the just rewards of imperial conquest".[55] About a century earlier, in the Late Republic, Cicero was very concerned about a similar distorting effect of the funeral orations

---

53 See Lange 2016a, 2016b.
54 Dio (Zonar. 7.21) τοιαῦτα μὲν ἦσαν πάλαι τὰ νικητήρια· αἱ δὲ στάσεις αἵ τε δυναστεῖαι πλεῖστα ἐνεωτέρισαν ἐπ' αὐτοῖς; see further Lange 2016b, 96.
55 Beard 2007, 1–2.

on the records of early Roman history, which often included false triumphs (*Brut.* 62):[56]

> *quamquam his laudationibus historia rerum nostrarum est facta mendosior. Multa enim scripta sunt in eis quae facta non sunt,* **falsi triumphi,** *plures consulatus...*
>
> Yet by these laudatory speeches our history has become quite distorted; for much is set down in them which never occurred, *false triumphs,* too large a number of consulships... (transl. G. Hendrickson)

As already observed, by Silius' time the collective memory of the Republican customs and rituals was lost for good. Obviously, the issue at stake was no longer the authenticity of the *Fasti Triumphales,* that is the official Roman records of triumphs from Romulus' kingship and onwards, but the gradual loss of the symbolic capital triumphs and funerals transmitted as ritual ceremonies and public spectacles. The false rituals examined so far in the *Punica,* some of them exaggerated by the trickeries and the fake religiousness of Rome's utmost enemy, appear to validate not just Fides' grudge against the people's horrific rites in *Pun.* 2, but even Lucan's denunciation of the Romans' unreligious conduct as exemplified in Caesar's neglect of the burial of Romans after Pharsalus (Luc. 9.175–179).[57] Similarly, the fact that Silius puts so much pressure on the prodigies that portended the Roman disaster at Trasimene is perhaps not at all irrelevant with the frequency and intensity of such supernatural phenomena during the last years of Nero's reign and particularly with their attribution by the masses to divine anger and punishment.[58]

Scholars have long pondered on Nero's possible "triumphal" celebrations after the assassination of his mother Agrippina in 59 CE, even if most of them agree that there was no public ovation.[59] On his part, Silius retains and amplifies the unsettling associations between funeral and triumphal imagery in many of his book closures only to mark their open-endedness and perhaps evoke some bad memories in readers who had experienced various ritual travesties under Nero or even Domitian. The former's stagecraft together with its whimsicality may particularly account for the ritual saturation and perversion observed in the closural episodes of the epic as well as for Hannibal's gradual slippage between

---

56 On this passage and similar ones see Lange 2016a, 30–31.
57 See Beard 2007, 36.
58 See Baier 2019, 312.
59 See Dio (Xiph.) 61.15.1; 16.1–4; 17.1; 18.3 and cf. Tac. *Ann.* 14.13 with Champlin 2003, 219–221; Lange 2016b, 100; Goldbeck 2016.

the victor and the victim in the role of religious actor. Some further examples from the *Zeitgeist* of Nero's last days may illustrate this point further.

Dio's account of the journey of the Armenian King Tiridates to Rome in 66 CE provides perhaps the most characteristic case. In an agreement to resolve the enduring Roman – Parthian conflict (58–63 CE) after his defeat by Corbulo's forces, Tiridates was invited to Rome supposedly to supplicate Nero and receive back his crown. According to Dio (63.2.1), however, his journey from Euphrates to Rome ended up in a triumphal procession ὥσπερ ἐν ἐπινικίοις instead of a due declaration of loyalty to the emperor.[60] The historian decries the senate's decision to grant a *triumphus Armeniacus* (see Pliny, *HN* 30.16), and castigates Nero because τὰ ἐπινίκια ἔπεμψε παρὰ τὸ νενομισμένον 'he conducted a triumph contrary to custom' (see Dio. 62.23.4), though there was no defeated enemy as, more or less, was the case with Scipio's triumph and Hannibal. Even more ludicrous and absurd was the emperor's mock triumph in 67 CE for his athletic and artistic victories at the Greek festivals. During the celebration for his return to Rome, the people of the city were astonished to see him riding in the very triumphal chariot that Augustus had used to celebrate his military victories.[61] Dio also reports (63.8) that the captives who constituted a standard part of a triumphal procession were substituted by Nero's defeated actors and music players at the festivals.[62] Once again, the historian mocks Nero, making it plain that the spectacle suggested a clear subversion or parody of a ritual celebration, when compared with the triumphs of Flaminius, Mummius, Agrippa and Augustus.[63] Could it be, therefore, that Nero's theatricality, as exemplified through his 'antitriumphs', is mirrored in Hannibal's self-fashioned rituals and his own self-portrayal as a religious actor in the *Punica*, an epic written by one of the emperor's last consuls? Or, conversely, are we supposed to take Silius' much-disputed account of Scipio's triumph as a moral, political and religious lesson to Nero

---

[60] See Suet. *Ner.* 13; Dio 63.2.1 καὶ ὁ Τιριδάτης ἐς τὴν Ῥώμην, οὐχ ὅτι τοὺς ἑαυτοῦ παῖδας ἀλλὰ καὶ τοὺς τοῦ Οὐολογαίσου τοῦ τε Πακόρου καὶ τοῦ Μονοβάζου ἄγων, ἀνήχθη, καὶ ἐγένετο αὐτῶν πομπὴ διὰ πάσης τῆς ἀπὸ τοῦ Εὐφράτου γῆς ὥσπερ ἐν ἐπινικίοις. For Tacitus' account of the same event, see *Ann*. 15.1–18, 24–31. On a discussion regarding whether this triumph was informal or not, see Griffin 1984, 226–227; Champlin 2003, 221–229; Beard 2007, 269–273; Lange 2016b, 110.

[61] See Suet. *Ner.* 25.1; Dio 63.20.3 with Miller 2000, 417–419; Lange 2016b, 111–112. See also Rüpke's paper in this volume who argues that the use of previously sacralised objects can further enhance the position of ritual actors.

[62] On top of that, a lyre player named Diodorus travelled in the same chariot with the emperor, just as a son of the triumphant general often did in the Republican era; see Beard 2007, 28–29.

[63] See again Dio. 63.8.2 with Lange 2016b, 111.

and his successors on how to conduct a genuine Roman triumph without reducing it to a cultural or artistic show-off?[64] One way or another, the false rituals of the *Punica* might parody the anti-closure/open-endedness of Nero's reign overall. If Tacitus and Suetonius are to be believed, there were many people who fooled others by pretending to be the emperor for almost twenty years after his fall. Suetonius further reports that people decorated his tomb with flowers, produced his statues and his edicts, as if he were still alive and would soon return to destroy his enemies.[65]

That said, we must concede that the Flavian triumphs did not lack their own embarrassing or unflattering moments. If we believe Suetonius (*Vesp.* 12), Vespasian must not have favoured triumphal processions at all, as he is reported to have been much exhausted and annoyed by the slow and tiresome parade during his triumph in 71 CE. As for his son Domitian, whom Silius hails in the course of Jupiter's theodicy as *Germanicus* (Sil. 3.607) for his supposed triumphs over the Chatti (83 CE) and the Dacians (86 CE), it is hard to believe that he was really worthy of such an honorific title (which, of course, evokes Scipio's cognomen *Africanus*).[66] Furthermore, Tacitus' (*Germ.* 37; *Agr.* 39) and Suetonius' (*Dom.* 6.1, 13.3) strong disapproval of Domitian's decision to claim a false triumph questions the sincerity not only of Jupiter's encomium in the *Punica*, but also of Martial's (2.2) and Statius' (*Silu.* 4.2) extravagant eulogies. Domitian's rather fanciful approach to ritual can be further deduced from the macabre banquet he hosted for the senators as part of his triumphal celebrations of 89 CE for his victories mentioned above. During that feast, which was supposed to honour fallen soldiers, Domitian exposed his autocratic sadism to his guests through the total abuse of funerary symbols.[67] Such an event might also have a heightened

---

64 See Edwards 1994, 90–91.
65 See *Hist.* 1.2 *ludibrium falsi Neronis*, 2.8 *Sub idem tempus Achaia atque Asia falso exterritae uelut Nero aduentaret, uario super exitu eius rumore eoque pluribus uiuere eum fingentibus credentibusque. ceterorum casus conatusque in contextu operis dicemus* [...] *multi ad celebritatem nominis erecti rerum nouarum cupidine et odio praesentium*. Suet. *Ner.* 57 *Et tamen non defuerunt qui per longum tempus uernis aestiuisque floribus tumulum eius ornarent ac modo imagines praetextatas in rostris proferrent, modo edicta quasi uiuentis et breui magno inimicorum malo reuersuri* [...] *Denique cum post uiginti annos adulescente me exstitisset condicionis incertae qui se Neronem esse iactaret*. For the impact of the false Neros in Silius' *Punica*, see Roumpou 2022, 278–281.
66 One has only to compare his victories to the far more deserved triumph of his brother Titus after his conquest of Jerusalem in 70 CE. See Joseph. *BJ* 7.121–157; Dio 66.12.1a. On this discussion see further Jacobs 2021, 163–164.
67 See the detailed account of Dio 67.9 and the related discussion in Beard 2007, 257–258. Domitian is reported to have decorated the dining room with black furniture and funeral

impact on Silius' depiction of Hannibal's exploitation of Roman funerary customs as a means of self-aggrandisement or macabre self-indulgence.

In the eyes of Silius, Domitian's own death and funeral might also constitute nothing but a sacrilege. According to Suetonius (*Dom.* 17), after he was assassinated by court officials, Domitian's corpse was carried away on a common bier, and cremated by his nurse Phyllis who mingled his ashes with those of his niece Julia at the Temple of the *gens Flauia*. The total absence of obsequies might even be contrasted to Nero's case, who was buried in the Mausoleum of the Domitii Ahenobarbi (Suet. *Ner.* 49) and retrospectively (and, probably, provocatively) received funeral offerings by Vitellius. According to Suetonius (*Vit.* 11), the ceremony was attended "by a great thong of the official priests", whereas at the accompanying banquet a flute-player was received with applause when he rendered Nero's songs; this enhances the impression that the mock funerals of the *Punica* may point exactly to the devaluation of such rituals in imperial times in comparison to the constructive contribution of these practices to the idea of *Romanitas* in Republican times.

6 Conclusions

To sum up, it is no mere coincidence that the ritual closures of the *Punica* suggest religious reflections rather than real rituals. In other words, when funerals and triumphs do take place in Silius' epic, this is only to confirm that in the poet's era ritual was gradually transformed from a religious ceremony into ritual discourse. While it goes without saying that the Flavian epics also reflect the tendency of many emperors to turn religion into politics,[68] it must be stressed that the agenda of such a discourse, at least on Silius' part, was not limited to the Flavian regime nor did it necessarily or exclusively have an anti-Neronian scope. In her seminal study of on ritual violence and perversion in the *Aeneid*, Vassiliki Panoussi has demonstrated that, although "in Virgil the sacrificial ritual often plays the same positive role that it does in Homer" and Aeneas "repeatedly displays his piety and technical expertise in a number of such occasions

---

lamps, while naked servants painted black emerged from the shadows bringing in gleaming dishes piled with black food. A row of gravestones inscribed with the guests' names was set before the dining couches which resembled those found in mausoleums etc. This was just another incident to showcase that in Silius' time rituals had lost their symbolic value, but humiliation could easily be their main target.

68 Baier 2019, esp. 316.

throughout the poem",⁶⁹ ritual impurity and pollution mark several episodes in order to affirm and justify Augustus' ideological and religious strategies.⁷⁰ Against this background, Silius' Hannibal may aspire to supplant Aeneas in "the sacrificial role of the *princeps* as a symbol of the religious unity of the empire", but the false rituals of the *Punica* are not as "regulated, prescribed and properly sanctioned" as those of the *Aeneid* and, above all, their perversion is not limited to sacrifice.⁷¹ For Valerius Maximus, the burial of Paulus, Gracchus and Marcellus made Hannibal believe that he was, in effect, burying the Republic, since these Romans symbolised 'a vestige of a bygone era'.⁷² In the *Punica*, though, Hannibal's implementation of funerary rituals as well as Scipio's quasi-funeral triumph may not only point to the idea that the first was clearing the path for the latter and the empire, as John Jacobs convincingly argues,⁷³ but also adumbrate an ongoing debate among the Romans about what nominated and eventually constituted a ritual like triumph.⁷⁴ In other words, even if the religious actors of the *Punica* supposedly consent to forms, Silius' readers are nonetheless invited to resist the authority their ritual practices seek to consolidate.⁷⁵ From this aspect, both Hannibal and Scipio fit the imperial discourse either as potential tyrants and proto-emperors or as engaging ritual actors. After all, if funerals shared one thing with triumphs as cultural spectacles and rituals, it was not only their "shifting and potentially controversial boundaries",⁷⁶ but also their staginess.⁷⁷

---

69 Panoussi 2009, 17.
70 See Panoussi 2009, 17–18 and 223–224. Note especially at pp. 20–35 her discussion of Iphigenia's sacrifice, the "preliminary deaths" of Mezentius and Pallas, and Turnus' *deuotio*.
71 Panoussi 2009, 17–18.
72 See Val. Max. 1.6.6 with Jacobs 2021, 138.
73 Jacobs 2021, 138.
74 See Lange 2016b, 112.
75 See Panoussi 2009, 222.
76 See Beard 2007, 270.
77 I am grateful to John Jacobs and Antony Augoustakis for their critical remarks as well as to the volume editor, Angeliki Roumpou, for her helpful comments to my contribution, which substantially improved its final version.

Helen Lovatt
Burning up, Melting down, Collapsing in: Fire Imagery, Narrative Articulation, Funerals, and the Incestuous Poetics of Statius' *Thebaid*

Abstract: This chapter explores fire imagery in Statius' *Thebaid*, its relationship to ritual and narrative articulation. Fire is often involved in Roman ritual, associated with catastrophic destruction alongside purification and release. The *Thebaid*'s complex narrative structure and temporality inspires much recent work (Simms, Chinn); lament and burial have also long shaped the poem's interpretation. I argue that one key tension of the *Thebaid*'s poetics is encapsulated in fire imagery: that between inward-pulling collapse (the burnt-out pyre) and unstoppable destruction and contagion (*urbs capta* and forest fire). These motifs draw on two important structural points in Virgil's *Aeneid*: the burning of Troy and the pyre of Dido, as well as their reworkings in Ovid, Lucan and Valerius Flaccus. This approach relocates the issue of closure in the *Thebaid* from the external *deus ex machina* figure of Theseus to the interior of the poem, focusing on: the contamination of beginnings and endings; the all-consuming pyre and grief for Opheltes; the contagion of Capaneus' fiery destruction; and the battle and lament narratives of book 12, as seen through imagery of fires building up and dying down. The chapter suggests that the incestuous subject matter of Thebes tends to collapse the *Thebaid* in on itself.

1 Introduction

Fire imagery is complex, polyvalent and powerful, and frequently intersects with ritual and contexts of narrative articulation, including closure. Its relationship to the poetics of release and binding is not straightforward, but fire often

---

Many thanks to Angeliki Roumpou for organising the conference and the volume so effectively and warmly, to Laila Dell'Anno for comments on an earlier draft, and to Tommaso Spinelli for sharing a pre-publication draft of his forthcoming book. The classic article by Knox 1950 on fire imagery in *Aeneid* 2 links fire to imagery of both destruction and renewal in the form of the serpent's ability to shed its skin.

https://doi.org/10.1515/9783110770483-009

stands for, or involves, a release of energy or an unbinding of materials or structures. The two central images of this chapter, funeral pyres and fires of destruction as part of *urbs capta* imagery, show fire acting to mark endings, consume material and cleanse pollution. If we take up the challenge posed by Rüpke in this volume, to think of ritual as a resonant event, an act of communication imbued with both risk and potential reward, an event that poses questions as well as offering a sense of emotional belonging, fire intersects in many ways with these ideas about ritual.[1] In the tortuous world of Statius' *Thebaid*, rituals are often problematic, asking questions, as Rüpke observes, and narrative structures rarely work as expected.[2] This paper builds on existing work on funerals, lament, and closure in the *Thebaid* to explore how fire imagery contributes to the complexity of the poem's narrative articulation, ritual scenes and their relationships to the Theban poetics of incest and politics of resistance.[3]

The phrase 'Burn it down' is a controversial gesture in activism.[4] It implies that in order to create meaningful political change it is necessary to radically erase existing structures. Conflagration and arson were also images and realities

---

[1] See Rüpke this volume, esp. page 17.

[2] Ten out of fifteen papers in Augoustakis 2013 focus on the *Thebaid*, with three more comparing it to other Flavian works, and the vast majority focus on the ineffectiveness of both ritual and divine apparatus in the poem, including Tuttle 2013; Hubert 2013; Gibson 2013; Parkes 2013; Dee 2013; Bernstein 2013; Ganiban 2013. In contrast, Bessone 2013 argues that Theseus and the *Ara Clementiae* provide sufficient reconstruction to balance out the negativity elsewhere in the poem. Keith 2013 argues that monstrous hybridity of the monsters at the beginning of the *Thebaid* shape the poetics of the rest of the poem.

[3] A recent flourish of work on Statius gives much to think about: Spinelli (forthcoming) chapter 2 discusses Statius' use of Ovidian conflagration imagery along with flood imagery to energise and problematise his narrative beginning; Chinn 2022 and Econimo 2021 both discuss visuality, with a focus on narrative structure; Agri 2022, 128–159 discusses fear as a structuring and causal element of the *Thebaid*'s psychology; Marinis/Papaioannou 2021 investigate various aspects of tragic narrative in the *Thebaid*; Hulls 2021 reconsiders Oedipus, Theseus and the poetics of the *Thebaid*; Simms 2020 explores the temporality of narrative in the *Thebaid* and shows effectively how the end falls into the beginning; Rebeggiani 2018 looks at Statius' relationship to Neronian culture, including Nero's use of solar imagery; Bessone 2011 argues that the combination of Theseus' clemency and Argia's heroism provide positive closure for the *Thebaid*.

[4] An editorial in *Eidolon* discussed the significance of the phrase; see Zuckerberg/Scullin et al. 2019, April 29. A series of discussions, initiated by Dan-el Padilla Peralta (Poser 2021, Feb. 2), discussed the necessity of making sweeping structural reform in order to move away from the inherent eurocentrism of Classics and its history of being used to support white supremacist ideology. Key interventions included: Hanink 2021, Feb. 11; further discussion and clarification in the detailed blog post by Kennedy/Planudes 2021.

of political unrest in ancient Rome, as Virginia Closs has well explored.[5] Closs argues that the *Aeneid* exploits the imagery of fire in fundamentally ambiguous ways: the epic 'strikes a delicate balance between suggesting the ultimate necessity of violence and destruction to resolve certain conflicts, and insistently exposing the human cost and inherent risks of employing such forces.'[6] Fire imagery in the *Thebaid* has been treated intermittently elsewhere: for instance, Spinelli discusses the Ovidian, cosmic resonances of the Phaethon image for understanding paternal relationships in the *Thebaid*.[7] The centrality of the fire — water dichotomy in Ovid's two destructions of the universe, as beginning and recurring imagery of narrative structure, underscores the Ovidian side of Statius' incestuous poetics.[8] Newlands points out the way that fire divides Atys and Ismene in their central episode of failed love.[9]

This chapter will explore the relationships between fire, ritual and narrative articulation in four sections: the failed or refused funerals that bring the ends of epic into middles and beginnings (anti-funerals); two particular fiery images in the funeral of Opheltes, and their connection to fire out of control and *urbs capta* imagery; the way that Statius' funeral pyres expand into the texts around them, with a case study of Capaneus (ante-funerals); and finally the narrative pattern of battle that begins with burning desire and ends with fire dying down, with a particular focus on book 12. Overall, I argue that one tendency of the *Thebaid* is for the narrative to collapse into its middle, in both parts and wholes, just as the Theban *mythos* always comes back to its origins in the story of Oedipus. Attempts to differentiate, order and control are thwarted by contamination, contagion and excessiveness, and one of the main vectors of these structural effects is the image of fire.

---

[5] Closs 2020, 45–66 on the *Aeneid*; Closs focuses mainly on the Neronian fire of 64 and its reception. For Flavian Rome (141–172), she examines Statius *Siluae* 2.7, Martial's *Epigrams* and the *Octavia*. This leaves a significant gap to explore similar themes in Flavian epic.
[6] Closs 2020, 66.
[7] Spinelli 2021, 104–107 argues that Statius' Jupiter displays a compulsion to repeat intergenerational trauma from previous epic and previous periods of Roman history.
[8] Spinelli (forthcoming) further explores the narrative articulation via Ovidian imagery of destruction by fire and flood in the early books of the *Thebaid*.
[9] Newlands 2016, 150: 'Fire is a powerful image for the transgression of familial bonds social mores.'

2 Anti-funerals: Failed, refused, faked and negated burial and the structure of the *Thebaid*

Achilles' refusal to bury Hector stands for the whole of the destruction caused by the Trojan war. Lucan gives his anti-hero, Pompey, a partial, unsatisfactory burial, which allows him to roam free as a spirit and inspire Cato to perpetuate civil war. Statius does not just 'hammer home' foreshadowings of Creon's refusal of burial to the Argives and Polynices, but he multiplies this failed burial at least sevenfold, as each hero dies and is not sufficiently, promptly or appropriately buried. Parkes lists these 'problematic' or 'perverted' funerals in her discussion of the necromancy of book 4 as a failed or perverted *katabasis*.[10] This section shows how fire imagery, especially images of unreliable ritual, gives these anti-funerals structural significance as images of the working of Statius' epic poetry.

Hypsipyle's fake funeral for her father Thoas combines the two key Virgilian fire tropes of *urbs capta* and Dido's pyre, emphasising the emptiness of ritual in the *Thebaid*. Hypsipyle, as narrator of her own past griefs, and saviour of her father, has long been seen as a version of Aeneas. She also matches Dido in other aspects, as queen welcoming the Argonauts. This sometimes operates in paradoxical ways, such as when the Lemnian women swear an oath to bind each other to their plan and seal it with human sacrifice of a child, evoking imagery of witchcraft, such as Dido uses as cover for her suicide (*Theb.* 5.152–163). This ritual avoids fire, focusing rather on blood and darkness. Hypsipyle represents herself as terrified by it, and compares herself to a deer pursued by wolves (5.165–169), also suggesting Dido, but Dido as victim of Venus and, inadvertently, Aeneas (*Aen.* 4.68–73).[11] Hypsipyle's smuggling of Thoas out of Lemnos particularly evokes Aeneas' rescue of Anchises (*Theb.* 236–264). Bacchus provides them with a path of flame as they leave (*mitis iter longae claruit limite flammae*, 'the gentle god brightened the way with a path of long flame', *Theb.* 5.286), in contrast to Aeneas who creeps through darkness, and is shocked into running by Anchises' sight of 'burning shields and flashing

---

10 Parkes 2013, 167–168. For Parkes, only the final burials at the very end of the poem are unproblematic.
11 There is a slight verbal echo, with the repetition of *cerua* in the same metrical location at *Theb.* 5.165 (*Aen.* 4.69). On Hypsipyle as unreliable narrator and doublet of both Dido and Aeneas, see Nugent 1996, with 61–62 on the oath and Hypsipyle's agency; 64 on *urbs capta* and repetitions of *Aen.* 2.

bronze' (*ardentis clipeos atque aera micantia*, *Aen.* 2.734). The light of dawn brings realisation and horror for the Lemnian women, leading to shame-faced, half-hearted funerals (*festinis ignibus urunt*, 'they burn in hurried fire', *Theb.* 5.301). In Hypsipyle's description of the bereaved city, it becomes an *urbs capta* without fire, but drenched in blood.

Hypsipyle builds her fake pyre in the innermost recesses of the palace (5.313), burns emblems for and belongings of Thoas, allowing a bloodied sword to stand in for a real killing, and prays to turn away the omen of this ritual from her father. So Dido builds a pyre supposedly intended to burn her memories of Aeneas (4.639–640), in the inner part of the house, transgressively (*interiora domus inrumpit limina*, 'she breaks through the inner thresholds into the house', *Aen.* 4.645), carries Aeneas' abandoned sword (646–647) and burns *exuuiae* ('spoils/reminders', 651). Dido's pyre stands as a synecdochic image for the ultimate destruction of Carthage by Roman forces, a mirror image of the destruction of Troy, and forms one of the ending points of the tetradic structure of the *Aeneid*, in apposition to the flaming figure of Augustus/Apollo watching the triumph on the shield of Aeneas at the end of book 8, and the soul of Turnus sent into the cold by *feruidus* ('burning', 'boiling', *Aen.* 12.951) Aeneas.[12] The importance of fire imagery in the Lemnian episode may partly relate to the island's sacred connection with Hephaestus/Vulcan. The myth of the Lemnian women has also been associated with a ritual in which new fire returns to the island, marking a new beginning.[13] Hypsipyle's fake funeral, too, articulates the epyllion of *Thebaid* 5, as Heslin has shown, in a way that is fundamentally different from Dido.[14] The fire cleanses her of responsibility in the eyes of the other Lemnians, and moves her from imitating Aeneas (as Valerius presents her heroism) to imitating Dido.

Heslin argues that Statius' Hypsipyle epyllion is fundamentally a rebuke to Valerius' *Argonautica* for not being innovative enough, and that it takes Virgil's revivifying of the sack of Troy and interweaves it with Catullus' encapsulation of both Argo, Theseus and the Troy narrative in poem 64.[15] 'Statius takes the Argo-

---

12 The complex intertextual relationship with Valerius' Lemnian episode can also be illuminated through the mutual reflections of fire imagery. For instance, there are multiple resonances of Valerius' Cyzicus episode, and both texts play with the limits of Apollonius' Lemnian episode, and how Apollonius covers up the Lemnian crime. On the relationship between the two episodes, see Clare 2004 and Gibson 2004. On the Argonaut myth and Statius, see Parkes 2009; 2014a; 2014b.
13 The classic article is Burkert 1970.
14 See Heslin 2018, 108.
15 See Heslin 2018, 118–120.

story, the *Thebaid*'s rival as the standard topic for collective epic at Rome, and turns it inside out'.¹⁶ Hypsipyle's pyre plays with interiority differently: in the heart of the story, the wood between the worlds, the innermost palace, is an absence, an empty pyre. Where Dido's pyre should not contain a body, but does, Hypsipyle's should contain a body, but does not. Where Valerius turns her into a hero, Statius makes her fundamentally unstable. The absence of Thoas' body casts Hypsipyle as innocent for the Argives, but guilty for the Lemnians, in breaking their oath. The fake ritual calls into question her subsequent narratives. The episode combines the pyre of Dido and the burning of Troy to focus in on intrafamilial violence, unreliable ritual and unresolvable interpretation. Like the wider *Thebaid*, the Lemnian epyllion threatens to collapse in on itself.¹⁷

The young hero Atys is brought dying into Thebes, so that he can violate his betrothed with death in marriage, but she only gets to close his eyes, not enact a ritual cleansing. In Ismene's dream, the transition to marriage becomes instead a transition to death: *subitusque intercidit ignis* ('A sudden fire split us apart', 8.631). The fire blurs the boundaries between the different rituals (wedding, funeral) and seems almost to blur the boundary between dream and reality: *turbata repente omnia*, ('suddenly all was upturned' 630–631) in the dream, becomes *subito cum pigra tumultu / expauit domus* ('when the sluggish house panicked with sudden turbulence', 646–647).¹⁸

The Parthenopaeus episode of book 9 begins with ritual which evokes death, based in water, but referring also to fire, and ends with a substitute and incomplete death ritual. Atalanta dreams primarily of tree destruction, especially

---

16 Heslin 2018, 120.

17 The incestuous elements are less prominent, although her emotional reunion after many years, with her sons, who she thought might be dead, does perhaps evoke Jocasta's reunion with Oedipus, and the confusion of family relationships is certainly seen in her usurpation of motherhood from Eurydice. Laila Dell'Anno (pers. comm.) points out that the potential echo in *Thoantis* (5.650) of the corpse she should have carried (that of Thoas) evokes the Lemnian slaughter, and its connection to the *Iliad*'s emphasis on her son Thoas (*Il.* 5.650–652) so that the replication and interweaving go beyond the *Thebaid* to pull in Trojan myth and *Argonautica* as well.

18 Laila Dell'Anno points out (pers. comm.) that there is a similar blurring between sleep and death at the moment of Opheltes' death 5.539–540: *fugit ilicet artus / somnus et in solam patuerunt lumina mortem* ('sleep flees suddenly from his limbs, and his eyes lie open only in death'). The fire imagery is incorporated through the snake, which has fiery eyes, poison and burns the grass (5.508 *liuida fax oculis*, 'livid flame in the eyes'; 5.522 *sicci nocens furit igne ueneni* 'it rages, harmful with the fire of its dry poison'; 5.527 *percussae calidis afflatibus herbae*, 'the turf struck dead by heated exhalations'). The connection between snakes and fire imagery is well-established; see Knox 1950.

her trophy-tree, but also of 'well-known images and likenesses of herself burnt up' (*effigiesque suas simulacraque nota cremari*, *Theb.* 9.582). At 9.887 Parthenopaeus himself refers back to Atalanta's dream, as if it were happening simultaneously, creating ring composition through self-aware characters. He sends her a lock of hair to burn instead of himself. His final instruction to Atalanta is as follows: 'But these weapons, unfortunate in their first campaign, burn them or hang them up as an accusation to ungrateful Diana' (*haec autem primis arma infelicia castris / **ure**, uel ingratae crimen suspende Dianae.*' *Theb.* 9.906–907). Just as Amphiaraus fails in his *katabasis*, and Parkes emphasises the importance of the semi-permeable boundary between the underworld and the world of the living in the *Thebaid*, so Parthenopaeus fails in his transition to manhood, the incomplete initiation matching the incomplete burial.[19] These few examples show how funeral ritual, and other rituals associated with fire (often alongside or in apposition to water), do not provide secure transition, in spatial, temporal, spiritual or narrative terms in Statius' *Thebaid*. The collapse of the battlefield itself at the transition between books 7 and 8, the intrusion of war into domestic space in the Atys and Ismene episode, and the failed cleansing of Atalanta, which forms a ring with Parthenopaeus' imagined funeral as he dies, all push towards simultaneity, the collapse inwards of narrative structure itself.

3 It's over before it's begun: incestuous poetics and the funeral of Opheltes

The funeral of the baby Opheltes in *Thebaid* 6 encapsulates beginning, middle and end, exemplifying the way that Statius' *Thebaid* falls into itself, just as the relationships of the Theban royal family are pushed too close and confused with each other through incest. The proem of the *Thebaid* begins with *fraternas acies* ('brotherly battle-lines', *Theb.* 1.1) inspired by the fire of the Muses (*Pierius menti calor incidit*, 'the Pierian heat falls on my mind', *Theb.* 1.3), and Statius outlines his project in this way: *limes mihi carminis esto / Oedipodae confusa domus* ('let the boundary of my song be the mixed-up house of Oedipus', *Theb.* 1.17). The Nemean episode has for a while now been seen as emblematic of the *Thebaid*'s poetics: by looking at this again through fire, ritual and narrative articulation, we can see in further detail how this works.[20] In the middle of the poem, Statius

---

19 Parkes 2013, 174.
20 Brown 1994; Soerink 2014.

draws on imagery of both opening and closing, so that we are encouraged to read every part of the poem as simultaneously beginning, middle and end.[21] The opening lines of book 6 emphasise the funeral and games as emblems and initiations of war, through imagery of sweat and fire: *quo Martia bellis / praesudare paret seseque accendere uirtus* ('through which martial virtue prepares to foresweat and sets itself alight', *Theb.* 6.3–4).[22] Where the *Iliad*'s funeral of Patroclus and games in book 23 fashion the end of the poem as substitute for the end of the war, and the funeral as funeral for Achilles, the funeral of Opheltes, also known as Archemorus ('beginning of grief'), stands in for the funerals of all the war dead, ending the war before it is begun.

The description of Opheltes' pyre and its building begins with a reminder that all of this will be burnt: *tristibus interea ramis teneraque cupresso / damnatus flammae torus et puerile feretrum / texitur* ('Meanwhile the couch condemned to the flame and the boyish bier are woven from sad branches and tender cypress', *Theb.* 6.54–56); decorated with *floribus morituris* ('flowers about to die', 58), the pyre building is described in exhaustive detail, recreating the ritual of building it. *Muneraque in cineres* ('gifts for ashes', 73) emphasise the conspicuous destruction of wealth and resources. The Argive army build the pyre as atonement both for the death of Opheltes and the killing of the sacred snake that caused his death, as an attempt to ward off their own imminent destruction: *cumulare pyram, quae crimina caesi / anguis et infausti cremet atra piacula belli* ('heap up the pyre, to burn up the crime of the slaughtered snake and the black offerings for an ill-omened war', *Theb.* 6.86–87). The building of the pyre itself threatens to be another act of sacrilege, giving previously untouched trees (93–95) as 'food for final flames' (100 *flammis alimenta supremis*). The Argive army also participate in the funeral rituals, not just cutting down the grove to build the pyre, and marching around it (*stantes inclinant puluere flammas*, 'they sway the standing flames with their dust', *Theb.* 6.216), circling three times, and crashing their weapons four times, beating their shields four times, but also adding their own items to the flames, as if attempting to avert their own inevitable deaths, or pre-mourning their own deaths.

Their own priest, presumably Amphiaraus, sets up an alternative, competing or additional fire to read omens for the war (*Theb.* 6.220–226):

---

[21] The idea of foreshadowing runs throughout the work of Vessey: Vessey 1970a; 1970b; 1973.
[22] On games as microcosm of the poem, see Lovatt 2005.

> semianimas alter pecudes spirantiaque ignis
> accipit armenta; hic luctus abolere nouique
> funeris auspicium uates, quamquam omina sentit
> uera, iubet: dextri gyro et uibrantibus hastis
> hac redeunt, raptumque suis libamen ab armis
> quisquis iacit, seu frena libet seu cingula flammis
> mergere seu iaculum summae seu cassidis umbram.

> Another fire receives half-dead herd animals and breathing
> Cattle; this the prophet orders to erase grief and omen
> Of fresh death, although he recognises the omens
> As true: they return in a right-hand circle past this one,
> Brandishing spears, and each man throws an offering seized
> From his own weapons, whether he offers reins, or a belt to the flames,
> Or whether he chooses to sink a javelin or the shade of his high helm.

The funeral pyre of Opheltes leads to another fire, which itself foreshadows further pyres. The sacrificial offerings of their own *exuuiae* (reminders of themselves) put the Argives in a liminal state between life and death. The two rituals become one, with the men marching fluidly from one circle into another, from clashing their weapons to brandishing them, the repeated *seu* clauses emphasising the deliberate repeated actions aimed at deflecting the ill omen that they are creating.

The excessiveness of all aspects of this funeral makes it a potentially dangerous ritual rather than a protective rite. The Argives stand guard around the flames partly to stop the excessive grief of the parents from leading to their suicide (6.202–203):

> iam face subiecta primis in frondibus ignis
> exclamat; labor insanos arcere parentes.

> Now the torch has crept up and fire shouts out
> from the first leaves; it is hard work to keep back the maddened parents.

The fire is personified while the humans require additional effort, as if keeping them from loading themselves as further fuel for the flames; their cries of grief are matched by the noise of the flames. Their excessive grief is further layered on in the gross consumption of wealth in the flames: *ditantur flammae; non umquam opulentior illis / ante cinis:* ('the flames are enriched; not ever before was anything more luxurious than those ashes', 206–207). The 'crackling' of fire (*crepitant*) becomes the cracking of gemstones; the flames flow in liquid silver (*liquescit / argentum*), brought out by the enjambement. Instead of clothes absorbing sweat from their human wearers, these clothes sweat gold. The fuel is made fat (*pinguescunt*) with exotic, expensive incense, and the whole becomes a bizarre banquet, moving from incense to honey and saffron, to wine, blood and milk.

Fire also features in the imagery used to describe this excessiveness.[23] Two striking similes emphasise the dangerous tendency of fire to grow out of control, destroying landscapes both natural and human. The Argive destruction of the wooded landscape to build the pyre is first compared to a forest fire and then to a captured city (*Theb.* 6.107–117):

> *dat gemitum tellus: non sic euersa feruntur*
> *Ismara cum fracto Boreas caput extulit antro,*
> *non grassante Noto citius nocturna peregit*
> *flamma nemus. linquunt flentes dilecta locorum*
> *otia cana Pales Siluanaque arbiter umbrae*
> *semideumque pecus, migrantibus aggemit illis*
> *silua, nec amplexae dimittunt robora Nymphae.*
> *ut cum possessas auidis uictoribus arces*
> *dux raptare dedit, uix signa audita, nec urbem*
> *inuenias; ducunt sternuntque abiguntque feruntque*
> *inmodici, minor ille fragor quo bella gerebant.*

> The land gives a groan: not so much is overturned Ismara
> Carried away when Boreas raises his head from his broken cave,
> Not more quickly with the South wind rioting does nocturnal flame
> Drive through the grove. Pales and Silvanus, judge of the shade,
> and the half-god herd, weeping, leave the places chosen
> for long-aged leisure, the woodland heaps up groans as they
> move on, nor do the Nymphs' embraces let go the oaks.
> As when a leader gives captured citadels to greedy victors
> To snatch, scarcely when the sign is heard, you would find
> No city left; they take, they raze, they drive away, they carry off
> Immoderate; that crash itself is less, with which they waged the war.

The destruction and desolation caused by the tree-felling in order to build the pyres is as complete as that caused by natural destruction (storm and forest fire, the Ovidian cosmic duo of water and fire, again) and the devastation of war (the looting of a city). This reverses *Aeneid* 2, in which the gods' destruction of Troy is compared to farmers felling an ancient ash tree (624–631). The multiple images of destruction contaminate each other and escalate in volume and intensity. The

---

[23] On the structural importance and complexity of Statius' visual imagery, see Chinn 2022, for instance 48–52 on Statius' retreating gaze and the visual sequencing of the prologue to catalogue in *Thebaid* 4. On ekphrasis in the *Thebaid*, see also Econimo 2021.

uprooted trees implicit in the storm simile make perfect sense given the context of tree-felling: this develops naturally into the forest fire image, since lightning strikes can cause wildfires, which are spread by the same strong winds (this time warm instead of cold). The misery of the woodland gods evicted from their territory and destroyed by the trees' destruction combines with the storm and fire imagery to evoke the people of a captured city. The completeness of destruction is emphasised by the very plain *nec urbem* ('no city') last in the line (115), and the string of third person verbs highlights the responsibility of the fighters for the destruction, while the enormous crash circles back towards the thunder of the starting imagery. Where epic similes usually compare human situations and actions to the natural world, here Statius reverses the flow, by comparing storm to war, and thus returning to the original comparison in which the Argive army are responsible for destroying the landscape. The images grow out of control, multiplying, contaminating each other, building energy and leading back to their own origin, all nevertheless focusing on the speed and completeness of destruction. The energy generated by the fiery clearance meta-poetically anticipates the re-starting of the epic narrative in book 7, just as Ovid's Phaethontic firestorm recapitulates the initiatory power of Virgil's sea storm.[24] However, the immensity of the funeral also foreshadows the total destruction of both Thebes and the Argive army, and the ritual fire blows out of control into the complete destruction of wildfire and the *urbs capta*.

The incommensurability of grief is at the root of the excessiveness and uncontainability of Opheltes' funeral. Despite, or because of, his tiny size, his loss is immeasurably awful for his parents and for the Argive army, for whom he represents their own deaths as well as the whole destructive war. It is impossible for the ritual to measure up. The ability of ritual to confer significance through social participation leads to a forest fire of grief, that spreads and contaminates. Opheltes' death stands in for, foreshadows, echoes and causes the deaths to come, encompassing the entire war in his miniature frame.

---

24 On Ovid's flood and fire as structuring the opening books of the *Thebaid*, see Spinelli (forthcoming).

4 Ante-funerals: untimeliness, narrative articulation, fire and weird ritual

'Foreshadowing' is a well-established aspect of Statius' Theban narrative. Andrew McClellan refers to the frequent proleptic reference to Creon's refusal of burial to the Argives as 'bludgeoning narrative anticipation'.[25] McClellan also shows how funeral rites are often evoked in imagery well beyond the bounds of the ritual itself, showing how Statius' poetry has a tendency to blur one aspect into another, collapsing narrative units together.[26] An example of this is the cremation of Capaneus. As we approach his climactic *aristeia*, imagery of thunderbolts and fire in the veins contaminate other situations and characters. Menoeceus in particular functions as an *alter ego* of Capaneus, his virtuous twin.[27]

The death of Capaneus is a clear articulating moment: the hero climbs the walls, threatening to use Jupiter's thunderbolt to renew his attack and relight his torch: *'his' ait 'in Thebas, his iam decet ignibus uti, / hinc renouare faces lassamque accendere quercum'* ('These', he said, 'against Thebes, these fires, now, ought to be used, I ought to renew my torch here and light up my exhausted oak.' *Theb.* 10.925–926). The narrative pauses on his burning body (*ardenti corpore*, 931), moving down from crest to shield to limbs. The men below are terrified by his fiery body, and the book finishes on the thought that he almost needed a second thunderbolt (*potuit fulmen sperare secundum*, 'he could have hoped for a second thunderbolt', 939). His falling body bridges the gap into the next book, where the thunderbolt is still consuming him, and he is still breathing his last and falling terrifyingly towards the earth (*Theb.* 11.1–4). The imagery of marking the walls (*signauit muros ultricis semita flammae*, 'he marked the walls with a path of avenging flame', 4), fragmenting the city (*lacerae complexus fragmina turris*, 'embracing pieces of torn-up tower', 9) and contaminating the fields (*hostiliaque urit / arua et anhelantem caelesti sulphure campum*, 'he burns the hostile fields and the gasping plain with heavenly sulphur', 16–17)

---

[25] McClellan 2019, 203. 'Statius, as narrator or through the voices of his characters, repeatedly refers to Creon's looming ban to the point of obsession'; McClellan 2019, 204.

[26] McClellan 2019, 215–220 discusses the anti-funerals as anticipations of Creon's refusal of burial. But this is to limit the temporal and thematic play and point it towards a culmination in the figures of Creon and Theseus that underestimates the way the *Thebaid* blurs both backwards and forwards.

[27] On Menoeceus as Capaneus' double, see Heinrich 1999, 186.

emphasises collapse.²⁸ The dizzying play of perspectives is multiplied by the similes, which compare his dead body first to Enceladus, happily viewed by the gods, pressed down by Aetna, exhausted after the gigantomachic battle at Phlegra (11.7–8), and second to Tityos, tortured by vultures tearing his innards, who themselves are horrified by the scale of his body as they emerge (11.12–15). The fire becomes both the cosmic destruction of a volcano and the internal fire of pain.²⁹ In a typically Statian inversion, the fields of Thebes are buried by Capaneus, rather than Capaneus being buried by the fields of Thebes.³⁰

Throughout book 10, characters are frequently hit by metaphorical thunderbolts, anticipating the fiery destruction of Capaneus, showing how the fire of his death contaminates the wider narrative. Menoeceus is described with a powerful thunderbolt image as Virtus inspires him to commit suicide by throwing himself off the walls of Thebes (*Theb.* 10.674–675):

fulminis haud citius radiis afflata cupressus
combibit infestas et stirpe et uertice flammas

No more quickly does a cypress, blown away by rays of a thunderbolt,
Drink up the hostile flames to both root and to peak

The swiftness of the flames is compared to the movement of light by the image of rays, and to forest fire blown by wind in the participle *afflata*, while *combibit* combines imagery of drinking and the integration of bodily functions. The roots and peak of the tree evoke the completeness of Menoeceus' possession by divine powers, while the hostile flames enclose the tree from tip to tip.³¹ The concluding phrase of the inspiration scene, as Menoeceus internalises the praise of those

---

28 See Sacerdoti 2018, 174–176 on the language of collapse, in relation to Statius' treatment of the eruption of Vesuvius.
29 On the potential importance of Vesuvius in Statius' poetics of trauma and renewal, see Sacerdoti 2018.
30 There is a clear connection to the figure of Prometheus in Valerius' *Argonautica*, the positive *exemplum* of Jupiter's mercy exercised by Hercules on his way to apotheosis. In a future article, I will discuss the deep and complex relationship between *Thebaid* and Valerius' *Argonautica* further.
31 The close relationship between fire and water imagery extends the contagion of Statius' poetics still further: in a sense it is arbitrary to attempt to separate out the fire elements of Statius' chemistry of destruction, and liquid imagery is also important in ritual contexts and at limits/moments of narrative articulation, purification and closure (rivers, blood), but this chapter does not have space to fully immerse itself in the interconnection of different elemental imagery. The Lucretian play of *ignis* and *lignis* makes a strong case for starting with fire in atomising poetic elements.

around him to solidify his suicidal determination, comes back to fire: *ignibus implet honestis* ('fills him with honourable fires', *Theb.* 10.685). It is as if Statius attempts to control the contagion of fire imagery with the adjective *honestis*, emphasising the respectability of Menoeceus' self-destructive impulse. The effect of the paradoxical valorisation is equally to ironise Menoeceus' desire for glory. Menoeceus and Capaneus contaminate each other, creating admirable villains and appalling heroes, so that both sides of the battle collapse together.

Earlier in book 10, thunderbolt imagery thematises revelation, involving viewers and readers in the *Thebaid*'s complex of fiery intoxication. Creon is hit by the realisation that Menoeceus is the subject of Tiresias' prophecy at 10.618 (*grandem subiti cum fulminis ictum*, 'hit by the great blow of a sudden thunderbolt'), joining in proleptically with the divine destruction of his son, which will then lead to his own killing by Theseus. Similarly, the Theban Amphion prefigures the futility of achievement in Statius' Theban war, as with Capaneus and Menoeceus, when he realises that his capture and killing of Hopleus and Dymas does not measure up to the wider destruction caused by the night raid (*Theb.* 10.467–472):

> *non longum caede recenti*
> *laetatus uidet innumeris feruere cateruis*
> *tellurem atque una gentem expirare ruina.*
> *qui tremor inicitur caeli de lampade tactis,*   470
> *hic fixit iuuenem, pariterque horrore sub uno*
> *uox, acies sanguisque perit*

> Not long did he rejoice at the fresh slaughter,
> He sees the earth boiling with innumberable squadrons
> And a whole people gasping their last in one destruction.
> A trembling falls on him, like those touched by light from the sky,
> Now it nails the young man, and his voice fails, equally under
> One shuddering, with his gaze and blood

This doubled moment of realisation, in which the Argive victory is compromised by the loss of Hopleus and Dymas, and the Theban success in killing Hopleus and Dymas is dwarfed by the mass slaughter of the night raid, forms the closural moment of this episode.[32] It emphasises the balanced contagious nature of mutual destruction, and replicates the overall structure of the war, in which initial Theban victory is doubled by Theban defeat at the hands of Theseus. The transition between Menoeceus' suicide and Capaneus' *aristeia* focuses on the

---

[32] On the importance of tragic *anagnorisis* in Flavian epic, see Cowan 2021.

lament of Eurydice, mother of Menoeceus, who connects the disorder of incest with the untimeliness of Menoeceus' death (10.796–797; 10.809–810):

> *non ego monstrifero coitu reuoluta nouaui*
> *pignora...*
>   *sponte en ultroque peremptus*
> *inrumpis maestas Fatis nolentibus umbras.*

> I did not renew in monster-bearing miscegenation
> pledges returning back ...
>   see, of your own accord, and destroyed by your wish
> you break in to the sad shades with the Fates unwilling.

Menoeceus in Eurydice's lament is both similar to and different from Polynices and Eteocles, out of time and out of place, disturbing the order of things. His death is against fate, like that of Dido, disruptive like that of Amphiaraus.

After Capaneus' death, fire, ritual and untimeliness are combined in the portrayal of Eteocles' attempt to propitiate Jupiter in gratitude for the thunderbolt (acting as transitional motif between the activities of the two Furies and the two brothers). As soon as Eteocles finishes his prayer, the fire embodies the destruction and violation of underworld powers in the *Thebaid* (11.226–227):

> *dixerat: ast illi niger ignis in ora genasque*
> *prosiluit raptumque comis diadema cremauit.*

> He had spoken: but black fire jumped forward into his face
> And cheeks, snatched and burnt the diadem from his hair.

Eteocles continues the disrupted ritual, like Hercules dying on Mount Oeta (11.234–238):

> *qualis ubi implicitum Tirynthius ossibus ignem*
> *sensit et Oetaeas membris accedere uestes,*
> *uota incepta tamen libataque tura ferebat*
> *durus adhuc patiensque mali; mox grande coactus*
> *ingemuit, uictorque furit per uiscera Nessus.*

> Just as when the Tirynthian feels the fire woven inside
> His bones and accepted the Oetean robes on his limbs,
> Nevertheless he continues the initiated prayers, the incense offered,
> Hard still and suffering pain; soon forced by greater pain
> He groaned, and Nessus rages victorious through his entrails.

The messenger emphasises untimeliness as he interrupts (11.242–243):

> '*rumpe pios cultus intempestiuaque, rector,*
> *sacra deum:*'

> 'Break dutiful worship, ruler, and untimely
> Rites of the gods:'

Eteocles is attempting to close the Capaneus episode, to shape the interpretation as favourable to his own cause, thinking that he is communicating with Jupiter, but his ritual is diverted by Tisiphone to Dis, and he is actually beginning the next battle, inevitably leading to his own journey downwards to Hades in contrast to Hercules' apotheosis. The fire in the bones continues imagery from Capaneus' death, and Eteocles' interrupted rites are broken like the course of Menoeceus' life. Imagery of contamination, matter and practice out of place and time, is combined with the intensity and uncontrollable nature of fire.

Capaneus' death therefore echoes backwards and forwards in the text, the climactic Argive *aristeia*, infecting other moments, often themselves transitional between scenes and characters, with the fire of divine destruction. This one example of the impressionistic blurring of Statius' poetry is particularly focused on fire, but it also brings out the way that untimeliness, or temporal disturbance, is one important characteristic of Statius' problematic rituals, denying them the power to bring closure and cohesion.

5 Burning up and dying down: books 10–12

The imagery of desire for fighting (and its waning) associates fire with narrative articulation.[33] At the beginnings of episodes and undertakings, Statius' fighters light up. For instance, as Capaneus finally gets into his *aristeia*, he is fiery and contaminated by fire (*Theb.* 10.842–844):

> *longeque timendus*
> *multifidam quercum flagranti lumine uibrat;*
> *arma rubent una clipeoque incenditur ignis.*

---

33 Hershkowitz 1994 shows how Statian narrative uses imagery of sexual arousal, climax and exhaustion to convey the waves of intensity and boredom that characterise the narrative of the *Thebaid*. This chapter argues that fire imagery matches and mixes in with those patterns, becoming part of the *Theban* complex of misdirected energy and fertility.

> Terrifying from afar
> He brandishes a many-forked oak blazing with light;
> His weapons grow red along with his shield fire is lit up.

The relationships between words in 844 blurs in the process of reading: we cannot tell clearly whether the arms and the shield are together, or Capaneus and the flame, or whether Capaneus will be the subject of *incenditur*, but then *ignis* turns up to bring it all together. This evokes the way fire spreads and takes over. Fire here acts as an image both for poetic intensity and inspiration, as well as battlefield violence and madness. The multiple nature of the torch, and its widespread terror-inducing effects, thematise the workings of Statian poetry and narrative.

It is not just Capaneus, with his fiery end, who embodies the poetics of fire. Similar imagery of burning to fight occurs at the beginning of other *aristeia* episodes: the transition back to the battlefield after Diana makes Parthenopaeus inviolable: *tunc uero exserto circumuolat igneus arcu, / nec se mente regit* ('then indeed he flies around fiery with his bow, nor does his mind control him, 9.736–737); after Thiodamas' speech, the Argives burn to join him (*talia uociferans noctem exturbat, euntque / non secus accensi proceres quam si omnibus idem / corde deus: flagrant comitare et iungere casus*, 'uttering such things, he threw the night into confusion, and they go afire no differently than if the god were the same for all in their hearts: they burn to accompany him and join the chance', 10.219–221); in the transition to Capaneus' *aristeia*, Adrastus and Polynices encourage the Argives (*sic ait; ardentes alacer succendit Adrastus / Argolicusque gener*, 'So he spoke; keen Adrastus and his Argive son-in-law lit up the burning men', 10.487–488). One fire word might be unremarkable, but *igneus* is strong, and the imagery of flying around (*circumuolat*) also evokes wildfire. In the other examples, Statius doubles and reinforces the fire imagery.

Creon's encounter with Eteocles, part of the sequence playing with delay and intense haste in book 11, in which he urges him into the fratricidal battle, forms a bridge between book 10 and 12, and continues the density of fire imagery.[34] Creon's grief for Menoeceus causes him to push Eteocles into battle and is presented in repeatedly fiery terms. He arrives burning: *sed ardens / ecce aderat luctu* ('but burning in grief, look, he was present', 11.262–263); Menoeceus burns him: *urit fera corda Menoeceus* ('Menoeceus burns his wild heart', 264); Creon accuses Eteocles of being like a plague from heaven, combining imagery of

---

34 On the theme of *mora* (delay) in the *Thebaid* and the way that book 12 speeds up the narrative and produces a compressed recapitulation of *Aeneid* 12, see Gervais 2017b.

plague-bearing star, thunderbolt and contagion: *urbem ... ceu caelo deiecta lues inimicaue tellus / hausisti* ('you have drained the city ... like a plague sent down from the sky or a hostile land', 273–275); he intensifies the accusation by focusing on the unburied Thebans: *hos ignis egentes / fert humus*, ('the ground bears these [Thebans] lacking fire', 276–277); he finishes the goading speech by describing Polynices as burning to kill him: *in te ardens frater* ('your brother burning against you', 295); finally Creon's wrath is boiling: *miseraque exaestuat ira* ('he boils over with wretched anger', 297). All this fire imagery leads up to a key snake image, in which Eteocles holds back his violent impulse against Creon, like a snake drinking its own venom (*Theb.* 11.308–314):

> sic iurgia paulum
> distulit atque ensem, quem iam dabat ira, repressit.
> ictus ut incerto pastoris uulnere serpens   310
> erigitur gyro longumque e corpore toto
> uirus in ore legit; paulum si deuius hostis
> torsit iter, cecidere minae tumefactaque frustra
> colla sedent, irasque sui bibit ipse ueneni.

> So he put off insults
> A little and re-sheathed the sword, which his anger was now providing.
> As when a serpent struck by a glancing wound from a shepherd
> Rises up in a coil and collects long poison from his whole body
> In his mouth; if the enemy twists his path a little
> Out of the way, the threats fall down, the neck swollen
> In vain settles, and the snake itself drinks the angers of its own poison.

The political opponent goading a young man into a fatal duel evokes Drances and Turnus in the *Aeneid*, but the snake image echoes Virgil's use of snake imagery in *Aeneid* 2, combining the description of Aeneas' mad dash to arms and his deception of Androgeos (*Aen.* 2.378–381) with Pyrrhus' rejuvenation and violence (*Aen.* 2.471–475).[35] By combining these images of destruction, drawing on the Virgilian *urbs capta*, Eteocles becomes the destroyer of his own city as well as the tyrant and the degenerate son. This image, further, creates a complex synergy between the final showdown of both *Aeneid* and *Thebaid*, and the

---

35 Verbal echoes include *repressit* at the end of the line (*Aen.* 2.378; *Theb.* 11.309); swelling: *tumentem* (*Aen.* 2.381); *tumidum* (*Aen.* 2.472); *tumefacta* (*Theb.* 11.313); *colla* (*Theb.* 11.314; *Aen.* 2.381); similar ideas include fleeing back (*refugit*, *Aen.* 2.380; *Theb.* 11.312–313); the snake rising up (*arduus*, *Aen.* 2.475; *serpens erigitur gyro* (*Theb.* 11.310–311); the poisonous nature of the snake (*uirus, ueneni; Theb.* 11.312, 314; hinted at in *mala gramina pastus*, *Aen.* 2.471; *nitens ... caerula*, 2.380–381).

initial destruction of the fall of Troy, making the *Aeneid* as Theban exemplar mimic the collapsible nature of Statian poetics. Rather than just abridging to speed up, intensify and polarise the final confrontation in book 12, as Gervais has persuasively shown, Statius also blurs the *Aeneid* into itself, stretching the poem's final duel over several books, and simultaneously condensing the *Aeneid* into different moments of truth. The snake image which describes Eteocles' anger encapsulates in miniature the pattern of swelling and subsiding, emphasised by Hershkowitz, and also apparent in the fire imagery of the final books. In book 12, in contrast, darkness dominates, fires struggle or are absent; the Theban burials do not have the hyperbolic firepower of Opheltes' funeral, and we subsequently see them dying down. The energy and force of the poem, its *calor* ('heat', *Theb.* 1.3) is sinking into smouldering embers. At the same time imagery of liquid decomposition grows stronger. Polynices relights Eteocles' pyre, and the final burials offer one last blaze of destruction, yet Statius' self-confessed incapacity to fully portray this grief and ritual is borne out by the relatively brief treatment.

The funeral of Menoeceus is restrained in comparison to the disproportionate excess of the funeral of Opheltes. Its main impact is to act as a contrast with Creon's refusal of burial to the Argives. The 'mountains are bereaved' of woods (*montibus orbatis*, 12.51), and the Theban pyres symbolise the destruction of both sides caused by the war: *ardent excisae uiscera gentis / molibus exstructis* ('the entrails cut out from the race are burning on built up piles', 12.53–54). The effort of building the pyres does not compensate for the deep hurts caused by the war. Meanwhile, the Argive ghosts protest their lack of burial: *nuda cohors uetitumque gemens circumuolat ignem.* ('The naked cohort flies around lamenting forbidden fire', 12.56). The phrase *circumuolat ignem* closely echoes *circumuolat igneus*, at the beginning of Parthenopaeus' *aristeia* (9.736). Although Menoeceus' pyre is not to be *uilem* ('common', 61), Creon makes it stand out by heaping it with military trophies, which do not fairly reflect the nature of his death (not unlike the irony of the enormous funeral for tiny Opheltes). A further reference to Hercules on Oeta (12.66–67, echoing 11.234–238) suggests apotheosis, but with high cognitive dissonance. The Tirynthian might be joyful that the stars are demanding him, but he is also in overwhelming pain, lying on the burning mountain (*in accensa iacuit Tirynthius Oeta*, 67). Creon responds by sacrificing live victims, like an Achilles or an Aeneas at the peak of their transgressive grief (68–70), and the height of the flames might evoke the fire and snake imagery of *Aeneid* 2 (*hic arduus ignis / palpitat,* 'here the high fire convulses' 12.70–71).[36] The connection back to Eteocles before the fratricide blurs the two tyrants together and foreshadows Creon's destruction, as well as bringing out the wrongness of the ritual. Creon blames Menoeceus' *ardor laudis* ('fire for praise', 72–73) for his death. The process of lamentation increases Creon's violence: *accensaque iterat uiolentius ira* ('and on fire with anger he begins again more violently', 12.93), emphasising the iterative, cumulative destruction of the Theban cycle of vengeance.[37] The attempt to generate poetic energy for the second war through fiery anger results in refusal of fire, allowing the liquid processes of decomposition to provide a different sort of contagion.

Argia's *aristeia,* her quest to bury Polynices, takes place across a landscape characterised by the failure of fire, blood-soaked and dark. After she splits from the other women, leaving them to go on to Athens, and supplicate Theseus, the next scene begins with darkness falling: the sun's burning chariot is hidden beneath the waves (12.228–229), but Argia does not register the night, and continues on (230–236). Not only does she lose her way in the dark, but the flame of the torch keeps failing: *et errantem comitis solacia flammae / destituunt gelidaeque facem uicere tenebrae!* ('And as she wanders the comfort of companion flame fails and cold shadows conquer the torch', 241–242). Her companion Menoetes points out the dying watch-fires: *cernis ut ingentes murorum porrigat umbras / campus et e speculis moriens intermicet ignis?* ('Do you see how the plain stretches out the huge shadows of the walls and the dying fire from the watch-towers flickers?' 251–252). His words outline their approach towards Thebes, but also create an otherworldly atmosphere in which time and space are distorted, and fire is overcome by darkness. Argia and the poem keep going by relighting the tired torch (*reficit spiramina fessi / ignis,* 'she rekindles the breath of tired fire', 268–269). The image comparing Argia to Ceres searching for Persephone (270–277) is lit by the fires of Aetna, and Enceladus gives fiery assistance, which the Stygian gloom attempts to suppress. The sequence in which Juno persuades Cynthia/Selene to provide light in order for Argia to find Polynices continues the emphasis on darkness and the failure of fire. When Argia finally catches sight of Polynices' cloak, it is 'drenched in blood' (*suffusaque sanguine,* 314). At the moment of Antigone's arrival on the scene, she is 'another groan and another torch' (*ecce alios gemitus aliamque ... facem,* 349–350). As Argia and Antigone exchange laments, two speeches, and the section itself, end

---

[36] *Arduus* is used of both snakes and flames in *Aen.* 2.328 and 475; see Knox 1950, 386–387; *palpito* often refers to repetitive movement in the agonies of death, cf. *Theb.* 8.439, 9.756.
[37] On cyclical or tragic causality in the *Thebaid,* see Marinis 2021 and Parkes 2021.

with fire: *Polynicis ad ignes* ('Polynices to the fires', 379); *accenso flebitis igne* ('You will weep when the fire is lit', 408). Meanwhile the next lines feature the Ismenos running with blood (*haud procul Ismeni monstrabant murmura ripas, / qua turbatus adhuc et sanguine decolor ibat*, 'not far away the murmurs made clear the banks of the Ismenos, where it flowed, stirred up still and discoloured by blood', 409–410). Fire and water, burning and cleansing, articulate the scenes. The comparison of Polynices to Phaethon, *Phaethonta sorores / fumantem lauere Pado* ('the sisters wash Phaethon's smoking body in the Padus', 413–414) equally brings together fire and water, cleansing and cremation. The sisters succeed in washing Polynices' body, but they struggle to find the heat to burn him (12.417–419):

> *ignem miserae post ultima quaerunt*
> *oscula; sed gelidae circum exanimesque fauillae*
> *putribus in foueis, atque omnia busta quiescunt.*

> they wretchedly seek fire after the final
> kisses; but the embers around them are cold and lifeless
> in the crumbling diggings, and all the pyres lie peaceful.

When they do succeed in bringing a fire back to life, it is famously the pyre of Eteocles, and becomes another illustration of the undying intra-familial violence that marks the house of Oedipus. The flames pour out, divided and double (431–432), becoming a second killing of the brothers in Antigone's anguished exclamation (437). Antigone too ends her speech of lament with fire: *saeuos mediae ueniemus in ignes*, 'we will come into the middle of the savage flames' (446). Like Opheltes' parents before them, and Evadne in the final scene, they threaten to break the boundaries between pyre and mourners, throwing themselves also onto the flames. The next section begins with the violence of the pyre infecting the Theban landscape: *uix ea, cum subitus campos tremor altaque tecta / impulit adiuuitque rogi discordis hiatus* ('She had scarcely said these things, when a sudden trembling attacked the plains and the high buildings and increases the chasm in the discordant pyre', 447–448). The lack of closure through burial is physically manifest in the abyss created between the flames and in the landscape, reminding readers of Amphiaraus' anti-funeral at the beginning of the war. Reignition threatens to throw us back into the centre of the epic, and into the underworld itself.

The counterpoint narrative of the alternative quest in which the other Argive women seek Theseus' help in enabling the burial of their husbands provides some balance: but it is notable that the *Ara Clementiae* is shaped by absence and negatives: it receives neither fire nor blood (*non turea flamma nec altus /*

accipitur sanguis, 'no flame with incense, no deep blood is received', 487–488). The final scene of funeral pyres, the climax of book 12 and the very last scene of the narrative also shows the contamination and redoubling of book 12, where the women too are drawn into the Theban vortex of destruction. The epic of lament threatens to be a whole new venture, unbounded itself. The lamenting women are described in military language, taking on Bacchic frenzy, shaking the stars with noise of lament, just like the noise of battle (*Theb.* 12.797–809):[38]

> *non ego, centena si quis mea pectora laxet*
> *uoce deus,* **tot busta** *simul uulgique ducumque,*
> **tot** *pariter* **gemitus** *dignis conatibus aequem:*
> **turbine quo sese caris instrauerit audax**   800
> **ignibus Euadne fulmenque in pectore magno**
> **quaesierit**; *quo more iacens super oscula saeui*
> *corporis infelix excuset Tydea coniunx;*
> *ut saeuos narret uigiles Argia sorori;*
> *Arcada quo planctu genetrix Erymanthia clamet,*   805
> *Arcada, consumpto seruantem sanguine uultus,*
> *Arcada, quem geminae pariter fleuere cohortes.*
> **uix nouus ista furor ueniensque implesset Apollo,**
> *et mea iam longo meruit ratis aequore portum.*

> Not I, even if some god loosened my hundred-fold chest
> with voice, could I equal so many pyres together of people
> and leaders, so many groans equal in worthy striving:
> in what whirlwind bold Evadne threw herself
> on the dear flames and sought out the thunderbolt
> in the great chest; in what way the tragic wife
> lying on top of the savage body excused the Tydean kisses;
> how Argia tells the tale of the savage guards to her sister;
> Arcadian, with what wailing the Erymanthian mother laments;
> Arcadian, preserving your appearance, with the blood drained out;
> Arcadian, whom equally the twin cohorts weep.
> Scarcely would a new madness and Apollo coming have sufficed for those things,
> And my ship has now long deserved harbour from that sea.

This mourning scene recapitulates in miniature the epic, which has just been recapitulated through the battle in *Thebaid* 12. As Evadne emulates Capaneus,

---

38 A recent intervention on this passage is Panoussi 2019, 103–113, who argues that women's ritual lament brings cohesiveness and a promise of reconciliation in the face of male violence. For me the blurring between the men and women, lament and death itself, including the self-immolation of Evadne, suggests rather a multiplication and continuation of grief, and the way the traumas of war echo down the generations.

by creating her own fiery death to match his, so Deipyle executes her own cannibalisation through grief, replicating Tydeus' gaping mouth in her kisses. The voice of Atalanta becomes the voice of the poet, and implicates anyone reading aloud in that new overwhelming madness, the fire of Apollo, which inspires this ongoing epic of grief. The overwhelming excess of mourning is divided into pyres and laments, and the final image sets the fires of Apollo in apposition to the sea of poetry. The contagion of fire is seen in the way lament spreads to both sides, while the women join or recuperate the men; Parthenopaeus' beauty and his effect on both sides of the war, continue his portrayal from book 9. It is not clear that these pyres (or laments) cleanse: rather the fire and the grief threaten to spread into the future (foreshadowing the next war, that of the *Epigonoi*).[39] As readers, we remain held at the moment of lament, with the ritual invocation of the dead Arcadian, not released from grief.

6 Conclusion

Elaine Fantham argued that the *Thebaid* was particularly characterised by lament.[40] McClellan takes her argument further by showing how Creon's refusal of burial echoes backwards through the poem, frequently mentioned and foreshadowed, so much so that he finds it overdone, almost oppressive. More than this, the *Thebaid* is structured not just by a series of deaths but also by a series of problematic, refused, incomplete or unsatisfying funerals. I have argued that Statius creates a sense of endlessness by an oversupply of endings, creating his particular refraction of Lucan's split voice of civil war. The Theseus episode's effectiveness as closural device is still being debated.[41] The *Thebaid* is also deter-

---

[39] Voigt 2016 argues that Statius offers a utopian female alternative to male epic, in which grief gives women agency. This is similar to the approach of Dietrich 1999. It does not sufficiently take into account the ways in which the women are implicated in the men's war, and even instigate it. The absence of Eriphyle, not perhaps surprising since Amphiaraus is already in the underworld, could be designed to avoid evoking the further tragic intergenerational destruction (Alcmaeon's killing of his mother and his subsequent death), or to elide it. This story also complicates the representation of Argia, whose complicity is greater in Statius, where she, not Polynices, offers the necklace to Eriphyle in return for Amphiaraus' participation.
[40] See Fantham 1999.
[41] Recent work on Theseus: Spinelli (forthcoming), chapters 2 and 3, argues that Theseus reestablishes boundaries, but also that he is bound up with Oedipus; Chinn 2022, 120–158 on the shield of Theseus, argues that '[t]he shields both problematise Theseus as an epic closural figure (via the Callimachean poetic "debate") and problematise the *Thebaid*'s status within the

minedly inward-looking, prophecies folding into themselves and endings blurred into beginnings.[42] The incestuous poetics of the *Thebaid* intensify the more than civil war into an inwardly retreating infinite *mise-en-abime*. In this literary universe neither [repeats of] the fall of Troy nor the death of Dido are allowed to be productive.[43] The recursive and iterative mode rules instead, and even those that try to break free from the pull of Thebes, such as Polynices in book 1, and the Argive women in book 12, end up sucked back in. It is no surprise, then, that fiery rituals in the *Thebaid* do not straightforwardly cleanse or provide space for renewal or reinvention. Instead, fire spawns further destruction, threatens to be (or actually is) out of control. Even building the pyre of Opheltes is an act of desecration, and the more the Argives attempt to control the ominous situation through ritual practice, the more they multiply and intensify the malevolent symbolism.

The tendency towards collapse and disintegration, along with the destabilisation of ritual practice, and the blurring of narrative divisions and thematic ideas, fundamentally setting epic teleology on fire, all of this suggests a dark political vision. The poetics of incest and the inward turn of the *Thebaid* in particular have implications for Statius' understanding of and relation to power. As a professional poet of Greek heritage, Statius stands at a distance from Roman senatorial concerns about imperial power, but he is significantly more disempowered than his contemporaries, Valerius Flaccus, Silius Italicus and Martial. The inward turn of the *Thebaid* brings out the way power reproduces itself, self-perpetuating, self-regarding.[44] Ritual can encode, create, and enable successful communication and community formation across power differentials (imperial,

---

epic genre (via the river Ismenos as a visual metapoetic metaphor)'. Hulls 2021, 151–163 attempts to go beyond a binary reading of Theseus; Simms 2020, 143–160, on the ambiguity and unexpectedness of Theseus; Rebeggiani 2018, 84–92 balances the identification of Theseus against the lack of golden age confidence in Statius' final lines, presenting Theseus as a potentially optimistic protreptic model for Domitian, within a fundamentally pessimistic model of Roman religion and politics. Bessone 2011, 128–199 argues that closure is created across the masculine of Theseus and the feminine of Argia.
42 Simms 2020, 24–29 shows how Statius' proem focuses on the myth's ending; Dalton 2020 shows how Statius scatters the limbs of the *Aeneid*'s opening throughout his epic.
43 'Time and again Statius highlights the perverted blurring of misery and violence as scenes of grieving everywhere spill over into violent acts, confrontations, and open warfare.' McClellan 2019, 232.
44 Cf. McClellan 2019, 214: 'Political reality too often actualised Lucan's 'tragic' vatic conception of the principate as an endless cycle of repeated self-evisceration.'

divine).⁴⁵ The collapse inwards, instability and perversion surrounding ritual in the *Thebaid* reflects a profound feeling of exclusion and alienation. But the *Thebaid* is not entirely a 'No-epic'.⁴⁶ There is a joy in darkly skewering the cognitive dissonances in a world overwhelmed by disempowerment.⁴⁷ The *Thebaid* hints towards modes of resistance and resilience, possibly even recuperation and rebuilding, but never fully commits to them or gives them straightforward traction. This ambivalence allows for the darkness of burning it down, but still contains the spark needed to re-emerge.

---

45 For a successful ritual action as part of 'ritualisation' and generally for the process of ritual communication, see Rüpke's contribution in this volume.

46 The works of Octavia Butler and her struggle to write readable, enjoyable books, while still remaining committed to her vision of how the world works, have strongly influenced my thoughts about politics, activism and literature. On 'Yes-novels' and 'No-novels' in Octavia Butler's working notes and archive materials, see George 2020 and Canavan 2016. On speculative fiction and activism, see Maree Brown 2017.

47 One might compare the too little too late, too much destruction not enough redemption, ending of Suzanne Collins' *Hunger Games* trilogy, which questions whether totalitarian power can ever be overturned, and whether humanity's hierarchical nature will inevitably encode existential threats to human race and planet. Collins' protagonist goes one further than Statius' traumatised lamenting heroines by using her final, closural arrow shot to kill off the wrong president, not the Eteocles/Creon figure, but the Theseus figure. In this way she brings her more than civil war to a close with a double defeat not unlike that of the *Thebaid*.

Michael Knierim
Narrative and Psychological Closure through Ritual at Cyzicus and Circe's Island

Abstract: This article examines Valerius Flaccus' Cyzicus episode and its Apollonian precedents through the lens of modern literature on trauma and Moral Injury. After slaughtering their friends unwittingly, the Argonauts are aghast. The funeral, though helpful, fails to produce psychological or literary closure as the Argonauts remain paralysed by grief and guilt. The quest and poem cannot proceed until a further ritual is performed by a legitimate and benevolent moral authority figure who can help the Argonauts lay aside their memories and bring closure. In contrast, the main purification in Apollonius Rhodius' Circe episode marks the closure of Medea's connection to family, language and people and the beginning of her life in exile. Circe's ritual does not reinforce group solidarity, and the moral authority is not benevolent but rejects Medea crushingly. Both episodes fit modern Moral Injury models. Apollonius does so in a negative way that leaves an isolated Medea full of wounds and the reader full of ominous expectations. Valerius does so in a positive way leading to a refreshing feeling of release for the Argonauts and the reader.

1 Introduction

Rituals and the moral authority figures who perform them play a significant role in the closure of psychological tensions in the main purification episodes of Valerius Flaccus and Apollonius Rhodius' *Argonauticas*. Resolution of tension and conflicts are types of literary closure listed by Don Fowler in his study of closure in the classics.[1] Since the chief tensions in these two epics involve the psychology of the characters, the way that they are resolved or complicated in purification episodes affects the interpretation of the poems as a whole.

Studying trauma in ancient epics can help to balance lingering Eurocentrism in modern trauma theory,[2] since ancient Greece and Rome are so different from modern European cultures. Different countries in our own time have different practices which influence their different rates of PTSD (post-traumatic

---

1 Fowler 2000, 242.
2 See Visser 2018, 126–127 on eurocentrism in trauma theory.

stress disorder) and Moral Injury.[3] The Greeks and Romans did not recognise psychological trauma of the kind that has become prominent since World War I,[4] and Jason Crowley argues that Greek hoplites were well insulated against trauma.[5] So it is worth considering the practices of other societies both modern and ancient which can contribute to the treatment and prevention of trauma.

Flavian and Hellenistic epic can also contribute to answering the call for more research on ritual in contemporary trauma theory.[6] Homer has inspired the psychologist Shay, author of *Achilles in Vietnam*, to better understand the causes of the destruction of character, but the *Iliad* does not contain the restorative rituals of the *Argonauticas*. Shay and others argue that group solidarity and reintegration into society, including ritual reintegration are critical for healing.[7] We will see that group rituals help to unite the Argonauts but leave Medea isolated.

This chapter will make use of the Moral Injury paradigm, since it conforms more closely to these ancient epics than does the more familiar PTSD. First, we will examine modern definitions of Moral Injury, its causes, symptoms and treatment. Then, we will see how this applies to Valerius' Cyzicus episode, where Jason and the Argonauts are paralysed by guilt and grief after unintentionally killing their hosts in a night-battle until Mopsus acts like a forgiving moral authority figure of Moral Injury and heals the group with a communal ritual. Then, Valerius' treatment will be compared to Apollonius' Cyzicus' episode with its ecstatic ritual elements. Finally, we will consider Medea, first Valerius' more hopeful version, then Apollonius' Circe episode which isolates Medea rather than reintegrating her.[8]

2 Moral injury: definitions

Moral Injury (MI) is a new paradigm that can overlap with PTSD but encompasses other causes, sub-threshold degrees of severity, more holistic treatments and community involvement. The 5th Edition of the *Diagnostic and Statistical Manual* of the American Psychological Association bases its diagnosis of post-

---

[3] DSM 5, entry on PTSD; Levine 2018, 227–228; Shay 1995, 202.
[4] Konstan 2014, 2.
[5] Meineck and Konstan 2014, 105–130.
[6] Visser 2018, 139.
[7] Levine 2018, 228–230; Nez/Avila 2018; Shay 2004, 152–153.
[8] Mehmel 1934, 35 already realised that Idmon's (sic!) purification of the Argonauts in V. Fl. recalled Circe in Ap. Rhod.

traumatic stress disorder on *experiencing* violence but says nothing about *betrayal* or *committing* violent acts against others including morally ambiguous acts. All of these are important to both major definitions of Moral Injury. The two models overlap, and I will make use of both.

According to Shay, "Moral injury is the sum total of the psychological, social and physiological consequences that a person undergoes when *all three* of the following are present:
1. Betrayal of what's right (the code of what is praiseworthy and blameworthy, part of the culture);
2. By someone who holds legitimate authority (legitimacy and authority are phenomena of the social system);
3. In a high-stakes situation (what's at stake clearly has links to the culture and social system, but must be present in the *mind* of the person suffering the injury)".[9] Jason will feel betrayed by gods and seers when they fail to prevent him from killing his friends at Cyzicus.

The Veterans Association researcher Litz and his colleagues, somewhat differently from Shay, define "potentially morally injurious experiences" as "[p]erpetrating, failing to prevent, bearing witness to, or learning about acts that transgress deeply held moral beliefs and expectations."[10] Drescher et al., part of Litz' school of thought, list additional events that can lead to moral injury: leadership failures, betrayal by peers and friendly fire.[11] Killing and failing to prevent killing are connected to increased risk of suicide.[12] Litz and Maguen note that, unlike PTSD, Moral Injury has no minimum threshold and is often characterised by "shame, guilt", and "self-handicapping behaviors such as retreating in the face of success..."[13] MI can also include "demoralization, which may entail confusion, bewilderment, futility, hopelessness, and self-loathing."[14] We will observe all of these in Valerius' Argonauts at Cyzicus.

Many of these symptoms are features of both PTSD and Moral Injury, though MI sufferers tend to have more guilt and shame while lacking the hypervigilance associated with fear-induced types of PTSD.[15] Often a person with MI thinks "I deserve to suffer" and feels that he or she needs to experience guilt in

---

9 Shay 2018, 302.
10 Litz et al. 2009, 700.
11 Drescher et al. 2011, 11.
12 Fontana 1992 cited in Litz et al. 2009, 697.
13 Maguen/Litz 2012, 1; Litz et al. 2009, 701.
14 Litz et al. 2009, 701.
15 See Litz et al. 2009, 697; Boudreau 2018, 54.

order to honour the dead.[16] Other characteristics of Moral Injury include: "negative changes in ethical attitudes and behavior... change in, or loss of spirituality... including negative attributions about God... guilt, shame, and forgiveness problems... reduced trust in others and in social/cultural contracts... or self-harm."[17] We will see that Valerius' Jason will wish to be dead in place of the dead and will lose trust in gods and seers; Medea in both epics will experience marked changes in attitudes and behaviour, difficulty trusting others and shame. Both characters will consider self-harm.

3 Valerius Flaccus: moral injury symptoms of Jason and the Argonauts at Cyzicus

The events at Cyzicus in Valerius Flaccus' *Argonautica* (2.630–633, 3.1–480) fit both Shay's definition of Moral Injury and Litz' since there has been betrayal of "what's right" by legitimate authorities in a high stakes situation *and* the Argonauts have transgressed deeply held moral beliefs: they have killed their hosts unwittingly in a night battle after adverse winds pushed them back to the same port without them realising it, while the gods did nothing to prevent this. Jason criticises the seers, and hence indirectly the gods for not warning him:[18] *tantumque nefas mens conscia uatum conticuit*, "the mind of the seers, (though culpably) aware, kept silent about such an abomination".[19] He feels betrayed by trusted, legitimate authorities in a situation that resulted in the death of his host and friend and much of his friend's people, high stakes indeed.[20] As for Litz' definition, killing one's friend and host is contrary to "deeply held ethical

---

16 Norman et al. 2014, 79, 82. See also Litz et al. 2009, 703.
17 Drescher et al. 2011, 9.
18 See Manuwald 1999, 93–95; Stover 2012, 126–148, esp. 147 presents the Cyzicans as "gigantomachic enemies of the Jovian order" deserving death, although the Argonauts do not know this. This does not affect my argument which concerns the internal feelings of the Argonauts.
19 Quotes from V. Fl. Book 3 are taken from Manuwald 2015. Translations are by author unless noted otherwise.
20 Mehmel 1934, 93–95 speaks of the "Sinnlosigkeit" of the Lemnian, Cyzican and Colchian civil wars and the arbitrary gods. See also Franchet d'Espèrey 1998; Fucecchi 1996, 102–103; Schenk 1991, 139–145; 1999, 74, 356; Heerink 2022. Though they refer to Valerius' narrative world, a psychological *feeling* of meaningless, is a major symptom of moral injury. See Shay 1995, 180. On meaningless killing in Apollonius' Cyzicus, see Hunter 1993, 43.

commitments" and friendly fire is listed as a cause of moral injury.[21] Difficulty distinguishing civilians from insurgents and actively participating in killing make matters worse for Jason as for modern soldiers.[22] The Argonauts fought tenaciously for their own survival, but when they discovered that they had killed their friends, not their Colchian enemies, the jarring contrast between what they had intended and what they actually did devastated them.[23]

Yet mourning and positive actions help the Argonauts overcome suicidal grief. At Cyzicus' funeral pyre Jason expresses his wish to be dead in Cyzicus' place.[24] In two studies cited by Litz et al. it was found that "combat guilt was the most significant predictor of both suicide attempts and preoccupation with suicide" and Litz adds "being the agent of killing or failing to prevent death or injury was associated with general psychological distress and suicide attempts".[25] This fits Jason, although he never attempts suicide like Ajax. Perhaps it was helpful for him to express his remorse and sadness in ritual lamentation surrounded by both his supportive men and the victim's people. According to Bernstein, Jason acts like a son to Cyzicus by lifting him onto the pyre (3.338–339). This kinship motif intensifies the pain and civil war quality of the episode.[26] Yet this also allows Jason to do something positive for his new kin. When Castor and Pollux help up Cyzicus' wife Clite, who has collapsed in grief upon her husband's body, they show their shared grief towards their unintended victims and do a positive action, something Moral Injury researchers agree is important for the inner healing of *perpetrators*.[27]

Even so, mourning at the funeral was not enough. They lost all *fiducia* ('confidence') and concern for *patria* ('homeland') and *amor laborum* ('love of

---

[21] Maguen/Litz, 2012, 2, 15–20% of American deaths in Vietnam were from friendly fire, Shay 1995, 125.
[22] Litz et al. 2009, 696–697. On night battles in Apollonius, see Lovatt 2018, 104–108.
[23] On Jason and Cyzicus' expectations dashed by fate, see Torres-Murciano 2007, 84–90. Seal 2014, 132–135 notes that the Argonauts unwittingly start an era of civil wars.
[24] Jason's lamentation lacks the controlling aggression that Augoustakis 2016a, 287–298 observes in other male laments in Flavian epic. See also Fantham 1999, 228 on anger and male grief in Flavian epic and ancient politics. Jason does express regret that he cannot fight Cyzicus' foes or bring him Colchian plunder (3.306–308). He blames gods and seers but makes no threats.
[25] Maguen/Litz 2012, 2.
[26] Bernstein 2008, 52–53. He also notes that the Argonauts fare remarkably well for kin-killers in epic. Stover 2012, 119–121, 123, notes that Valerius' Cyzicans feel similarity and kinship Greek guests and exchange gifts, unlike Apollonius'.
[27] Lapsley/Karakashian 2018, 234–235; Litz et al. 2009, 701; Manuwald 1999, 92. Whether this was helpful for Clite's healing is a different matter.

deeds'), could not escape *imagine caesorum* ('the image of the slain') nor did they feel that they had wept or done enough for them in their desire for *segni luctu* ('sluggish grief') (3.362–368). This fits with the demoralised self-handicapping observed by Litz et al.[28] It also partly fits with Shay's picture of a morally injured Achilles who "is tortured by guilt and the conviction that he should have died rather than his friend," and "goes berserk and commits atrocities against the living and the dead",[29] losing all interest in home-coming like many Vietnam berserkers.[30] Though Jason has the first part of Achilles' reaction, he does not go berserk, instead he seeks out a benevolent moral authority who prescribes a healing ritual of a kind not seen in Homer.

4 Valerius Flaccus: Mopsus, a benevolent moral authority

Jason goes to a benevolent moral authority figure, Mopsus, a fellow Argonaut and a priest of Apollo whose authority is further enhanced by a secret purification ritual from a mysterious figure named Celaeneus and his strong grasp of the context and purpose of the rituals and of the fate of murdered souls and murderers. Since he is a member of the Argonauts, though he took no part in the battle except as a witness,[31] he has a strong connection with his men (3.98–99). All this makes him a legitimate moral authority that the men would listen to. A benevolent moral authority is a prominent part of Litz' treatment protocol for Moral Injury known as Adaptive Disclosure, in which the sufferer has a real or imaginary dialogue with a compassionate and respected person from their past such as a "parent, teacher, leader, friend", someone who never failed them.[32] This moral authority figure is distinct from the therapist who tries to facilitate the encounter.[33] The goal is to get the forgiveness of the authority figure without dismissing the gravity of what has been done since the forgiveness needs to be

---

[28] Litz et al. 2009, 701.
[29] Shay 1995, xx–xxi cited by Pryer 2018, 64.
[30] Shay 1995, 51–53, 73.
[31] Cf. Manuwald 1999, 165–167.
[32] Litz et al. 2009, 703–704; 2016, 126–127.
[33] Litz et al. 2016, 124–133. Of course a modern therapist embodies the considerable authority of science, medicine, the Veterans Association, and the government. However, soldiers with MI may feel betrayed by these, and other forms of authority can have more personal impact.

believable and too much justification can lead to perpetuating the behaviour.³⁴ Jason does not need to tell Mopsus about the battle since he was there. He merely asks for the meaning of the slaughter, and of their present fear and lack of interest in *lares* and *fama* ('household gods', i.e. home; and fame) (3.373–376). Mopsus never condemns Jason or uses harsh language in his reply.

Similarly a modern therapist too should put things in perspective, not excusing bad actions but placing them in context so that the perpetrator will not overgeneralise from something done in the heat and confusion of war, but will be able to recover something of his or her old self.³⁵ Mopsus does not explicitly speak this way, yet the rite does mark off their past actions from their future life. The explanatory context that he gives involves a theological picture of the world that is connected to practical consequences through ritual. Other forms of modern trauma theory emphasise the inexpressible, incomprehensible nature of trauma. In these views, simply describing the event and making it into an intelligible narrative helps to achieve psychological closure.³⁶ The incomprehensibility of trauma seems to be a Euro-centric trope rather than a universal,³⁷ yet Jason's insistent questions for meaning are answered by Mopsus' religious/ philosophical explanation. Instead of explaining away or too easily excusing the Argonauts' shame, he takes it seriously, yet puts it in context while honouring the dead.³⁸

In Mopsus' view, guilty murderers are troubled by ghosts, unwitting killers are troubled by their own consciences. Even so, his ritual resembles one for guilty murderers, including diverting the wrath of the ghosts.³⁹ Johnston notes that often the same ancient Greek rites were intended to honour, placate and ward off the dead, and that those who died by violence were more likely to haunt their murderers (3.377–416).⁴⁰ Thus, Mopsus was covering every eventuality. Yet using the same rites for justified and unjustified killers also accords

---

34 Litz et al. 2016, 118, 128.
35 Litz et al. 2009, 701, 703.
36 Tuval–Mashiach et al. 2004, 281.
37 Visser 2018, 128.
38 See Castelletti 2012, 319–322 for a Greek acrostic in the ritual description where the first letters of lines 3.340–344 spell out "*Aidos*". For my purposes, this expresses the Argonauts' shame and connects them with Medea's *Aidos* and *pudor*. On *aidos* and *pudor*, see Eigler 1991, 163, 168.
39 See Manuwald 2015, 166–167, 174; Stover 2012, 172 n. 70; Boyancé 1972, 324–325.
40 Johnston 1999, 38, 47–48, 73–74 and 78–79.

well with modern MI theory, since even the most justified of killings can leave moral scars.[41]

5 Valerius Flaccus: a healing communal ritual

Mopsus purifies himself at night before leading the Argonauts through an elaborate purification at dawn (3.417–429). Marching in their weapons and armour they are purified by laurel and prostrate together before the rising sun; animals are slaughtered and the pollution from their armaments is transferred by touch to the meat which is thrown away (3.430–442).[42] Mopsus is assisted by another seer, Idmon, whose participation increases the communal nature of the ritual (3.176).[43] Mopsus sets up wooden effigies of warriors and calls upon the dead to spend their anger on these and be at peace rather than plaguing the Argonauts.[44] After a final offering is accepted by chthonic snakes, ('*umbrarum famuli*', 458), Mopsus tells the men to get on the ship and go and not to look back. The Argonauts are then described as *alacres* ('joyful', 462), and there is a *laetae concordia uocis* ('harmony of joyful voice[s]') (464), as they enter into a light-hearted rowing contest, thus resuming their quest and their thirst for heroic deeds.[45]

Purification ceremonies can mark transitions in time,[46] and leaving without looking back is common in rituals dealing with the dangerous dead.[47] Here the combination gives emphatic closure to the psychological wounds of the Argonauts and the Cyzicus episode. The epic, which was in danger of being shut down on the shores of the Propontis, has opened up again. The horror, chaos and kin-slaying in the dark are balanced by Jason's questions at night and Mopsus' ritual preparation. The dawn of horrible realisation is balanced by a dawn of purification. In their victory the Argonauts had chased the spirits (*manes*)

---

[41] See Boudreau 2018, 53–54.
[42] On *lustramina* as the meat, see Manuwald 2015, 182; Schaaf 2014, 200–201 notes that in Chthonic offerings the meat is usually burned, not eaten.
[43] See Manuwald 2015, 111–112 on Ornytus; Kleywegt 1991, 230 on Mopsus and Idmon in both epics. Idmon was also polluted by killing a host, but is able to do a positive action through ritual like Castor and Pollux at Cyzicus' funeral as noted above.
[44] Stover 2012, 175 n. 76, discusses these and the statue of Rhea in Apollonius.
[45] Stover 2012, 176–177 notes the importance for societies to forget after civil wars in order to heal, citing Virgil, Statius and Lucan.
[46] Parker 1983, 24.
[47] Johnston 1999, 38, 47–48, 73–74 and 78–79; Manuwald 2015, 181–182.

of the slain (3.219) then were haunted by them, but now have appeased them. Mopsus performed the purification from on top of the funeral mound of the slain (3.433–434), presumably near the battlefield near the shore where the Argonauts have been paralysed all this time. These pairs balance the poem and restore balance to the characters.

However, the closure is not perfect since there are foreboding intertextual references connecting Cyzicus and Clite with Absyrtus, Jason and Medea.[48] In Apollonius, Jason and Medea had given a weapon and one of Hypsipyle's cloaks to Absyrtus to lure him to his death (4.423).[49] Valerius' Jason had received armaments and a cloak from Cyzicus made by Clite (3.9, 25, 10). Later Jason puts one of Hypsipyle's cloaks on Cyzicus' pyre (3.340–342).[50] Clite here does not kill herself as in Apollonius but she does lament Cyzicus as her *coniunx pariter fraterque parensque* ('equally husband, brother and parent' 3.323) just as Apollonius' Medea had referred to herself as Jason's κούρη τε δάμαρ τε / αὐτοκασιγνήτη τε ('daughter, wife and sister', 4.368–369) while she was pleading with him to kill her brother rather than abandon her. Apollonius' death of Absyrtus, like Valerius' Cyzicus episode took place at night accompanied by a battle and involved sacrilege against a goddess because it took place in Artemis' temple whereas Valerius' Cyzicus had profaned the goddess Cybele (4.452–491). Later Valerius' Absyrtus will participate in a civil war against family, starting out as a friend to Jason, but then turning against him, as Valerius' Cyzicus starts as a friend but becomes an unwitting enemy.[51] An attentive reader aware of Apollonius would have noticed these sinister parallels. Cyzicus is a stand in for Absyrtus, and thus this will be the primary purification ceremony in the epic.[52] Cyzicus and Clite are linked to Jason and Medea and that pair's lost innocence with ominous implications.[53] Even so, the ritual has succeeded in alleviating surface psychological tensions for now.[54]

---

[48] For more parallels between Apollonius' Cyzicus and Absyrtus, see Hunter 1993, 42–43.
[49] On Jason's treachery, see Zissos 2017, 209. On Hypsipyle's cloak, Hamvas 2016, 366–367; Bulloch 2006.
[50] For more on the cloaks, see Zissos 2017, 211 n. 32, 227.
[51] For parallels between Valerius' Cyzicus and Colchis wars and Perses, see Schenk 1991, 150–153; Stover 2012, 149–150.
[52] For a simile linking Apollonius' fights against Cyzicus and Absyrtus, see Clare 2002, 190–196.
[53] Beye 1969, 42 notes that Apollonius' text compares the young Cyzicus to the youthful Jason.
[54] According to Stover 2012, 170, 179 this episode shows a *uates'* ability "to bring... closure to the traumatised participants of civil war".

6 Valerius Flaccus: comparison with Apollonius' Cyzicus episode in Book 1.936–1152

Moral Injury is less prominent in Apollonius' treatment of the Cyzicus episode although the Argonauts express sorrow and participate in three days of mourning ceremonies with Cyzicus' people. Marching around the tomb in armour is mentioned as well as funeral games. No speeches are reported. Clite commits suicide, rather than living to be helped up by the Dioscuri. This is part of a trend of less successful healing in Apollonius versus Valerius as we will see with Medea. The slaughter is less severe, since the Argonauts only kill twelve named Cyzicans besides the king, whereas in Valerius they seemed close to wiping out the male population. Later, Apollonius' Argonauts are held back for twelve days, one for each named man that they killed as Clauss observes.[55] Thus their delay is connected to the killing, however, they are held back by contrary winds, not feelings of grief and guilt as in Valerius. One could argue that the funeral had already accomplished a successful healing of the Argonauts, but their depth of grief was not emphasised as much as in Valerius, nor were they given quasi kin status.[56] Jason, instead of going to Mopsus at night, tormented by doubts and existential questions, is sound asleep when Mopsus wakes him up to tell him of an omen. Yet when Mopsus reveals that they need to perform ceremonies for Rhea, some of the rituals are similar, and Clauss sees them as a blood-purification ceremony.[57]

The most striking features of Apollonius' rites are the armed dance and the clashing of weapons and armour to drown out the sounds of the mourning people of Cyzicus, which could have been apotropaic against ghosts stirred up by the laments.[58] Yet there is something heartless about drowning out the noise of their victims, whose trauma will be embodied in mourning rituals for generations.[59] The Argonauts' psychological turmoil if they have any, is resolved by this, but it leaves tension in the narrative and the reader.

The armed marching and dancing of the Argonauts, their singing and their rowing contest could also have benefited their mental health (1.1153–1171).

---

[55] Clauss 1993, 166.
[56] Stover 2012, 123 also notes that Apollonius' episode lacks the bonding exchange of gifts.
[57] Connected to Dardanus, founder of such ceremonies by Clauss 1993, 168, 171. Polt 2013, 340, 344–345 sees it as blood-purification for killing the earth-born.
[58] Boyancé 1972, 318–319. On apotropaic elements in V. Fl.'s ritual, see 325, 331, 334.
[59] On the mourning *aitia*, see 4.1061–1077 and Thalmann 2011, 91–100; van Groningen 1962. Apollonius' text comes from Race 2014.

Newhouse notes that the vigorous exercise and camaraderie of extreme sports like white-water rafting help veterans to process adrenaline influenced combat memories and balance cortisol levels.[60] The Argonauts invoke the Idaean Dactyls who are often confused with the Corybantes whose armed dance is strongly connected to the healing of madness and to Orpheus in ancient sources (1.1125–1131).[61] Their shield clashing gives rise to the custom of Phrygian drumming to Rhea in whose honour the Argonauts sing and feast (1.1134–1151). Gimpel, an art therapist, points out the power of group music therapy to focus veterans on the present, putting away the past, while promoting "group cohesion, intimacy", "support and relationships".[62] Another study "described the action of controlling and modulating one's muscles when drumming as a metaphor for learning how to modulate one's emotions".[63] The exercise component might not have been a conscious part of the design of either poet, just a physical reality of their societies. The group solidarity though, is striking, and is markedly different from Medea, particularly Apollonius' Medea, as we will see.[64] Further, all of these actions would give new, positive associations to their guilty weapons and armour while teaching them, through their muscles and bodies to put aside sorrow, something that is relatively explicit in Valerius and is hinted at in Apollonius.

Though Valerius had some subtly sinister intertextual references, they were much less prominent than the callousness of Apollonius' Argonauts. Rhea's nature rejoices and the Argonauts sail away, but Apollonius' Cyzicans will grieve for centuries.

7 Valerius Flaccus: Medea

Valerius' Medea meets many of both Shay's and Litz' criteria for Moral Injury, yet her prognosis is relatively hopeful.[65] When the goddesses appear in disguise in books 6 and 7 and try to use divine powers and persuasion to get Medea to do something that she thinks is wrong, they use the forms of two authoritative

---

60 Newhouse 2018, 155–157.
61 Ustinova 1998, 503–505, 507–509, 510, 517; Nock 1941, 580.
62 Gimpel 2016, 38.
63 Gimpel 2016, 37 citing Burt 1995.
64 On group solidarity and ritual in Apollonius, see Lye 2012, 232–236.
65 The Moral Injury paradigm arose from studying soldiers but can also apply well to civilians; see Antonelli 2017.

females in her life: her older sister, and her aunt.⁶⁶ When they tell her to give up her father and her fatherland for the sake of a stranger, they are figures of legitimate authority, betraying "what's right" in a high stakes situation which fits Shay's definition.⁶⁷ She also sees her father betray Jason.⁶⁸ As Litz et al. noted, witnessing betrayals of "what's right" can also cause the symptoms of MI.⁶⁹

According to Drescher et al. MI is often characterised by changes in attitudes and behaviour.⁷⁰ When Medea, finally overpowered by the goddesses, starts to help Jason by giving him everything that had once been sacred to her, she declares herself *nocens* ('wicked/guilty'), the beginning of the shame and guilt of moral injury (7.461).⁷¹ Zissos notes that after this, "significant inversions in her sentiments and conduct promptly emerge" as her first action is to use magic to coerce Jason's love.⁷² The coercion itself might or might not have been against her moral code, but in doing so she *is* distancing herself further from her family by connecting herself with a foreign man which *is* against her code. Stocks observes that Valerius emphasises Medea's relationship with her father and that even though Aeetes deserved to be betrayed and Jason's cause was righteous, her betrayal of her father is still a breach of *pietas*.⁷³ Fucecchi describes Medea's struggle against Venus as an ἀριστεία (a feat of heroic might) though she ultimately loses. She had wished to dedicate herself to Hecate in virginity,⁷⁴ but now her ethical commitments are overthrown by the raw power of the gods as she is pushed to do things that she would not have chosen.⁷⁵ Similarly, Medea

---

66 On the sisters, see Keith 2016, 249–254 though she neglects the mother-like aspect in Apollonius (3.732–735). Presumably Valerius' Chalciope is still older than Medea and thus a moral authority.
67 Elm von der Osten 2007, 119–122 notes that Venus/Circe persuades her to betray her kin which is exactly what Apollonius' Circe condemns her for.
68 Stover 2011, 189–190 notes that Venus/Circe will use this in her persuasive arguments to convince Medea.
69 Litz et al. 2009, 697–698, 700.
70 Drescher et al. 2011, 9.
71 Citations from V. Fl. Book 7 are taken from Perutelli 1997. On this passage, its context and similes, see Elm von der Osten 2007, 127–129; Salemme 1991, 14–17, 61–66.
72 Zissos 2012, 115.
73 Stocks 2016, 52–54.
74 Fucecchi 2014, 128–129; 1996, 103–105, 160–165; Lovatt 2006, 67–78.
75 On the gods' role vs. Medea's agency, see Mehmel 1934, 55, 89–91, 94; Salemme 1991, 53–54; Ferenzci 1998, 338–346; Schenk 1999, 355–357, 361–366. They emphasise the gods' power; for Salemme her culpability is ambiguous; for Ferenzci she is a doomed hero; Eigler 1991, 160–172 reads Valerius' gods as allegories for psychological forces, with Medea as both perpetrator and victim. Elm von der Osten 2007, 181–182, 185 sees Venus in transition from person to allegory. See also 104–105, 153 on culpability, similes, and how Medea becomes "irrevocably

describes herself as *noxia* ('harmful/guilty') after betraying her pet dragon which trusted her (8.106).[76]

Yet Valerius holds out hope for Medea's future healing.[77] Valerius' prophecies often reference alternate versions of the myth and contradict his main narrative,[78] but prophecies that go beyond the ending of his poem are probably not meant to be contradicted, and his poem would likely have ended long before the child-slaying foreshadowed in the sculptures of the Colchian temple (V. Fl. 5.430–455) and in Mopsus' grim prophecy at the wedding (8.247–251).[79] However, he also foreshadows her later return with Medus, her future son by Aegeus, to Colchis where she will restore her deposed father (5.683–687).[80] Indeed, Zissos is able to call Medea's elopement with Jason a "divinely-induced aberration in an otherwise exemplary story of filial loyalty" pointing out her strong moral code and commitment to family and country.[81]

Regardless of what Valerius intended for her role in Absyrtus' death, Medea will be reconciled with her birth family, receiving forgiveness from some of those that she had betrayed, including representatives of Absyrtus. She will also receive forgiveness from her father, a presumably benevolent moral authority figure for her by this time. Forming connections with people that one respected before the moral injury occurred is a very important step in healing modern

---

guilty", unable to "return to a sorrow-free life". For my purposes, it does not matter whether Valerius' gods are meant as real or allegorical, nor whether Medea is responsible. What matters is that she *feels* responsible.

76 Line numbers of V. Fl. Book 8 are from Castelletti 2022. On Valerius' allusions to variant versions of the myth, see Zissos 2016, 112–114. For Apollonius and his predecessors, see Fantuzzi 2008, 295–296.
77 Perutelli 1994, 49 thinks she is more "closely bound to moral principles", particularly familial *pietas*, than Apollonius' Medea.
78 See Zissos 2016.
79 On Mopsus' ominous wedding visions, see Elm von der Osten 2007, 147–153. Salemme 1991, 78–80 examines ominous similes of the wedding episode. On more inauspicious similes of Jason and Medea in Valerius, see Salemme 1991, 10–12, 25–33, 33–37, 44; Perutelli 1994, 42–43, 49–50; Elm von der Osten 2007, 99–105, 138–143; Davis 2014, 201–203, 209–210; Buckley 2016, 77–79; Battistella/Milić Galli 2020, 209–218, 231. The wedding's Cybele and Bellona similes also recall those goddesses' roles at Cyzicus. Since, as Elm von der Osten noted above, Cybele purifies herself of all sadness from her killing of Attis, yet will go on to inspire frenzy in others, this may imply that purification can lead to emotionally happy repeat offenders. See also Heerink 2022 on how the Argonauts enter meaningless war in Colchis *after* their purification.
80 The line numbers in Book 5 are from the 1913 Teubner edition. Mozley's 1937 Loeb edition reads *luet* for *libet*, emphasising her atoning suffering already implied by *impia*. On the return, see Zissos 2012, 97–98.
81 Zissos 2012, 99.

MI.⁸² Receiving forgiveness from victims, even if only in imagination is another step,⁸³ as is performing reparations when possible.⁸⁴ Even if his moral authority as *paterfamilias* has been compromised by his treachery, Aeetes would still count as someone from her past to rebuild a restorative relationship with. Whatever guilt or grief she may feel from killing her older children at Corinth may well be displaced by securing a strong position for Medus her younger child in Colchis. So unlike Apollonius' poem, her prognosis is good in Valerius.

8 Apollonius: Medea and moral injury

Apollonius' Medea has an even more severe case of Moral Injury than Valerius'. As Valerius' Jason wished he was dead after violating deeply held ethical standards, so Apollonius' Medea wished to die before breaking her own rules and betraying her family by helping Jason (3.771–801).⁸⁵ Her main motivations are her desire for Jason on the one hand and her fear of her father and her αἰδώς ('shame') on the other. She actually pulls out her box of deadly herbs to kill herself, but is stopped by Hera, fear of death and love of life (802–819). After betraying her family, she again considers killing herself out of fear, but Hera steers her towards flight instead (4.20–25). Later, Medea feels deeply betrayed when the Argonauts consider relinquishing her to Absyrtus' Colchians, and she rages with a desire to destroy herself and the ship.⁸⁶ She foresees shame and punishment for herself if she is returned to Colchis, and she terms her past

---

82 Litz et al. 2009, 702, 704.
83 Litz et al. 2016, 132–133.
84 Litz et al. 2009, 704.
85 On Apollonius' psychological subtly, see Phinney 1967, esp. 340. On her dilemma, see Hunter 1987, 138.
86 According to Salemme 1991, 85–87 Apollonius' Medea wanted to sink the boat and kill herself with everyone else (4.391–394) but Valerius' is likened to a non-violent Bacchante content to die upon seeing Tempe or Pelion. I note that such a simile contains a threat of an unintentionally violent Agave. These words come near to where Valerius' epic cuts off at a moment of maximum confusion, tension and sense of betrayal, when Medea interrupts Jason while the Latin reveals some room for excruciating confusion: *sic fata parantem / reddere dicta uirum furiata mente refugit* (8.445–446). The crucial word here is *reddere* which means "to give back". Until the following word *dicta* is heard, there is a brief moment during which Jason might be preparing to give *her* back (to the Colchians). The word *dicta* makes clear that he is preparing to give back *words*, i.e., he is going to answer her. But she turns away and is not listening to him. So perhaps she thinks that he is preparing to give *her* back. The order in which the Latin is auditorily processed admirably reflects Medea's fears and her act of turning away.

deeds δεινά ('terrible') (4.380). Even though all she has done has been to help Jason and to flee from her father in fear, she feels shame for betraying her family already.

This Moral Injury is greatly amplified when Jason and Medea decide to murder her brother Absyrtus. She entraps him by promising to plot with him to betray Jason (4.435–440).[87] Thus there is also some underhandedness on Absyrtus' part and Medea witnesses this moral betrayal on top of the ones committed by her against her family and by the Argonauts against her. When Jason ambushes Absyrtus in the temple of Artemis, Medea is present at his death. She turns her eyes away, as if she tried to prevent her own traumatisation, but she becomes a tactile witness since Absyrtus' last act is to use his hands to throw his own gushing blood at his sister, thus tainting her with blood-pollution and ensuring that her last memory of him is of him seeking supernatural vengeance against her (4.464–476). Absyrtus receives no funeral, no armed dance, no Colchian "tree-burial", just an unmarked grave, nothing to placate the dead. Jason performs a brutal μασχαλισμός: cutting off the corpse' extremities to cripple any vengeful ghost;[88] he then laps up and apotropaically spits out Absyrtus' blood and ἄγος ('pollution') three times,[89] which can hardly have been a healing experience for Medea (4.477–478). Different cultures are different, but this is extreme by ancient standards.[90] The fact that the μασχαλισμός is described as θέμις "what's right" for those who murder by treachery, either shows just how twisted and *not right* things are, or if we interpret it as "what's usual" then we have a major change in attitudes and behaviours for Jason and Medea, another symptom of MI (4.479).[91] Then she helps the Argonauts to surprise and slaughter her own people in a night battle (4.482–489). Medea has committed treachery, witnessed a family member sacrilegiously killed, seen her future husband commit murder and mutilate her brother's remains. She does not mourn. She meets many criteria for both PTSD and Moral Injury.[92]

---

87 See Byre 1996, 10–11, 14 on the cloak as trap.
88 See Johnston 1999, 158.
89 Ceulemans 2007, 104–105.
90 Hunter 2008, 145 sees precedents for the μασχαλισμός in the epic cycle. But epics are full of extremes.
91 On the MI symptom, see Drescher et al., 2011, 9. On the irony of θέμις here, see Mori 2008, 188 and n. 8, 201–215.
92 Exposure to human remains and witnessing traumatic actions are listed in the DSM V entry on PTSD.

9 Apollonius: Circe, not a benevolent moral authority (4.659–752)

Jason and Medea's purification by Circe, closes off the section of narrative travels after Absyrtus' murder during which they are ritually impure and silent. It restores their speech and ability to participate in public life and ritual. The kinslaying on an island in a sacred temple of Artemis is balanced by a purification by kin at a sacred hearth on an island. However, it achieves no closure whatsoever for their psychological tensions or the readers' ominous expectations. When Jason and Medea go to Circe to be purified of murder, the other Argonauts stay on the beach. The guilty pair go alone silently to the hearth where Jason plants the murder weapon in the ashes. Circe pours piglet blood over them, calling upon Kathartic Zeus with libations, πέλανοι ('batter or cakes') and wineless offerings and prayers, while her servant nymphs carry out the λύματα ('remnants of purification') (4.706–712).[93]

Afterwards Medea gives her aunt a somewhat dishonest, self-justifying account, afraid of her reaction. In properly conducted Exposure Therapy, often a part of the Adaptive Disclosure method described above,[94] the patient should try to really face the negative experience honestly in order to get past shame and fears of rejection so that one can bring out all the beliefs and ideas associated with the experience and process them.[95] Litz et al. note the usefulness for MI recoverers to seek out people they respect from their old life and to form positive healing relationships with them, but one should start with those who will be easier to relate to and more understanding.[96] Unfortunately for Medea, Circe is too close to the victim, too upset over his death and over Medea's betrayal of her family.[97] Medea would have needed some more neutral figure to talk to, and she was not ready to face what she had done or to begin the difficult work of rebuilding family connections. So, Medea may have been right to try to hide things from her aunt, although it did not help. Circe expresses disgust for Medea's actions, never mentioning the murder, but only Medea's flight from her father and her association with a stranger. Circe tells the younger woman to leave and never come back. Medea covers her eyes with her robe as she is seized

---

93 See Knight 1995, 195 and Clare 2002, 254 on the importance of Circe's ritual knowledge.
94 See "Valerius Flaccus: Mopsus, A Benevolent Moral Authority" above.
95 Litz et al. 2009, 701, 703.
96 Litz et al. 2009, 702, 704.
97 Plantinga 2007, 560–561 notes the problems from a related purifier.

by ἀμέγαρτον ἄχος, 4.749 ("sad distress"). We do not even know whether she tells Jason what she is hearing, since she and her aunt were talking in Colchian, although Jason could probably tell something from the gestures and tone.[98] He does at least take her hand. This is as much solidarity as Medea receives in the course of the ritual and its aftermath.

It would have been contrary to pollution laws for Circe to allow killers of her kin to remain under her roof; it was usual for killers to go into exile and seek purification there where they would generally be admitted into the new society.[99] In *the Laws*, Plato does unusually prescribe purification for murderers *before* their exile, similar to what Circe does which is the only known case of purification followed by expulsion in myth, although the host could refuse the purification as happened to Ixion.[100] Circe would probably have refused if she had recognised Medea earlier.[101]

Though the ritual does seem to reconcile Jason and Medea to the gods, and their sea misfortunes cease, it is a disaster for Medea emotionally and socially. She will never meet her family or speak her native language or have anyone she can really trust ever again in Apollonius' epic. That part of her life has been closed off. Litz notes the usefulness of self-transcendence and a spiritual *community* for the healing process citing Drescher's definition of spirituality as "an individual's understanding of, experience with, and connection to that which transcends the self".[102] Both Circe and Mopsus' rituals involve the transcendent gods, but Mopsus' has more in the way of *community*. Valerius' Argonauts were solidified as a group, putting the people and the grievous events at Cyzicus behind them. In Apollonius, the close of Circe's rite emphasises the closing off of connections, but not in a healing way.[103] His Medea will express her isolation from country, parents and home in her speeches in Phaeacia, while calling upon queen Arete and all the Argonauts *except* Jason to help her and not to betray her to the Colchians (4.1011–1057).[104] Medea has difficulty trusting the Argonauts,

---

98 On the use of Colchian and Jason's exclusion, see Plantinga 2007, 555–557; Hunter 1993, 137, 146–147.
99 Parker 1983, 123, 370, 374. Plantinga 2007, 561 also notes this.
100 Parker 1983, 374–375.
101 See Mori 2008, 222. Cf. Parker 1983, 374.
102 Drescher 2006, 337 cited in Litz et al. 2009, 704.
103 See Plantinga 2007, 563.
104 Hunter 1987, 133 n. 30 sees in this the "increased seriousness of Medea's position."

especially Jason, a fear which Euripides' sequel largely justifies. Destruction of trust is important in Shay's type of Moral Injury.[105]

10 Apollonius: Medea, trust and Talos

In her last appearance in the epic, Medea destroys Talos the faithful bronze guardian of Crete. Arguably this was a good tactical decision, since the Argonauts were tired and thirsty and Talos was preventing their landing by throwing πέτρας (huge rocks). Perhaps they could have sailed around. But those with Moral Injury can be more aggressive,[106] and the way that Medea destroys him involves unleashing pure hatred from her eyes which startles and frightens even the narrator. She invokes the 'life-devouring spirits of death' (Κῆρας θυμοβόρους) and the 'fleet hounds of the underworld' (Ἀίδαο θοὰς κύνας). She is θεμένη κακὸν νοὸν ('putting on a bad mind'), and πρῖεν χόλον ('gnashed bitter gall'), ἐχθοδοποῖσιν ὄμμασι ('with eyes full of hate'), ἐπιζάφελον κοτέουσα ('violently raging') at 4.1638–1688.

Cassidy rightly observes that this scene foreshadows Medea's future marriage with Achilles in the underworld as Jason leads her forward to the bow of the ship where, in a violent rage, she destroys a powerful bronze warrior by its achilles' heel. Given that Achilles is Shay's archetypal Iliadic berserker, and that Medea summons rage-filled magical powers like those felt by invincible berserkers in the heat of battle in Vietnam, Medea will be a good match for Achilles.[107] But Shay notes that berserkers always suffer permanent psychological damage.[108] Perhaps some could wield such magic without meeting a tragic fate, but not Medea.

Thus, Apollonius paints a bleak picture for Medea's future. Though it cannot quite follow Euripides since Theseus and thus Aegeus are in the past,[109] the key event of Medea's child-slaying is foreshadowed by the ominous simile of the "mother of dead children" at 3.747–748. In Euripides, when Jason the last person

---

105 Shay 2004, 166. This passage refers to "complex PTSD", an earlier name for MI. See also Litz et al., 2016, 122 for more on betrayal type MI.
106 Drescher et al. 2011, 9.
107 Cassidy 2019, 445 where she emphasises that Talos does not deserve punishment. Fantuzzi 2008, 300 thinks that Medea's action was gratuitous against a non-threat.
108 Shay 1995, 77–98, 200–201.
109 See Book 1.101–104.

she has left finally betrays her, Medea will live for nothing but vengeance like Achilles and the Vietnam berserkers.[110]

11 Ritual healing, ghosts, dances and benevolent moral authority in modern times

As this paper nears its own closure, it should be noted that ritual healing of Moral Injury is a feature of more recent times. In *War and Moral Injury: a Reader*, Chester Nez, a Navajo Code-Talker and World War II veteran, tells how after coming back to the reservation from the Pacific, he was haunted by nighttime visions of Japanese soldiers. Because of the secrecy surrounding the Code-Talkers, he was not allowed to speak about the war to anyone except in the most general terms. Finally, he told his sister about the specters, and his family hired a hand-trembler to diagnose the problem: ghosts. Then they put on an elaborate ceremony involving several nights of sacred chants, dances and sand paintings. The hand-trembler, his family members and the ritual singer functioned as moral authorities, but all the many Navajo participants in the ceremony were to bring *hozoji* that is "kindness, compassion and good will" with them, emphasising the harmonious community.[111] He says that it worked. He did not see those sights again for many years.[112] The same ceremony often used to be performed for Navajo men returning from war and for children returning from boarding school who had had experiences of isolation, cultural dislocation and abuse rivaling Medea's.[113]

12 Conclusion

We have seen prominent themes of solidarity/isolation and acceptance/rejection in the purification rituals and those who perform them in the ancient epics. These coincide with the more hopeful depiction of recovery from Moral Injury in Valerius vs. Apollonius, though Valerius' account of the Cyzicus episode does have some subtly ominous intertextual references.

---

110 On Euripides, see Lush 2014.
111 Nez/Avila 2018, 143.
112 Nez/Avila 2018, 144.
113 Nez/Avila 2018, 142. For more examples, see also Pacello 2018, 120.

Different cultures deal with Moral Injury differently, some more effectively than others. Since Moral Injury research is still in its infancy,[114] there is much to be learned. Phenomena similar to MI are clearly illustrated in both Valerius' and Apollonius' epics.[115] Both of the two main ceremonies mark an end. The one in Valerius Flaccus brings a healing closure to the Argonauts' feelings of guilt and grief from the Moral Injury of the slaying of their hosts. The Circe episode in Apollonius marks the end of Medea's relationship with her family, her people and her language as well as the intensification of her suffering from Moral Injury. Comparison with modern material suggests that the ancient poets had a good understanding of what we call psychological trauma and of ways of responding to it.

The poets can also contribute to the modern discussion. Valerius Flaccus in particular points a positive way forward embodying many of the principles of current Moral Injury research with effective community action, whereas Apollonius shows us the effects of its absence. Clearly ancient Greek epic, and Sophoclean tragedy are having an impact through the work of Shay, Meagher and others. Maybe it is time for Flavian and Hellenistic poets to have their say too.

---

[114] See Drescher et al. 2011, 8–9 and Litz et al. 2009, 704–705.

[115] This essay has focused on rituals in epic, but they had precedents in Greek and Roman culture. For Mopsus see Manuwald 1999, 176 on a lustration of Octavian's army; Boyancé 1972, 341 and Stover 2012, 174–175 on banishing ghosts at the Lemuria; and Parker 1983, 22–23 on marching armies between halves of a sacrificed animal. For Circe see Parker 1983, 370 ff.

Marco Fucecchi
Compage soluta: Collapsing Universe and the Boundaries of Epic Poetry (Lucan, Silius, Statius and Claudian's *De raptu*)

Abstract: Imperial epic associates ancient myths of fraternal strife, and mostly the related historical theme of Roman civil war, with images of collapsing universe. Cosmic dissolution, transgression of the boundaries between underworld, earth, sea and sky and the consequent return of the elements into primeval chaos are usually introduced at the beginning (or even at the end) of war narratives and other stories dealing with the gods' fight for supremacy. This analysis concentrates on the occurrence, in such contexts, of the phrase *compage soluta* ("when the framework <of the world> is dissolved"), which describes the loosening and breaking of the aethereal bonds that maintain the structure of the universe. The first simile of Lucan's *Bellum Ciuile* (1.72 ff.) offers the starting point for a wide-ranging exploration involving other epic-historical contexts — such as Hannibal's last threatening words in Silius' *Punica* (17.606b ff.), which also indirectly announces Rome's future internal crisis —, as well as mythical episodes centred on Pluto's 'periodic' attempts to subvert Jupiter's power by stirring up the forces of Hell: from Statius *Thebaid* 8 (much indebted to Homer *Iliad* 20) and Claudian's *De raptu* 1, with the puzzling interlude provided by Eumolpus' *Bellum Ciuile* in Petronius' *Satyricon*.

1 Introduction

Latin epic tends to associate ancient mythical and historical war narratives with images of cosmic dissolution, which can be endowed with an introductory (or even ending) role and certainly are located in crucial places within the poems. Civil war in particular — together with its more emblematic counterpart, gigantomachy — is often connected to the collapse of the universe: the breaking of the boundaries between underworld, earth, sea and sky prefigures the return of the natural elements into primordial chaos.

I am sincerely grateful to Angeliki Roumpou for inviting me to participate in this volume. I would like to thank Darcy Krasne for her kind help in revising (and improving) the whole paper and, mostly, for sharing her thoughts about the topic I have tried to deal with.

In this paper, I shall focus on a single phrase — the ablative absolute *compage soluta* — which, in such contexts, graphically illustrates the loosening of the very structure of the cosmos: its range of occurrence encompasses texts dealing more or less directly with civil war, from the epic poems of the 1st century CE (Lucan's *Pharsalia*, Statius' *Thebaid*, Silius' *Punica*) to Claudian's *De raptu Proserpinae*. I am aware that the relationship between fraternal strife and cosmic dissolution is a great (and debated) problem, which goes well outside the limited scope of my research.[1] Be that as it may, if this essay manages to illustrate the need for further work on this topic, it will have served its purpose.

2 Lucan's first simile

Lucan's *Pharsalia* starts out with a clear connection between gigantomachy and civil war.[2] Here, I will consider in particular the first simile of the poem (1.72b ff.), where the analogy between civil war and cosmic collapse (as an extreme form of boundary transgression) is fully exploited.[3] After the proem and the *laudes Neronis*, Lucan meditates on the causes of the war between Caesar and Pompey: he "feels inspired to reveal the causes of such great events" (67 *fert animus causas tantarum expromere rerum*) as an introduction to the main narrative. The historical fact turns out to be a catastrophe of cosmic scale. It is the hostile chain of destiny (1.70a *inuida fatorum series*) that led Rome to self-destruction, as usually happens to everything that reaches the height of greatness and success (70b–71 ... *summisque negatum / stare diu*, "the speedy fall which no eminence can escape").[4] The narrator describes Rome, at the middle of the 1st century BC, as no longer able to sustain her own greatness: the *caput mundi* is sinking into civil war under the weight of her good fortune (71–72...

---

1 Suffice it to say that the topic is also relevant to Valerius Flaccus' *Argonautica*, a poem that I do not include in this survey because it contains no occurrence of the clause *compage soluta*. However, cf. Krasne 2018b, 363–364 "the Argo's voyage causes the very bindings of the cosmos to collapse, turning the constituent parts of the world against each other in a sort of cosmic civil war". For further, brief, remarks on Valerius' *Argonautica*, see below (n. 45).
2 Luc. 1.36 *non nisi saeuorum ... post bella gigantum*. See also 3.316; 4.593 ff.; 7.145 ff.
3 For links to Lucretius' and Virgil's cosmic imagery, see Hardie 1986 (esp. ch. 5); Roche 2005; Nelis 2014.
4 Sen. *Controu.* 1 *praef.* 7 "perhaps it is just Fate, whose grim law is universal and everlasting — things that get to the top sink back to the bottom, faster than they rose" (transl. Winterbottom); Narducci 2002, 42.

nimioque graues sub pondere lapsus / nec se Roma ferens).⁵ The consequence of all this is the destruction of the state, which is compared with the final conflagration of the universe.⁶ This corresponds to the Stoic *ekpyrosis*, whose first step will be the dissolution of the cosmic framework (Luc. 1.72b–80):

> ... *sic, cum compage soluta*
> *saecula tot mundi suprema coegerit hora*
> *antiquum repetens iterum chaos, omnia mixtis*
> *sidera sideribus concurrent, ignea pontum*   75
> *astra petent, tellus extendere litora nolet*
> *excutietque fretum; fratri contraria Phoebe*
> *ibit et obliquum bigas agitare per orbem*
> *indignata diem poscet sibi, totaque discors*
> *machina diuolsi turbabit foedera mundi.*   80

> Just as when, once the whole structure has dissolved, the final hour closes out the long ages of the universe, seeking again the ancient chaos, stars will collide with stars, blazing planets will plummet into the sea, and the earth will refuse to stretch out the shore and will shake off the ocean. Phoebe, disdaining to drive her two-horse chariot cross-ways across the sky, will go against her brother and demand the day for herself. The whole discordant machine will overturn the laws of a universe ripped apart[7]

This simile formally puts together the past — that of Rome (the world city)'s destruction caused by civil war (68–69 *quid in arma furentem / impulerit populum, quid pacem excusserit orbi*) — and the (hopefully far) future of the cosmic deflagration at the end of a Great Year (72 ff. *cum ... coegerit ... concurrent... petent... nolet* etc.). Even more interesting is the way Lucan projects the human events onto a cosmic scenario, as already happened in Seneca's tragedies, where the *nefas* usually assumes the dimension of a universal catastrophe:[8] this

---

5 For the topos, see Liv. *praef.* 4; Hor. *Epod.* 16.2; Sen. *Ag.* 87 ff.
6 Cicero (*Rep.* 3.34) already compared the destruction of a state (*ciuitas*) to the decay and dissolution of the whole universe (Degl' Innocenti Pierini 1999, 20). Seneca (*Clem.* 1.4.1) defines the Emperor as the *desmos* (*uinculum*) and *pneuma* (*spiritus uitalis*) preserving the stability of the cosmos. In the famous speech of Petilius Cerialis in Tacitus' *Historiae* the Roman state is described as a *compages,* coalesced throughout the centuries: "it cannot be destroyed without overwhelming its destroyers" (*Hist.* 4.74 *octingentorum annorum fortuna disciplinaque compages haec coaluit, quae conuelli sine exitio conuellentium non potest*).
7 Translation is by Roche 2009 with adaptations.
8 Rosenmeyer 1989; Schmitz 1993.

represents — as Narducci rightly observed — a typical mark of the tragic character of Lucanean epos.⁹

But now it is time for a closer look at this first occurrence of the phrase *compage soluta*. The noun *compages* (from *cum* + *pingere* lit. "putting together") can mean in a concrete sense: 1) "joint, bond" — more often in the plural — connecting the parts of every kind of (natural) structure, from the animal or human body to the whole universe; 2) the framework itself, the structure of a 'body':¹⁰ for Lucan, see e.g. 1.502 *nondum sparsa compage carinae* (the hull of a boat); 2.486–487 *atque omnis trahe, gurges, aquas, ut spumeus alnos / discussa compage* (a bridge) *feras*; 3.490 *nunc aries .../ ...compagem soluere muri* (the city-walls) / *temptat*; until 5.119 *compages humana* (the human body).¹¹ More specifically, in a cosmological sense, these two notions correspond respectively to: 1) (as plural) the bonds ensuring the cohesion of the universe, where all things are bound together (e.g. Manil. 2.802–803 *totus in illis / nititur aeternis ueluti compagibus orbis*, the cardinal points, "by which the celestial circle is totally held in position as by eternal supports"); 2) the whole framework of the universe, the structure composed of the natural elements, as is the case in Lucan's simile and at least two of the other occurrences of *compage soluta* that we are going to deal with: Statius *Theb.* 8.31 and Silius *Punica* 17.607.¹²

The imagery of cosmic dissolution inherent to *compage soluta* is "central to the meaning of the first seven books of the *Bellum ciuile*", as Michael Lapidge

---

9 Narducci 2002, 48. In the present paper I cannot tackle controversial matters such as the sense of the *laudes Neronis* or Lucan's judgement on Roman empire. As for the dialectic relationship between the *Bellum Ciuile* and the Stoic orthodoxy, see Narducci 2002; Roche 2005; 2009.

10 *TLL* 3.1998,45 ff. 'res ex diuersis partibus compacta', where we also find Tac. *Hist.* 3.27 *soluta compage scutorum* (68 f.), apparently the first occurrence of this way of defining the wall of shields (cf. Amm. Marc. 14.2.10; 16.12.44; 24.4.15; Oros. *Hist.* 6.7.9).

11 Both *TLL* 3.1997, 79 ff. and *OLD* s.v. *compages* §1 register, at first, the abstract meaning, i.e. the action of holding together or the construction (*actio compingendi*), or rather the status, the condition of being composed.

12 At *TLL* 3.1999, 41–50 (*de mundo*) we have e.g. Lucan. 5.632–633 *arduus axis / insonuit motaque poli compage laborat* and the two aforementioned passages of Statius and Silius; the first place is reserved for Manilius 2.802–803 (see above for the other meaning); however, what seems to me more striking is the omission of Lucan 1.72. See also *TLL* 3.1999, 50 ff. 'de terra', where we find e.g. Sen. *Oed.* 580 *tellus... compage rupta sonuit* and Stat. *Theb.* 8.144 *rupta ... soli compage*, together with Sen. *QNat.* 6.32.4 *ruptis compagibus dehiscens solum*. Darcy Krasne rightly points out to me the interesting case of Apuleius' *Mund.* 32 **soluta conpage** *simulacri totius incolumitas interiret* (translating ps-Aristotle's [*Mund.*] 400a.2 τὸ σύμπαν ἄγαλμα λύειν τε καὶ συγχεῖν), where the philosopher is discussing Pheidias' statue of Athena as a metaphor for the integrity of the cosmos.

observed forty years ago.[13] Lucan offers an example of poetic transposition of Greek technical terms introduced by the Stoic philosopher Chrysippus (III BC), whose cosmological theory becomes familiar at Rome through the mediation of Cicero's writings,[14] and is still dominant in the Stoicism of the 1st century CE.[15] According to Chrysippus, the universe (*synolos*)[16] is held together by the all-pervasive *pneuma*, while the cosmic conflagration (*ekpyrosis*) is the periodic release (*analysis, analyein* i.e. *soluere*) of the bindings (*desmoi*) which give coherence and continuity (*synècheia*) to the connection (*symplokè*) of all things (*syndoùmena*), i.e. the structure of the universe.[17] However, while the Stoic *ekpyrosis* originates from "the periodic need of the universe to be purified and renewed",[18] Lucan shows that civil war is rather caused by *furor*, which destroys human as well as cosmic bonds.[19] This brings about another important deviation from Chrysippus' theory: the lack of hints at rebirth or regeneration of the universe after the *ekpyrosis*.[20] Lucan refutes the Stoic providentialism as still represented e.g. by the *mundus renouaturus* promised in Seneca's *Consolatio ad Marciam*.[21] In historical terms, this Lucanean deviation results in severing (or strongly problematising, at least) the 'providential' connection between the end of Roman Republic and the beginning of the Empire.

---

13 Lapidge 1979, 346 who also records a number of occurrences of the 'dissolution theme' in the *Bellum ciuile* (367 ff.). For *soluere* in a similar context, see Latinus' words in Virg. *Aen.* 12.204–205 ... *non, si ... caelumque in Tartara soluat*, "not even a force that could ... make heaven collapse into Tartarus' dark pit" (transl. Ahl).
14 See e.g. Balbus' speech in *De natura deorum* Book 2; Lapidge 1979, 350; Cicero (*Nat. D.* 2.19) translates Chrysippus' *pneuma diēnekès* with *continuatus spiritus*.
15 For Lucan the three main sources of the Stoic cosmological vocabulary are, according to Lapidge 1979, 351, Cornutus' *Theologia Graeca*, the *Astronomica* of Manilius — "the first Latin poet who attempts to reproduce the Stoic theory of cosmic coherence together with the metaphor of cosmic binding" (Lapidge 1980, 819) — and, obviously, his uncle Seneca's writings.
16 Lapidge 1979, 347 ff. (part. 348 n. 21); apparently Chrysippus does not use the term *sympagìa*, from which the Latin calque *compages* originates, nor other derivatives from *sympēgnymi* (e.g. the adjective *sympagēs*, 'joined together, compacted': Plat. *Ti.* 45b; 46c; 56e).
17 The *machina mundi* (Lucr. 5.96; see also Manil. 2.807), which is related to other images like the "chain" (gr. *heirmòs*) or the "weaving together" of fates (*symplokè*; *fatorum series*: Lapidge 1979, 349 n. 32).
18 Lapidge 1979, 367 n. 85.
19 Luc. 7.136 *aethera... cadentem*; 2.289 *mundum... cadentem* and 290 *ruat... aether* (Narducci 2004, 16 ff.); for Seneca's tragedies, see above, n. 8.
20 Schotes 1969, 25; Narducci 2002, 46 f. and Narducci 2004, 15 f.
21 *Marc.* 26.6 from which Lucan draws the image of stars colliding with stars. Seneca's tragedy, conversely, offers a less optimistic perspective, which is rightly considered a fundamental influence on Lucan: e.g. Sen. *Thy.* 827 ff. and Narducci 2004, 18.

By contrast, the final conflagration as a return of the elements into chaos (1.74 *antiquum repetens iterum chaos*, i.e. the primordial stew from which everything arose), rather than into fire, should not be considered as properly unorthodox from a Stoic viewpoint.[22] Lucan's simile fits well with Chrysippus' conception of the "chaotic" result of *ekpyrosis*, as we can infer from Plutarch's testimony.[23] And it is probably following in Chrysippus' footsteps that the Stoic philosopher of the Neronian age, Annaeus Cornutus, states that chaos represents "the generative moisture from which the universe derived or even the fire itself which, when quenched, will in turn regenerate a universe".[24] Lucan may have become familiar with Chrysippus' theory and vocabulary when attending Cornutus' school, together with Persius the satirist.[25] A further point in this direction comes from Persius himself, who — in his third satire — uses the rare collocation *compage soluta* as comic metaphor:[26] the floppy, loosed neck of a student snoring and yawning in a philosophical (Stoic) school is projected onto the image of the 'dissolution' of the cosmic structure (Pers. 3.58–59 *stertis adhuc laxumque caput compage soluta / oscitat hesternum dissutis undique malis*, "you are still snoring and your lolling head with its joint dissolved is yawning yesterday's yawn, with your jaws completely unstitched").[27]

3 A step backwards: from Lucan to Augustan poetry

Regardless of their Stoic 'purity' (or lack thereof),[28] Lucan's *ekpyrosis* and return into chaos do not represent mere terms of comparison, distanced in the undetermined future: on the contrary, they prove to be literally true at the very time of the civil war between Caesar and Pompey. The recurrence of images of cosmic collapse before the fateful day of Pharsalus retrospectively enhances the struc-

---

22 Cf. Ov. *Met.* 2.298 f.; Lapidge 1979, 361.
23 Plut. *De Stoic. rep.* 1053B 6 (= *SVF* 2.605).
24 Lapidge 1979, 362 quoting *Theol. Gr.* 28.5 ff.; Boys-Stones 2018, 85. For the problem of regeneration, see below.
25 Suet. *Vit. Persii* 5; Lapidge 1979, 352, *contra* Most 1989, 2054 f.
26 Biggs 2020, 38.
27 Biggs 2020, part. 38–40.
28 E.g. Nelis 2014 also underlines Empedoclean influences.

tural role played by the comparison of *Bellum Ciuile* 1.72 ff. in the narrative strategy.[29]

The storm which strikes the vessel of Caesar and Amyclas at the end of book 5 (5.597 ff.) is one of the anticipatory signs of the imminent catastrophe.[30] Separate seas are carried away by the contrasting winds; the Tyrrhenian sea migrates to the Aegean, the Adriatic to the Ionian; mighty waves from the ocean bury the lofty peaks of the mountains: all this sounds like a repetition of the Great Flood (620 ff.). After ignoring the warnings issued by Amyclas, who is invited to believe in the power of his unknown passenger (578 ff.), Caesar faces the cataclysm with firm confidence in the support of his ally Fortuna. At 632 ff. the storm is said to endanger the stability of cosmos: *tum superum conuexa tremunt atque arduus axis / intonuit **mota**que poli **compage** laborat. / Extimuit natura chaos; rupisse uidentur / concordes elementa moras rursusque redire / nox manes mixtura deis,* "the dome of the gods quaked, the lofty sky thundered and was troubled, **when the heaven's framework**[31] **was shaken**. Nature dreaded chaos: it seemed that the elements had burst their harmonious bonds, and that Night was returning, to blend the shades below with the gods above".[32] While the storm is raging, Caesar launches his titanic challenge towards the gods, whose hostility he does not fear (654–671). In fact, contrary to the great flood sent by Jupiter — the first return into primeval chaos in the world's history –,[33] neither the outbreak nor the end of the apocalyptic storm of Lucan's book 5 can be traced back to divine intervention. And it is thanks to Fortuna's help that the greatest wave (*decimus… fluctus*) finally sets Caesar down again on the land of Epirus: the end of the storm and the miraculous landing near his camp will lead him to recover all his power as well as his good fortune (677 *fortunamque suam tacta tellure recepit*).

Thus, the great storm of the Amyclas episode can be conceived of as an instance of (or a hint at) the cosmic collapse (*soluta compage*) announced by the poem's first simile. At the same time, it also reenacts — and even overturns — other 'chaotic' epic openings. The first that comes to mind is the release of the

---

29 Lapidge 1979, 362 ff.
30 Lapidge 1979, 367 f.; Tarrant 2002, 358–359 also quotes Sen. *Ag.* 485 ff.
31 In *TLL* 3.1999.44 f. this passage is classified (less probably, in my opinion) under the examples of *compages* as *iunctura*.
32 Translation is by Duff with adaptations.
33 The first consequence of the flood is the loosening of the boundaries between earth and sea: Ov. *Met.* 1.291–292.

winds from Aeolus' cave in Virgil's *Aeneid* book 1.[34] The storm triggered against the Trojans by the Lord of the winds, incited by Juno's rage, would have completely destroyed Aeneas' fleet, if it were not for Neptune's intervention that restored order (141) and saved the life and destiny of the Trojan hero (142 ff.). In the first (political) simile of the *Aeneid* (148 ff.), the sea god is compared to a respected statesman who manages to appease the crowd in tumult with his words (153 *ille regit dictis animos et pectora mulcet*). By escalating "the catastrophic destruction of political strife to a cosmic scale",[35] Lucan's first simile thus inverts the tone and outcome of the emblematic image created by Virgil.

A few verses later in *Aeneid* 1, a second divine scene confirms that Jupiter is keeping control of the situation. His prophecy reassures Venus about the accomplishment of fate: with the advent of Caesar Augustus, the gates of war, "grim with iron and close-fitting bars (*compagibus artis*), shall be closed" (1.293 f.). According to the ancient Roman ritual here referred to, the plural *compages* means the doorposts binding the temple of Janus, where *Furor* is imprisoned, its hands bound back by bronze chains (294–296). Conversely, at the outset of Lucan's *Pharsalia*, the promise of Virgil's Jupiter (peace all over the world conquered by Rome) is recalled only indirectly, as an almost desperate wish, by the author of Nero's eulogy (1.61b–62 … *pax missa per orbem / ferrea belligeri compescat limina Iani*, "let Peace fly over the earth and shut fast the iron gates of the warlike Janus"): the jussive subjunctive (*compescat*) meaningfully takes the place of the future indicative (*claudentur*).[36]

But let's come back again to Virgil. As we know, at the beginning of *Aeneid*'s second half, the gates of Janus' temple are opened by Juno, who slips down from the sky to trigger war in Latium (*Aen.* 7.621–622 *impulit ipsa manu portas, et cardine uerso / Belli ferratos rumpit Saturnia postis* "with her own hands dashed in the lingering doors, and on their turning hinges Saturn's daughter burst open the iron-bound gates of war"). Just before, however, the Augustan narrator has introduced an aetiological celebration of the still extant temple (607 *sunt geminae portae*) together with the description of the hundred bars of bronze and iron firmly closing the *Portae Belli* under Janus' (and Augustus')

---

34 81 ff. … *cauum conuersa cuspide montem / impulit in latus; ac uenti uelut agmine facto, / qua data porta, ruunt et terras turbine perflant*, "he (= Aeolus) pointed his spearhead down, then pierced through the hollow flank of the mountain. The winds, like legions marshalled for battle, stream through the portal supplied, blast out across earth in tornadoes" (transl. Ahl).
35 Roche 2005, 60 and n. 20 (with bibl.).
36 Roche 2009, 143–144 *ad* 60–62: "Nero did in fact close the doors of the Temple of Janus after the supplication of the Parthian king Tiridates in AD 66"; see also Hor. *Epist.* 2.1.253 ff.; Aug. *Anc.* 13. On the Empedoclean implications of Lucan's image of *pax*, see Nelis 2014.

strict surveillance: another image of firmness which almost has the power, if not to undermine Juno's effort in advance, at least to relegate the goddess' hostility to a remote (and no longer effective) past.[37]

By stressing Juno's antagonistic role, the episodes of *Aeneid* 1 and 7 — situated at the opening of the poem's first and second half — both emphasise the cosmic dimension of the goddess' (vain) attempts at breaking the course of fate. Lucan, for his part, enters the field of cosmological poetry more explicitly: his first simile illustrates a catastrophe that is the outcome of the irrational fury of civil war and not the effect of divine intervention. Thus, he provides a further, idiosyncratic response not only to Virgil's *Aeneid*, but also to the openings of Ovid's *Metamorphoses* and *Fasti*, placed respectively under the sign of Greek Chaos and its Latin counterpart, the god Janus (Ov. *Fast.* 1.103 *me Chaos antiqui... uocabant*). Lucan displays Ovid's influence early, by announcing that his *animus* (and not the Muse) pushes him to set forth the causes of the great events (1.67 *fert animus...*)[38] and, soon after, by depicting a cosmic collapse that interacts with Ovid's description of primordial Chaos (*Met.* 1.5–20).[39] Richard Tarrant is probably right in suggesting that Lucan's picture of cosmic dissolution, as a return to primordial chaos, reverses the progression of the *Metamorphoses* from chaos to cosmos.[40] Tarrant likewise observes, however, that Ovid's own epic poem already thematises — especially in the first two books — the actual danger

---

[37] Juno's gesture in *Aeneid* 7 literally transfers to Rome's prehistory the foundational myth of the opening of the gates of War, which Ennius, in Book 7 of his *Annales*, had traced back to the second half of III BC (fr. 225 f. S. *postquam Discordia taetra / Belli ferratos postes portasque refregit*, "... after foul Discord broke open the ironclad doors and doorposts of war"; transl. Warmington). If Ennius' *Discordia* mirrors the Empedoclean *Neikos* (Nelis 2014 cf. Enn. *Ann.* 220–221 S.), the opening of the gates of war by Juno paves the way to the forces of Chaos, leading to a "civil war" *ante litteram* between Latins and Trojans.

[38] *Causas tantarum expromere rerum* (67) is also indebted to Virg. *Aen.* 1.8–11, and *immensum opus* (68) to *Aen.* 7.45 *maius opus moueo*.

[39] *Antiquum repetens iterum chaos* (74) recalls Ov. *Met.* 1.5 ff. *ante mare et terras et quod tegit omnia caelum / unus erat toto naturae uultus in orbe, / **quem dixere chaos**: rudis indigestaque moles / nec quicquam nisi pondus iners congestaque eodem / non bene iunctarum discordia semina rerum* and 2.298 f.; Roche 2009, 147 ff. (see above, n. 22).

[40] Tarrant 2002, 356 ff. reads Lucan's *antiquum ... chaos* (74) not just as a chronological remark ("primeval"), but rather as a metaliterary pun (the chaos previously described by Ovid). According to him, "two features of Ovid's account of chaos that have been mentioned earlier make Lucan's reference to the episode especially fitting": the blurring of boundaries and the confusion of categories, on one side, and the depiction of chaos in terms that evoke dispute and conflict (*pugnare, lis*), on the other: chaos is the most graphic example of *concordia discors* and, as such, it represents the logical result of the collapse of a "discordant cosmos": Luc. 1.79 f. *discors / machina diuolsi... mundi*.

of the return of cosmos into chaos, as is highlighted by episodes of potential regression like gigantomachy (*Met.* 1.151 ff.), the Flood (*Met.* 1.262 ff.) and Phaethon (*Met.* 1.747–779 and 2.1–400).[41] Thus, it is not by chance that Lucan alludes to at least two of these Ovidian episodes in the *laudes Neronis*[42] before introducing his own equivalent to the great flood: the *ekpyrosis*, used as a term of comparison for civil war, and whose representation seems almost 'contaminated' by elements related to inundation.[43]

Furthermore, the way Ovid, as master of the Roman calendar, introduces the god Janus in *Fasti* 1 prefigures the same itinerary from the primordial past — when the double-faced god (65 *Iane biceps* and 89 *Iane biformis*) hosted in Latium the god Saturnus, cast out of Olympus — to the glorious (and golden) future of Augustan Rome, where Janus himself enjoys living in a splendid marble temple. The god recollects the cosmogonic separation and the birth of the elements from the one mixed whole (106 *unus aceruus*), which discord (107 *rerum…lite suarum*) led to dissolution (108 *massa soluta*):[44] after being "a mere ball, a shapeless lump" until that time, "he assumed the face and limbs of a god" (111–112 *tunc ego, qui fueram globus et sine imagine moles, / in faciem redii dignaque membra deo*), with all his peculiarity (113–114 *nunc quoque, confusae quondam nota parua figurae, / ante quod est in me postque uidetur idem*). Since then, Janus has been charged with the guardianship of the universe (119 *me penes est unum uasti custodia mundi*), playing the role of war's jailer (123–124 *sanguine letifero totus miscebitur orbis, / ni teneant rigidae condita Bella serae*). The self-presentation of this elegiac Janus is another famous cosmological "start" which Lucan aims to challenge: in *Bellum ciuile*'s first simile, internal discord brings about the destruction of the universe (*soluta compage*), while in Ovid's *Fasti*,

---

41 Tarrant 2002, 350: "Read in isolation, Ovid's creation story leaves the impression that primeval chaos yields, definitively and finally, to cosmos. But as Ovid's poem continues, the clear-cut divisions established at the outset are undone or threatened at several levels". On the trajectory of Ovid *Met.* 1 from cosmogony to cosmic dissolution, see also Nelis 2009.
42 Luc. 1.36 *non nisi saeuorum … post bella gigantum* (see above, n. 2) and 48 ff. *seu te flammigeros Phoebi conscendere currus* etc.; on the presence of Phaethon's myth (and its various interpretations) in the *laudes Neronis*, see Roche 2009, 153 *ad* 74.
43 1.76 f. *… tellus extendere litora nolet / excutietque fretum* "earth, refusing to spread her shores out flat (= she will heave them up), will shake off the ocean"; see Roche 2009, 155 *ad loc.* who, however, finds "insupportable" Getty's interpretation, according to which *fretum* is nominative and the meaning is "the land will refuse to stretch out its coastline (i.e. will no longer have a demarcated coastline), the restraint of which the sea will throw off".
44 For *lis* as synonym of the Greek *eris*, see *Met.* 1.21 *hanc deus et melior litem natura diremit*.

the dissolution of the primordial mass (*Fast.* 1.108 *massa soluta*) is the prelude to the birth of the natural elements.[45]

4 A step forward: from Lucan to Flavian epic and beyond

The dialectical tension between images of release — opening — dissolution, on the one hand, and binding — closure — (re)construction on the other (i.e. between chaos and cosmos), will exert its influence throughout the epic tradition. Lucan's image of a collapsing universe inspires other literary representations of cataclysms as well as other occurrences of the ablative absolute *compage soluta*, from Flavian poetry through the late antique revival of the epic genre. In the poems of Statius and Silius — while keeping its original function as cosmological metaphor — this phrase is also charged with further implications, due to the formal restoration of the divine machinery.

4.1 Statius' *Thebaid* 8: Hades' declaration of war

At the end of Statius' *Thebaid* Book 7 (816–823), during the first battle at Thebes, Amphiaraus, the Argive seer and priest of Apollo, is swallowed up by the earth with his chariot. The sudden breaking of the ground causes a traumatic, perturbing osmosis between the upperworld (earth and heaven) and the underworld. At the outset of *Thebaid* 8 we have a brief preliminary sketch of the underworld's reaction to this event. The unexpected arrival of the still alive warrior raises astonishment and fear in the shades (*manes*) (8.4 "horror seizes them all", *horror habet cunctos*), while Charon, the ferryman of the dead, is rather worried about the violation of the laws of nature, not to mention "the lack of

---

[45] The term *massa* is found in a line reported in the margin of Carrio's *uetus codex* (C) of Valerius Flaccus' *Argonautica* (1.829b *primae... massae*): the context of ll. 828–831 is that "the underworld is so vast that in the event of cosmic disintegration, it would absorb all shattered matter and remain intact" (Zissos 2008, 413). Furthermore, if in 829 Heinsius' correction *soluere* for MSS *uoluere* is right, we would have the collocation *soluere molem*, which corresponds to *soluta compage* (the universe, swallowed by chaos, i.e. the chasm of the underworld: Zissos 2008, 414; Krasne 2018b, 368–370).

proper procedure".⁴⁶ Then, the narrative focus switches to the king of the underworld: surrounded by his attendants and advisers (Furies, the personification of Death, Minos, Radamanthus), the god is judging the dead with no pity (21 ff. *forte sedens media regni infelicis in arce / dux Erebi populos poscebat crimina uitae, / nil hominum miserans iratusque omnibus umbris*, "by chance the leader of Erebus was sitting in the middle of the fortress of his luckless kingdom and was insistently asking the people for the misdeeds they had committed whilst alive, with no pity for humankind and angered at all the shades"). Thus, Amphiaraus' irruption breaks the atmosphere of a common working day in the tyrannic court: though unaccustomed to feeling fear, Hades is shocked by the sudden breaking of "the upper structure" and the view of the stars (31–33 ... *ille autem* **supera compage soluta** / *nec solitus sentire metus expauit oborta / sidera*).⁴⁷

Very soon, however, fear gives way to wrath. The god presumes an attack by one of his brothers, Jupiter or Neptune: in his eyes, such a dramatic transgression of the boundaries between life and death cannot mean anything but an act of hostility. Then, in a long tirade (34–79), he declares war for his own part (37 *congredior*), threatening the return of the universe into chaos (37 *pereant agedum discrimina rerum* "let the natural boundaries collapse") and promising the mobilisation of his army (Giants, Titans, Furies etc.) against the Olympians (42 ff.).⁴⁸ By taking that sudden earthquake as *casus belli*, Hades shows himself ready not only to defend his own kingdom, but also to expand its boundaries to the upperworld (46 f. *pandam omnia regna, / si placet, et Stygio praetexam Hyperiona caelo* "if it pleases me, I shall extend all of my kingdom and cover Hyperion [=the Sun] with a Stygian sky"): his aim is to counter the offence received by bringing Chaos on earth.⁴⁹ In fact, the chthonic forces have already

---

46 Augoustakis 2016b, 71; Stat. *Theb.* 8.18–20 *umbriferaeque fremit sulcator pallidus undae / dissiluisse nouo penitus telluris hiatu / Tartara et admissos non per sua flumina manes*, "the pale furrower of the shade-bearing water cries out that Tartarus has been rent asunder to its depths by a strange fissure of the earth and that ghosts have been admitted some other way than by his own river".
47 See Augoustakis 2016b, 76–77. The addition of an attribute (*supera*) to *compage soluta* may underline the referential value of Lucan's phrase (the collapse of the sky: *TLL* 3,1999,45f.), but could also be a way to take on Hades' subterranean viewpoint: in that case, the collapse of the "upper structure" could mean, literally, the breaking of the ground.
48 His speech ends by recalling the most emblematic image and motif of gigantomachy: 79 ... *iungere Pelion Ossae* "to join Pelion with Ossa" Augoustakis 2016b, 98 f.
49 Statius accepts the assimilation between chaos and the underworld that relies upon the etymology of *Chaos* from *cháskein* ("open the mouth wide; yawn etc.") and alludes to the 'voracity' of Hades' realm. At *Theb.* 8.52–53 Hades, referring to the violation of his own realm, asks provocatively: *anne profanatum totiens Chaos hospite uiuo / perpetiar?* "should I endure that

launched a first (still unprovoked) attack to the upperworld at the beginning of Book 2, when Tisiphone, answering Oedipus' curse, drives Laius' shade to Eteocles' palace in a remake of the opening scenes of Seneca's *Agamemnon* and *Thyestes*.⁵⁰ Now, it is the king of the underworld himself who sends the fury as his avenger (8.65 *i, Tartareas ulciscere sedes*), asking her to pave the way to the fratricide (67–68 *triste, insuetum, ingens quod nondum uiderit aether, / ede nefas,* "bring forth some ghastly horror, huge and unwonted, such as the sky has never yet beheld").⁵¹

In such a context — which develops (and extremises) the reaction of fear of the Homeric Hades to the earthquake provoked by Poseidon⁵² — the phrase *soluta compage* becomes the hub of a dynamic intertextual relationship. First of all, it is the signpost to Statius' translation of Lucan's cosmic collapse into a mythical scenario. At the beginning of *Thebaid* 8, the breaking of the ground awakens Hades' rage against Jupiter: the renewed sibling rivalry turns out to be a counterpart to the fraternal strife between Eteocles and Polynices.⁵³ At the same time, Statius' recollection of the primeval contest between the divine brothers enacts the specific (though covert) allusion made by Lucan when — among the causes of Roman civil war — he mentioned the internecine fight for power engaged by the triumvirs (1.84–85 *tu causa malorum / facta tribus dominis communis, Roma*):⁵⁴ here the Neronian poet was implicitly hinting at the ancestral partition of the world between Jupiter, Poseidon and Hades.⁵⁵ Statius' Hades remembers that circumstance with bitterness, because he received the worst of the lots (*Theb.* 8.38–39 *magno me tertia uictum / deiecit fortuna polo,*

Chaos is so often violated by a living visitor?"; see also 4.520 *panditur Elisium chaos* with Parkes 2012. Hesiod already located chaos beneath the earth (according to West on *Th.* 116, and his interpretation of χάσμα at *Th.* 740), while Virgil associated its name with underworld entities such as Erebos, Phlegethon, Hecate; however, the assimilation *Chaos* ~ underworld seems to actually start with Ovid's *Metamorphoses* (e.g. *Met.* 10.30; 14.404; Tarrant 2002, 359 "Ovid is apparently the first writer to make chaos a quasi-synonym for Tartarus or Erebus").

50 Gervais 2017a, 97–98 and 2021, 129 ff. also highlights other (epic) intertexts of Statius' episode, such as its reworking of a *Leitmotiv* of Augustan epic, the evocation of the Fury (from Virgil's *Aeneid* 7.341 ff. to Ovid's *Metamorphoses* 4.432 ff., where Juno respectively asked Allecto and Tisiphone for help).
51 Bessone 2011, 99.
52 Hom. *Il.* 20.61–65; the same reaction occurs at Ov. *Met.* 5.366–368 (esp. 356 ... *rex pauet ipse silentum*), where the earthquake is caused by Typhoeus.
53 Augoustakis 2016b, xxiii f. with other bibliography.
54 After the first cause, the *inuida fatorum series* (70), Lucan introduces the second: the triumvirate and the division of power (84–97).
55 Hom. *Il.* 15.185–189; see Roche 2009, 160.

"the third lot cast me defeated from the mighty sky"):[56] now, he fears that he is going to lose control even over his own domain (40 *nec iste meus*). To sum up, we can say that Statius literally reconstructs and actualises the mythical background of Theban fraternal strife, which Lucan — who instead illustrates the cosmological impact of Roman civil war by drawing upon the imagery of natural philosophy — had only alluded to.

Thus, by exploiting the allusive potential of the phrase *compage soluta*, which Lucan used at the outset of his *Bellum ciuile* for its emblematic flavour, Statius highlights that the narrative action of the *Thebaid* is properly entering its crucial phase here, at the beginning of Book 8:[57] the way Hades himself announces the *aristeiai* of Book 8–11 at the end of his speech (69–79) shows that we are dealing with a new proem of the *Thebaid*. Moreover, this also seems to mark a turning point in the relationship between the Olympians and the king of the underworld. When Jupiter sends Mercury to evoke Laius' shade from the underworld (*Theb.* 1.292 ff.), we may think of an 'implied collaboration' between the two, as happens in Virgil and Ovid when Juno evokes, respectively, Allecto and Tisiphone. Rather, in Statius' *Thebaid* 8 it is matter of 'competition' and primacy: what is at stake is universal power.

4.2 Appendix: a Latin 'precursor'

Statius' Hades finds a special antecedent in the *pater Ditis* who appears at the outset of the most famous example of mock-epic in Latin literature: Eumolpus' *Bellum ciuile* in Petronius' *Satyricon*. After the diatribe of an external voice against the moral decadence of Rome, victim of luxury (119),[58] the narrative action begins when the king of the underworld raises his head from the gate of hell, near Lake Avernus (120.76 *Ditis pater extulit ora*). In his speech (79–99), on the eve of the civil war between Caesar and Pompey, Ditis laments to Fortuna the attacks brought against his reign by the greedy Romans, whose engineering works challenge his own realm (90 *en etiam mea regna petunt*, "they grasp even at my kingdom");[59] now, he wants to take vengeance on them and finally, after a long time, drench his mouth with their blood. Thus, he tries to bring the goddess

---

[56] Augoustakis 2016b, 80.
[57] In Virgil's *Aeneid*, too, after Allecto's evocation by Juno in book 7, Turnus gives the signal of war at 8.1 f., soon after Juno's opening of the Gates of war.
[58] On the imagery of consumption in Petronius, see Connors 1998, 109 f.
[59] This may remind us of Hades' comment at Stat. *Theb.* 8.39–40 ... *mundumque nocentem / seruo. Nec iste meus* (see above, page 192).

to his own side: she, too, has been probably the victim of Rome's excessive weight and is no longer able to lift her soon-to-perish mass (82–83 *ecquid Romano sentis te pondere uictam, / nec posse ulterius perituram extollere molem?*). At the end of the speech, Hades/Ditis personally breaks the ground to shake hands with his new ally (121.100–101 *dextrae coniungere dextram / conatus rupto tellurem soluit hiatu*), who shares his anger (121.105–106 *nec enim minor ira rebellat / pectore in hoc*). Soon after, however, when a sudden roar of thunder comes from the sky, split by a blaze of lightning, the Lord of the underworld sinks, pale with terror: he still fears the flame of his brother Jupiter (120.124–125 *subsedit pater umbrarum, gremioque reducto / telluris pauitans fraternos palluit ictus*). Upset and afraid for the kingdom and his own safety, as in *Iliad* 20, Ditis abandons the stage, without launching any challenge against Jupiter (as in Statius' *Thebaid*). He and his ally, Fortuna, fade into the background, leaving room for other (human and, perhaps, also divine) actors. However, their desire for slaughter will be satisfied:[60] after all, civil war is an inescapable destiny.

5 Searching for a wife (and reconstructing a background): Hades in Claudian's *De raptu*

Some centuries after Statius' poem, Claudian opens his *De raptu Proserpinae* with a further representation of Hades' anger, which — in the mythical chronology, at least — predates the Theban war. The late antique poet reconstructs a typical 'a posteriori' background to the opening scene of *Thebaid* 8 (where Proserpina is already Queen of the Underworld), bringing again to the fore the internecine strife between divine brothers as well as Hades' threat to the stability of cosmos.[61] However, unlike what happens in *Thebaid* 8 — where the sudden earthquake provides the *casus belli* and fuels Hades' thirst for revenge –, Claudian has the angry king of Erebus formally play the role of the 'aggressor'.

At the outset, Hades is said to be already preparing war against the Olympians (*De Rapt.* 1.33 *proelia moturus Superis*), and for a very peculiar reason (33 f.):

---

60 Answering Hades' exhortation (94 ff.), Fortuna's last words invite the god to open up the doors of his thirsty kingdom in order to receive the huge number of victims (116 *pande, age, terrarum sitientia regna tuarum* etc.).
61 Claudian may develop a hint made by Statius' Hades in his speech: *Theb.* 8.61–62 *ast ego uix unum, nec celsa ad sidera, furto / ausus iter Siculo rapui conubia campo*, "yet I have scarcely dared one trip by stealth, and not even to the high stars, when I snatched my bride from the Sicilian plain".

"he is unmarried and has long wasted the years in childless state, brooking no longer to lack the joys of wedlock and a husband's happiness nor ever to know the dear name of father" (...*quod solus egeret / conubiis sterilesque diu consumeret annos / impatiens nescire torum nullasque mariti / inlecebras nec dulce patris cognoscere nomen*).[62] In fact, the proem starts by asking "with what torch the god of love overcame Dis" (25 f. *qua lampade Ditem / flexit Amor*). In the rest of the *De raptu*, however, there is neither any reference to Cupid's ambush nor to Hades' falling in love as narrated by Ovid in *Met*. 5.379 ff. In Claudian's poem the love theme is actually undermined (as the absence of Venus may suggest) and Hades' hostility has political roots: once again, it is matter of supremacy. For that purpose, the god mobilises the whole infernal army against Jupiter (1.37–41). The destruction of the entire universe seems imminent: the Titans would see the daylight again, while all the elements break their bonds, the laws of nature, causing the dissolution of the cosmos.[63]

When Hades' army is about to attack, Lachesis' intervention persuades him to address a formal request to Jupiter (67 *posce Iouem, dabitur coniunx*, "ask of Jove, he will give you a wife"), thus preventing the catastrophe.[64] In fact, the message that the god of the underworld summons Mercury to carry to Jupiter still shows his bitter grudge against his brother (93 ff.).[65] More than a request, it

---

[62] Chaos, i.e. the Underworld, will be his wife's dowry! (28 *dotale Chaos*), see Onorato 2008, 186 ff. On the first scene of Claudian's *De raptu* (as well as for his use of the phrase *compage soluta*), I find many good observations in the doctoral thesis by Riccardo Brolese (see esp. Brolese 2011, 124 ff.).

[63] 1.42–47 *paene reluctatis iterum pugnantia rebus / rupissent elementa fidem penitusque reuulso / carcere laxatis pubes Titania uinclis / uidisset caeleste iubar rursusque cruentus / Aegeon positis aucto de corpore nodis / obuia centeno uexasset fulmina motu*, "Almost had the elements, once more at war with reluctant nature, broken their bond; the Titan brood, their deep prison-house thrown open and their fetters cast off, had again seen heaven's light; and once more bloody Aegaeon, bursting the knotted ropes that bound his huge form, had warred against the thunderbolts of Jove with hundred-handed blows" (transl. Platnauer); see Wheeler 1995; Brolese 2011, 128–129.

[64] In Lachesis' words the 'dissolution theme' comes up again, too: 63–65 *ne pete firmatas pacis dissoluere leges, / quas dedimus neuitque colus, neu foedera fratrum / ciuili conuerte tuba*, "seek not to break the established treaty of peace which our distaffs have spun and given thee, and overturn not in civil war the compact fixed betwixt thee and thy two brothers".

[65] Hades plays the victim: 94 f. ... *sic nobis noxia uires / cum caelo Fortuna tulit?*, "did injurious fortune rob me at once of power and light?"; 99 ff. *nonne satis uisum, grati quod luminis expers / tertia supremae patior dispendia sortis / informesque plagas, cum te laetissimus ornet / signifer et uario cingant splendore Triones? / sed thalamis etiam prohibes?*, "is it not enough that deprived of the pleasant light of day I submit to the ill fortune of the third and final choice and

definitively sounds like an ultimatum (113 ff. *si dicto parere negas, patefacta ciebo / Tartara, Saturni ueteres laxabo catenas, / obducam tenebris solem,* **compage soluta** */ lucidus umbroso miscebitur axis Auerno*, "if you refuse to listen to my word, I will throw open Hell and call forth her monsters, will break Saturn's old chains, and shroud the sun in darkness. **The framework of the world shall be *loosened*** and the shining heaven mingle with Avernus' shades"). With the phrase *compage soluta*, accurately placed at the end of his message, this 'late antique Hades' hints at the words used by the narrating voice when introducing the speech of the god's *alter ego* in Statius' *Thebaid* Book 8 (31 ff., see above).[66] In so doing, however, Claudian's character highlights the fact that — unlike what happened (i.e. will happen) with Amphiaraus' descent into his kingdom — this time the god of the underworld is not going to wait for his brother's offence: on the contrary, the cosmic catastrophe will be the signal of the attack he brings to the upperworld.

Once again, however, war will not actually take place, because Jupiter will listen to Hades' request. When the god of the underworld breaks the natural barrier that detained him in his prison (2.170–171 *prohibebant undique rupes / oppositae solidaque deum compage tenebant*), and beneath his stroke "Trinacria looses her rocky bonds and yawns wide with cavernous cleft" (2.186–187 *duros Trinacria nexus / soluit et immenso late discessit hiatu*), Jupiter remains inactive, if not properly taking on the 'orchestration' of Proserpina's kidnapping: displaying a good deal of diplomacy, the Olympian king averts the risk of war, thus saving the cosmic order.[67]

Given these implications, Claudian's plot seems to have been influenced more by the opening of Statius' *Thebaid* 8 than by the Ovidian scene of Hades' falling in love in *Met*. 5. Though explicitly evoked, the spectre of a catastrophe is soon neutralised in the *De raptu* to leave room for a further, indirect celebration of Jupiter's superiority, which is also legitimated by the god's political skills and *savoir-faire*.[68]

---

these hideous realms, whilst thee the starry heavens adorn and the Wain surrounds with twinkling brilliance — must thou also forbid our marriage?...".
66 Onorato 2008, 198–199; Brolese 2011, 128–131 (with other bibl.).
67 However, for a hint at the war theme, see 2.151 ff. with Brolese 2011, 133–138.
68 This aspect distinguishes Claudian's Jupiter from his 'Statian self', whose aim is to reaffirm his own authority by taking revenge on the impious Thebes (*Theb*. 1.241 ff. *ultorem... Iouem; ... noua sontibus arma / iniciam regnis, totumque a stirpe reuellam exitiale genus*). In the *Thebaid* Jupiter and Hades appear as enemies (like the Theban brothers), but they unknowingly work in close collaboration (Ganiban 2007, 120 "there is strife between Dis and Jupiter, but it is extremely

6 "I will never die": cosmic dissolution and threat in Hannibal's last words at Zama

Another difference between Claudian's and Statius' episodes concerns the imagery itself of the catastrophe they evoke (*compage soluta*). While in *Thebaid* 8 the sudden breaking of the ground is a *fait accompli* that unleashes Hades' fury, in Claudian the cataclysm is threatened by the god himself. In so doing, Claudian seems to combine Statius' influence with that of another Flavian intertext: Silius' *Punica*, where the nightmare of civil war is often (and not only indirectly) evoked. In book 17, almost at the end of the narrative, Hannibal speaks for the last time in the poem and issues a final challenge to Jupiter, while leaving the battlefield at Zama (Sil. 17.606–609a): **caelum licet omne soluta / in caput hoc compage ruat** *terraeque dehiscant, / non ullo Cannas abolebis, Iuppiter, aeuo, / decedesque prius regnis, quam nomina gentes / aut facta Hannibalis sileant,* "though the earth yawn asunder, **though all the framework of heaven break up and fall upon my head**, never shall you, Jupiter, wipe out the memory of Cannae, but you shall step down from your throne before the world forgets the name or the achievements of Hannibal"; and, a few lines later (613b ff.): ... *mihi satque superque / ut me Dardaniae matres atque Itala tellus, / dum uiuam, expectent nec pacem pectore norint,* "(it will be) enough, and more than enough (for me), if Roman mothers and the people of Italy dread my coming while I live, and never know peace of mind". With these words, Hannibal definitively abandons the scene: he manages to escape capture, and for the Romans, he will remain a perpetual 'bogeyman', casting his shadow over their fate.[69] Thus, Claudian's Hades not only provides the 'a posteriori' background to his 'self' of Statius' *Thebaid* 8: in his threats carried out against Jupiter we can also hear the echo of the last (and irreconcilably obstinate) words pronounced by Silius' Hannibal, the champion of the Chaos, i.e. of the obscure forces of the Underworld,[70] the titan who wanted to conquer the Capitol, thereby dethroning Rome's Jupiter.

By combining these two influences, the poet of the *De raptu* also reproduces the technique of multiple intertextuality adopted by Silius towards Lucan's *Bellum ciuile*. As is well known, the 'decline theme' associates the late Hannibal

---

one-sided. Jupiter's seeming ignorance of Dis reflects the general weakness of all the heavenly gods... They act in ignorance of hell's significant involvement in the fraternal war").
69 Horsfall 1973, 138; Stocks 2014, 27–29.
70 As is shown by his oath in Dido's temple in *Punica* 1.

of Silius' *Punica* with Lucan's Pompey. At the battle of Zama, standing on a hill, Hannibal looks down at the inescapable defeat (Sil. 17.597–599 *at fessum tumulo tandem regina propinquo / sistit Iuno ducem, facies unde omnis et atrae / apparent admota oculis uestigia pugnae*, "but at last Hannibal was weary; and Juno, the queen of heaven, made him sit down on a hillock hard by, whence he had a clear view of all that awful battle and could trace every detail"). By assuming this pose, he looks like Pompey just prior to taking flight from the battlefield at Pharsalus (Luc. 7.649 ff. *stetit aggere campi*... 652 f. *tot telis sua fata peti, tot corpora fusa / ac se tam multo pereuntem sanguine uidit*). Hannibal, too, will soon afterwards leave the stage. In his last words, however, we do not find any resignation: on the contrary, we still recognise the titanic rebel whom we know from the previous books (Sil. 17.606 f. *caelum licet omne soluta / in caput hoc compage ruat*, "though all the framework of heaven break up and fall upon my head"). These words remind us of Lucan's Caesar's polemical address to the gods during the storm (Luc. 5.659 f. *licet ingentis abruperit actus / festinata dies fatis, sat magna peregi* ... 670 f. ... *desint mihi busta rogusque, dum metuar semper terraque expecter ab omni*). If this indifference towards death at sea underlines Caesar's display of superiority over the power of fate, in Silius' *Punica* the concessive clause (*caelum licet... ruat*) actually sanctions Hannibal's defeat. Nonetheless, neither of the two 'titans' — the winner (Lucan's Caesar), as well as the defeated one (Silius' Hannibal) — refrains from issuing his challenge towards the gods and fate. Both characters embody paradoxical versions of the Stoic *sapiens*, i.e. the man who does not care about death, not even when facing earthquakes or other cataclysms, according to the famous image which concludes Book 6 of Seneca's *Naturales Quaestiones* (6.32.4): "he who can despise life may look unmoved upon the tossing of the sea... even though by some upheaval of the world the tide has turned the whole Ocean bodily upon the land. Unmoved he will behold the fierce forbidding aspect of the thundering heavens, yes, **though heaven itself be crushed** and unite its fires for the destruction of mankind and of itself first of all (***frangatur licet caelum*** *et ignes suos in exitium omnium, in primis suum misceat*); unmoved he will behold earth's framework rent and earth's foundations yawning beneath (*ruptis compagibus dehiscens solum*), though the realms of the nether world be uncovered (*illa **licet** inferorum regna **retegantur***)...".[71]

---

[71] See also Papaioannou in this volume for Valerius' portrayal of Aeson as the ideal Stoic wise and Pelias as the typical Stoic villain.

7 Brief conclusion

With Seneca's prose passage we have reached the end of this rapid survey. Images of cosmic dissolution characterise very crucial points — mostly openings and closures — of Latin war epic since the 1st century CE. My particular aim was only to highlight the recurring presence, in such contexts, of the phrase *compage soluta,* which shows how this kind of poetry is indebted to Stoic philosophy and its imagery, although without displaying too many preoccupations of orthodoxy. Latin poets seem fascinated with exploiting the Stoic conceptual frame in order to emphasise (and thematise) the destructive potential of obscure, irrational forces. In their texts, these forces can be embodied respectively by great historical characters undaunted by cosmic dissolution (like Lucan's Caesar and Silius' Hannibal), or by the gods of the underworld, like the Furies and even Hades himself, who — from Petronius and Statius to Claudian — seems to change his attitude and finally display the ambition to take control over the entire universe. As an indirect consequence, this highlights the inability of the Olympian gods to effectively tame the forces of the underworld. Perhaps this operation may represent, on the literary level, the first step of a process of relativisation of the traditional divine apparatus whose ultimate target (starting with Flavian epic, at least) is the construction of a new (human) authority as well as of a more 'human' power (mirrored in epic characters like Statius' Theseus or Silius' Scipio) that can actually resist the forces of chaos. This will be the decisive factor that — more than Jupiter's power — may ensure the renewal and the perpetuation of the Empire.

Damien P. Nelis
Epilogue

The very fact that it is possible to spend the quiet days at the back end of 2022 reading a volume entitled *Ritual and the Poetics of Closure in Flavian Literature* must be a sign of the times. The essays collected here by Angeliki-Nektaria Roumpou do indeed offer satisfyingly complex and thought-provoking discussions of different kinds of ritual and various ways of thinking about closure. Students and scholars interested in Valerius Flaccus, Statius, Silius Italicus, and Martial will have to set aside some time for this book, among all the other books, papers, and commentaries that already await their attention or are about to land in their in-trays or computers during 2023. The first days of January have already delivered 'Festivals in Statius' *Thebaid*: Uncelebrating Vergil', by A. Walter.[1] But beyond learning so much about the connections between closure and ritual, this reader has also come away from these chapters with a better appreciation of Flavian poetics as a whole. Investigating closure means looking at so many aspects of a text, as amply illustrated in the preceding pages. One must not forget all the texts that have been lost, as Michael Dewar has recently reminded us,[2] thus making generalisations hazardous, but who would have thought that such a relatively small corpus of texts would respond so richly to analysis from this double perspective? Much has already been written about both topics independently of each other, of course. The volume edited by A. Augoustakis, *Ritual and Religion in Flavian Epic* (Oxford 2013) drew attention to one part of the story, while the citation rate of an essay such as that by S. Braund, 'Ending epic: Statius, Theseus and a merciful release',[3] may suffice to illustrate the interest of scholars of Flavian literature in the subject of closure.

It may seem obvious to say that a book like this would not have been possible without all the excellent scholarship of recent decades that has so immeasurably improved and enriched our reading of the Latin poetry of the late first century CE. It is true of any serious research in literary studies that it builds on what has gone before, but a survey of the bibliography at the close of this volume brings out in an extraordinarily striking and vivid manner the ways in which the study of a relatively narrow topic like the relationship between closure and ritual is possible today because of the findings of an intimidatingly

---
1 See Walter 2022.
2 See Dewar 2016.
3 See Braund 1996.

large amount of recent work on all sorts of other aspects of the same literary corpus. So many names and titles come immediately to mind that it is not easy to draw up a list of favourite contributions. But one name that comes to mind at once is that of D.P. Fowler. If it was possible for Philip Larkin to joke that sexual intercourse began in nineteen sixty-three, it seems reasonable to suggest that, for many, closure began in nineteen eighty-nine. That was the year in which Fowler published his 'First thoughts on closure', a typically brilliant piece, combining theory and practice, postmodernist provocation and old-fashioned scholarship. Few articles unite passing reflections on both Gestalt psychology and on the ending of the second book in the Alexandrian edition of Sappho, while celebrating the fact that literary critics have started to look to their ends. Given the sophisticated fluency with which the authors in this volume handle the complexities of closure, it is worth remembering that some of us at least had never even heard of closure until we picked up volume twenty-two of *Materiali e discussioni*.[4] Some will say, 'speak for yourself', but much has certainly changed over the last thirty years or so. Fowler's original piece, to be followed by his 'Second Thoughts on Closure' and 'Postmodernism, Romantic Irony and Classical Closure', all three to be found in his *Roman Constructions. Readings in Postmodern Latin* (Oxford 2000) was truly an education for the uninitiated. Angeliki-Nektaria Roumpou's volume is on one level a direct result of Fowler's article. He explicitly set it up as a piece that might come to the aid of graduate students looking for a research topic. Being so far ahead of the field, he was in a perfect position to summarise the state of play in both ancient and modern literature, while proposing all sorts of avenues for future work on both Greek and Latin texts, wittily describing it as 'one of those annoying pieces which suggest that it would be a good idea of somebody else did some work'. Well, at least some of that work has now been done. But whereas Fowler was intent in opening up the terms of the debate, striving to encourage Classicists to engage with modern literary theory, the brief set before the authors invited to speak at the 'Zoom seminar' (another sign of the times) on "The Poetics of Release and Binding: Resolution and Constraint as Modes of Closure in Flavian Literature", that has given rise to these essays represented a narrowing down of the focus. Perhaps it is a testament to Fowler's success in educating a generation of scholars that made this restriction both possible and attractive. We can now at least take it for granted that when you ask a group of Latinists to think about closure, they will know what you are talking about. Taking that as a given, one of the attractive features on display here, alongside the many convincing investigations into the

---

4 This is the volume in which D. Fowler's article 1989 is published.

intricacies of closure, or, to be more accurate, of the ways in which it is in various ways postponed, problematised and undercut, is the space given to investigating what we mean by ritual. On the one hand, we probably all think we know instinctively what the term means, and most readers probably immediately see common sense in linking ritual to closure. Irene de Jong, for example, writes in her *Narratology and the Classics. A Practical Guide* of 'a repertoire of ending *topoi*, like death, return, reunion, marriage, …'.[5] When she goes on to provide a precise example, she chooses the end of Homer's *Iliad*, which 'is marked by the ending *topos* of the burial of Hector…'.[6] As many have pointed out, it can hardly be coincidental that that poem had begun with the bodies of men left as 'the spoil for dogs and birds' (*Il.* 1.4–5). The ghastly failure to provide ritual burial at the start is answered by the insistence on proper burial at the close. As in so many areas, Homer sets the terms of the debate. But what exactly are we talking about when we easily think of a marriage and a funeral as obvious examples of ritual, and why do we think of them, at least on some level, as satisfactorily closural? After all, the ending of Homer's *Iliad* is one of the great literary examples of problematic closure, as Fowler discussed in his essay.[7] It is particularly useful for literary scholars to be offered the opportunity to run their ideas about ritual up against the thinking of an expert in the history of religion, with J. Rüpke's paper providing much food for thought. This is not the first occasion for such collaborative work, given the publication, among many other scholarly contributions but especially chapter four of D. Feeney's *Literature and Religion at Rome. Cultures, Contexts, and Beliefs* (Cambridge 1998), of another collection of conference papers, *Rituals in Ink*, arising from a meeting in Stanford in 2002 and published in 2004, edited by Barchiesi/Rüpke/Stephens. For this kind of work rigorous analysis of the category of ritual is of course crucial. As far as this reader is concerned, complacent enough about closure, lazily under-informed about theories of ritual, it was eye-opening to read about 'special actions' in relation to time and space, to be provoked into thinking about ritual as a problem-solving exercise in very specific cases, to be invited to consider that the analysis of ritual communication should involve thinking hard about the investments made by the originators of such a strategy. Latinists are used to thinking of the poet as a priest-like *uates* figure, and also about the processes and forms of authority, communication, invention, and occasion that lie at the heart of the experience of interpreting literary works that represent religious

---

5 de Jong 2014, 89.
6 de Jong 2014, 90.
7 Fowler 1989, 245–246.

activity (on which see recently A. Gramps, *The Fiction of Occasion in Hellenistic and Roman Poetry*, Berlin/Boston 2021). But ritual needs the same kind of careful handling as closure, and one of the lessons of this volume will be that literary scholars must not work with a stable, unproblematic definition of the former in order to do exciting things with the latter.

Many of the points made in this collection strike home with particular force in relation to Virgil's *Georgics*, a poem that seems to be almost hyper-closural. It comes to an end with both the ritual of *bugonia*, bringing resolution to the immediate problem of Aristaeus in the form of the loss of his bee-hives, and a formal *sphragis*, identifying the author and the contexts and settings in which he wrote the work. The way in which the last line of the poem, (*Geo* 4.566) *Tityre, te patulae cecini sub tegmine fagi*, rewrites the first line of the *Bucolics*, *Tityre, tu patulae recubans sub tegmine fagi*, even goes so far as to bring to a close the poet's whole career up to this point. When one adds the fact that Virgil is also alluding to the end of the *Aetia* of Callimachus, it becomes hard to resist the idea that this is an experiment in the combination of 'ending *topoi*', to use de Jong's term, one that may well have been influential for later authors interested in exploring connections between ritual and closure. But, of course, matters are not so simple, and closure is not so complete as it may seem, because Virgil has already used the prologue of the third book of the *Georgics*, a proem right in the middle, to look forward to the writing of a future epic. And in preparing in this way generic elevation towards the *Aeneid* he is in fact inverting Callimachus' downward generic shift from elegy to iambic at the end of the *Aetia*. Consideration of Virgil's complex and influential machinations, which bring the handling of the closure of a single work into dialogue with a whole corpus and the construction of a literary career, leads on naturally to thoughts about the importance of the Augustan model for the understanding of Flavian procedures. As the recent volume by R. Marks and M. Mogetta reminds us (*Domitian's Rome and the Augustan Legacy*, Ann Arbor 2021, including, by the way, a paper entitled 'Augustan to the End'), comparison with Augustan precedent remains a dominant critical move when it comes to assessing the Flavian achievement. It comes as no surprise, therefore, to see the authors of the essays in this volume taking due account of their Augustan predecessors. As in so much work on Latin literature, analysis of intertextual engagement with the literary tradition is pervasive. Studying the links between ritual and closure in a text that is a rewriting of another text in which ritual and closure were already interconnected obviously has some validatory force for the subject itself. But beyond that basic point, there is the added possibility that the very repetition of forms of closure across literary history helps consolidate appreciation of a repertoire of topoi among good readers. As in the practice of ritual itself, repetition leads to consolidation, and so Flavian audiences may have been well-informed interpreters of ritual and closure because the very intertextual nature of the works they were studying forced them to see such works as the *Argonautica* or the *Thebaid* or the *Siluae* in literary historical terms. In addition, appreciation of the complexities of Flavian allusion to aspects of ritual and closure in Augustan texts can lead us on to think hard about the history of Roman religion through the first century of imperial rule. Ritual is not a timeless category, thus making it vital to pay attention to change, if we are to understand how it functions in a given society at a given time.

If, after reading this volume, anyone is moved to consider putting together a collection entitled *Ritual and the Poetics of Closure in Augustan Literature*, how similar or different would that volume be, in comparison to this one? Would readings of Virgil, Horace, Propertius, Tibullus, and Ovid be underpinned by similar techniques of reading? Quite probably, and intertextuality would almost certainly be in play. Just as it comes as no surprise to see in this volume frequent reference to the *Aeneid*, for example, so a book on Augustan poetry would almost certainly look back more than once to the ending of the first edition of Ennius' *Annales*, with its celebration of the triumph of Fuluius Nobilior, and probably also to the whole closing section of Catullus 64, with its emphasis on the perversion of ritual norms. In addition, one would surely find in any Augustan prequel demonstration of the fact that closure does not occur only at the end of individual works of literature, but that it can be active at almost any point, most obviously at book ends, and here one would expect sophisticated readings of Ovidian techniques throughout his career, which, alongside Virgil's, were clearly influential on the Flavians. Studying closure, as these papers reveal, means thinking about the poetics of segmentation, to how we define unity, to how we relate the part to the whole, while paying attention to ancient techniques of narrative structuring and the ways in which larger episodes function in relation to complete narratives. One thinks immediately of C. McNelis's *Statius' Thebaid and the Poetics of Civil War* (Cambridge 2007), a book that still has much to teach us.

One way in which a volume on Augustan poetry could potentially differ from this one is by a greater emphasis on the manipulation and reinvention of ritual from the late forties BCE on. The fact that 'what could be defined as Augustus' religious policy already was entirely enacted between 43 and 28 BC (when he was still Octavian)', as John Scheid has pointed out,[8] raises some interesting

---

8 Scheid 2005c, 178.

questions and at the very least discourages lazy use of the term 'Augustan'. It would take another book to work out the relationship between the evolutions of Augustan rituals and the ways in which they are imitated and reworked in the Flavian period, and a study of that kind would in turn open up the way to a wide-ranging study of the similarities and differences between the ways in which Augustan and Flavian authors write about early imperial religion. It is surely one of the merits of this collection that a relatively small number of papers potentially opens up such broad avenues for future research. It is nice to think that D. Fowler would have approved of the fact that his thoughts on closure were not the end.

List of Contributors

Theodoros Antoniadis has studied Classics at the Universities of Thessaloniki (BA, PhD) and Toronto (MA). He has published various articles on Neronian Literature and Flavian Epic in peer-reviewed journals and conference proceedings, while his current research focuses primarily on the *Punica* of Silius Italicus. He is currently Assistant Professor of Latin at the Aristotle University of Thessaloniki.

Laila Dell'Anno is a PhD student at the University of Cambridge. In her dissertation, she explores the *Siluae* as a consciously designed poetry book with the aim of recalibrating their scholarly reception. Her research interests extend beyond the poetry of the Augustan and Flavian periods to a comparative and theoretical approach to classical, early modern, and modern literature.

Marco Fucecchi is Associate professor of Latin language and literature at the University of Udine (Italy). His research interests include Latin literature from the Augustan age to the 1st century CE, with particular regard to epic poetry. He is the author of some monographs on Flavian epic poems (Valerius Flaccus' *Argonautica* and Silius Italicus' *Punica*) as well as many articles on various topics in Latin literature.

Alison Keith teaches Classics and Women's Studies at the University of Toronto, where she is the Director of the Jackman Humanities Institute. She has written extensively about the intersection of gender and genre in Latin literature and Roman society, and has authored or edited books on Ovid and his reception, Vergil and Latin epic, Propertius and Roman literary cultures, Roman dress, women and war in antiquity, and motherhood in antiquity.

Michael Knierim holds an MA in Classics from the University of Kentucky and is now pursuing a PhD in Classical Philology at the University of Illinois in Urbana-Champaign with an interest in ancient religion, trauma-theory, epic poetry, historiography and comparative literature. He has given talks on Apollonius Rhodius, Theocritus and Sanskrit epic poetry.

Helen Lovatt is Professor of Classics at the University of Nottingham and has published widely on Flavian epic and its reception, especially Statius. Major works include: *Statius and Epic Games: Sport, Politics and Poetics in the Thebaid* (Cambridge 2005), *The Epic Gaze: Vision, Gender and Narrative in Ancient Epic* (Cambridge 2013) and a cultural history of the Argonaut myth, *In Search of the Argonauts* (London 2021). Her current work focuses on *The Power of Sadness in Virgil's Aeneid*, and further work on the Argonaut tradition, *Argonauts Crossing*.

Margot Neger gained her PhD in 2011 from the University of Munich with a thesis on Martial (published as *Martials Dichtergedichte. Das Epigramm als Medium der poetischen Selbstreflexion*, Tübingen 2012). After some years as a postdoc at the University of Salzburg, she published a second monograph on Pliny the Younger (*Epistolare Narrationen. Studien zur Erzähltechnik des jüngeren Plinius*, Tübingen 2021). In August 2019 she joined the Department of Classics and Philosophy at the University of Cyprus as an Assistant Professor. Her research-interests are ancient epigram and epistolography, literature of the Imperial age, late antique poetry, narratology, generic interaction, and ancient literary criticism. She is also co-editing a volume on Intertextuality in Pliny's *Epistles* (in print at Cambridge University Press).

Damien P. Nelis is Professor of Latin at the University of Geneva. From 1999 to 2005 he was Professor of Latin in Trinity College Dublin. He works mainly on Latin poetry, with a special interest in its Hellenistic background. He is currently working on a digital edition of the *Achilleid* of Statius and on a study of Vergil's *Georgics*.

Sophia Papaioannou is Professor of Latin Literature at the National and Kapodistrian University of Athens, Faculty of Philology. Her research interests include Ancient Epic, Latin poetry, and Roman Comedy, and she has published many books and articles on these topics. She has recently co-edited (with Agis Marinis) the volume *Elements of Tragedy in Flavian Epic* (De Gruyter 2021) and she is currently working on the reception of the Latin tradition in Nonnus' *Dionysiaca*.

Angeliki-Nektaria Roumpou is a Research Fellow in Latin language and literature in the Academy of Athens, working on the connection between ritual and textual closure in Flavian epic. She is currently writing a commentary on Silius Italicus' *Punica* 17 (OUP) and preparing the first Greek translation, introduction and commentary on Silius Italicus' *Punica* 1.

Jörg Rüpke is Fellow in Religious Studies and Vice-director of the Max Weber Centre for Advanced Cultural and Social Studies of the University of Erfurt, Germany. Together with Susanne Rau he is now Co-director of the Kolleg-Forschergruppe 'Urbanity and Religion: Reciprocal Formations'. His research focused on the ancient Mediterranean and appropriate conceptual tools has widened to questions of religious change in urban environments. His monographs include *Religions of the Romans* (2007), *Fasti sacerdotum* (2008), *The Roman Calendar from Numa to Constantine* (2011), *Religion in Republican Rome. Rationalization and Ritual Change* (2012); *Religiöse Erinnerungskulturen: Formen der Geschichtsschreibung in der römischen Antike* (2012); *Ancients and Moderns: Religion* (2013), *From Jupiter to Christ* (2014), *Religious Deviance in the Roman World* (2016), *On Roman Religion: Lived Religion and the Individual in Ancient Rome* (2016), *Pantheon* (2018), *Peace and War in Ancient Rome* (2019), *Urban religion: A Historical Approach to Urban Growth and Religious Change* (2020), and *Religion and its History* (2021). He has edited the *Companion to Roman Religion* (2007) and the *Companion to the Archaeology of Religion in the Ancient World* (2015, with Rubina Raja).

Clayton Schroer is currently Visiting Assistant Professor of Classics at Emory University in Atlanta, Georgia (USA). He is currently completing his monograph on postcolonial readings of exile in Silius Italicus' *Punica* and Latin Epic more broadly. His research interests include Latin literature of the early Empire, postcolonialism, and Classical receptions in American space programs.

Bibliography

Adamietz, J. (1976), *Zur Komposition der Argonautica des Valerius Flaccus*, Munich.
Adler, E. (2003), *Vergil's Empire: Political Thought in the Aeneid*, Lanham, MD/New York.
Agri, D. (2022), *Reading Fear in Flavian Epic: Emotion, Power and Stoicism*, Oxford.
Ahl, F. (1986), "Statius' *Thebaid*: A Reconsideration", *Aufstieg und Niedergang der römischen Welt* 2.32.5, Berlin/Boston, 2803–2912.
Ahl, F./Davis, M./Pomeroy, A.J. (1986), "Silius Italicus", *Aufstieg und Niedergang der römischen Welt* 2.32.5, Berlin/Boston, 2492–2561.
Alexiou, M. (1974), *The Ritual Lament in Greek Tradition*, Cambridge.
Ambühl, A. (2010), "Sleepless Orpheus: insomnia, love, death and poetry from antiquity to contemporary fiction", in: E.J. Scioli/Ch. Walde (eds.), *'Sub imagine somni': Nighttime Phenomena in Greco-Roman Culture*, Pisa, 259–284.
Ando, C. (2001), "The Palladium and the Pentateuch: towards a sacred topography of the later Roman empire", *Phoenix* 55, 369–410.
Antonelli, M. (2017), "Moral Injury", *The American Journal of Psychoanalysis* 77.4, 406–416.
Appadurai, A. (1986), *The Social Life of Things: Commodities in Cultural Perspective*, Cambridge.
Armitage, D. (2017), *Civil War: A History in Ideas*, New Haven.
Asper, M. (1997), *Onomata allotria. Zur Genese, Struktur und Funktion poetologischer Metaphern bei Kallimachos*, Stuttgart.
Augoustakis, A. (2008), "An insomniac's lament: the end of poetic power in Statius' *Siluae* 5, 4", in: C. Deroux (ed.), *Studies in Latin Literature and Roman History 14*, Brussels, 339–347.
Augoustakis, A. (2010), *Motherhood and the Other: Fashioning Female Power in Flavian Epic*, Oxford.
Augoustakis, A. (ed.) (2013), *Ritual and Religion in Flavian Epic*, Oxford.
Augoustakis, A. (2015a), "Valerius Flaccus in Silius Italicus", in: M. Heerink/G. Manuwald (eds.), *Brill's Companion to Valerius Flaccus*, Leiden, 340–358.
Augoustakis, A. (2015b), "Campanian Politics and Poetics in Silius Italicus' *Punica*", *ICS* 40.1, 155–169.
Augoustakis, A. (2016a), "Burial and Lament in Flavian Epic: Mothers, Fathers, Children", in: N. Manioti (ed.), *Family in Flavian Epic*, Leiden, 276–300.
Augoustakis, A. (2016b), *Statius, Thebaid 8. Edited with Introduction, Translation, and Commentary*, Oxford.
Augoustakis, A. (2017), "Burial scenes: Silius Italicus' *Punica* and Greco-Roman historiography", in: F. Bessone/M. Fucecchi (eds.), *The Literary Genres in the Flavian Age: Canons, Transformations, Reception*, Berlin/Boston, 299–316.
Augoustakis, A./Froedge, S./Kozak, A./Schroer, C. (2019), "Death, Ritual, and Burial from Homer to the Flavians", in: C. Reitz/S. Finkmann (eds.), *Structures of Epic Poetry*, Vol. II.2: *Configuration*, Leiden, 483–522.
Augoustakis, A./Bernstein, N.W. (2021), *Silius Italicus' Punica: Rome's War with Hannibal*, London/New York.
Austin, R.G. (1971), *P. Vergili Maronis Aeneidos Liber Primus*, Oxford.
Baier, T. (2019), "Flavian Gods in Intertextual Perspective. How Rulers Used Religious Practice as a Means of Communicating", in: N. Coffee et al. (eds.), *Intertextuality in Flavian Epic Poetry: Contemporary Approaches*, Berlin/Boston, 305–322.

Balland, A. (2010), *Essai sur la société des épigrammes de Martial*, Paris.
Barchiesi, A. (1997), "Endgames: Ovid's *Metamorphoses* 15 and *Fasti* 6", in: D.H. Roberts/F.M. Dunn/D. Fowler (eds.), *Classical Closure: Reading the End in Greek and Latin Literature*, Princeton, 181–208.
Barchiesi, A. (2005), "The Search for the Perfect Book: a PS to the New Posidippus", in: K. Gutzwiller (ed.), *The New Posidippus: A Hellenistic Poetry Book*, Oxford, 20–42.
Barchiesi, A. (2020a), "Ovid, Boccaccio and the equites. Autography and the Question of the Audience", in: M. Möller (ed.), *Excessive Writing. Ovids Exildichtung*, Heidelberg, 137–156.
Barchiesi, A. (2020b), "Testo e frammento nell' *Achilleide* di Stazio", in: M. Papini (ed.), *Opus imperfectum. Monumenti e testi incompiuti del mondo Greco e romano*, Roma, 287–300.
Barchiesi, A. (2021), "*Rege sub uno*: on the politics of Statius' *Achilleid*", in: C.W. Marshall (ed.), *Latin Poetry and its Reception. Essays for Susanna Braund*, London/New York, 56–74.
Barchiesi, A./Hardie, P. (2010), "The Ovidian career model: Ovid, Gallus, Apuleius, Boccaccio", in: P. Hardie/H. Moore (eds.), *Classical Literary Careers and their Reception*, Cambridge, 59–88.
Barchiesi, A./Rüpke, J./Stephens, S. (eds.) (2004), *Rituals in Ink: A Conference on Religion and Literary Production in Ancient Rome held at Stanford University in February 2002*, Stuttgart.
Barich, M.J. (1982), *Aspects of the Poetic Technique of Valerius Flaccus*, PhD Thesis, Yale University.
Barney, S.A. et al. (2006), *The Etymologies of Isidore of Seville*, Cambridge.
Battistella, C./Milić Galli, L. (2020), "Foreshadowing Medea: Prolepsis and Intertextuality in Valerius Flaccus", in: N. Coffee et al. (eds.), *Intertextuality in Flavian Epic: Contemporary Approaches*, Berlin, 205–241.
Beard, M. (2007), *The Roman Triumph*, Cambridge.
Bernstein, N.W. (2008), *In the Image of the Ancestors: Narratives of Kinship in Flavian Epic*, Toronto.
Bernstein, N.W. (2013), "Ritual Murder and Suicide in the *Thebaid*", in: A. Augoustakis (ed.), *Ritual and Religion in Flavian Epic*, Oxford, 233–248.
Bernstein, N.W. (2017), *Silius Italicus Punica 2. Edited with an Introduction, Translation and Commentary*, Oxford.
Bernstein, N.W. (2018a), "Continuing the *Aeneid* in the First Century: Ovid's 'Little *Aeneid*', Lucan's *Bellum Ciuile*, and Silius Italicus' *Punica*", in: R. Simms (ed.), *Brill's Companion to Prequels, Sequels, and Retellings of Classical Epic*, Leiden, 248–266.
Bernstein, N.W. (2018b), "*Inuitas maculant cognato sanguine dextras*: civil war themes in Silius's Saguntum episode", in: L.D. Ginsberg/D.A. Krasne (eds.), *After 69 CE – Writing Civil War in Flavian Rome*, Berlin/Boston, 179–198.
Bessone, F. (2011), *La Tebaide di Stazio: Epica e potere*, Pisa.
Bessone, F. (2013), "Religion and power in the *Thebaid*", in: A. Augoustakis (ed.), *Ritual and Religion in Flavian Epic*, Oxford, 145–162.
Beye, C.R. (1969), "Jason as love-hero in Apollonios' *Argonautika*", *Greek, Roman and Byzantine Studies* 10.1, 31–55.
Bianconi, C. (2005), "Il patrono come amicus e come dominus in Marziale", *Maia* 57, 65–94.
Biggs, T. (2020), "*Lucanus Mirabatur Adeo Scripta Flacci*: Lucan and Persius", in: L. Ziontek/M. Thorne (eds.), *Lucan's Imperial World. The Bellum Ciuile in its Contemporary Context*, London, 33–50.

Bitto, G. (2018), "Schlaflos mit Kallimachos: eine Interpretation von Statius *Silu*. 5,4", in: S. Finkmann/A. Behrendt/A. Walter (eds.), *Antike Erzähl- und Deutungsmuster: zwischen Exemplarität und Transformation*, Berlin/Boston, 285–310.

Bitto, G. (2020), "Leser im Bcc. Zu den Praefationes von Statius' *Silvae*", in: G.M. Müller/ S. Retsch/J. Schenk (eds.), *Adressat und Adressant in antiken Briefen*, Berlin/Boston, 181–204.

Blidstein, M. (2018), "Loosing Vows and Oaths in the Roman Empire and Beyond: Authority and Interpretation", *Archiv für Religionsgeschichte* 20.1, 275–303.

Bömer, F. (1957/58), *Publius Ovidius Naso. Die Fasten*, 2 vols., Heidelberg.

Bömer, F. (1986), *P. Ovidius Naso, Metamorphosen. Buch XIV–XV*, Heidelberg.

Borg, B.E. (2014), "Eine Frage von Leben und Tod: Pathos und Leidenschaft auf den mythologischen Sarkophagen Roms", in: M. Clemenz et al. (eds.), *IMAGO. Interdisziplinäres Jahrbuch für Psychoanalyse und Ästhetik*, Gießen, 77–92.

Borgeaud, P. (2009), *Violentes émotions: approches comparatistes*, Genève.

Boudreau, T. (2018), "The Morally Injured", in: R. Meagher/D. Pryer (eds.), *War and Moral Injury: A Reader*, Oregon, 51–59.

Bowden, H. (2013), "Seeking certainty and claiming authority: the consultation of Greek oracles from the Classical to the Roman imperial periods", in: V. Rosenberger (ed.), *Divination in the Ancient World: Religious Options and the Individual* (*Potsdamer Altertumswissenschaftliche Beiträge* 46), Stuttgart, 41–59.

Bowie, M.N.R. (1988), *Martial Book XII: A Commentary*, Diss. Oxford.

Boyancé, P. (1972), "Un rite de purification dans les *Argonautiques* de Valerius Flaccus", *Etudes sur la religion romaine. Publications de l'École française de Rome* 11, Rome, 317–345.

Boys-Stones, G. (2018), *The Greek Theology, Fragments, and Testimonia. Translated with an Introduction and Notes*, Atlanta.

Brandt, J.R./Iddeng, J.W. (eds.) (2012), *Greek and Roman Festivals: Content, Meaning, and Practice*, Oxford.

Braund, S. (1996), "Ending epic: Statius, Theseus and a merciful release", *Proceedings of the Cambridge Philological Society* 42, 1–23.

Briscoe, J. (2008), *A Commentary on Livy Books 38–40*, Oxford.

Brolese, R. (2011), *Conpage soluta. Ricerche sul De raptu Proserpinae di Claudiano*, PhD diss., University of Udine.

Brookes, I.N. (1992), *A Literary Commentary on the Fifth Book of Ovid's Fasti*, PhD diss. University of Newcastle.

Brown, J. (1994), *Into the Woods: Narrative Studies in the Thebaid of Statius with Special Reference to Books IV–VI*, PhD diss., Cambridge.

Buckley, E. (2016), "Over her live body: marriage in Valerius Flaccus' *Argonautica*", in: N. Manioti (ed.), *Family in Flavian Epic*, Leiden, 61–88.

Buckley, E. (2018a), "Ending the *Argonautica*: Giovanni Battista Pio's *Argonautica*-Supplement (1519)", in: R. Simms (ed.), *Brill's Companion to Prequels, Sequels, and Retellings of Classical Epic*, Leiden/Boston, 295–315.

Buckley, E. (2018b), "Flavian Epic and Trajanic historiography: speaking into the silence", in: A. König/C. Whitton (eds.), *Roman Literature under Nerva, Trajan and Hadrian: Literary Interactions, AD 96–138*, Cambridge, 86–125.

Bulloch, A. (2006), "Jason's Cloak", *Hermes* 134.1, 44–68.

Buongiovanni, C. (2012), *Gli Epigrammata Longa del decimo libro di Marziale: Introduzione, Testo, Traduzione e Commento. Testi e Studi di Cultura Classica*, Pisa.
Burkert, W. (1970), "Jason Hypsipyle and new fire at Lemnos", *The Classical Quarterly* 20, 1–16.
Byre, C.S. (1996), "The Killing of Apsyrtus in Apollonius Rhodius' *Argonautica*", *Phoenix* 50.1, 3–16.
Canavan, G. (2016), *Modern Masters of Science Fiction: Octavia E. Butler*, Champaign, IL.
Cancik, H. (1965), *Untersuchungen zur lyrischen Kunst des P. Papinius Statius*, Hildesheim.
Cancik, H. (1985), "Rome as sacred landscape: Varro and the end of Republican religion in Rome", *Visible Religion* 4/5, 250–265.
Canobbio, A. (2007), "Dialogando col lettore. Modalità comunicative nei finali dei libri di Marziale", in: A. Bonadeo/E. Romano (eds.), *Dialogando con il passato: permanenze e innovazioni nella cultura latina di età flavia*, Firenze, 207–231.
Canobbio, A. (2011), *M. Valerii Martialis Epigrammaton liber quintus. Introduzione, edizione critica, traduzione e commento*, Napoli.
Carradice, I.A./Buttrey, T.V. (2007²), *The Roman Imperial Coinage: From AD 69 to 96, Vespasian to Domitian* 2.1, London.
Caseau, B. (1999), "Sacred Landscapes", in: G.W. Bowersock/P. Brown/O. Grabar (eds.), *Late Antiquity: A Guide to the Postclassical World*, Cambridge, MA, 21–59.
Cassidy, S. (2019), "Wedding Imagery in the Talos Episode: Apollonius Rhodius, *Argonautica* 4.1653–88", *The Classical Quarterly* 68.2, 442–457.
Castelletti, C. (2012), "A 'Greek' Acrostic in Valerius Flaccus (3.430–4)", *Mnemosyne* 65, 319–323.
Castelletti, C. (2022), *Valerius Flaccus, Argonautica, Book 8. Edited with Introduction, Translation, and Commentary*. Ed. by A. Augoustakis, M. Fucecchi and G. Manuwald, Oxford.
Ceccarelli, L. (2008), "Religious Landscape. A case-study from Latium Vetus", in: O. Menozzi/M.L. Di Marzio/D. Fossataro (eds.), *SOMA 2005: Proceedings of the IX Symposium on Mediterranean Archaeology Chieti (Italy), 24 – 26 February 2005*, Oxford, 333–339.
Ceulemans, R. (2007), "Ritual mutilation in Apollonius Rhodius' *Argonautica*: A contextual analysis of IV, 477–479 in search of the motive of the μασχαλισμός", *Kernos* 20, 97–112.
Champlin, E. (2003), *Nero*, Cambridge.
Chaniotis, A. (2009), "The Dynamics of Rituals in the Roman Empire", in: O. Hekster/S. Schmidt-Hofner/C. Witschel (eds.), *Ritual Dynamics and Religious Change in the Roman Empire*, Leiden, 3–29.
Chaniotis, A. (ed.) (2011), *Ritual Dynamics in the Ancient Mediterranean: Agency, Emotion, Gender, Representation*, Stuttgart.
Chaniotis, A. (ed.) (2013a), *Emotions in Greece and Rome: Texts, Images, Material Culture* (Unveiling emotions 2), Stuttgart.
Chaniotis, A. (ed.) (2013b), *Unveiling Emotions: Sources and Methods for the Study of Emotions in the Greek World* (Heidelberger althistorische Beiträge und Studien 52), Stuttgart.
Chaudhuri, P. (2014), *The War with God: Theomachy in Roman Imperial Poetry*, Oxford.
Cheong, P.H./Huang, S./Poon, J.P.H. (2011), "Religious Communication and Epistemic Authority of Leaders in Wired Faith Organizations", *Journal of Communication* 61.5, 938–958.
Chidester, D. (2018), *Religion: Material Dynamics*, Berkeley.
Chinn, C.M. (2022), *Visualizing the Poetry of Statius: An Intertextual Approach*, Leiden.
Citroni, M. (ed.) (1975), *M. Valerii Martialis Epigrammaton Liber I*, Florence.

Citroni, M. (1989), "Marziale e la letteratura per i Saturnali (poetica dell'intrattenimento e cronologia della pubblicazione dei libri)", *Illinois Classical Studies* 14, 201–226.
Citroni, M. (1992), "Letteratura per i Saturnali e poetica dell'intrattenimento", *Studi Italiani di Filologia Classica* 10, 425–447.
Citroni, M. (2002), "L'immagine della Spagna e l'autorappresentazione del poeta negli epigrammi di Marziale", in: G. Urso (ed.), *Hispania terris omnibus felicior. Premesse ed esiti di un processo di integrazione, Atti del convegno internazionale, Cividade de Friuli, 27–29 Settembre 2001*, Pisa, 281–301.
Clare, R.J. (2002), *The Path of the Argo: Language, Imagery, and Narrative in the Argonautica of Apollonius Rhodius*, Cambridge.
Clare, R.J. (2004), "Tradition and originality: Allusion in Valerius Flaccus' Lemnian episode", in: M. Gale (ed.), *Latin Epic and Didactic Poetry*, Swansea, 125–148.
Clauss, J.J. (1993), *The Best of the Argonauts: The Redefinition of the Epic Hero in Book 1 of Apollonius' Argonautica*, Berkeley.
Closs, V. (2020), *While Rome Burned: Fire, Leadership and Urban Disaster in the Roman Cultural Imagination*, Ann Arbor.
Coleman, K. (2005), "Martial, Book 6: A Gift for the *Matronalia*?", *Acta Classica* 48, 23–35.
Connors, C. (1998), *Petronius the Poet: Verse and Literary Tradition in the Satyricon*, Cambridge.
Corrigan, K. (2013), *Virgo to Virago: Medea in the Silver Age*, Newcastle.
Courtney, E. (1990), *P. Papini Stati Siluae*, Oxford.
Cowan, R. (2021), "Knowing me, knowing you: epic anagnorisis and the recognition of tragedy", in: A. Marinis/S. Papaioannou (eds.), *Elements of Tragedy in Flavian Epic*, Berlin/Boston, 43–64.
Criado, C. (2000), *La teología de la Tebaida Estaciana: El anti-virgilianismo de un classicista*, Hildesheim.
Dalton, H.E.B. (2020), "Transforming *arma uirumque*: Syntactical, morphological and metrical dis-*membra*-ment in Statius' *Thebaid*", *The Classical Quarterly* 70, 286–309.
Damschen, G./Heil, A. (2004), *Marcus Valerius Martialis, Epigrammaton liber decimus: Das zehnte Epigrammbuch*, Frankfurt am Main.
Darwall-Smith, R.H. (1996), *Emperors and Architecture: A Study of Flavian Rome*, Brussels.
Davis, P.J. (2014), "Medea: From Epic to Tragedy", in: M. Heerink/G. Manuwald (eds.), *Brill's Companion to Valerius Flaccus*, Leiden, 192–210.
Davison, W.P. (1983), "The Third-Person Effect in Communication", *The Public Opinion Quarterly* 47.1, 1–15.
Day, J.W. (2019), "The Origins of Greek Epigram: The Unity of Inscription and Object", in: C. Henriksén (ed.), *A Companion to Ancient Epigram*, Hoboken, 231–247.
Dee, N. (2013), "Wasted water: the failure of purification in the *Thebaid*", in: A. Augoustakis (ed.), *Ritual and Religion in Flavian Epic*, Oxford, 181–198.
Degl'Innocenti Pierini, R. (1999), *Tra filosofia e poesia. Studi su Seneca e dintorni*, Bologna.
de Jong, I. (2014), *Narratology and the Classics. A Practical Guide*, Oxford.
Delz, J. (1987), *Sili Italici, Punica*, Stuttgart.
Dewar, M. (2016), "Lost Literature", in: A. Zissos (ed.), *A Companion to the Flavian Age of Imperial Rome*, Malden, 449–483.
Dietrich, J. (1999), "*Thebaid*'s Feminine Ending", *Ramus* 28, 40–53.

Dominik, W.J. (2003), "Hannibal at the Gates: Programmatizing Rome and *Romanitas* in Silius Italicus' *Punica* 1 and 2", in: A.J. Boyle/W.J. Dominik (eds.), *Flavian Rome: Culture, Image, Text*, Leiden, 469–497.
Dominik, W.J. (2012), "Critiquing the critics: Jupiter, the Gods and free will in Statius' *Thebaid*", in: T. Baier (ed.), *Götter und menschlicher Willensfreiheit: von Lucan bis Silius Italicus* (Zetemata – Monographien zur klassischen Altertumswissenschaft), München, 187–198.
Dominik, W.J. (2018), "Civil war, parricide, and the sword in Silius Italicus' *Punica*", in: L.D. Ginsberg/D.A. Krasne (eds.), *After 69 CE. Writing Civil War in Flavian Rome*, Berlin/Boston, 271–294.
Döpp, S. (1993), "Saturnalien und lateinische Literatur", in: S. Döpp (ed.), *Karnevaleske Phänomene in antiken und nachantiken Kulturen und Literaturen*, Trier, 145–177.
Dorcey, P.F. (1992), *The Cult of Silvanus. A Study in Roman Folk Religion*, Leiden.
Drescher, K.D. (2006), "Spirituality in the face of terrorist disasters", in: L.A. Schein et al. (eds.), *Psychological Effects of Catastrophic Disasters: Group Approaches to Treatment*, New York, 335–381.
Drescher, K.D. et al. (eds.) (2011), "An exploration of the viability and usefulness of the construct of moral injury in war veterans", *Traumatology* 17.1, 8–13.
Econimo, F. (2021), *La parola e gli occhi. L'ekphrasis nella Tebaide di Stazio*, Pisa.
Edgeworth, R.J. (1992), *The Colors of the Aeneid*, New York.
Edwards, C. (1993), *The Politics of Immorality in Ancient Rome*, Cambridge.
Edwards, C. (1994), "Beware of imitations: theatre and the subversion of imperial identity", in: J. Elsner/J. Masters (eds.), *Reflections of Nero: Culture, History, & Representation*, London, 83–97.
Ehlers, W.W. (ed.) (1980), *Gai Valeri Flacci Setini Balbi Argonauticon libros octo*, Stuttgart.
Eigler, U. (1988), *Monologische Redeformen bei Valerius Flaccus*, Frankfurt.
Eigler, U. (1991), "Medea als Opfer Die Götterintrige im VII und VIII Buch der *Argonautica* (VII 1 – VIII 67)", in: v. M. Korn/H.J. Tschiedel (eds.), *Ratis Omnia Vincet: Untersuchungen zu den Argonautica des Valerius Flaccus*, Hildesheim/Zurich/New York, 155–172.
Elm von der Osten, D. (2007), *Liebe als Wahnsinn: Die Konzeption der Gottin Venus in den Argonautica des Valerius Flaccus*, Stuttgart.
Ernout, A./Meillet, A. (1959⁴), *Dictionnaire étymologique de la langue latine. Histoire des mots*, Rev. with additions and corrections by J. André, Paris.
Fairclough, H.R. (1916), *Virgil. Eclogues. Georgics. Aeneid: Books 1–6*. Revised by G.P. Goold, Cambridge, MA.
Fantham, E. (1999), "The Role of Lament in the Growth and Eclipse of Roman Epic", in: M. Beissinger/J. Tylus/S. Wofford (eds.), *Epic Traditions in the Contemporary World: The Poetics of Community*, Berkeley, 221–235.
Fantham, E. (2009), *Latin Poets and Italian Gods*, Toronto.
Fantham, E. (2010), "*Discordia fratrum*: aspects of Lucan's conception of civil war", in: B. Breed/C. Damon/A. Rossi (eds.), *Citizens of Discord: Rome and its Civil Wars*, Oxford, 207–221.
Fantuzzi, M. (2008), "Which magic, which eros? Apollonius' *Argonautica* and the different narrative roles of Medea as a sorceress in love", in: T. Papanghelis/A. Rengakos (eds.), *Brill's Companion to Apollonius Rhodius*, Leiden, 289–310.
Favro, D./Johanson, C. (2010), "Death in Motion: funeral processions in the roman forum", *Journal of the Society of Architectural Historians* 69.1, 12–37.
Fearnley, H. (2003), "Reading the imperial revolution: Martial, *Epigrams* 10", in: A.J. Boyle/W.J. Dominik (eds.), *Flavian Rome*, Leiden, 613–635.

Feeney, D.C. (1982), *A Commentary on Silius Italicus Book 1*, PhD diss., Oxford.
Feeney, D.C. (1991), *The Gods in Epic: Poets and Critics of the Classical Tradition*, Oxford.
Feeney, D.C. (1998), *Literature and Religion at Rome. Cultures, Contexts, and Beliefs*, Cambridge.
Feeney, D.C. (2007), *Caesar's Calendar: Ancient Times and the Beginnings of History*, Berkeley.
Ferenzci, A. (1998), "Medea – Eine Heldin", in: U. Eigler/E. Lefèvre (eds.), *Ratis Omnia Vincet: Neue Untersuchungen zu den Argonautica des Valerius Flaccus*, Munich, 337–346.
Finkmann, S. (2019), "Necromancies in ancient epic", in: C. Reitz/S. Finkmann (eds.), *Structures of Epic Poetry*, Vol. II.2, Berlin/New York, 747–798.
Flores Militello, V. (2019), *Tali dignus amico. Die Darstellung des patronus-cliens-Verhältnisses bei Horaz, Martial und Juvenal*, Tübingen.
Fowler, D. (1989), "First thoughts on closure: problems and prospects", *Materiali e discussioni per l'analisi dei testi classici* 22, 75–122.
Fowler, D. (1995), "Martial and the book", *Ramus* 24, 31–58.
Fowler, D. (1997), "Second thoughts on closure", in: D.H. Roberts/F.M. Dunn/D. Fowler (eds.), *Classical Closure: Reading the End in Greek and Latin Literature*, Princeton, 3–22.
Fowler, D. (2000), *Roman Constructions: Readings in Postmodern Latin*, Oxford.
Fowler, D. (2000a) = Fowler 1989.
Fowler, D. (2000b) = Fowler 1997.
Franchet d'Espèrey, S. (1988), "Une étrange descente aux enfers: le suicide d'Eson et Alcimède (Valerius Flaccus, *Arg.* I 730–851)", in: D. Porte/J.P. Néraudau (eds.), *Hommages à Henri Le Bonniec: Res Carae*, Brussels, 193–197.
Franchet d'Espèrey, S. (1998), "L'univers des *Argonautiques* est-il absurde?", in: U. Eigler/E. Lefèvre (eds.), *Ratis Omnia Vincet: Neue Untersuchungen zu den Argonautica des Valerius Flaccus*, Munich, 213–222.
Franklinos, T. (2018), "Ovid, *Ex Ponto* 4: an intratextually cohesive book", in: S. Harrison/S. Frangoulidis/T.D. Papanghelis (eds.), *Intratextuality and Latin Literature*, Berlin/Boston, 289–306.
Fratantuono, L.M./Smith, R.A. (2015), *Virgil, Aeneid 5. Text, Translation and Commentary*, Leiden.
Frazer, J.G. (1976), *Ovid V: Fasti*, Cambridge, MA.
Friedländer, L. (1886), *M. Valerii Martialis Epigrammaton Libri mit erklärenden Anmerkungen versehen*, Leipzig.
Fucecchi, M. (1993), "Lo spettacolo delle virtù nel giovane eroe predestinato. Analisi della figura di Scipione in Silio Italico", *Maia* 45, 17–48.
Fucecchi, M. (1996), "Il Restauro dei Modelli Antichi: Tradizione Epica e Tecnica Manieristica in Valerio Flacco", *Materiali e Discussioni per l'Analisi dei Testi Classici* 36, 101–165.
Fucecchi, M. (2014), "War and Love in Valerius Flaccus' *Argonautica*", in: M. Heerink/G. Manuwald (eds.), *Brill's Companion to Valerius Flaccus*, Leiden, 115–135.
Fucecchi, M. (2018), "Flavian Epic: Roman ways of metabolizing a cultural nightmare", in: L.D. Ginsberg/D.A. Krasne (eds.), *After 69 CE: Writing Civil War in Flavian Rome*, Berlin, 25–49.
Fucecchi, M. (2019), "Hannibal as (anti-)hero of *Fides* in Silius' *Punica*", in: A. Augoustakis/E. Buckley/C. Stocks (eds.), *Fides in Flavian Literature*, Toronto, 187–207.
Fucecchi, M. (2020), "Constructing (super-)characters: the case study of Silius' Hannibal", in: N. Coffee et al. (eds.), *Intertextuality in Flavian Epic Poetry: Contemporary Approaches*, Berlin/Boston, 259–281.
Fusi, A. (2006), *M. Valerii Martialis Epigrammaton liber tertius. Introduzione, edizione critica, traduzione e commento*, Hildesheim/Zurich/New York.

Fusi, A. (2011), "Marziale e il fantasma di Scorpo. Nota a 10.48.23", in: P. Mastandrea/R. Perrelli (eds.), *Latinum est, et legitur: metodi e temi dello studio dei testi latini*, Amsterdam, 261–280.
Gaertner, J.F. (2008), "Livy's Camillus and the Political Discourse of the Late Republic", *The Journal of Roman Studies* 98, 27–52.
Gaffney, G.E. (1976), *Mimic Elements in Martial's Epigrammaton Libri XII*, diss. Vanderbilt University, Nashville, TE.
Galán Vioque, G. (2002), *Martial, Book VII. A Commentary*, Leiden/Boston/Köln.
Galli, D. (2007), *Valerii Flacci Argonautica I: Commento*, Berlin.
Ganiban, R. (2007), *Statius and Virgil: The Thebaid and the Reinterpretation of the Aeneid*, Cambridge.
Ganiban, R. (2013), "The death and funeral rites of Opheltes in the *Thebaid*", in: A. Augoustakis (ed.), *Ritual and Religion in Flavian Epic*, Oxford, 249–265.
George, M. (2008), "The Dark Side of the Toga", in: J. Edmondson/A. Keith (eds.), *Roman Dress and the Fabrics of Roman Culture*, Toronto, 94–112.
George, L. (2020), *A Handful of Earth, A Handful of Sky*, Canada.
Georgoudi, S./Koch-Piettre, R./Schmidt, F. (eds.) (2012), *La Raison des signes: Présages, rites, destin dans les sociétés de la Méditerranée ancienne*, Leiden.
Gervais, K. (2017a), *Statius Thebaid 2: Edited with an Introduction, Translation, and Commentary*, Oxford.
Gervais, K. (2017b), "*Odi(tque moras)*: abridging allusions to Vergil, *Aeneid* 12 in Statius, *Thebaid* 12", *American Journal of Philology* 138, 305–329.
Gervais, K. (2021), "Senecan heroes and tyrants in Statius' *Thebaid* 2", in: S. Papaioannou/ A. Marinis (eds.), *Elements of Tragedy in Flavian Epic*, Berlin/Boston, 129–148.
Gibson, B. (1996), "Statius and insomnia: allusion and meaning in *Siluae* 5.4", *The Classical Quarterly* 46.2, 457–468.
Gibson, B. (2006), *Statius, Siluae 5*, Oxford.
Gibson, B. (2013), "Hymnic Features in Statian Epic and the *Siluae*", in: A. Augoustakis (ed.), *Ritual and Religion in Flavian Epic*, Oxford, 127–144.
Gimpel, T. (2016), "The Military, Moral Injury, and Music Therapy", *Music & Medicine* 8.1, 35–40.
Goldbeck, F. (2016), "Die Triumphe der julisch-claudischen Zeit", in: F. Goldbeck/J. Wienand (eds.), *Der Römische Triumph in Prinzipat und Spätantike*, Berlin/Boston, 103–122.
Goldman-Petri, M. (2021), "Domitian and the Augustan Altars", in: R. Marks/M. Mogetta (eds.), *Domitian's Rome and the Augustan Legacy*, Ann Arbor, 32–56.
Gordon, R. (2013), "'Will my Child Have a Big Nose?': Uncertainty, authority and narrative in katarchic astrology", in: V. Rosenberger (ed.), *Divination in the Ancient World: Religious Options and the Individual* (*Potsdamer Altertumswissenschaftliche Beiträge* 46), Stuttgart, 93–137.
Gosden, C./Marshall, Y. (1999), "The Cultural Biography of Objects", *World Archaeology* 31.2, 169–178.
Gramps, A. (2021), *The Fiction of Occasion in Hellenistic and Roman Poetry*, Berlin/Boston.
Greensmith, E. (2020), *The Resurrection of Homer in Imperial Greek Epic: Quintus Smyrnaeus' Posthomerica and the Poetics of Impersonation*, Cambridge.
Grewe, S. (1998), "Der Einfluss von Senecas *Medea* auf die *Argonautica* des Valerius Flaccus", in: U. Eigler/E. Lefèvre (eds.), *Ratis omnia vincet. Neue Untersuchungen zu den Argonautica des Valerius Flaccus*, Munich, 173–190.

Grewing, F. (1997), *Martial, Buch VI (Ein Kommentar)*, Göttingen.
Grewing, F. (1998), "Etymologie und etymologische Wortspiele in den Epigrammen Martials", in: F. Grewing (ed.), *Toto notus in orbe: Perspektiven der Martial-Interpretation*, Stuttgart, 315–356.
Grewing, F./Acosta-Hughes, B./Kirichenko, A. (eds.) (2013), *The Door Ajar. False Closure in Greek and Roman Literature and Art*, Heidelberg.
Grewing, F. (2020), "A Saturnalian poet as a literary critic. The carnivalesque poetics of Martial's *Apophoreta* 183–196", *Thersites* 11, 176–204.
Griffin, M. (1984), *Nero: The End of a Dynasty*, London.
Griffin, M. (2000²), "The Flavians", in: A. Bowman/P. Garnsey/D. Rathbone (eds.), *The Cambridge Ancient History*, Cambridge 11, 1–83.
Gummere, R. (1917), *Seneca, Lucius Annaeus. Ad Lucilium Epistulae Morales*, Cambridge, MA.
Gunderson, E. (2021), *The Art of Complicity in Martial and Statius. Martial's Epigrams, Statius' Siluae, and Domitianic Rome*, Oxford.
Hahn, J./Gotter, U. (2008), *From Temple to Church: Destruction and Renewal of Local Cultic Topography in Late Antiquity*, Leiden.
Halbwachs, M. (1925), *Les Cadres sociaux de la mémoire*, Paris.
Hamvas, G. (2016), "Il Vestiario di Giasone: Mantelli negli *Argonautica* di Valerio Flacco", *Acta Antiqua Academiae Scientiarum Hungaricae* 56.3, 359–367.
Hanink, J. (2021), *A New Path for Classics. Chronicle of Higher Education*, Washington.
Hardie, A. (1983), *Statius and the Siluae. Poets, Patrons and Epideixis in the Graeco-Roman World*, Liverpool.
Hardie, P. (1986), *Virgil's Aeneid: Cosmos and Imperium*, Oxford.
Hardie, P. (1993), *The Epic Successors of Virgil. A Study in the Dynamics of a Tradition*, Cambridge.
Hardie, P. (1997), "Closure in Latin epic", in: D.H. Roberts/F.M. Dunn/D. Fowler (eds.), *Classical Closure: Reading the End in Greek and Latin Literature*, Princeton, 139–162.
Heerink, M. (2020), "Replaying Dido: Elegy and the Poetics of Inversion in Valerius Flaccus' *Argonautica*", in: N. Coffee et al. (eds.), *Intertextuality in Flavian Epic Poetry: Contemporary Approaches*, Berlin, 187–203.
Heerink, M. (2022), "Civil War and Trauma in Valerius Flaccus' *Argonautica*", in: M. Heerink/E. Meijer (eds.), *Flavian Responses to Nero's Rome*, Amsterdam, 163–184.
Heil, A. (2013), "*Maronis mentula*. Vergil als Priapeen-Dichter bei Martial (Mart. 9, 33)", *Philologus* 157, 111–118.
Heinrich, A. (1999), "*Longa retro series*: Sacrifice and repetition in Statius' Menoeceus episode", *Arethusa* 32, 165–195.
Henderson, J. (1993), "Form Remade: Statius' *Thebaid*", in: A.J. Boyle (ed.), *Roman Epic*, London, 162–191.
Henderson, J. (2007), "Bringing it all Back Home: Togetherness in Statius' *Siluae* 3.5", *Arethusa* 40.2, 245–277.
Hendrickson, G.L./Hubbell, H.M. (1962), *Cicero Brutus*, Cambridge, MA.
Henriksén, C. (2006), "Martial's modes of mourning. Sepulchral epitaphs in the Epigrams", in: R.R. Nauta/H.-J. van Dam/J.J.L. Smolenaars (eds.), *Flavian Poetry*, Leiden/Boston, 349–367.
Hernández González, F. (2008), "Avitus, el amigo del poeta latino Marcial", *Fortunatae* 19, 27–39.
Hersch, K.K. (2010), *The Roman Wedding: Ritual and Meaning in Antiquity*, Cambridge.

Hershkowitz, D. (1994), "Sexuality and madness in Statius' *Thebaid*", *Materiali e discussioni per l'Analisi dei Testi Classici* 33, 123–147.
Hershkowitz, D. (1998), *Valerius Flaccus' Argonautica: Abbreviated Voyages in Silver Latin Epic*, Oxford.
Heslin, P. (2009), *The Transvestite Achilles: Gender and Genre in Statius' Achilleid*, Cambridge.
Heslin, P. (2018), "A Perfect Murder: The Hypsipyle Epyllion", in: N. Manioti (ed.), *Family in Flavian Epic*, Leiden, 89–121.
Hinds, S. (1993), "Medea in Ovid: scenes from the life of an intertextual heroine", *Materiali e discussioni per l'analisi dei testi classici* 30, 9–47.
Hinds, S. (1998), *Allusion and Intertext: Dynamics of Appropriation in Roman Poetry*, Roman Literature and its Contexts, Cambridge.
Hodder, I. (2012), *Entangled: An Archaeology of the Relationships between Humans and Things*, Chichester.
Holzberg, N. (1997), *Ovid: Dichter und Werk*, München.
Holzberg, N. (2002), *Martial und das antike Epigramm*, Darmstadt.
Holzberg, N. (2004/05), "Martial, the Book, and Ovid", *Hermathena* 177/178, 209–224.
Holzberg, N. (2011), "Applaus für Maro. Eine "augusteische" Interpretation von Mart. 9, 33", in: A. Heil et al. (eds.), *Noctes Sinenses. Festschrift for Fritz-Heiner Mutschler zum 65. Geburtstag*, Heidelberg, 68–73.
Höschele, R. (2010), *Die blütenlesende Muse: Poetik und Textualität antiker Epigrammsammlungen*, Tübingen.
Höschele, R. (2013), "*Sit pudor et finis*: false closure in ancient Epigram", in: F. Grewing/B. Acosta-Hughes/A. Kirichenko (eds.), *The Door Ajar. False Closure in Greek and Roman Literature and Art*, Heidelberg, 247–262.
Hooper, W.D., rev. Ash, H.B. (1934), *Marcus Porcius Cato, On Agriculture*, Cambridge, MA.
Hope, V.M. (2009), *Roman Death: The Dying and the Dead in Ancient Rome*, London.
Hope, V.M./Huskinson, J. (eds.) (2011), *Memory and Mourning: Studies on Roman Death*, Oxford.
Horsfall, N.M. (1973), "Three notes on Horace's *Epodes*", *Philologus* 117, 136–138.
Horsfall, N. (2000), *Virgil, Aeneid 7: A Commentary*, Leiden.
Howell, P. (1980), *A Commentary on Book One of the Epigrams of Martial*, London.
Howell, P. (1998), "Martial's return to Spain", in: F. Grewing (ed.), *Toto notus in orbe: Perspektiven der Martial-Interpretation*, Stuttgart, 173–186.
Hubert, A. (2013), "*Malae preces* and their articulation in the *Thebaid*", in: A. Augoustakis (ed.), *Ritual and Religion in Flavian Epic*, Oxford, 109–126.
Hulls, J.M. (2010), "Replacing history: inaugurating the new year in Statius, *Siluae* 4.1", in: J.F. Miller/A.J. Woodman (eds.), *Latin Historiography and Poetry in the Early Empire: Generic Interactions*, Leiden, 87–104.
Hulls, J.M. (2011), "Poetic monuments: grief and consolation in Statius *Siluae* 3.3", in: V.M. Hope/J. Huskinson (eds.), *Memory and Mourning: Studies on Roman Death*, Oxford, 150–175.
Hulls, J.M. (2021), *The Search for the Self in Statius' Thebaid: Identity, Intertext and the Sublime*, Berlin.
Hunter, R. (1987), "Medea's flight: the fourth book of the *Argonautica*", *The Classical Quarterly* 37.1, 129–139.
Hunter, R. (1993), *The Argonautica of Apollonius: Literary Studies*, Cambridge.

Hunter, R. (2008), "The poetics of narrative in the *Argonautica*", in: T. Papanghelis/A. Rengakos (eds.), *A Companion to Apollonius Rhodius*, Leiden/Boston, 115–146.
Insoll, T. (ed.) (2001), *Archaeology and World Religion*, London.
Insoll, T. (2004), *Archaeology, Ritual, Religion*, New York.
Insoll, T. (2009), "Materiality, belief, ritual-Archaeology and material religion: an introduction", *Material Religion* 5, 260–265.
Insoll, T. (ed.) (2011), *The Oxford Handbook of the Archaeology of Ritual and Religion*, Oxford.
Jacobs, J. (2009), "*Anne Iterum Capta Repetentur Pergama Roma?*: the fall of Rome in the *Punica*", PhD diss., New Haven.
Jacobs, J. (2021), *An Introduction to Silius Italicus and the Punica*, London.
Jenkyns, R. (2013), *God, Space, and City in the Roman Imagination*, Oxford.
Johannsen, N. (2006), *Dichter über ihre Gedichte: die Prosavorreden in den 'Epigrammaton libri' Martials und in den 'Siluae' des Statius. Hypomnemata* 166, Göttingen.
Johnston, S.I. (1999), *Restless Dead: Encounters between the Living and the Dead in Ancient Greece*, Berkeley.
Juhnke, H. (1972), *Homerisches in römischer Epik flavischer Zeit: Untersuchungen zu Szenennachbildungen und Strukturentsprechungen in Statius' Thebais und Achilleis und in Silius' Punica*, München.
Kaliwoda, U. (1998), "Die persönliche Religiosität Martials", *Grazer Beiträge* 22, 197–210.
Kaster, R.A. (2011), *Macrobius, Saturnalia*. 3 vols., Cambridge, MA.
Kay, N. (1985), *Martial Book XI: A Commentary*, London.
Keith, A. (2013), "Medusa, Python and Poine in Argive religious ritual", in: A. Augoustakis (ed.), *Ritual and Religion in Flavian Epic*, Oxford, 303–318.
Keith, A. (2016), "Sisters and their secrets in Flavian epic", in: N. Manioti (ed.), *Family in Flavian Epic*, Leiden, 248–275.
Keith, A. (2018), "Historical Roman courtesans", in: R. Berg/R. Neudecker (eds.), *The Roman Courtesan: Archaeological Reflections of a Literary Topos*, Acta Instituti Romani Finlandiae 46, Rome.
Keith, A. (2018[2019]), "Epicurean principle and poetic program in Martial, *Epigrams* 10.47–48", *Phoenix* 72.3-4, 319–37.
Keith, A. (2021), "Martial's retirement and other Epicurean postures in Book 10", in: L. Curtis/I.P. Garrison (eds.), *The Lives of Latin Texts: Papers presented to Richard J. Tarrant*, Cambridge, MA, 173–204.
Kennedy, R.F./Planudes, M. (2021), "Changing "Classics": What Do We Want? Not What Some People Keep Saying We Want", *Classics at the Intersections*. https://rfkclassics.blogspot.com/2021/02/changing-classics-what-do-we-want-not.html, last access 21.03.2023.
Kermode, F. (2000 [1966]), *The Sense of an Ending. Studies in the Theory of Fiction: with a New Epilogue*, Oxford.
Kleywegt, A.J. (1991), "Die 'Anderen' Argonauten", in: M. Korn/H.J. Tschiedel (eds.), *Ratis Omnia Vincet: Untersuchungen zu den Argonautica des Valerius Flaccus*, Hildesheim, 225–237.
Kleywegt, A.J. (2005), *Valerius Flaccus, Argonautica, Book 1: A Commentary*, Leiden.
Kline, A.S. (tr.) (2002), *Vergil, The Aeneid. A translation into English prose* (Poetry in Translation), https://www.poetryintranslation.com/PITBR/Latin/Vergilhome.php, last access 21.03.2023.
Klodt, C. (2005), "*Ad uxorem* in eigener Sache: as Abschlussgedicht der ersten drei Silvenbücher des Statius vor dem Hintergrund von Ovids 'Autobiographie' (*Trist.* 4. 10) und seinen

Briefen an die Gattin", in: M. Reichel (ed.), *Antike Autobiographien: Werke – Epochen – Gattungen*, Köln/Wien/Böhlau, 186–222.
Knight, V. (1995), *The Renewal of Epic: Responses to Homer in the Argonautica of Apollonius*, Leiden/New York.
Knox, B.M.W. (1950), "The serpent and the flame. The imagery of the second book of the *Aeneid*", *American Journal of Philology* 79, 379–400.
Knox, P.E. (1995), *Ovid, Heroides. Select Epistles*, Cambridge.
Koeppel, G.M. (1969), "Profectio und Aduentus", *Bonner Jahrbücher* 169, 130–194.
Koeppel, G.M. (1980), "A Fragment from a Domitianic Monument in Ann Arbor and Rome", *Bulletin/Museums of Art and Archaeology, University of Michigan* 3, 9–29.
Kolb, M.J. (1994), "Monumentality and Rise of Religious Authority in Precontact Hawai'i", *Current Anthropology* 35.5, 521–547.
Kolosova, O.G. (2000), "*Callaicum mandas siquid ad Oceanum*... Zur Zeit und Ursace der Heimkehr Martials", *Gerión* 18, 323–341.
Konstan, D. (2014), "Introduction. Combat trauma: the missing diagnosis in ancient Greece", in: P. Meineck/D. Konstan (eds.), *Combat Trauma and the Ancient Greeks*, New York, 1–14.
Kranemann, B. (2017), "Liturgie, Körper, kulturelles Gedächtnis: Nonverbale Erinnerungsformen im Gottesdienst", *Bibel und Liturgie: ... in kulturellen Räumen* 90.1, 23–31.
Krasne, D.A. (2018a), "Distance learning: competing philosophies at sea in book 2 of Valerius Flaccus' *Argonautica*", *Phoenix* 72, 239–265.
Krasne, D.A. (2018b), "Valerius Flaccus' collapsible universe: patterns of cosmic disintegration in the *Argonautica*", in: L.D. Ginsberg/D.A. Krasne (eds.), *After 69 CE – Writing Civil War in Flavian Rome*, Berlin/Boston, 363–385.
Kunze, M. (1992), "Weihrelief an Kybele", in: Staatliche Museen zu Berlin (ed.), *Die Antikensammlung im Pergamonmuseum und in Charlottenburg*, Mainz, 128–129.
Kytzler, B. (1955), *Statius-Studien: Beiträge zum Verständnis der Thebais*, PhD diss., Berlin.
Laguna Mariscal, G. (1990), "La *Silva* 5.4 de Estacio: plegaria al sueño", *Habis* 21, 121–138.
Laguna Mariscal, G. (1992), *Estacio, Silvas III, Introducción, Edición Crítica, Traducción y Comentario*, Madrid.
Lange, C.H. (2016a), "The late Republican triumph: continuity and change", in: F. Goldbeck/ J. Wienand (eds.), *Der Römische Triumph in Prinzipat und Spätantike*, Berlin/Boston, 29–58.
Lange, C.H. (2016b), "Mock the triumph: Cassius Dio, triumph and triumph-like celebrations", in: C.H. Lange/J.M. Madsen (eds.), *Cassius Dio: Greek Intellectual and Roman Politician*, Leiden, 92–114.
Lapidge, M. (1979), "Lucan's Imagery of Cosmic Dissolution", *Hermes* 107, 344–370.
Lapidge, M. (1980), "A Stoic Metaphor in late Latin poetry: the binding of the cosmos", *Latomus* 39, 817–837.
Lapsley, M./Karakashian, S. (2018), "Owning the past, healing the future", in: R. Meagher/ D. Pryer (eds.), *War and Moral Injury: A Reader*, Oregon, 231–235.
Larash, P. (2010), "Antulla's Tomb and Martial's: poetic closure in book 1", *Acta Classica Debrecenensis* 46, 41–56.
Latour, B. (ed.) (2011), *Jubilieren: Über religiöse Rede*, trans. Achim Russer, Berlin.
Laudizi, G. (1989), *Silio Italico: Il Passato Tra Mito e Restaurazione Etica*, Galatina.
Lazzarini, C. (2012), *L'addio di Medea: Valerio Flacco, Argonautiche 8.1–287*, Pisa, Hildesheim.
Leary, T. (1996), *Martial Book XIV: the Apophoreta. Text with Introduction and Commentary*, London.

Leary, T. (2001), *Martial. Book XIII: The Xenia. Text with Introduction and Commentary*, London.
Leberl, J. (2004), *Domitian und die Dichter. Poesie als Medium der Herrschaftsdarstellung*, Göttingen.
Leibinger, H. (2000), *Kultische Situation in lyrischer und epischer Dichtung: Untersuchungen zum Realitätsbezug in einigen Gedichten von Horaz, Properz, Tibull, Statius und Claudian*, Tübingen.
Lejavitzer, A. (2001), "Marcial: tiempo y celebración en los epigramas", *Nova Tellus. Anuario del Centro de Estudios Clásicos* 19.2, 175–185.
Leonhard, C. (2005), "'Als ob sie mir ein Opfer dargebracht hätten'. Erinnerungen an den Tempel in der Liturgie der Synagoge", in: A. Gerhards/S. Wahle (eds.), *Kontinuität und Unterbrechung: Gottesdienst und Gebet in Judentum und Christentum*, Paderborn, 107–122.
Levine, S. (2018), "Legal War, Sin and 'Moral Injury' in the Age of Modern Warfare", in: R. Meagher/D. Pryer (eds.), *War and Moral Injury: A Reader*, Oregon, 219–230.
Lévy, C. (2013), "Note sur l'évolution sémantique de silva de l'époque républicaine à Saint Augustin", in: P. Galand/S. Laigneau-Fontaine (eds.), *La Silve. Histoire d'une écriture libérée en Europe, de l'Antiquité au XVIIIe siècle*, Turnhout, 45–56.
Lévy, J./Lussault, M. (eds.) (2013), *Dictionnaire de la géographie et de l'espace des sociétés* (Nouvelle éd. revue et augmentée), Paris.
Liberman, G. (ed.) (2010), *Stace, Silves*, Paris.
Lindsay, W.M. (1929[2]), *M. Val. Martialis Epigrammata. Recognovit brevique adnotatione instruxit*, Oxford.
Littlewood, J. (2011), *A Commentary on Silius Italicus' Punica 7*, Oxford.
Littlewood, J. (2017), *A Commentary on Silius Italicus' Punica 10*, Oxford.
Litz, B.T./Stein, N./Delaney, E./Lebowitz, L./Nash, W.P./Silva, C./Maguen, S. (2009), "Moral Injury and Moral Repair in War Veterans: A Preliminary Model and Intervention Strategy", *Clinical Psychology Review* 29, 695–706.
Litz, B.T./Lebowitz, L./Gray, M.J./Nash, W.P. (2016), *Adaptive Disclosure: A New Treatment for Military Trauma, Loss, and Moral Injury*, New York.
Lorenz, S. (2002), *Erotik und Panegyrik. Martials Epigrammatische Kaiser*, Tübingen.
Lorenz, S. (2003), "Martial: 1970–2003. 1. Teil", *Lustrum* 45, 167–277.
Lorenz, S. (2004), "Waterscape with black and white: epigrams, cycles and webs in Martial's *Epigramaton liber quartus*", *AJPh* 125, 255–278.
Lorenz, S. (2006), "Martial 1970–2003 (2. Teil und Schluss)", *Lustrum* 48, 109–223, 233–247.
Lorenz, S. (2009), "Der "ernste" Martial: Tod und Trauer in den Epigrammen", *Gymnasium* 116, 359–380.
Lorenz, S. (2019), "Micro to Macro: Martial's Twelve Books of Epigrams", in: C. Henriksén (ed.), *A Companion to Ancient Epigram*, Hoboken, 521–539.
Lovatt, H.V. (1999), "Competing endings: re-reading the end of the *Thebaid* through Lucan", *Ramus* 28.2, 126–151.
Lovatt, H.V. (2005), *Statius and Epic Games: Sport, Politics and Poetics in the Thebaid*, Cambridge.
Lovatt, H.V. (2006), "The Female gaze in Flavian epic: looking out from the walls in Valerius Flaccus and Statius", in: R.R. Nauta/J.J.L. Smolenaars/H. van Dam (eds.), *Flavian Poetry*, Leiden, 59–78.
Lovatt, H.V. (2007), "Statius, Orpheus, and the Post-Augustan *Vates*", *Arethusa* 40.2, 145–163.

Lovatt, H.V. (2018), "Apollonius Rhodius *Argonautica* 4 and the epic gaze: there and back again", in: A. Kampakoglou/A. Novokhatko (eds.), *Gaze, Vision, and Visuality in Ancient Greek Literature*, Berlin/Boston, 88–112.
Lühr, G. (1880), *De P. Papinio Statio in Silvis priorum poetarum Romanorum imitatore*, diss., Konigsberg.
Lush, B. (2014), "Combat trauma and psychological injury in Euripides' *Medea*", *Helios* 41.1, 25–57.
Lye, S. (2012), "Rewriting the gods: religious ritual, human resourcefulness, and divine interaction in the *Argonautica*", in: M.A. Harder/R.F. Regtuit/G.C. Wakker (eds.), *Gods and Religion in Hellenistic Poetry* (Hellenistica Groningana 16), Leuven, 223–247.
MacCormack, S.G. (1990), "*Loca sancta*: The organization of sacred topography in late antiquity", in: R.G. Ousterhout (ed.), *The Blessings of Pilgrimage* (Illinois Byzantine Studies 1), Urbana, 7–40.
Maguen, S./Litz, B. (2012), "Moral injury in veterans of war", *PTSD Research Quarterly* 23.1, 1–6.
Malaspina, E. (2006), "Hyle-silva (et alentour). Problèmes de traduction entre rhétorique et métaphore", *Interférences Ars Scribendi* 4, 1–10.
Malaspina, E. (2013), "La formation et l'usage du titre *siluae* en latin classique", in: P. Galand/ S. Laigneau-Fontaine (eds.), *La Silve. Histoire d'une écriture libérée en Europe de l'Antiquité au XVIIIe siècle*, Turnhout, 17–44.
Manuwald, G. (1999), *Die Cyzicus-Episode und ihre Funktion in den Argonautika des Valerius Flaccus*, Göttingen.
Manuwald, G. (2000), "Der Tod der Eltern Iasons. Zu Valerius Flaccus, *Arg.* 1.693–850", *Philologus* 144, 325–338.
Manuwald, G. (2015), *Valerius Flaccus. Argonautica Book III*, Cambridge.
Manzo, A. (1995), "La fonte greca degli epigrami sepolcrali di Marziale", in: L. Belloni/ G. Milanese/A. Porro (eds.), *Studia classica Johanni Tarditi oblata*, 755–768.
Maree Brown, A. (2017), *Emergent Strategy: Shaping Change, Shaping Worlds*, Chico, CA.
Marinis, A./Papaioannou, S. (eds.) (2021), *Elements of Tragedy in Flavian Epic*, Berlin.
Marinis, A. (2021), "Eteocles and Polynices in Statius' *Thebaid*: revisiting tragic causality" in: A. Marinis/S. Papaioannou (eds.), *Elements of Tragedy in Flavian Epic*, Berlin, 149–170.
Markland, J. (1827 [1728]), *P. Papinii Statii libri quinque Siluarum*, London.
Marks, R. (2003), "Hannibal in Liternum", in: P. Thibodeau/H. Haskell (eds.), *Being There Together. Essays in Honor of Michael C.J. Putnam*, Afton, 128–144.
Marks, R. (2005), *From Republic to Empire. Scipio Africanus in the Punica of Silius Italicus*, Frankfurt am Main.
Marks, R. (2018), "*Sparsis Mauors agitates in oris*: Lucan and civil war in *Punica* 14", in: L.D. Ginsberg/D.A. Krasne (eds.), *After 69 CE: Writing Civil War in Flavian Rome*, Berlin, 51–68.
Marks, R. (2019), "Fides, Pietas, and the outbreak of hostilities in *Punica* 1", in: A. Augoustakis/ E. Buckley/C. Stocks (eds.), *Fides in Flavian Literature*, Toronto, 171–186.
Marks, R. (2020), "Searching for Ovid at Cannae: A Contribution to the Reception of Ovid in Silius Italicus' *Punica*", in: N. Coffee et al. (eds.), *Intertextuality in Flavian Epic Poetry: Contemporary Approaches*, Berlin, 87–106.
Marks, R./Mogetta, M. (eds.) (2021), *Domitian's Rome and the Augustan Legacy*, Ann Arbor.
Masters, J. (1992), *Poetry and Civil War in Lucan's Bellum Ciuile*, Cambridge.
Mayer, R. (1981), *Lucan, Civil War VIII, Edited with an Introduction, and Commentary*, Warminster.
Mayer, R. (1994), *Horace, Epistles Book I*, Cambridge.

McClellan, A. (2019), *Abused Bodies in Roman Epic*, Cambridge.
McGuire, D.T. (1985), *History as Epic: Silius Italicus and the Second Punic War*, diss. Cornell University.
McGuire, D.T. (1990), "Textual strategies and political suicide in Flavian epic", in: A.J. Boyle (ed.), *The Imperial Muse: Ramus Essays on Roman Literature of the Empire, ii. Flavian Epicist to Claudian*, 21–45, Bendigno.
McGuire, D.T. (1997), *Acts of Silence. Civil War, Tyranny, and Suicide in the Flavian Epics*, Hildesheim.
McNelis, C. (2007), *Statius' Thebaid and the Poetics of Civil War*, Cambridge.
Mehmel, F. (1934), *Valerius Flaccus*, Hamburg.
Meid, W. (1957), 'Das Suffix –no– in Götternamen', *Beiträge zur namenforschung* 8, 72–108.
Meineck, P./Konstan, D. (eds.) (2014), *Combat Trauma and the Ancient Greeks. The New Antiquity*, New York.
Merli, E. (1993), "Ordinamento degli epigrammi e strategie cortigiane negli esordi dei libri I–XII di Marziale", *Maia* 45, 229–256.
Merli, E. (1998), "Epigrammzyklen und 'serielle Lektüre' in den Büchern Martials. Überlegungen und Beispiele", in: F. Grewing (ed.), *Toto notus in orbe. Perspektiven der Martial – Interpretation*, Stuttgart, 139–156.
Meyer, E. (1983^2), *Einführung in die lateinische Epigraphik*, Darmstadt.
Miller, J.F. (2000), "Triumphus in Palatio", *American Journal of Philology* 121, 409–422.
Mindt, N. (2013), *Martials 'epigrammatischer Kanon'*, München.
Moreno Soldevila, R. (2006), *Martial, Book IV: A Commentary*, Leiden.
Moreno Soldevila, R./Marina Castillo, A./Fernández Valverde, J. (2019), *A Prosopography to Martial's Epigrams*, Berlin.
Mori, A. (2008), *The Politics of Apollonius Rhodius' Argonautica*, Cambridge.
Most, G.W. (1989), "Cornutus and Stoic Allegories. A Preliminary Report," *Aufstieg und Niedergang der römischen Welt* II 36.3, Berlin/New York, 2014–2069.
Mozley, J.H. (ed. tr.) (1934), *Valerius Flaccus: Argonautica*, Cambridge, MA.
Narducci, E. (2002), *Lucano. Un'epica contro l'impero. Interpretazione della Pharsalia*, Roma/Bari.
Narducci, E. (2004), "Lo sfondo cosmico della Pharsalia", in: P. Esposito/E.M. Ariemma (eds.), *Lucano e la tradizione dell'epica latina*, Napoli, 7–20.
Narlikar, A. (2020), *Poverty Narratives and Power Paradoxes in International Trade Negotiations and Beyond*, Cambridge.
Nasse, C. (2012), *Erdichtete Rituale: Die Eingeweideschau in der lateinischen Epik und Tragödie (Potsdamer altertumswissenschaftliche Beiträge* 38), Stuttgart.
Nauta, R. (2002), *Poetry for Patrons. Literary Communication in the Age of Domitian*, Leiden.
Neger, M. (2012), *Martials Dichtergedichte. Das Epigramm als Medium der poetischen Selbstreflexion*, Tübingen.
Neger, M. (2019), "*Laudabo digne non satis tamen Baias*: Martial's Epigrammatic Campania", in: A. Augoustakis/J. Littlewood (eds.), *Campania in the Flavian Poetic Imagination*, Oxford, 83–98.
Nelis, D. (2001), *Vergil's Aeneid and the Argonautica of Apollonius Rhodius*, Leeds.
Nelis, D. (2009), "Ovid, *Metamorphoses* 1.416–51: noua monstra and the foedera naturae", in: P. Hardie (ed.), *Paradox and the Marvellous in Augustan Literature and Culture*, Oxford, 248–267.

Nelis, D. (2014), "Empedoclean epic: How far can you go?", *Dictynna* 11. (http://dictynna. revues.org/1057, last access 21.03.2023).
Newlands, C. (2009a), "Statius' Programmatic Apollo and the ending of Book 1 of the *Thebaid*", in: L. Athanasaki/R.P. Martin/J.F. Miller (eds.), *Apolline Politics and Poetics*, Athens: European Cultural Centre of Delphi, 353–378.
Newlands, C. (2009b), "Statius' Prose Prefaces", *Materiali e discussioni per l'analisi dei testi classici* 61, 229–242.
Newlands, C. (2010), "'*Fastos adulatione foedatos?*' (Tac. *Hist.* 4.40.2): Stazio sui *Fasti* di Ovidio", in: G. La Bua (ed.), *Vates operose dierum: Studi sui Fasti di Ovidio, Testi e studi di cultura classica* 48, Pisa, 155–168.
Newlands, C. (2011), *Statius Siluae Book II*, Cambridge.
Newlands, C. (2016), "Fatal Unions: Marriage at Thebes" in: N. Manioti (ed.), *Family in Flavian Epic*, Leiden, 143–173.
Newhouse, E. (2018), "Recovering from Moral Injury", in: R. Meagher/D. Pryer (eds.), *War and Moral Injury: A Reader*, Oregon, 147–157.
Newmyer, S.T. (1979), *The Siluae of Statius: Structure and Theme*, Leiden.
Nez, C./Avila, J. (2018), "Code Talker", in: R. Meagher/D. Pryer (eds.), *War and Moral Injury: A Reader*, Eugene, OR, 137–144.
Nilsson, M.P. (1921), "Saturnalia", *Realencyclopädie der classischen Altertumswissenschaft* II A.1, 201–211.
Nock, A.D. (1941), "A Cabiric Rite", *American Journal of Archaeology* 45.4, 577–581.
Norden, E. (1956), *Agnostos Theos. Untersuchungen zur Formengeschichte religiöser Rede*, Darmstadt.
Norman, S.B./Wilkins, K.C./Myers, U.S./Allard, C.B. (2014), "Trauma Informed Guilt Reduction Therapy with Combat Veterans", *Cognitive and Behavioral Practice* 21, 78–88.
Ogden, D. (2019), *Greek and Roman Necromancy*, Princeton.
O'Hara, J.J. (1996), *True Names: Vergil and the Alexandrian Tradition of Etymological Wordplay*, Ann Arbor.
O'Keefe, T. (2010), *Epicureanism*, Berkeley/Los Angeles.
Onorato, M. (2008), *Claudio Claudiano, De Raptu Proserpinae*, Napoli.
Östenberg, I. (2009), *Staging the World: Spoils, Captives, and Representations in the Roman Triumphal Procession*, Oxford.
Östenberg, I. (2019), "*Damnatio Memoriae* inscribed: the materiality of cultural repression", in: A. Petrovic/I. Petrovic/E. Thomas (eds.), *The Materiality of Text – Placement, Perception, and Presence of Inscribed Texts in Classical Antiquity*, Leiden, 324–347.
Pacello, C. (2018), "Moral trauma and nuclear war", in: R. Meagher/D. Pryer (eds.), *War and Moral Injury: A Reader*, Oregon, 114–120.
Pagán, V.E. (2000), "The Mourning after: Statius *Thebaid* 12", *American Journal of Philology* 121, 423–452.
Panoussi, V. (2009), *Greek Tragedy in Vergil's Aeneid: Ritual, Empire, and Intertext*, Cambridge.
Panoussi, V. (2013), "Dancing in Scyros: Masculinity and Young Women's Rituals in the *Achilleid*", in: A. Augoustakis (ed.), *Ritual and Religion in Flavian Epic*, Oxford, 335–351.
Panoussi, V. (2019), *Brides, Mourners, Bacchae: Women's Rituals in Roman Literature*, Baltimore.
Papaioannou, S. (2021), "Apollonius' 'Further Voices': Cameo Appearances of Greek Tragedy in Valerius Flaccus' *Argonautica*", in: A. Marinis/S. Papaioannou (eds.), *Elements of Tragedy in Flavian Epic*, Berlin/Boston, 65–89.

Parker, G. (2014), "*Tarda solacia*: liminal temporalities of Statius' prose prefaces", in: L. Jansen (ed.), *The Roman Paratext: Frame, Texts, Readers*, Cambridge, 112–128.
Parker, R. (1983), *Miasma: Pollution and Purification in Early Greek Religion*, Oxford.
Parkes, R. (2012), *Statius, Thebaid 4*, Oxford.
Parkes, R. (2013), "Chthonic ingredients and thematic concerns: the shaping of the necromancy in the *Thebaid*", in: A. Augoustakis (ed.), *Ritual and Religion in Flavian Epic*, Oxford, 165–180.
Parkes, R. (2021), "Finding the tragic in the epics of Statius", in: A. Marinis/S. Papaioannou (eds.), *Elements of Tragedy in Flavian Epic*, Berlin/Boston, 107–128.
Patzelt, M. (2018), *Über das Beten der Römer. Gebete im spätrepublikanischen und frühkaiserzeitlichen Rom als Ausdruck gelebter Religion*, Berlin/Boston.
Paule, M. (2014), "*Quae Saga, Quis Magus*: On the Vocabulary of the Roman Witch", *The Classical Quarterly* 64.2, 745–757.
Peirano, I. (2012), "'Sealing' the book: The sphragis as paratext", in: L. Jansen (ed.), *The Roman Paratext: Frame, Texts, Readers*, Cambridge, 224–242.
Pellucchi, T. (2012), *Commento al libro VIII delle Argonautiche di Valerio Flacco*, Zurich/New York.
Pepe, C./Moretti, G. (2015), *Le parole dopo la morte: Forme e funzioni della retorica funeraria nella tradizione greca e romana* (Labirinti 158), Trento.
Perutelli, A. (1982), "Pluralità di modelli e discontinuità narrativa: l'episodio della morte di Esone in Valerio Flacco (1.747 sgg.)", *Materiali e Discussioni per l'analisi dei testi classici* 26, 123–140.
Perutelli, A. (1994), "Il sogno di Medea da Apollonio Rodio a Valerio Flacco", *Materiali e Discussioni per l'Analisi dei Testi Classici* 33, 33–50.
Perutelli, A. (1997), *Argonauticon Liber 7*, Firenze.
Petersmann, H. (1973), "Zu einem altrömischen Opferritual (Cato *de agricultura* c. 141)", *Rheinisches Museum* 116, 238–255.
Phinney, E. (Jr.) (1967), "Narrative Unity in the *Argonautica*, The Medea-Jason Romance", *Transactions and Proceedings of the American Philological Association* 98, 327–341.
Plantinga, M. (2007), "Hospitality and rhetoric: the Circe episode in Apollonius Rhodius' *Argonautica*", *The Classical Quarterly* 57.2, 543–564.
Polt, C.B. (2013), "The Origin of the Idaean Dactyls (Apollonius *Argonautica* 1.1129–31), *Classical Philology* 108.4, 339–346.
Pomeroy, A.J. (1986), "Somnus and Amor; the Play of Statius, *Siluae* 5,4", *Quaderni Urbinati di Cultura Classica* 24, 91–97.
Pontiggia, L. (2018), "La folgore di Giove e la teomachia di Capaneo nella *Tebaide* di Stazio", *Materiali e discussioni per l'analisi dei testi classici* 80, 165–192.
Promey, S.M. (2014), "Religion, Sensation, and Materiality. An Introduction", in: S.M. Promey (ed.), *Sensational Religion. Sensory Cultures in Material Practice*, New Haven, 1–21.
Pryer, D.A. (2018), "What we don't talk about when we talk about war", in: R. Meagher/D. Pryer (eds.), *War and Moral Injury: A Reader*, Eugene, OR, 60–73.
Putnam, M. (2011), *The Humanness of Heroes: Studies in the Conclusion of Virgil's Aeneid*, Amsterdam.
Race, W. (2014), *Apollonius Rhodius, Argonautica*, Cambridge, MA.
Raja, R./Rüpke, J. (2015a), "Appropriating religion: methodological issues in testing the 'Lived Ancient Religion' approach", *Religion in the Roman Empire* 1.1, 11–9.

Raja, R./Rüpke, J. (eds.) (2015b), *A Companion to the Archaeology of Religion in the Ancient World*, Malden.
Raja, R./Rüpke, J. (2015c), "Archaeology of religion, material religion, and the ancient world", in: R. Raja/J. Rüpke (eds.), *A Companion to the Archaeology of Religion in the Ancient World*, Malden, 1–25.
Rebeggiani, S. (2018), *The Fragility of Power: Statius, Domitian and the Politics of the Thebaid*, Oxford.
Reeve, M. (1977), "Statius' *Siluae* in the fifteenth century", *The Classical Quarterly* 27, 202–225.
Reinmuth, O.W. (1933), "Vergil's use of '*interea*': a study of the treatment of contemporaneous events in roman epic", *American Journal of Philology* 54, 323–339.
Reitz, C. (1982), *Die Nekyia in den Punica des Silius Italicus*, Frankfurt am Main.
Richlin, A. (1992a), *Pornography and Representation in Greece and Rome*, Oxford.
Richlin, A. (1992b), *The Garden of Priapus. Sexuality and Aggression in Roman Humor*, Oxford.
Rieger, A.K. (2016), "Waste matters: life cycle and agency of pottery employed in Graeco-Roman sacred spaces", *Religion in the Roman Empire* 2.3, 307–339.
Rieger, A.K. (2018), "Imagining the absent and perceiving the present: an interpretation of material remains of divinities from the rock sanctuary at Caesarea Philippi (Gaulanitis)", in: M. Arnhold/H. O' Maier/J. Rüpke (eds.), *Seeing the God: Image, Space, Performance, and Vision in the Religion of the Roman Empire*, Tübingen, 27–58.
Rieger, A.K. (2020), "Introduction to section 2: a 'thing' called body: Expressing religion bodily", in: V. Gasparini et al. (eds.), *Lived Religion in the Ancient Mediterranean World: Approaching Religious Transformations from Archaeology, History and Classics*, Berlin, 201–208.
Rimell, V. (2008), *Martial's Rome*, Cambridge.
Ripoll, F. (1998a), *La Morale Héroïque Dans les Épopées Latines d'Époque Flavienne: Tradition et Innovation*, Leuven/Paris (Bibliothèque d'études classiques 14).
Ripoll, F. (1998b), "La *Thébaide* de Stace entre épopée et tragédie", in: M.H. Garelli-François (ed.), *Rome et le tragique. Colloque international 26, 27, 28 mars 1998, Pallas* 49, 323–340.
Ripoll, F. (2008), "La 'tragédie' d'Éson au chant I des *Argonautiques* de Valérius Flaccus", *Les Études Classiques* 76, 383–396.
Rist, J.M. (1980), "Epicurus on Friendship", *Classical Philology* 75, 121–129.
Roberts, D.H./Dunn, F.M./Fowler, D. (1997), *Classical Closure: Reading the End in Greek and Latin Literature*, Princeton.
Roberts, D.H. (1993), "The frustrated mourner: strategies of closure in Greek Tragedy", in: R.M. Rosen/J. Farrell (eds.), *Nomodeiktes: Greek Studies in Honor of Martin Ostwald*, Ann Arbor, 573–589.
Roberts, D.H. (1997), "Afterword: ending and aftermath, ancient and modern", in: D.H. Roberts/F.M. Dunn/D. Fowler (eds.), *Classical Closure: Reading the End in Greek and Latin Literature*, Princeton, 251–273.
Roche, P. (2005), "Righting the reader: conflagration and civil war in Lucan's *De Bello Ciuili*", *Scholia* 14, 52–71.
Roche, P. (2009), *Lucan. De bello ciuili, Book 1. Edited with Introduction, Text, and Commentary*, Oxford.
Rodríguez-Almeida, E. (1989), "Due note marzialiane: I «balnea quattuor in campo» e le «sellae paterclianae» subcapitoline", *Mélanges de l'école française de Rome* 101.1, 243–254.

Roman, L. (2001), "The representation of literary materiality in Martial's *Epigrams*", *The Journal of Roman Studies* 91, 113–145.
Rosa, H. (2016a), "Religion als Form des In-der-Welt-Seins: Latours andere Soziologie der Weltbeziehung", in: L. Henning (ed.), *Bruno Latours Soziologie der "Existenzweisen". Einführung und Diskussion*, Bielefeld, 251–260.
Rosa, H. (2016b), "Einem Ruf antworten: Bruno Latours andere Soziologie der Weltbeziehung", *Soziologische Revue* 39.4, 552–560.
Rosa, H. (2019), *Resonance: A Sociology of the Relationship to the World*, trans. J.C. Wagner, Cambridge.
Rosati, G. (2013), "Un aedo in posa. Stazio e la coscienza di un poeta professionista", in: H. Casanova-Robin/A. Billault (eds.), *Le poète au miroir de ses vers, Études sur la représentation du poète dans ses œuvres*, Grenoble, 81–100.
Rosenmeyer, T.G. (1989), *Senecan Drama and Stoic Cosmology*, Berkeley/Los Angeles/London.
Rossi, A. (2004), "Parallel Lives: Hannibal and Scipio in Livy's third decade", *Transactions of the American Philological Association* 134.2, 359–381.
Roumpou, A.N. (2018), *Silius Italicus' Punica 17.341–654: A Literary Commentary*, PhD diss., University of Nottingham.
Roumpou, A. (2019), "Triumph, closure, and the power of the individual in Silius Italicus's *Punica* 17", *Illinois Classical Studies* 44.2, 385–407.
Roumpou, A.N. (2022), "Hannibal redivivus: fear and haunting memory in Silius Italicus", in: A. Augoustakis/M. Fucecchi (eds.), *Silius Italicus and the Tradition of the Roman Historical Epos*, Leiden, 266–283.
Rüpke, J. (2001), "Antike Religionen als Kommunikationssysteme", in: K. Brodersen (ed.), *Gebet und Fluch, Zeichen und Traum: Aspekte religiöser Kommunikation in der Antike*, Münster, 13–30.
Rüpke, J. (2004), "*Acta aut agenda*: relations of script and performance", in: A. Barchiesi/J. Rüpke/S.A. Stephens (eds.), *Rituals in Ink: a Conference on Religion and Literary Production in Ancient Rome held at Stanford University in February 2002*, Stuttgart, 23–43.
Rüpke, J. (2005), "Gäste der Götter – Götter als Gäste: zur Konstruktion des römischen Opferbanketts", in: S. Georgoudi/R. Koch Piettre/F. Schmidt (eds.), *La cuisine et l'autel: Les sacrifices en questions dans les sociétés de la Méditerranée ancienne*, Turnhout, 227–239.
Rüpke, J. (2007), "Religion medial", in: J. Malik/J. Rüpke/T. Wobbe (eds.), *Religion und Medien: Vom Kultbild zum Internetritual* (Vorlesungen des Interdisziplinären Forums Religion der Universität Erfurt 4), Münster, 19–28.
Rüpke, J. (2012), *Antike Epik: Eine Einführung von Homer bis in die Spätantike*, Marburg.
Rüpke, J. (2013), "Was ist ein Heiligtum? Pluralität als Gegenstand der Religionswissenschaft", in: A. Adogame/M. Echtler/O. Freiberger (eds.), *Alternative Voices: A Plurality Approach for Religious Studies. Essays in Honor of Ulrich Berner* (Critical Studies in Religion/Religionswissenschaft 4), Göttingen, 211–225.
Rüpke, J. (2016), *On Roman Religion: Lived Religion and the Individual in Ancient Rome. Townsend Lectures/Cornell Studies in Classical Philology*, Ithaca/London.
Rüpke, J. (2018), *Pantheon: A New History of Roman Religion*, Princeton.
Rüpke, J. (2021), *Ritual als Resonanzerfahrung* (Religionswissenschaft heute 15), Stuttgart.
Rüpke, J./Scheid, J. (eds.) (2010), *Bestattungsrituale und Totenkult in der römischen Kaiserzeit/Rites funéraires et culte des morts aux temps impériales* (Potsdamer Altertumswissenschaftliche Beiträge 27), Stuttgart.

Sacerdoti, A. (2014), "*Quis magna tuenti/somnus*? Scenes of sleeplessness (and intertextuality) in Flavian poetry", in: A. Augoustakis (ed.), *Flavian Poetry and its Greek Past*, Leiden/Boston, 13–29.
Sacerdoti, A. (2018), "*Semirutos … de puluere uultus*: Vesuvius, Statius and trauma", in: A. Augoustakis/J. Littlewood (eds.), *Campania in the Flavian Poetic Imagination*, Oxford, 167–180.
Sacerdoti, A. (2019), *Tremefacta quies (Ach. 1, 242): spazi di transito nella Tebaide di Stazio e nei Punica di Silio Italico*, Naples.
Salemme, C. (1991), *Medea: Un Antico Mito in Valerio Flacco*, Naples.
Sanderson, E.C. (2022), "Kin conflicts and stasis: civil war on Peuce in Valerius Flaccus' *Argonautica*", *The Classical Quarterly* 72.1, 1–13.
Scaffai, M. (1986), "Il Tiranno e le sue Vittime nel libro 1 degli *Argonautica* di Valerio Flacco", in: *Munus Amicitiae: Scritti in Memoria di Alessandro Ronconi*, Florence, 233–261.
Schaaf, I. (2014), *Magie und Ritual bei Apollonios Rhodios: Studien zu ihrer Form und Funktion in den Argonautika*, Berlin.
Scheid, J. (2005a), "Les dieux du Capitole: un exemple des structures théologiques des sanctuaires romains", in: X. Lafon/G. Sauron (eds.), *Théorie et pratique de l'architecture romaine: la norme et l'expérimentation. Études offertes à Pierre Gros*, Aix-en-Provence, 93–100.
Scheid, J. (2005b), *Quand faire, c'est croire. Les rites sacrificiels des Romains* (Collection historique), Paris.
Scheid, J. (2005c), "Augustus and Roman Religion", in: K. Galinsky (ed.), *The Cambridge Companion to the Age of Augustus*, Cambridge, 175–194.
Scheidegger Laemmle, C. (forthcoming), Posthumous Poetics? *Siluae* V and the 'Literary Politics' of Statius' Oeuvre, forthcoming.
Scheidegger Laemmle, C. (2016), Werkpolitik in der Antike: Studien zu Cicero, Vergil, Horaz und Ovid. *Zetemata* 152, München.
Schenk, P. (1991), "Cyzicus, Perses und das Eingreifen der Götter", in: M. Korn/H.J. Tschiedel (eds.), *Ratis Omnia Vincet: Untersuchungen zu den Argonautica des Valerius Flaccus*, Hildesheim, 139–153.
Schenk, P. (1999), *Studien zur poetischen Kunst des Valerius Flaccus: Beobachtungen zur Ausgestaltung des Kriegsthemas in den Argonautica* (Zetemata 102), Munich.
Scherf, J. (2001), *Untersuchungen zur Buchgestaltung Martials*. Beiträge zur Altertumskunde 142, Munich/Leipzig.
Schetter, W. (1960), *Untersuchungen zur epischen Kunst des Statius* (Klassisch-Philologische Studien 20), Wiesbaden.
Schmitz, C. (1993), *Die kosmische Dimension in der Tragödien Senecas*, diss. Berlin/New York.
Schöffel, C. (2002), *Martial, Buch 8. Einleitung, Text, Übersetzung, Kommentar*, Stuttgart.
Schotes, H.A. (1969), *Stoische Physik. Psychologie und Theologie bei Lucan*, diss. Bonn.
Schroer, C.A. (2020), "*Quid restat profugis*? Exile and power in Silius Italicus' *Punica*" PhD diss., University of Illinois at Urbana, Champaign.
Schroer, C.A. (2021), "*Quid restat profugis*? Victorious exile in Silius Italicus' *Punica*", in: R. Marks/M. Mogetta (eds.), *Domitian's Rome and the Augustan Legacy*, Ann Arbor, 192–207.
Schütz, A. (1981), *Der sinnhafte Aufbau der sozialen Welt: Eine Einleitung in die verstehende Soziologie*, Frankfurt am Mein.

Scott, B. (2012), *Aspects of Transgression in Valerius Flaccus' Argonautica*, PhD Thesis, Liverpool.
Scullard, H.H. (1973), *Roman Politics: 220–150 B.C.*, Oxford.
Scullard, H.H. (1981), *Festivals and Ceremonies of the Roman Republic*, London.
Seal, C. (2014), "Civil war and the Apollonian model in Valerius' *Argonautica*", in: A. Augoustakis (ed.), *Flavian Poetry and its Greek Past*, Leiden, 113–135.
Shackleton Bailey, D.R. (1993), *Martial, Epigrams*. 3 vols., Cambridge, MA.
Shackleton Bailey, D.R. (2000), *Valerius Maximus. Memorable Doings and Sayings*, 2 vols., Cambridge, MA.
Shackleton Bailey, D.R. (2015), *Statius – Siluae*, Cambridge, MA.
Shay, J. (1995), *Achilles in Vietnam: Combat Trauma and the Undoing of Character*, New York.
Shay, J. (2004), *Odysseus in America: Combat Trauma and the Trials of Homecoming*, New York/London.
Shay, J. (2018), "Moral leadership prevents moral injury", in: R. Meagher/D. Pryer (eds.), *War and Moral Injury: A Reader*, Oregon, 301–306.
Showerman, G. (1914), *Ovid. Heroides. Amores*. Trans. by Grant Showerman. Revised by G.P. Goold, Cambridge, MA.
Simms, R. (ed.) (2018), *Brill's Companion to Prequels, Sequels, and Retellings of Classical Epic*, Leiden.
Simms, R. (2020), *Anticipation and Anachrony in Statius' Thebaid*, London.
Skutsch, O. (1985), *The Annals of Q. Ennius, Edited with Introduction and Commentary*, Oxford.
Smith Herrnstein, B. (1968), *Poetic Closure: A Study of How Poems End*, Chicago.
Soerink, J. (2014), *Beginning of Doom. Statius Thebaid 5.499–753. Introduction, Text, Commentary*, PhD diss., Rijksuniversiteit Groningen.
Sommerstein, A./Torrance, I.C. (eds.) (2014), *Oaths and Swearing in Ancient Greece. Beiträge zur Altertumskunde* 307, Berlin.
Spaltenstein, F. (1986/90), *Commentaire des Punica de Silius Italicus*, 2 vols., Geneva.
Spaltenstein, F. (2002), *Commentaire des Argonautica de Valérius Flaccus (livres 1 et 2)*, Brussels.
Spinelli, T. (2021), "*Crudelis uincit pater*: Oedipal paternities in Statius' *Thebaid*", *Classical Journal* 117, 97–119.
Spinelli, T. (forthcoming), *Statius and Ovid: Poetics, Politics and Intermediality in the Thebaid*, Cambridge.
Spisak, A.L. (1998), "Gift-giving in Martial", in: F. Grewing (ed.), *Toto notus in orbe: Perspektiven der Martial-Interpretation*, Stuttgart, 243–255.
Spisak, A.L. (2007), *Martial: A Social Guide*, London.
Stavrianopoulou, E. (2006), *Ritual and Communication in the Graeco-Roman World*, trans. Antique Centre International d'Etude de la Religion Grecque (Kernos: Supplément; 16), Liège.
Steinsapir, A.I. (2005), *Rural Sanctuaries in Roman Syria. The Creation of a Sacred Landscape*, Oxford.
Sterbenc Erker, D. (2009), "Woman's tears in ancient roman ritual", in: T. Fögen (ed.), *Tears in the Graeco-Roman World*, Göttingen, 135–160.
Stocks, C. (2014), *The Roman Hannibal: Remembering the Enemy in Silius Italicus' Punica*, Liverpool.
Stocks, C. (2016), "Daddy's little girl? The father/daughter bond in Valerius Flaccus' *Argonautica* and Flavian Rome", in: N. Manioti (ed.), *Family in Flavian Epic*, Leiden, 41–60.

Stocks, C. (2019), "Broken bonds: Perfidy and the discourse of civil war", in: A. Augoustakis/ E. Buckley/C. Stocks (eds.), *Fides in Flavian Literature*, Toronto, 21–44.
Stover, T. (2011), "Unexampled exemplarity: Medea in the *Argonautica* of Valerius Flaccus", *Transactions of the American Philological Association* 141.1, 171–200.
Stover, T. (2012), *Epic and Empire in Vespasianic Rome: A New Reading of Valerius Flaccus' Argonautica*, Oxford.
Strathern, A. (2019), *Unearthly Powers: Religious and Political Change in World History*, Cambridge.
Strunk, T.E. (2017), *History after Liberty: Tacitus on Tyrants, Sycophants, and Republicans*, Ann Arbor.
Suarsana, L./Werlen, B./Meusburger, P. (eds.) (2017), *Knowledge and Action* (Knowledge and Space 9), Cham.
Summers, W.C. (1894), *A Study of the Argonautica of Valerius Flaccus*, Cambridge.
Tafaro, A. (2016), "Cross-references between epitaphs and funerary epigrams: a case study of Scorpus the charioteer in Martial 10.50–10.53", *Appunti romani di filologia: studi e comunicazioni di filologia, linguistica e letteratura greca e latina*, 61–76.
Tarrant, R. (2002), "Chaos in Ovid's *Metamorphoses* and its Neronian influence", *Arethusa* 35, 349–360.
Taves, A. (2009), *Religious Experience Reconsidered: A Building Block Approach to the Study of Religion and Other Special Things*, Princeton.
Thalmann, W. (2011), *Apollonius of Rhodes and the Spaces of Hellenism*, Oxford.
Themann-Steinke, A. (2008), *Valerius Maximus: Ein Kommentar zum zweiten Buch der 'Facta et dicta memorabilia'*, Trier.
Tipping, B. (2010), *Exemplary Epic: Silius Italicus' Punica*, Oxford.
Torres-Murciano, A.R. (2007), "*Meus hic ratibus qui pascitur ignis* (Val. Flac. 2.658), o Cízico: un Héctor frustrado", *Cuadernos de Filología Clásica: Estudios Latinos* 27.2, 81–92.
Toynbee, J.M. (1996), *Death and Burial in the Roman World*, Baltimore.
Triplett, K. (2010), "Gründungslegenden in der Erinnerungspflege japanisch-buddhistischer Tempel – am Beispiel des Tsubosakasan Minami Hokkeji", in: P. Schalk et al. (eds.), *Geschichten und Geschichte: Historiographie und Hagiographie in der asiatischen Religionsgeschichte* (Historia religionum), Uppsala, 140–180.
Tsfati, Y. (2011), "Third Person Effect", *Oxford Bibliographies*, 1–2.
Tuttle, A. (2013), "Argive augury and portents in the *Thebaid*", in: A. Augoustakis (ed.), *Ritual and Religion in Flavian Epic*, Oxford, 71–87.
Tuval-Mashiach, R./Freedman, S./Bargai, N./Boker, R./Hadar, H./Shalev, A.Y. (2004), "Coping with Trauma: Narrative and Cognitive Perspectives", *Psychiatry* 67.3.
Tweed, T.A. (2011), "Space", *Material Religion* 7, 116–123.
Ustinova, Y. (1998), "Corybantism: the nature and role of an ecstatic cult in a Greek polis", *Horos* 10–12, 503–520.
Vallat, D. (2008), *Onomastique, Culture et Société dans les Épigrammes de Martial*, Brussels.
van der Keur, M. (2015), *A Commentary on Silius Italicus' Punica 13. Intertextuality and Narrative Structure*, PhD diss. Amsterdam.
van Gennep, A. (1909), *Les Rites de Passage*, Paris.
van Groningen, B.A. (1962), "Un passage difficile d'Apollonios de Rhodes (*Argonautiques* I 1071–1077)", *Mnemosyne* 15.3, 268–270.
van Nuffelen, P. (2012), "Playing the ritual game in Constantinople (379–457)", in: L. Grig/ G. Kelly (eds.), *Two Romes: Rome and Constantinople in Late Antiquity*, Oxford, 183–200.

von Albrecht, M. (1964), *Silius Italicus: Freiheit Und Gebundenheit Römischer Epik*, Amsterdam.
Vessey, D. (1970a), "The games in *Thebaid* VI", *Latomus* 29, 426–441.
Vessey, D. (1970b), "The significance of the myth of Linus and Coroebus in Statius *Thebaid* 1.557–672", *American Journal of Philology* 91, 315–331.
Vessey, D. (1973), *Statius and the Thebaid*, Cambridge.
Vessey, D. (1974), "Silius Italicus on the Fall of Saguntum", *Classical Philology* 69, 28–36.
Visser, I. (2018), "Trauma in non-western contexts", in: R. Kurtz (ed.), *Trauma and Literature*, Cambridge, 124–139.
Voigt, A. (2016), "The power of the grieving mind: female lament in Statius' *Thebaid*", *Illinois Classical Studies* 41, 59–84.
Voisin, P. (2016), "Un moment unique dans la rhétorique des Vies Parallèles: quand le rituel de l'éloge et du blâme fait place à un double éloge croisé!", *Revue des Études Latines* 94, 121–139.
Vollmer, F. (1898), *P. Papinii Statii Silvarum libri*, Leipzig.
Walter, A. (2022), 'Festivals in Statius' *Thebaid*: uncelebrating Vergil', *Vergilius* 68, 57–76.
Weinrich, I. (2020), "The materiality of sound, mediation, and practices of listening. Observations from historic and contemporary muslim practices", *Entangled Religions* 11.3, https://er.ceres.rub.de/index.php/ER/article/view/8555/8120, last access 21.03.2023
Werlen, B. (ed.) (2008), *Sozialgeographie. Eine Einführung*, Bern.
Werlen, B. (2017), "Action, knowledge, and social relations of space", in: L. Suarsana/B. Werlen/P. Meusburger (eds.), *Knowledge and Action* (Knowledge and Space 9), Cham, 31–56.
Werlen, B. (2021), "World-relations and the production of geographical realities: on space and action, city and urbanity", *Religion and Urbanity online*.
West, M. (1966), *Hesiod. Theogony. Edited with Prolegomena and Commentary*, Oxford.
West, M. (2011), *The Making of the Iliad*, Oxford.
West, M. (2013), *The Epic Cycle: A Commentary on the Lost Troy Epics*, Oxford.
West, S. (2007), "Terminal Problems", in: P.J. Finglass/C. Collard/N.J. Richardson (eds.), *Hesperos Studies in Ancient Greek Poetry Presented to M.L. West on his Seventieth Birthday*, Oxford, 3–21.
Westall, R. (2014), "Triumph and closure: between history and literature", in: C.H. Lange/F.J. Vervaet (eds.), *The Roman Republican Triumph: Beyond the Spectacle*, Rome, 33–52.
Wheeler, S.M. (1995), "The underworld opening of Claudian's *De raptu Proserpinae*", *Transactions of the American Philological Association* 125, 113–134.
White, P. (1972), *Aspects of Non-Imperial Patronage in the Works of Martial and Statius*, diss. Harvard University.
White, P. (1975), "The Friends of Martial, Statius and Pliny, and the dispersal of patronage", *Harvard Studies in Classical Philology* 79, 265–300.
Williams, G. (1958), "Some Aspects of Roman Marriage Ceremonies and Ideals", *Journal of Roman Studies*, 48, 16–29.
Williams, R.D. (1960), *P. Vergili Maronis Aeneidos Liber Quintus*, Oxford.
Wray, D.L. (2007), "Wood: Statius's *Siluae* and the poetics of genius", *Arethusa* 40.2, 127–143.
Wulfram, H. (2008), *Das römische Versepistelbuch: eine Gattungsanalyse*, Berlin.
Zissos, A. (2008), *Valerius Flaccus' Argonautica Book 1: Edited with Introduction, Translation, and Commentary*, Oxford.
Zissos, A. (2012), "The king's daughter: Medea in Valerius Flaccus' *Argonautica*", *Ramus* 41.1–2, 94–118.

Zissos, A. (2014), "Stoic thought and Homeric reminiscence in Valerius Flaccus' *Argonautica*", in: M. Garani/D. Konstan (eds.), *The Philosophizing Muse: The Influence of Greek Philosophy on Roman Poetry*, Cambridge (Pierides 3), 269–297.

Zissos, A. (2016), "Allusion and narrative possibility in the *Argonautica* of Valerius Flaccus", in: A. Augoustakis (ed.), *Flavian Epic*, Oxford, 111–126.

Zissos, A. (2017), "Generic attire: Hypsipyle's cloaks in Valerius Flaccus and Apollonius Rhodius", in: F. Bessone/M. Fucecchi (eds.), *The Literary Genres in the Flavian Age: Canons, Transformations, Reception*, Berlin, 201–228.

Zissos, A. (2019), "Closure and segmentation: endings, medial proems, book divisions", in: C. Reitz/S. Finkmann (eds.), *Structures of Epic Poetry*, Berlin/Boston, 531–564.

Zuckerberg, D./Scullin, S. et al. (2019), "Burn it all down?" *Eidolon* (https://eidolon.pub/burn-it-all-down-82f5edb16e, last access 24.05.2023).

Thematic Index

Absyrtus 93, 169, 173, 175, 176
Acastus 80, 82–83, 91
Achilles 77, 126, 138, 142, 153, 166, 178–179
Adrastus 23, 151
Aeetes 92–93, 115 n.13, 172, 174
Aegeus 173, 178
Aeneas 2, 50 n.27, 80 n.3, 84, 90–91, 103, 126–127, 133, 138, 138 n.11, 139, 152–153, 188
–shield of 127, 139
Aeson 8, 80 n.3, 80 n.5, 81–84, 87–89, 91–93, 91 n.40, 115 n.13, 199 n.71
Aetna 147, 154
Aeolus 90, 90 n.38, 188
Aethon 28
Africa 95
Aithiopis of Arctinus 2, 2 n.6
Athenians 23
Agency 4, 15, 16 n.8, 17–21, 48 n.17, 138 n.11, 157 n.39, 172 n.75
–agent 21, 35, 165
Agrippa 130
Agrippina 129
Ajax 165
Alcimede 8, 80 n.5, 81–87, 84 n.20, 85 n.21, 86 n.23, 86 n.25, 88 n.31, 91, 93, 115 n.13
Alcmaeon 157 n.39
Allecto 114 n.9, 193 n.50, 194, 194 n.57
Amphiaraus 15, 22–23, 117 n.18, 141–142, 149, 157 n.39, 191–192, 197
–anti-funeral of 155
Amphion 148
Amyclas 11, 187
Anchises 36, 127, 138
Androgeos 152
Anthropology 6, 59
Antigone 154–155
Antulla 34–37, 42
Apollo 40–41, 54, 139, 156–157, 166, 191
Apotheosis 147 n.30, 150, 153
Appius (ghost of) 124
Aposiopesis 75

Archemorus (see Opheltes) 142
Ardea 108 n.41
Arete (queen) 177
Argia 23, 136 n.3, 154–157, 157 n.39, 158 n.41
Argives 3, 22, 23, 140, 143, 151, 158
Army 142, 145
–refusal of burial to 138, 146, 153
–women 23, 155, 158
Argonautic
–expedition 82, 87, 92
–journey/voyage 82, 82 n.11
–legend 8, 79 n.2, 93
–narrative 82 n.11
Ariadne 91
Artemis (temple of) 169, 175, 176
Atalanta 140–141, 157
Athena 14, 184 n.12
Athens 154
Attis 50, 173 n.79
Atys 137, 140–141
Augustus 2 n.3, 20 n.21, 108 n.42, 127, 130, 133, 188–189
–Augustus/ Apollo 139
–triple triumph of 127–128
Autonoe (see also Deiphobe) 86

Bacchus 28, 63, 92, 127 n.51, 138
–triumph of 127, 127 n.51
Baetis 125
Boii 117
Burial 1, 2 n.6, 3, 5–6, 18 n.17, 22–23, 83, 114, 114 n.12, 119 n.25, 121, 124, 124 n.39, 129, 133, 135, 138 n.10, 153, 155, (tree-burial) 175, 203
–failed 138
–incomplete 141
–mock 118
–refusal of 138, 146, 146 n.26, 153, 157
–unsatisfactory 138

Caesar (Julius) 11, 88, 101–102, 120, 129, 182, 186–187, 194, 199, 200
Caieta (nurse) 84

Calpe 125
Camillus 95–97, 101–102, 105, 107
–exile of 108 n.41
–*reditus* of 99–100
Campania 46, 98
Cannae 108, 119–123, 122 n.33, 198
Capaneus 14, 117 n.18, 135, 137, 146–151, 156–157
–*aristeia* of 146, 148, 150–151
–death of 146, 149
Carthage 95, 105, 113 n.4, 121, 125, 139
Catharsis (lack of) 4, 87
Castor and Pollux/Dioscuri 165, 168 n.43, 170
Cato
–the Elder 52, 54
–the Younger 33–34, 138
Celaenus 166
Ceres 39, 58, 154
Chalciope as moral authority 172 n.66
Chaos 4, 11, 168, 181, 183, 186–192, 189 n.37–40, 190 n.41, 192–193 n.49, 196, 196 n.62, 198, 200
–and disorder 9, 116
–and order 8, 93, 188
Chatti 131
Cincinnatus 125 n.43
Circe 10, 85–86, 161–162, 162 n.8, 172 n.67, 176–177, 176 n.93, 180, 180 n.115
Civil war 3, 5, 6, 11, 81, 92–93, 92 n.43–44, 102, 114, 117 n.18, 119 n.23, 127, 138, 157–158, 159 n.47, 164 n.20, 165, 165 n.23, 168 n.45, 169, 169 n.54, 181, 182, 182 n.1, 183, 185, 186, 189, 189 n.37, 190, 193–195, 196 n.64, 198
–discord 101, 102
Claudius Etruscus 98–99, 99 n.17
Clite 165, 165 n.27, 169, 170
Closure 4–11, 5 n.27, 13–14, 17, 27, 29, 35–37, 45, 45 n.7, 52 n.39, 58–59, 58, 59, 59 n.1, 67, 74, 75, 79, 79 n.2, 81–84, 84 n.15, 87, 89, 95–97, 99–100, 102, 104, 107, 108, 109, 115 n.13, 116, 124–125, 125 n.43, 125 n.45, 129, 132, 135–136, 136 n.3, 147 n.31, 150, 158 n.41, 161, 169, 169 n.54, 191, 200, 201–206
–ambiguous 8, 9, 113, 119

–defiance of 3
–denied 150
–fragmented 80
–healing 10, 180
–hinder 3
–incomplete 8, 9
–lack of 93, 155, 176
–liberating 114
–literary 161
–open 43
–psychological 161
–poetics of 1, 5, 111
–problematic 3, 5, 203
–psychological 161, 167–168
–thwart of 1
–undermined 2
Coda (see *sphragis*) 68 n.34, 81–82, 105
Colchis 90, 92, 169 n.51, 173–174, 173 n.79
Collapse 141, 147–148, 147 n.28, 158
–cosmic 11
–inner (or inwards) 6, 10, 135, 140–141, 159
–narrative 97, 136
Conflagration (see also *ekpyrosis*) 136, 136 n.3, 183, 186
Contagion 135, 137, 147 n.31, 148, 152, 154, 157
Contamination 135, 137, 150, 156
Continuation(s) 2, 2 n.5, 2 n.7, 3, 6, 8, 9, 14, 31, 82, 97, 102, 109, 156
Corbulo 130
Cordus 123
Cornelia 123, 123 n.37
Corybantes 171
Cretheus 83–84, 87, 115 n.13
–as ritual actor 84
Creon 23, 138, 146, 146 n.25, 146 n.26, 148, 151–154, 157, 159 n.47
Cupid 196
Cybele (or Kybele) 28, 38–39, 39 n.61, 50, 169, 173 n.79
Cynthia/Selene 154
Cyzicus 10, 139 n.12, 161–165, 164 n.20, 165 n.23, 165 n.24, 168, 168 n.43, 169, 170, 173 n.79, 177, 179
–funeral of 168 n.43

Dacians 131
Dardanus 170 n.57
Death 1, 3, 6, 8, 10, 22, 23, 24, 24 n.29, 34–37, 64, 67, 69, 71–77, 77 n.62, 79, 80 n.3, 81–83, 84 n.15, 88–90, 88 n.32, 93, 106, 108, 111, 114–119, 115 n.13, 119 n.22, 121, 124, 126, 128, 132, 133 n.70, 140, 140 n.18, 142–143, 145, 146–147, 149–150, 153–154, 154 n.36, 156 n.38, 157–158, 157 n.39, 164, 164–165 n.18, 165 n.21, 169, 173–176, 178, 192, 199, 203
–and closure 81, 84 n.15, 89, 106
Deiphobe (see Sibyl) 86
Deuotio 119 n.24, 124 n.38, 133 n.70
Deipyle 157
Destruction 6 n.29, 44, 111, 114, 119, 120, 146, 135–139, 137 n.8, 140, 142, 144–145, 147–150, 152–154, 156, 157 n.39, 158, 159 n.47, 162, 178, 183, 183 n.6, 188, 199
–of the Empire 6, 182,
–of the universe/cosmic 137, 147, 190, 196
Diana 52, 52 n.35, 53, 90, 141, 151
Dido 84, 90–91, 91 n.39, 92 n.42, 135, 138–140, 138 n.11, 149, 158, 198 n.70
Dionysios Scytobrachion 81
Dionysus (see also Bacchus) 50, 54
Dis 150
Disruption 3
–cultural 6
–of order 4, 111
–structural 6
Dissolution 5, 10, 11, 185 n.13, 190–191, 196 n.64
–cosmic dissolution/of the universe 11, 181–184, 183 n.6, 186, 189, 190 n.41, 196, 198, 200
Domitian 4, 28, 28 n.5, 31 n.26, 37–38, 44, 60, 65, 76, 97, 98 n.15, 99, 104, 104 n.31, 111, 127, 129, 131–132, 132 n.67, 158 n.41
–as Jupiter *Terrestris* 61 n.7
–death of 76, 132
–(false) triumph of 97–98, 98 n.14, 104 n.31, 131

Drances 152
Drusus, funeral of 111, 128
Ducarius 117
Dymas 148

Ebro river 125
ekpyrosis 183, 185–186, 190
Enceladus 147, 154
Endings 1–8, 2 n.4, 2 n.6, 5 n.27, 15, 42, 79, 93, 96, 109, 125 n.45, 135, 136, 139, 142, 157–158, 158 n.42, 159 n.47, 173, 181, 202–205
–abrupt 87
–ambiguous 9, 111
–cathartic 87
–complicating 3
–false 5
–incomplete 9, 111
–lost 1
–open 3, 5, 8, 9, 14, 78, 79 n.1, 93, 124, 129
Epicurean 7, 48, 48 n.19, 50, 57, 57 n.54, 57 n.56
–αταραξια (*quies*) 57, 57 n.52
–Epicureanism 57
–*otium* 45
Epicedion–epicedia 60–62, 65, 68, 68 n.35, 70, 71, 73, 74, 98, 60
Erichtho 83, 85–86, 86 n.23
Eriphyle 157 n.39
Eteocles 24, 149–155, 159 n.47, 193
Eurydice 140 n.17, 149
Evadne 155–156, 156 n.38
Exile 9, 95–108, 96 n.7, 99 n.17, 106 n.37, 106 n.39, 108 n.41, 161, 177
–poetry of 7, 68, 70

Fabius Cunctator 119, 119 n.24, 122, 122 n.33, 124
Faenius Telesphorus 34–37, 35 n.43
–as an agent 35
Fasti Triumphales 129
Faustinus 34–37, 35 n.45, 35 n.47
Festivals 20 n.21, 23, 27–34, 31 n.28, 32 n.32, 54–55, 57 n.56, 63, 91, 130, 201
see also 'Floralia'
see also 'Matronalia'

236 — Thematic Index

see also 'Nemean games'
See also 'Saturnalia'
Fides 111–116, 113 n.4, 113 n.6, 116 n.15, 119, 129
Fire 7 n.29, 9–10, 47, 91, 115, 135–155, 137 n.5, 137 n.8, 137 n.9, 139 n.12, 140 n.18, 147 n.31, 157–158, 165, 165 n.21, 186, 199
–and narrative articulation 136–137, 141, 150
–as ending marker 136
–failure of 154
Flaminius 9, 116–119, 116 n.16, 123, 123 n.35, 130
–as an anti-*uates* 117
–impiety of 116
Flavian 95, 97, 104, 127, 132, 180, 198, 204–205
–culture 3, 5, 6, 9, 100, 113 n.4
–dynasty 127
–emperors 98
–empire 5
–epic 3, 4 n.16, 5, 8, 9, 11, 13, 14, 80, 111, 117, 117 n.18, 124, 132, 137 n.5, 148 n.32, 162, 165 n.24, 191, 200
–era/period 1, 3 n.10, 6, 10, 206
–literature/texts 1, 3, 4, 5, 6, 7, 11, 98, 99 n.17, 113 n.4, 136 n.2, 201, 206
–Rome 5, 137 n.5
–society 30
–triumph 131
–world 11
Flora 27, 33–34, 49, 54–55, 54 n.42
Floralia 33–34, 54–55
Fratricide/fraternal conflict 3, 8, 81, 92, 92 n.44, 93, 141, 154, 181–182, 193–194, 198 n.68
Fuluius Nobilior 2, 205
Funeral 1, 2, 4, 7, 9, 15, 22–23, 27, 30, 35, 62, 73–74, 83–84, 114–115, 114 n.10, 120, 120 n.27, 121–125, 123 n.37, 127–129, 132–133, 135–136, 139–143, 145, 153, 156–157, 161, 165, 169–170, 175, 203
–ante-funerals 137, 146
–anti-funerals 137–138, 146 n.26, 155
–denied 119, 122

–failed 137
–fake/quasi-/pseudo- 114, 116, 125, 133, 138, 139
–games 142, 142 n.22, 170
–incomplete 10, 157
–mock 9, 111, 126, 132
–problematic 10, 157
Furies 11, 39 n.61, 149, 192, 200
See also 'Allecto'
See also 'Tisiphone'

Gades 125
Garamantes 125
Gauls 99, 101
Gigantomachy 181–182, 190, 192 n.48
Glaucias (Melior's boy)/*puer* 8, 61, 72, 73 n.46
–*alter ego* of Statius 73
–dealth of (*puer*) 74
Gracchus 119, 122 n.31, 123 n.35, 124
–burial of 124 n.39, 133
–funeral of 119 n.25

Hades 11, 150, 191–198, 192 n.47, 192 n.49, 194 n.59, 195 n.60, 195 n.61, 196 n.65, 197 n.68, 200
Hamilcar 106, 106 n.38
Hasdrubal 122 n.32
Hannibal 9, 11, 18, 88 n. 32, 95, 96 n.7, 97, 102–107, 105 n.32, 106 n.36, 109, 111–126 116 n.15, 122 n.31, 122 n.33, 123 n.35, 124 n.39, 130, 132, 133, 181, 198–200
–as religious actor 120, 124–125, 130
–impiety of 113, 116
Hanno 125
Hecate 39 n.61, 172, 193 n.49
Hector 1, 117 n.18, 126
–burial of 2 n.6, 138, 203
–funeral of 2 n.6
Hera (see also Juno) 174
Hercules 60, 111–113, 118, 127, 127 n.51, 147 n.30, 149–150, 153
Hopleus 148
Hypsipyle 138–140, 138 n.11, 169, 169 n.49
–agency of 138 n.11

Idmon 162 n.8, 168, 168 n.43
Initiation 19, 61, 141
Ino 92
Iphigenia, sacrifice of 133 n.70
Ismene 137, 140–141
Ismenos (river) 155, 158 n.41
Ixion 177

Janus 40–41, 53, 188–190, 188 n. 36
Jason 10, 79–87, 80 n.3, 81 n.8, 89, 90 n.36, 92–93, 92 n.43, 115, 162–170, 165 n.23–24, 169 n.49, 169 n.53, 172–179, 173 n.79, 174 n.86, 177 n.98
Jocasta 140 n.17
Jupiter 4, 15, 22, 28, 39–40, 49–53, 60–61, 92, 112, 103, 126, 131, 137 n.7, 146, 147 n.30, 149–150, 181, 187–188, 192–198, 197 n.68, 198 n.68, 200
–*Optimus Maximus* 52 n.32, 61
–*Terrestris* 61 n.7
Juno 38–39, 66, 82, 85–86, 106, 115, 117, 154, 188–189, 189 n.37, 193 n.50, 194, 194 n.57, 199
–*Juno Lucina* 32

Kalends of March 32, 49, 52, 52 n.39
Katabasis 36, 79, 83, 83 n.12, 84, 141
–failed/perverted 138
Kepotaphium 35, 37

Lachesis 196, 196 n.64
Lacuna 76–77, 77 n.63, 95 n.1
Laius 85 n.22, 193–194
Lament 1, 4 n.17, 9, 62, 72, 75, 78, 78 n.69, 81, 84, 87–88, 101, 135–136, 149, 154–157, 156 n.38, 165, 165 n.24, 170
Laudatio funebris 120, 122, 122 n.34
Laudes Neronis 182, 184 n.9, 190, 190 n.42
Lemnian women 138–139
Liternum 96 n.7, 106, 106 n.37, 106 n.39, 108 n.41
Lotis (nymph) 55
Lustratio 53
(see also 'purification')

Magic 19, 79, 81, 85–86, 172, 178
Manto 86
Marcellus 119, 199 n.25, 122 n.33, 124
–burial of 124 n.39, 133
Marius 125 n.43
Marriage 84, 89, 93, 140, 178, 196 n.65, 203
(see also 'wedding')
Mars 40 n.66, 49, 52–53
Μασχαλισμός 175, 175 n.90
Matronalia 32–33
Medea 10, 79–81, 85–93, 85 n.21, 86 n.25, 90 n.35–36, 91 n.39, 161–162, 164, 167 n.38, 169–180, 172 n.66, 172 n.68, 172–173 n.75, 173 n.77, 173 n.79, 174 n.86, 177 n.104, 178 n.107
–as angry lion 87–89
–as Dido 84, 91
Medus 173–174
Melanippus 22
Menoeceus 146–151, 146 n.27, 153–154
–death of 149
–funeral of 153
Menoetes 154
Mercury 85 n.22, 194, 196
Metellus 108
Minerva 22, 24
Moors 125
Mopsus 81, 168 n.43, 170, 173, 173 n.79, 176 n.94, 177, 180 n.115
–as moral authority figure 10, 162, 166–169
Moral authority 10, 161, 162, 166, 172 n.66, 173–174, 176, 176 n.94, 179
Moral injury 10, 161–166, 164 n.20, 170–175, 171 n.65, 178–180
Mourning 6, 8, 23, 34, 62–63, 72, 74, 78, 83, 126 n.48, 142, 156–157, 165, 170, 170 n.59
Mummius 130

Necromancy 8, 79, 83–85, 83 n.12, 85 n.21–22, 86 n.24, 93, 138
Nemea (river) 23
Nemean games 23, 72
Neoptolemus 88
Neptune 39, 188, 192

Nero 9, 20 n.21, 111, 113, 127, 129–132, 136 n.3, 188, 188 n.36
–false Neros 131, 131 n.65
See also '*laudes Neronis*'
New beginnings 3, 5, 15, 37, 139
Novius Vindex 60
Numidians 125

Oath (swearing) 1, 1 n.2, 7, 27, 37–39, 43, 108 n.41, 138, 138 n.11, 198 n.70
–and closure 37
–breaking of 140
–false 38
Oedipus 136 n.3, 137, 140 n.17, 141, 155, 157 n.41, 193
Opheltes 15, 22, 135, 145, 155, 158
–death of 140 n.18, 142, 145
–funeral of 137, 141–143, 145, 153
Orpheus 71–72, 171

Parthenopaeus 24, 140–141, 151, 153, 157
Patroclus, funeral 142
Paulus 119–123, 123 n.35, 125 n.45
–as religious actor 122
–burial of 18, 119 n.25, 121, 133
–funeral of 120, 123, 125 n.45
Perses (brother of Aeetes) 92, 169 n.51
Pelias 8, 80 n.3, 82–83, 87–89, 88 n.32, 91–93
–as Stoic villain 88, 199 n.71
Persephone 154
(see also 'Proserpina')
Peuce (island) 89, 90 n.36, 93
Phaethon 137, 155, 190, 190 n.42
Pharsalus 120, 121, 129, 186, 199
Phlegethon 193 n.49
Phlegra 147
Phyllis 38–39
Phyllis (Domitian's nurse) 132
Priam 88–89
Priapus 49, 54–56, 55 n.46, 56 n.48–49
PTSD (post-traumatic stress disorder) 161–163, 162 n.3, 175, 175 n.92, 178 n.105
Polydamas 117 n.18
Polynices 23, 138, 149, 151–155, 157 n.39, 158, 193

–as Phaethon 155
Pompey 123, 182, 186, 194, 199
–burial of 138
–funeral of 123
Prayer 7, 23, 28, 38, 40–41, 40 n.66, 53, 57, 61, 149, 176
–failed 4
Priest 20, 23, 28, 54, 71–72, 74, 118, 132, 142, 166, 191, 203
–priestly roles 19, 56
Promachus 83
–death of 89
Prometheus 147 n.30
Propaganda 97–98, 104 n.31
Prophecy 1, 108 n.42, 148, 158, 173, 188
Proserpina 39, 89–90, 195, 197
Punic Wars
–First 99, 126 n.46
–Second 125–126
Purification 1, 10, 38, 53, 111, 113, 120 n.27, 127, 135, 147 n.31, 161, 162 n.8, 166, 168–170, 170 n.57, 173 n.79, 176–177, 179
(see also '*lustratio*')
Pyrene (mountain) 125

Reditus 5, 9, 95, 97–108
–and closure 102, 104, 109
Religion 3–6, 4 n.16, 15–17, 17 n.10, 18 n.15, 21, 21 n.24, 27–28, 49 n.21, 132, 158 n.41, 203, 205–206
–and ritual 4, 6, 7, 45, 119
Religious communication 14, 16 n.8, 17 n.12, 18–20, 18 n.17, 25, 122
–actor 18 n.17, 21, 84 n.17, 111, 120, 120 n.27, 122, 124–125, 130, 133
–authority 20, 20 n.22
–language 38 n.55, 38 n.57, 49 n.21
–media 16–17, 19
–practice 1, 5, 7, 9, 42–43, 111, 116, 158
–roles 17
Remus 108 n.42
Resolution 1, 3–4, 8–9, 93, 95, 111, 114, 161, 202, 204
Resonance theory 16–17, 22
Restoration 1, 2, 2 n.3, 10–11, 191
Rhea 168 n.44, 170–171

Ring composition 8, 80, 80 n.5, 81–82, 141
Rite of passage/*rite de passage* 7, 59–61, 60 n.3, 60 n.5, 61, 63, 70, 73–74
Ritual 14 n.4, 15, 18–25, 20 n.19, 21 n.24, 27–29, 33–34, 37–38, 41–42, 43–46, 48–51, 49 n.21, 52 n.40, 54, 56–58, 59–61, 63, 70–72, 74, 79–86, 81 n.8, 84 n.15, 88, 90 n.36, 93, 95–97, 102–104, 108–109, 111–112, 115, 115 n.13, 117–133, 126 n.46, 132 n.67, 135–143, 136 n.2, 145–147, 147 n.31, 149–150, 153–154, 156 n.38, 157–159, 159 n.45, 161–162, 165–70, 167 n.38, 168 n.43, 170 n.58, 171 n.64, 176–177, 176 n.93, 179, 180 n.115, 188, 201, 203–206
–actors 6, 19–21, 84, 111, 122, 125, 130 n.61, 133
–communication 4 n.15, 6, 14, 16, 23, 25, 122 n.34, 158, 203
–crisis 4, 127
–denied 4, 119, 122
–disturbance of 28
–false 9, 111, 113, 115–117, 119, 123–124, 123 n.35, 126, 127–129, 131, 133
–healing 166, 168–169, 179
–incomplete 4, 9, 10, 111, 140–141, 157
–mocked 4–5, 7, 42, 116, 118–119, 126, 128, 130, 132
–negation of 15
–performance of 1, 7, 9, 27, 29, 56–57, 83, 88, 111
–perverted 1–5, 9, 111, 117 n.18, 119, 138, 124 n.38
–pollution 115, 133, 136, 175
–problematic 9, 84, 84 n.16, 116, 136, 150
–reintegration 162
–reversed 9, 111, 119
–studies 13–14, 17
–temporality of 14
–theory 6, 13–14, 17, 203
Ritualisation 13, 16, 19, 21, 23, 24, 111, 159 n.45
Romulus 108 n.42, 129

Sacralisation 16, 20, 20 n.20, 49 n.20
–of atmosphere 18
–of objects 20, 130 n.61
–of space 17, 20–21
–sacrality 19
Sacrilege 8, 15, 22, 28, 93, 128, 132, 142, 169
Sacrifice 1–3, 4 n.16, 7, 25, 28, 40–41, 43, 48 n.17, 49, 51–52, 57, 79, 81, 83, 116, 119 n.24, 124 n.38, 133, 133 n.70
–animal 23, 117 n.19, 180 n.115
–human 5, 117 n.19, 138
–incomplete 5
–mock 117
–perverted 5
–sacrificial victim 2, 88, 153
Saguntum 111, 113–115, 113 n.6, 121
Satricus 99–100
Saturnalia 7, 27–33, 29 n.13, 31 n.26, 37, 60, 61 n.8, 63
Scipio (Africanus) 5, 9, 11, 95–97, 96 n.7, 100–108, 105 n.32, 106 n.36–37, 106 n.39, 108 n.41, 119, 122, 122 n.33, 124–127, 130–131, 133, 200
–as a proto-princeps (or a proto-autocrat) 127, 133
–The Younger 125 n.43
Sibyl 86
Sicily 89–90
Siluanus 49–53, 52 n.32, 52 n.35, 52 n.40, 54 n.42
Sol 92
Solymus 99
Somnus 60 n.5, 75
Spectacle 9, 111, 113, 120, 123, 129, 130
Sphragis 68 n.34, 75–76, 76 n.56, 204
Stoicism 185–186, 185 n.15, 199, 200
–providentialism 185
–*sapiens* 199
Suicide 5, 9, 80 n.3, 81, 81 n.8, 83, 88, 88 n.28, 88 n.31, 91 n.40, 113–114, 124 n.38, 138, 143, 147–148, 163, 165, 170
–Stoic 88
Supplication 88 n.36, 112
Syphax 125

Tagus (Spanish king) 47, 122 n.32
Talos 178, 178 n.107
Tiresias 86, 148
Thebans 22–23, 148, 152
Thebes 23, 135, 140, 145–147, 154, 158, 191, 197 n.68
Theron 118–119, 119 n.22, 122
Theseus 4, 11, 91, 125, 135, 136 n.2-3, 139, 146 n.26, 148, 154–155, 157, 157 n.41, 159 n.47, 178, 200, 201
Thiodamas 151
Third-person phenomenon 6, 14, 24–25, 145
Thoas 138–140
Tiridates 130, 188 n.36
Tisiphone 114–115, 116 n.15, 150, 193–194, 193 n.50
Titus 98 n.15, 131 n.66
Tityos 147
Transcendence 6, 13–14, 16, 22, 177
–transcendent actors 16
Trasimene 116, 118, 121, 122 n.33, 129
Trauma 10, 137 n.7, 147 n.29, 156 n.38, 161–162, 167, 170, 180
–trauma theory 161–162, 161 n.2, 167
Treaty 23, 196 n.64
Trebia 118
Triumph 9, 87, 95, 97, 99–101, 104, 104 n.30, 107, 111, 125, 125 n.43, 125 n.46, 126 n.46, 127–129, 130 n.60, 131–133, 139, 205
–anti-triumph 102, 130
–Domitian's triumph 97–98, 98 n.14, 104 n.31, 130–131, 131 n.66

–Nero's 20 n.21, 129
–of Augustus 127–128, 139
–of Flaminius 117
–of Scipio 5, 9, 95–96, 100–104, 107–108, 119, 124–126, 130–131, 133
–triumphal procession/parade 1, 2, 9, 87, 96–99, 98 n.11, 104, 111, 116, 126, 126 n.48, 127, 130–131
Troy 135, 139, 140, 145, 153, 158
Turnus 2, 80 n.3, 126, 133 n.70, 139, 152, 194, 157
Tydeus 15, 22, 24, 157
Typhoeus 193 n.52

Valerius Corvinus 116–117
Venus 39, 126, 138, 172, 172 n.67–68, 172 n.75, 188, 196
Vespasian 98 n.15, 127, 131
Vesta 55
Vesuvius 147 n.28–29
Victoria 52
Vitellius 132
Volteius 124 n.38

Wedding 55, 60 n.5, 84, 90, 90 n.36, 93, 140, 173, 173 n.79
(see also 'marriage')
Witchcraft 5, 85 n.21, 86, 138
Witch 85, 85 n.21, 85 n.22, 86 n.23

Zama 95, 106, 119, 125 n.45, 126, 198–199
Zeus (Kathartic) 176
(see also 'Jupiter')

Index of Sources

Ammianus Marcellinus
14.2.10	184 n.10
16.12.44	184 n.10
24.4.15	184 n.10

Apollodorus
1.9.27	81

Apollonius Rhodius
1.46–47	86
1.936–1152	170–171
1.1125–1131	171
1.1134–1151	171
1.1153–1171	170
3.732–735	172 n.66
3.747–748	178
3.771–801	174
3.802–819	174
4.20–25	174
4.310	89
4.368–369	169
4.380	175
4.391–394	174 n.86
4.423	169
4.435–440	175
4.464–476	175
4.477–479	175
4.482–489	175
4.659–752	176–178
4.706–712	176
4.749	177
4.1011–1057	177
4.1638–1688	178

Appian
Hannibalic War
50	119 n.25

Apuleius
De Mundo
32	184 n.12

Augustus
Monumentum Ancyranum
13	188 n.36

Cato
De argicultura
83	53
141	53, 40 n.66

Catullus
Carmina
28.13	48
63.3	50
64	139, 205
64.53–55	91
95.8	30

Cicero
Ad Atticum
6.3.3	104 n.30

Brutus
62	129

De diuinatione
1.77–78	117 n.17

Natura Deorum
2.19	185 n.14

De Re publica
3.34	183 n.6

De Senectute
75	119 n.25

Pro Quinctio
19.60	99

Philippics
13.9	104 n.30

Claudian
De raptu Proserpinae
1.25	196
1.28	196 n.62
1.33–36	196
1.37–41	196
1.42–47	196 n.63
1.63–65	196 n.64
1.67	196

1.93	196	**Hesiod**	
1.94–95	196 n.65	*Theogonia*	
1.99–103	196 n.65	116	193 n.49
1.113–116	196	740	193 n.49
2.170–171	197	*Opera et dies*	
2.186–187	197	109–201	113 n.3

Dio Cassius

Zonar. 7.21	128 n.54	**Homer**	
Zonar. 8.17	125 n.46	*Iliad*	
Xiph. 61.15.1	129 n.59	1.4–5	203
15.28–29	108 n.41	2.337–341	1
Xiph. 16.1–4	129 n.59	3.103–107	1
17.1	129 n.59	5.650–652	140 n.17
18.3	129 n.59	12.233–243	117 n.18
57–56 (frag.)	126 n.47	15.185–189	193 n.55
62.23.4	130	19.32	36
63.2.1	130, 130 n.60	20.61–65	193 n.52
63.8	130	23.327–328	50 n.27,
63.8.2	130 n.63	24.785–804	1, 2 n.6
63.20.3	130 n.61	*Odyssey*	
66.12.1a	131 n.66	4.86	36
67.7.4	104 n.31		
67.9	132 n.67	**Horace**	
		Carmina	
Diodorus Siculus		3.30	35, 44, 68, 68 n.33, 71
4.50	81	*Epistulae*	
		1.16.57–62	40–41
Diogenes Laertius		1.20.12	30 n.21
10.10	57 n.56	2.1.253	188 n.36
10.120a	57 n.53 and n.56	2.1.269–270	30 n.21
10.120b	57 n.54 and n.56	*Epodi*	
		16.2	183 n.5
Ennius		*Satires*	
Annales		1.119	29
7.220–221	189 n.37	*Sermones*	
7.225	189 n.37	1.120	31
9.299	98 n.11		
15	2, 14	**Isidorus**	
		Etymologiae	
Frontinus		14.8.30	49 n.21
Strategemata		17.6.6	49–50
4.7.39	108 n.41	17.6.7	49 n.21
		Josephus	
		Bellum Iudaicum	
		7.121–157	131 n.66

Index of Sources

Livy
praef. 4	183 n.5	3.490	184
1.38.4	98 n.11	4.253–336	112 n.1
3.26.29	125 n.43	4.503–504	124 n.38
4.10.7	98 n.11	4.593	182 n.2
5.49.7	98 n.11, 99	5.119	184
7.11.11	104 n.30	5.578	187
9.5.9	98 n.11	5.597	187
22.2.11–13	117 n.17	5.620	187
22.3.4–14	116 n.16	5.632–633	184 n.12, 187
22.52.6	119 n.25	5.654–671	187
22.53.10–12	108 n.41	5.659–670	199
25.17.4–7	119 n.25	5.677	187
27.28.1–2	119 n.25	6.80–116	112 n.1
28.38.4–5	126 n.47	6.605	85
30.45	125 n.43	6.628	85
30.45.1	100	6.651	85
31.20.3	104 n.30	6.762	85
38.50.7	105	7.136	185 n.19
41.28.9	98 n.11	7.145	182 n.2
44.22.17	98 n.11	7.649–653	199
45.39.2	104 n.30	7.789–794	120 n.27
45.39.11	98 n.11	7.794–799	121 n.29
		8.72–742	123, 123 n.37
		9.175–179	129

Lucan
1.36	182 n.2, 190 n.42	**Lucretius**	
1.48	190 n.42	3.52–54	117 n.19
1.61–62	188	5.96	185 n.17
1.67	182, 189		
1.68–69	183	**Macrobius**	
1.70	193 n.54	*Saturnalia*	
1.70–72	182	1.8.5	31 n.28
1.72b–80	183		
1.72	181–183, 184 n.12, 187	**Manilius** *Astronomica*	
1.76–77	190 n.43	2.802–803	184, 184 n.12
1.79	189 n.40	2.807	185 n.17
1.84–85	193		
1.84–97	193 n.54	**Martial**	
1.502	184	*Epigrammata*	
1.730–751	83	1 praef. 12–21	54
2.289–290	185 n.19	1 praef. 15–16	3
2.486–487	184	1.1.2	35
3.73–75	101	1.1.5–6	35
3.79	101	1.1.14–15	33
3.316	182 n.2	1.25	35
3.342–350	112 n.1	1.35	55, 56 n.49

1.39.5–6	40 n.64	6.24	29 n.13
1.88	35 n.41	6.28–29	35 n.41
1.112–118	35	6.49	56 n.49
1.113	35 n.44	6.61.7	30 n.21
1.114	7, 27, 34–37	6.72–73	56 n.49
1.115	35–36	6.83.1–2	99 n.17
1.116	7, 27, 34–37	7.18	32 n.30
1.117	37	7.28.7–8	29 n.13
1.117–118	34, 35 n.44	7.36	29 n.13
2.2	131	7.53	29 n.13
2.14	28 n.19	7.58	32 n.30
2.24.1–4	99 n.17	7.72	29 n.13
2.25	32 n.30	7.91	29 n.13
2.34	32 n.30	7.91.4	56 n.49
2.40	40 n.63	7.96	35 n.41
2.85	29 n.13	8 *praef.*	33 n.36, 37–38
2.93.1	33 n.36	8.3.1–2	33 n.36
3.24	28, 40 n.65	8.40	56 n.49
3.24.13–14	28	8.65	98
3.29	31 n.28	8.65.11	104 n.30
3.51	32 n.30	8.80	38
3.54	32 n.30	8.81	7
3.58.47	56 n.49	8.81.1–7	38
3.90	32 n.30	8.82	38
4.14	29 n.13, 30	9.4	32 n.30
4.19.3	29 n.13	9.33	40 n.62
4.19.3–4	31 n.25	9.37	32 n.30
4.31	76 n.54	9.48	77 n.62
4.31.4	76 n.54	9.78	32 n.30
4.38	32 n.30	9.86	35 n.41
4.46	29 n.13	9.90.15	32 n.32
4.58	32 n.30	9.102	41
4.80	40 n.62 and n.63	10.2.1	33 n.36
4.88	7, 29 n.13, 30, 37	10.2.1–4	43
4.88.1–4	30–31	10.2.9–12	44
4.89	31	10.12	44
5.2.5–6	33 n.36	10.13	44
5.18	29 n.13	10.18	29 n.13
5.19.3	104 n.30	10.24.1–3	32 n.32
5.19.11–14	29 n.13	10.29	29 n.13
5.30	29 n.13	10.30	44
5.49.8–10	29 n.13	10.37	44
5.78	28 n.10	10.37.19–20	44 n.5
5.84	7, 29 n.13, 31–33, 37	10.47.5	46 n.9
		10.73.5–7	48 n.17
6.1.1	33, 33 n.36	10.74	43, 45, 45 n.8, 47–48, 47 n.14
6.16	56 n.49		

10.74.1–6	45	**Orosius**	
10.74.7–12	46	*Historiae*	
10.75	32 n.30	6.7.9	184 n.10
10.78	43, 45		
10.86	45	**Ovid**	
10.87.6–7	29 n.13	*Amores*	
10.92	7, 43, 45, 48, 48 n.18, 57–58	2.12.5	104 n.30
		Epistulae ex Ponto	
10.92.3–12	49	1.1.72	30 n.21
10.92.4	50, 50 n.27	1.2.48	101
10.92.6	50–51	4.12	77 n.54
10.92.7	51	4.14	77 n.54
10.92.9–10	52	*Fasti*	
10.92.11	54	1.65	190
10.92.12	55	1.89	190
10.92.13–19	56	1.103	189
10.95	32 n.30	1.106–124	190–191
10.96	43, 45, 47–48	1.391–440	55
10.96.1–6	47	1.433–444	55
10.96.7–12	47–48	1.440	40 n.65
10.96.13–14	48	2.69–70	51
10.103	43, 45, 58	3.1–2	52
10.104	43, 45	3.295–299	51
11.2	29 n.13	3.786	39 n.60
11.15	29 n.13	5.183–378	33 n.39
11.18.22	56 n.49	5.349	34 n.40
11.19	32 n.30	6.319–348	55
11.34	40 n.62	6.339–344	55
11.51.2	56 n.49	*Heroides*	
11.67	40 n.62	2.35–45	38–39
11.72	56 n.49	2.44	39
11.108.4	41	*Metamorphoses*	
12.4(5).1	33 n.36	1.5–20	189
12.18	46, 46 n.12, 47	1.21	190 n.44
12.18.13–16	46	1.151	190
12.62.11–16	29 n.13	1.262	190
12.77	28	1.291–292	187 n.33
12.81	29 n.13	1.747–779	190
12.90	7, 39–41	2.1–400	190
13.1.1	30	2.298	186 n.22
14.1.1	30	4.432	193 n.50
14.1.5–6	29	5.366–368	193 n.52
14.37	30 n.21	5.379	196
14.70	56 n.49	8.801–804	112 n.1
14.223	7, 29, 37	10.30	193 n.49
		13.421	101
		13.448	117 n.19

14.404	193 n.49	**Polybius**	
15.876	76	3.80.3–82.8	116 n.16
15.879	36	6.53.1–3	122 n.34
Tristia		11.33.7	126 n.47
3.14.45–46	70		
4.10	69	**Propertius**	
		3.5.25–46	57 n.57
Persius		3.21.25–26	57 n.57
3.58–59	186		
		Sallust	
Petronius		*Bellum Catilinae*	
Satyrica		61	119 n.23
79–99	194–195	*Bellum Iugurthinum*	
116	195 n.60	114	125 n.43
119	194		
120.76	194	**Seneca the Elder**	
120.79–99	194–195	*Controuersiae*	
121.116	195 n.60	1 *praef.* 7	182 n.4
120.124–125	195		
121.100–101	195	**Seneca the Younger**	
121.105–106	195	*Ad Marciam*	
		3.1	111
Plato		26.6	185 n.21
Laws	177	*Agamemnon*	
Symposium		87	183 n.5
223c	29	485	187 n.30
Timaeus		*Consolatio ad Marciam*	
45b;	185 n.16	3.1	128
46c;	185 n.16	*De beneficiis*	
56e	185 n.16	5.17.3	113 n.3
		De clementia	
Pliny the Elder		1.4.1	183 n.6
Naturalis Historia		*De ira*	
19.173	14	3.26.4	113 n.3
30.16	130	*Epistulae*	
		87.23–24	128
Pliny the Younger		*Medea*	
Panegyricus		800	89
16.3	104	862	89
		Oedipus	
Plutarch		580	184 n.12
De Stoicorum repugnantiis		*Phoenissae*	
1053B 6 (=SVF 2.605)	186 n.23	322-324	101 n.24
Marcellus		*Quaestiones Naturales*	
30.1–2	119 n.25	6.32.4	184 n.12, 199
		Thyestes	
		827	185 n.21

Servius
ad Aeneid
1.2	108 n.41
1.310	49, 49 n.21
1.441	49 n.21
5.129	50

Silius Italicus
1.8–11	113 n.5
1.14	95
1.152–154	122 n.32
1.268	113 n.5
1.296–302	113 n.5
1.625–626	99
1.626	99 n.19
2.264–269	119, 122 n.32
2.460	111
2.465–474	112
2.494–503	112
2.496	116
2.510–512	114
2.526–542	114
2.599–608	114
2.618	114
2.650	114
2.656	114
2.681–682	115, 118 n.21
2.686–688	118 n.21
2.693–695	115
2.696–707	116
2.699–707	106
3.572–573	126
3.607	131
4.709–710	117
5.24–129	116
5.66–69	117 n.17
5.70–74	117 n.17
5.77–91	117
5.127–129	118
5.652–655	117
5.655–666	118
5.658–666	118, 123
6.689–691	106
7.1	122 n.33
7.6–7	122 n.33
7.6–8	119 n.24
7.557–563	99
7.746–750	119 n.24
7.748–749	127 n.51
9.66–177	99
9.157–158	99
10.208	95 n.2
10.305	125 n.45
10.415–448	108
10.420	108
10.438–439	108
10.449–453	120
10.503–577	120
10.504–506	123
10.518–520	119 n.25
10.518–523	121–122
10.558–569	121–122
10.565–567	123
10.572–574	120 n.26, 122
12.473–474	119 n.25
12.473–478	124 n.39
12.478	122. n.31
13.466–487	124
13.514–515	107
13.515	95
13.714–716	123 n.35
13.874–893	106
15.381–396	124 n.39
15.383–387	120 n.26
15.385–387	119 n.25
15.394–396	119 n.25
17.216–217	103
17.220–223	102–103
17.223–224	103 n.27
17.233	103
17.235	103
17.289	95
17.292	95, 95 n.1
17.378	103 n.29
17.381–382	103
17.538	106
17.597–599	199
17.606–607	199
17.606–609	198
17.607	184
17.613–615	198
17.618	125 n.45
17.618–619	95
17.618–624	125

17.625	95, 102, 107, 109, 126	4 *praef.* 16–19	65
		4 *praef.* 24	76 n.54
17.625–628	100	4.1	61 n.7
17.625–654	125	4.1–3	65 n.21
17.626	96, 100	4.2	60–61, 131
17.627	102 n.26, 103, 126	4.2.10–16	60–61
		4.3	76 n.57
17.627–628	101, 127 n.50	4.3.120	72 n.45
17.635–642	125	4.4	76 n.57, 77 n.61
17.643–644	105–106, 125–126	4.4.94–96	77 n.61
		4.6	60
17.647–650	127	4.7	77 n.61
17.651–654	96	4.7.23–24	77
		4.9.10	30 n.21
Statius		5 *praef.* 8–9	66
Achilleis	3, 4, 8, 69 n.35, 76–77, 77 n.61	5.1	69, 76 n.57
		5.1.10–15	69 n.41
Siluae		5.1.12	68 n.33
1 *praef.* 3	73 n.46	5.1.15	68 n.33
1.1.1–3	71 n.43	5.1.94–97	66
1.1.91–94	69 n.41	5.1.101–107	66
1.2	60	5.2	77 n.61
1.2.114	72 n.45	5.2.168–174	65–66
1.5.64–65	98 n.16	5.2.177	66
1.6.4	31 n.28	5.3	60, 67 n.27, 68–69, 71–74
1.6.93–97	63		
2 *praef.* 1–4	62 n.10	5.3–5	64, 68 n.34
2 *praef.* 7–9	73 n.46	5.3.5–7	70
2 *praef.* 15–18	65 n.21	5.3.10	69
2 *praef.* 21	76 n.54	5.3.41–45	72
2.1	60, 61, 72	5.3.47–63	71
2.1.1–35	62	5.3.213–214	69
2.1.15–18	73	5.4	60 n.5, 74 n.47, 75
2.1.20	62 n.11		
2.1.33–34	68 n.35	5.4.11–13	75
2.3	56 n.47, 60	5.5	8, 60, 72–73, 77–78, 77 n.62
2.3–5	65 n.21		
2.6	60, 76	5.5.1	68
2.7	60, 137 n.5	5.5.24–27	77 n.63
3 *praef.* 4	73 n.46	5.5.33–34	78
3.1	60	5.5.38	69
3.1.114	72 n.45	5.5.40	69
3.3	60, 98	5.5.43–45	73–74
3.3.37–39	69 n.41	5.5.46–52	73
3.3.171	104 n.30	5.5.49–52	70
3.3.182–183	99	5.5.72	76 n.54
4 *praef.* 1–4	65 n.21	5.5.86	76

Thebais

1.1	141	8.4	191
1.3	141, 153	8.18–20	192 n.46
1.17	141	8.21–23	192
1.241–243	197 n.68	8.31	184
1.292	194	8.31–79	192, 197
2.19–22	85 n.22	8.38–40	194, 194 n.59
2.704–742	24	8.52–53	192 n.49
2.726	24	8.61–62	195 n. 61
3.653–655	117 n.18	8.65–68	193
3.696	23	8.69–79	194
3.712–720	23	8.144	184 n.12
4.13–15	23	8.439	154 n.36
4.520	193 n.49	8.630–631	140
4.824	23	8.646–647	140
4.825–843	23	8.715	22
4.839–841	23	8.759	22
5.152–163	138	8.760–767	15, 22
5.165	138 n.11	9.1–31	15, 22
5.165–169	138	9.582	141
5.236–264	138	9.736	153
5.286	138	9.736–737	151
5.301	139	9.756	154 n.36
5.313	139	9.885–907	24
5.508	140 n.18	9.887	141
5.522	140 n.18	9.906–907	141
5.527	140 n.18	10.219–221	151
5.539–540	140 n.18	10.467–472	148
5.650	140 n.17	10.487–488	151
5.741–743	23	10.618	148
5.750–752	22	10.674–675	147
6.1–248	15	10.685	148
6.3–4	142	10.796–797	149
6.24–250	23	10.809–810	149
6.54–56	142	10.842–844	150–151
6.73	142	10.883–939	15
6.86–87	142	10.925–926	146
6.93–95	142	10.931	146
6.100	142	10.939	146
6.107–117	144	11.1–4	146
6.202–203	143	11.7–8	147
6.206–207	143	11.9	146
6.216	142	11.12–15	147
6.220–226	142–143	11.16–17	146
7.1–226	15, 24	11.226–227	149
7.816–823	191	11.234–238	149, 153
8.1–126	15, 24	11.242–243	150
		11.262–264	151

11.273–275	152	Nero	
11.276–277	152	13	130 n.60
11.295	152	25.1	130 n.61
11.297	152	49	132
11.308–314	152	57	131 n.65
11.309	152 n.35	*Persius*	
11.310–314	152 n.35	5	186 n.25
12.51	153	*Vespasianus*	
12.53–54	153	12	131
12.56	153	*Vitellius*	
12.66–67	153	11	132
12.70–71	153–154		
12.72–73	154	**Tacitus**	
12.93	154	*Agricola*	
12.228–229	154	39	131
12.230–236	154	39.1	104 n.31
12.241–242	154	*Annales*	
12.251–252	154	14.13	129 n.59
12.268–277	154	15.1–18	130 n.60
12.314	154	15.24–31	130 n.60
12.349–350	154	16.6	116
12.379	154	*Germania*	
12.408	154–155	37	131
12.409–410	155	*Historiae*	
12.413–414	155	1.2	113, 131 n.65
12.417–419	155	2.8	131 n.65
12.431–432	155	3.27	184 n.10
12.437	155	4.74	183 n.6
12.446–448	155		
12.487–488	155–156	**Tibullus**	
12.579	104 n.30	1.1.2	37
12.782–785	23		
12.787–788	23, 127 n.51	**Valerius Flaccus**	
12.789–796	23	1.21–37	92
12.791–793	23	1.211–226	81
12.793–794	78	1.277–282	92
12.797–809	156	1.498–567	92
12.808–809	77	1.503–527	92
12.816	36 n.51	1.536–556	92
		1.574–658	81
Suetonius		1.693–699	82
Caligula		1.700–703	91
47	104 n.30	1.700–721	81
Domitianus		1.722–723	80 n.3
6.1	131	1.730–740	83
13.3	131	1.736–737	85
17	132	1.741–746	87

RESUELVA SU PASADO
ESTUDIO DE CASOS CON LA TERAPIA EMDR

Acerca del Libro

Este libro es un compendio de estudios de casos de personas tratadas con la Terapia EMDR. Las sesiones fueron grabadas y transcritas, ilustrando una variedad de diagnósticos así como la velocidad de resolución al usar los protocolos de Terapia EMDR que se ofrecen en la formación básica de esta aproximación terapêutica.

Aunque muchos profesionales van a poder aprovechar su contenido, el libro se destina al público en general a fin de que conozcan la fuerza y el poder de cambio que la Terapia EMDR produce en nuestros cerebros, y consecuentemente, en nuestra conducta, emociones, sensaciones y decisiones de vida. Aquí se podrá ver como es posible evitar la evolución de cuadros de estrés pos-traumático; la resolución de fobias que fueron fuente de trastornos durante años; cómo resolver dilemas; las experiencias traumáticas escolares que pueden ser superadas; y finalmente, cómo fortalecer los recursos que promueven la resiliencia.

Acerca de la Autora

Durante más de 30 años, Esly Regina Carvalho, Ph.D., doctora y profesora de psicología, se ha dedicado al área de la salud emocional: como psicóloga en la práctica clínica; como facilitadora, ofreciendo formación en diferentes modalidades terapéuticas, tales como EMDR, Brainspotting y Psicodrama; como autora, compartiendo y socializando su experiencia con los demás; y a través de presentaciones públicas, conferencias y estudios tanto en Brasil como en otros países de América Latina, Estados Unidos, Portugal y España, ayudando a las personas a vencer los desafíos de la vida.

www.traumaclinicedicoes.com.br

ISBN 9781941727591

1.741–748	83	8.134–174	81
1.749–817	83	8.144–170	86 n.25
1.755	85	8.217–467	93
1.757–761	87	8.243–260	90 n.36
1.780	85	8.247–251	81, 173
1.818–826	83, 115 n.13	8.263	93
1.825–826	80 n.3	8.277	93
1.827–847	115 n.13	8.312–317	93
1.827–850	83	8.318–384	81
1.828–831	191 n.45	8.444–449	92, 92 n.42
1.832–839	84	8.445–446	174 n.86
1.835–842	84	8.453–457	87–88
1.842–845	84		
1.847	82	**Valerius Maximus**	
2.1–5	81–2	1.6.6	133 n.72
2.4	82	2.8.5	126 n.47
2.585–612	92	2.10.8	33–34
3.9–10	169	5.1.ext.6	120 n.26
3.25	169	5.12.7	108 n.41
3.98–99	166		
3.176	168	**Velleius Paterculus**	
3.219	169	2.12.1	125 n.46
3.306–308	165 n.24		
3.323	169	**Virgil**	
3.338–339	165	*Aeneid*	
3.340–342	169	1.2–3	108 n.41
3.340–344	167 n.38	1.8–11	189 n.38
3.362–368	166	1.55	90
3.373–376	167	1.60	90 n.38
3.377–416	167	1.81–83	188 n.34
3.417–429	168	1.141–153	188
3.430–442	168	1.223	95
3.433–434	169	1.292–293	108 n.42
3.458	168	1.293–296	188
3.462	168	1.496–506	90
3.464	168	2.328	154 n.36
4.452–491	169	2.378	152 n.35
5.341–349	89–90	2.378–381	152
5.430–455	173	2.380–381	152 n.35
5.683–687	173	2.471	152 n.35
6.439–448	85	2.471–475	152
6.446–448	85	2.472	152 n.35
7.163	101	2.475	152 n.35, 154 n.36
7.198–199	86		
7.440	101	2.624–631	144
7.461	172	2.734	139
8.106	173	4.68–73	138

4.69	138 n.11	7.621–622	188
4.160	90	8.1	194 n.57
4.169–170	90	8.714–715	100 n.22, 127 n.50
4.172	90		
4.300–303	91	8.714–728	127
4.590–627	91 n.40	11.54	97–98
4.639–640	139	12.204–205	185 n.13
4.645–651	139	12.946–947	80 n.3
5.46–48	36	12.949	2
5.129	50 n.27	12.951	139
6.637–644	84	12.951–952	80 n.3
6.660–665	84	*Eclogues*	
6.801–805	127	1.1	204
6.893–897	84	6.54	50
7.45	189 n.38	7.1	50
7.47	50 n.28	10.75	29
7.331–440	114 n.9	*Georgics*	
7.341	193 n.50	4.566	204
7.607	188		

www.ingramcontent.com/pod-product-compliance
Lightning Source LLC
Chambersburg PA
CBHW020226170426
43201CB00007B/336